Commercial-Investment Real Estate Council Series

Anderson, *Success Strategies for Investment Real Estate: The Professional's Guide to Better Service and Increased Commissions*

Arnold, *Commercial Investment Real Estate, Book I, 2nd edition*

Arnold, *Commercial Investment Real Estate, Book II, 3rd edition*

Carn, et al., *Real Estate Market Analysis*

McCurry, *Commercial Real Estate*

Messner, Boyce, Trimble, Ward, *Analyzing Real Estate Opportunities: Market and Feasibility Studies*

Messner, Lyon, Ward, Freedenberg, *Real Estate Investment and Taxation, 4th edition* (previously published as *Marketing Investment Real Estate*)

Nourse, *Managerial Real Estate: Corporate Real Estate Asset Management*

Real Estate Investment and Taxation

Fourth Edition

Stephen D. Messner
Victor L. Lyon
Robert L. Ward
Charles Freedenberg

COMMERCIAL-INVESTMENT REAL ESTATE COUNCIL™ of the
REALTORS NATIONAL MARKETING INSTITUTE® of the
NATIONAL ASSOCIATION OF REALTORS®, Chicago, Illinois

PRENTICE HALL Englewood Cliffs, New Jersey 07632

Library of Congress Cataloging-in-Publication Data

Real estate investment and taxation / Stephen D. Messner . . . [et al.].
  —4th ed.
       p. cm.
     Includes bibliographical references.
     ISBN 0-13-763053-0 :
     1. Real property and taxation—United States.   2. Real estate
investment—United States.   3. Real property tax—United States.
I. Messner, Stephen D.
HJ4181.R37 1991
332.63'24—dc20

89-48290
CIP

Editorial/production supervision
  and interior design: **Eleanor Ode Walter**
Cover design: **20/20 Services, Inc.**
Manufacturing buyer: **Mary Ann Gloriande**

 © 1991, 1987 by Prentice-Hall, Inc.
A Division of Simon & Schuster
Englewood Cliffs, New Jersey 07632
Previously published as *Marketing Investment Real Estate* and copyright 1985,
1982, 1976, 1975 by the COMMERCIAL-INVESTMENT REAL ESTATE
COUNCIL™ of the REALTORS NATIONAL MARKETING INSTITUTE® of
the NATIONAL ASSOCIATION OF REALTORS®.

Printed in the United States of America

10 9 8 7 6 5 4 3 2 1

ISBN   0-13-763053-0

Prentice-Hall International (UK) Limited, *London*
Prentice-Hall of Australia Pty. Limited, *Sydney*
Prentice-Hall Canada Inc., *Toronto*
Prentice-Hall Hispanoamericana, S.A., *Mexico*
Prentice-Hall of India Private Limited, *New Delhi*
Prentice-Hall of Japan, Inc., *Tokyo*
Simon & Schuster Asia Pte. Ltd., *Singapore*
Editora Prentice-Hall do Brasil, Ltda., *Rio de Janeiro*

Contents

Contents

Preface

This book concerns itself with the process of including real estate in a total investment program in order to achieve an investor's goals. As we move into the decade of the 1990s, this task is becoming increasingly important and relevant. Income-producing and/or speculative real estate have long been recognized as having a useful investment potential for a broad range of investors with different needs and investment objectives. Now, even greater numbers of investors and institutions are turning to real estate over other forms of direct and indirect investment media because of the flexibility and return potential that it offers when transactions are properly structured.

The national economy has experienced only modest levels of inflation during the past several years, yet many forms of real estate investments represent an ideal hedge against the shrinking purchasing power of the dollar. In addition, real estate is often purchased because of the tax advantages it holds for certain categories of investors. Also, real estate has long been linked with the advantages associated with leveraged financing; even during periods of tight money it is possible to finance real estate purchases through lender participation.

All of these developments create new opportunities for well-qualified investment real estate brokers to provide counsel to a growing number of clients. To meet the investment objectives of their clients, brokers must be aware of market developments and be equipped with the specialized tools of analysis necessary to cope with ever-changing market conditons. It is to this end that this book was written.

Understanding and knowledge of the new techniques and tools presented here will assure the broker a viable role in the client team—attorney, accountant and REALTOR®. The broker's role is multifaceted; it can be the traditional one of the seller's agent or one of providing counseling services for which a fee rather than a commission is paid. Whatever the case, it is clear that the role of the commercial-investment real estate broker is expanding in both breadth and complexity.

Thorough mastery of investment principles and techniques and their applications can best be achieved through the educational courses which lead to the professional designation CCIM (Certified Commercial-Investment Member) of the REALTORS NATIONAL MARKETING INSTITUTE®. These courses constitute the best in professional education and training and produce some of the most competent real estate investment brokers in the country. *Real Estate Investment and Taxation* 4th ed. is the primary textbook for these courses.

However, *Real Estate Investment and Taxation* is also intended to be an independent entity. It can be used before, during and after the courses or can stand on its own. While primarily addressed to the commercial-investment real estate broker for use in marketing real estate to clients, it will also be of value to investors and their direct advisors. Accountants and attorneys will find this book a reference of great value in their work for real estate investment clients. In any case, it is intended to be read from cover to cover so that the comprehensiveness of a thorough, uniform analytical approach is understood. Only then should it be used as a reference in checking a particular tax treatment or financing technique to be applied to a specific property.

By using the methods described in this book, knowledgeable brokers will be able to extend their skills to serve many more clients than in the past and serve all their clients in a more professional manner than has ever before been possible.

About the Authors

REALTOR Stephen D. Messner, D.B.A., is a Professor of Finance and Real Estate in the School of Business Administration at the University of Connecticut. He also served as the Associate Dean and Acting Dean from 1985 to 1989; the Head of the Finance Department from 1972 to 1985; and Assistant Director and Director of the Center for Real Estate and Urban Economic Studies from 1966 to 1977. Dr. Messner co-authored the first, second, and third editions of *Marketing Investment Real Estate* and *Analyzing Real Estate Opportunities*, both published by the COMMERCIAL-INVESTMENT REAL ESTATE COUNCIL of the REALTORS NATIONAL MARKETING INSTITUTE. He also co-authored two editions of *Industrial Real Estate*, published by the Society of Industrial Realtors, and has contributed numerous articles to *Real Estate Today* and the *Commercial Investment Real Estate Journal*. He has authored more than 100 books, articles, and monographs and has served as the CIREC educational consultant since 1972. In 1987, he received the Victor L. Lyon Award for outstanding contributions to the CCIM program. Dr. Messner holds the CCIM and SRPA designations.

REALTOR Victor L. Lyon is Chairman of the Board and Founder of Lyon Commercial Real Estate, Inc. and is a past president of REALTORS NATIONAL MARKETING INSTITUTE. A co-author of the earlier editions of *Marketing Investment Real Estate,* REALTOR Lyon, a Certified Commercial Investment Member (CCIM) and Certified Real Estate Managing Broker (CRB), is a senior instructor for the Commercial Investment Courses of the Marketing Institute. In addition, he has attained the designations of the American Institute of Real Estate Appraisers (MAI), the Society of Real Estate Counselors (CRE), the Real Estate Securities and Syndication Institute (SRS), and the Society of Real Estate Appraisers (SRPA). Mr. Lyon is a recipient of the Distinguished Service Award (1981) and the Educator of the Year Award (1988) from the NATIONAL ASSOCIATION OF REALTORS.

REALTOR Robert L. Ward is the owner of his own commercial/investment real estate brokerage company, The Robert L. Ward Company, specializing in income property brokerage. He is past chairman of the Commercial-Investment Council of the REALTORS NATIONAL MARKETING INSTITUTE and a Senior Instructor of the Commercial-Investment Real Estate Council courses. REALTOR Ward was chosen by his fellow instructors as the Instructor of the Year in 1986. He also received the Victor L. Lyon Award in 1988 for outstanding contributions to the CCIM program. REALTOR Ward has authored a sales training manual for the Florida Association of REALTORS, and co-authored books: *Analyzing Real Estate Opportunities* and the first edition of *Marketing Investment Real Estate,* used in real estate courses throughout the nation.

REALTOR Charles Freedenberg, CCIM, J.D. is a commercial real estate broker with the firm of Craig L. Michalak, Inc. Commercial Real Estate in Bellevue, Washington, specializing in investment real estate and consulting. He is a senior instructor in the Commercial Investment Real Estate Council's commercial investment real estate courses. He is also on their Long Range Planning committee and a member of their governing council. Prior to his involvement with commercial real estate, Mr. Freedenberg served for over six years with the Internal Revenue Service. He has had several articles published and is widely known for his tax law and tax application seminars which have been given throughout the United States.

Acknowledgments

The preparation of the fourth edition of *Real Estate Investment and Taxation* involved the efforts of several individuals who provided suggestions, reviewed draft materials, typed a succession of drafts, did editorial work and performed other important tasks. Rather than list the many, many people who were involved in various degrees with the production of this book, the authors would like to single out three individuals who deserve special thanks and recognition.

Celene Bielefeld, an MBA student at the University of Connecticut, assisted in making the changes necessary to update illustrations and numerical examples so that they reflect the most recent market and tax information. She also drafted new segments for this edition; in particular, the lease-versus-buy materials.

Robert Dubil, a Ph.D. candidate at the Wharton School and an MBA graduate from the University of Connecticut, helped collect data to update several of the sections of this edition and prepared the background materials on securitization.

Finally, Beth Wingren, also an MBA student at the University of Connecticut, coordinated the entire revision process (nearly 600 pages) and managed to keep the four authors nearly on schedule.

Glastonbury, CT
1990

1
Nature and Scope
of Investments

INTRODUCTION

This is a text about real estate investments, the impact of the federal income tax on such investments and a rational approach to analyzing and comparing the relative benefits of real estate investment opportunities. In a broader sense, it is a book on real estate investment decision-making, since the goal of the analysis generally is to help an investor make a choice from alternative investments. It is appropriate at the outset, however, to consider the larger scope of investment, including how and why investing is undertaken, the problems of investment risks, basic investment characteristics or attributes and investment alternatives. Such analysis will enable the real estate broker or investor to compare different types of available investments and the expected results of each. The real estate broker must be familiar with the entire spectrum of investments to make a meaningful analysis of the present or potential position of a client or prospect.

INVESTING IN THE 1990s

At no time over the past 50 years has it been more important to understand the principles of real estate investment analysis and decision-making. As we entered the 1990s, investors faced unparalleled problems. The United States economy went through a recession accompanied by double-digit inflation, and public efforts to fight both economic foes caused major upheavals in the money and capital markets. By 1987 interest rates were reduced significantly, but at the expense of a huge budget deficit. Ronald Reagan's attempted supply-side economics, fiscal policy, the resulting deficits, the Wall Street Stock Market crash of October 1987, and major tax reforms set the stage for a new real estate and investment arena in the 1990s.

Most small investors were in a quandary, having to choose from an ever-growing array of investment alternatives—precious metals, gems, art, railroad cars, oil drilling interests, plus a variety of new securities and funds (trusts).

Securitization (liquid pools of smaller debt pieces with reduced risk sold to investors) was, perhaps, the single most important change in real estate financing during the decade of the 1980s. Since 1984, the market for commercial mortgage securities has been increasing steadily. In addition, the general trend of reducing special tax benefits or shelters and plugging tax loopholes for investors, which was prevalent in the 1970s, continued to influence the relative desirability of certain investments.

The 1980s represented the decade of the tax paradox. Real estate retained many of the tax advantages lost by other forms of investment in the 1970s. The Economic Recovery Act of 1981 added even further advantages to real estate as an investment. The Deficit Reduction Act of 1984 produced minor reductions in these advantages, but real estate investments retained the major tax advantages gained in earlier years. Enter the Tax Reform Act of 1986, the impact of which has yet to be fully felt. A decline in interest rates, an increase in rent, changes in the value of existing properties and implications for individual investors reverberated throughout the industry. With increased taxation of new investments, real estate as the ultimate tax shelter is in decline, a complete turnaround from the beginning of the decade.

The extremely volatile and uncertain market conditions, coupled with a significant increase in the nature and choice of investment vehicles and the 1986 tax reforms, create an intensely competitive environment for the real estate broker. As the 1980s came to a close, the fear of recession in the United States persisted. This fear continues to ripple through all aspects of investment, influencing the actions of major institutions and manufacturing firms as well as individual investors. The broker must be able to understand the investment implications of a variety of investments to best serve the investor.

NATURE OF INVESTING

What Is an Investment?

The answer to this question is understood by most people probably in only a general way. One dictionary, for example, defines an investment as an "expenditure of money for income or profit; capital outlay." Most people understand that investment involves the commitment of money or other property (the capital outlay) in the hope of earning future income or profit on that outlay. However, specific investments and the elements affecting them raise more complex questions for which answers may not be as readily available.

The range of possible investments is, of course, quite broad. Placing money into a savings account is an investment, as is the purchase of corporate or government bonds. The purchase of some types of life insurance is considered an investment insofar as there is a buildup in cash surrender value. Similarly, the purchase of an annuity is a form of investment. The purchase of stock in a corporation or a mutual fund is an investment, as is the contribution of capital to a proprietorship or partnership business. Last, but not least, real estate, in its many forms, is an investment.

When an individual commits funds for a property with the combined expectation of direct benefit from use plus future investment return, the classification of the activity is somewhat less well defined than the examples above. This phenomenon is common with commercial-investment property (vacation rental property, an owner-occupied duplex, owner-occupied retail buildings and the like) and can also be found with certain other tangible property (paintings, jewelry, antiques and other collector items). The problem here is much more than simply one of definition; it centers on the decision-making criteria used in acquiring or disposing of the property, which may be confounded by the multiple objectives of use and investing.

The *primary* purpose of a pure investment is future income or profit. The profit or income an investor expects from an investment can take two basic forms: (1) income earned in the form of interest, dividends or rents; (2) profit realized from appreciation in value (when the investment property is sold for more than it cost).

Who Invests?

One quite remarkable feature of the economic system of the United States, with its ability to produce an enormous and varied quantity of goods and services, is that a major portion of this capacity is made possible by private investments. In a private enterprise economy such as ours, the buildings and machines necessary for production can be purchased only through sacrifices in present consumption and through the desire and ability of some to save and to invest their savings for the future.

The overwhelming majority of the population is engaged in some form of investing. As disposable personal income in the United States has risen, so have the number and proportion of people who have funds in excess of their current consumption requirements. Indeed, for the past several decades, the number of savers and investors has grown at a rate much higher than the population itself. Today in our economy, savings and investment capital emanate not from a select few but from the large and growing number of middle-income individuals and families.

Accompanying this growth in the number of investors has been the growth in the country's financial intermediaries: banks, life insurance companies, savings and loan associations, pension funds and so on. This growth has been in the size and, consequently, the importance of such institutions and in the variety of investment vehicles they offer. Recent changes have occurred to cause increasing numbers of investors to channel their funds directly into investments such as real estate, tangible personal property, open-market securities (U.S. Treasury Bills) and commercial mortgage securities, without using financial intermediaries.

The forecast for the future seems clear enough. There will be even greater numbers of investors. Investors will be more sophisticated and will have increasing amounts of information and media to aid them in their investment pursuits. Finally, there will be an ever-increasing number of investors seeking to invest their funds directly rather than through financial intermediaries, and they will face an ever-expanding selection of investment alternatives.

Why Do People Invest?

While the answer to this question seems all too obvious, the point should be emphasized that ''making a profit'' is neither a definitive enough nor comprehensive enough goal to be helpful in assessing the rationale for investing. In our free enterprise economy, individuals interact with business firms by supplying both labor and capital in exchange for wages, salaries, interest and dividends. The cash receipts from business are then used by individuals to meet and satisfy basic consumption needs and desires. Consumption, however, has a variety of monetary costs. While food and clothing typically can be purchased with current earnings, other items such as housing, automobiles, education and the like, can be purchased only through borrowing or savings or both. Most individuals save a portion of current income so that they might provide for future consumption; as a result, these people face investment decisions regularly. Thus, it is to make future consumption possible that people save and invest in the present.

People purchase commercial-investment real estate for a variety of reasons. Obviously, some people buy property because they intend to use it themselves. But even those who purchase income-producing property to rent to others may have reasons other than dollar return when they make the acquisition. Pride of ownership—the romance of brick and mortar—can be an important factor in purchasing commercial property. An investor may take great pride in the purchase of a locally prominent office building that can be shown off to friends.

Other investors look to commercial property to provide gainful employment through management, construction, repair and other uses. Monetary return may be of secondary importance to this group of buyers. Still other buyers may have a combination of goals in mind when selecting commercial real estate, including portfolio diversification, control of a highly leveraged property and tax shelter.

INVESTMENT ALTERNATIVES

A large number of investment alternatives are available to the typical investor; these alternatives can be categorized in several ways. Here is one way to categorize investment alternatives:

> Direct investment alternatives
>   Fixed principal investments
>   Cash
>   Corporate bonds

Government bonds
Money market instruments
Savings accounts
Savings certificates
Variable principal securities
Common stocks
Convertible securities
Futures
Options
Preferred stocks
Warrants
Real assets
Art, antiques and other valuables
Business ventures
Commodities
Currencies
Mortgages
Real estate
Indirect investment alternatives
Collateralized mortgage obligations
Insurance company portfolios
Investment companies
Master limited partnerships
Mutual funds
Pension funds
Real estate investment trusts
Real estate mortgage investment conduits
Trust funds

The primary division between types of investments—direct and indirect—differentiates between those investment alternatives in which the individual makes the actual investment decisions. Indirect investments are those in which the individual has little or no say.

Of the direct investments, the fixed-principal investments are those in which the principal amount or terminal value is known (fixed) with complete certainty. Perhaps the best example of this class is the bond that has a set value at maturity.

Variable-principal securities have no fixed or certain terminal value, and the laws of supply and demand produce periodic changes in principal value (price). Common stock, for example, has neither a fixed income nor a fixed market price.

Nonsecurity investments include a broad range of vehicles, but their common characteristic is that while they are direct investments under the definition used above, they are not classified as securities. One might argue that the mortgage instrument is a near-security in that it is traded in secondary markets, but there are many types of mortgage loans and many different ways to invest directly in mortgages. The other nonsecurities are more clearly of the tax-sheltered variety, in which certain of the income tax provisions can offer significant tax advantages to classes of investors.

With indirect investment alternatives, individuals have virtually no, or at most very little, influence or control over the actual selection of investments. Some have called this the "money management industry," which is growing rapidly in our economy.[1]

INVESTMENT ATTRIBUTES

Although it is generally true that the primary reason individuals and institutions invest is to create future wealth and thus provide for future consumption, there are a variety of other reasons. Because particular investors have different needs and desires that must be satisfied by the investments they undertake, it follows that there are basic factors or attributes of each investment that somehow relate to its ability to meet a particular investor's objectives. As a practical matter, many institutional investors are restricted to some extent in the type of investments they make. In some cases they are legally restricted; but equally important to individuals as well as institutional investors are such factors as habits, historical precedent, tradition and, simply, sound judgment; those factors prompt investors to limit their selection to certain investments.

Investment attributes are directly related to investment objectives. Rational financial planning requires that each investor carefully consider and specifically identify individual investment objectives within the context of personal needs, along with any legal restrictions that might be faced when the investment is made for others. Thus, we might think of attributes in terms of the ability of an investment to provide investment benefits.

For the typical investor the five most important investment attributes are the following:

Risk
Liquidity
Return
Manageability
Taxability

Risk

In terms of relative importance, risk may be the most important attribute of an investment for most investors. Risk is generally defined in terms of the degree of certainty with which return from the investment is expected. An extreme example would be cash which remains uninvested. The return is absolutely certain to be *zero*; there is complete safety and, thus, no risk. Most investors think of certainty of receiving principal invested back as their highest priority and are concerned only secondarily with receipt of income.

Risk may be further defined according to type. There are four distinct categories:

Purchasing power risk relates to the extent to which an investment is subject to losses (or gains) in the purchasing power of dollar amounts received as income or as return of principal. With price levels moving steadily upward, most investors have come to think of this form of risk as almost sure uncertainty as to *loss* of purchasing power, referring to this as "inflation risk." This attitude has been substantially reinforced by the double-digit inflation of the late 1970s and early 1980s. It should be remembered, however, that there have been periods of downward price movement (during the Depression of the 1930s and in some isolated instances in the mid-1970s), and during these periods purchasing power actually increased.

Most commonly, high purchasing power risk is associated with those investments offering a fixed income, even though this risk affects income and principal in the same way. Investments with a high degree of purchasing power risk are bonds, mortgages, savings accounts and other fixed (or limited) income investments. Investing in common stock and real estate is generally considered the most practical and effective protection against this form of risk.

Fixed income investments are not protected against inflation or loss of purchasing power. Once an annuity with a fixed dollar amount is purchased, that is the dollar amount which will be received regardless of future changes in the purchasing power of the dollar received. This also holds true for the interest rate called for in bonds; only the *amount* specified by the bond will be paid at each interest period (the interest rate will not go up). Furthermore, the amount received at maturity will be the amount paid for the bond except when purchased at a discount. Preferred stock falls into the same category as bonds since the dividends called for are generally fixed as a percentage of the par value of the stock.

Common stock, on the other hand, is deemed to be a hedge against inflation on the theory that the market value of the stock will reflect any inflationary factors in the economy. This may hold true for the entire spectrum of common stocks but may not apply to any one particular stock. Furthermore, when interest rates increase in an inflationary period, common stock prices may decline, as was dramatically demonstrated in 1974.

Various business investments may reflect the pressures of inflation since the price at which the products or services are sold by the business will be subject to the same inflationary pressures.

Real estate prices generally have reflected the inflationary spiral in recent years. It also has become quite common for real estate leases to include escalation clauses calling for increased rents to offset increases in the cost of living.

Financial risk is measured in terms of the uncertainty concerning the financial ability of the investment to return principal and income in the future. The popular rating systems, such as Moody's and Standard and Poor's, base their grading systems of securities on the relationship between the amount of funds an issuer has to satisfy security holders and the amount of funds required to meet those demands.

Business risk is often confused with "financial risk" because the two are so closely related. Business risk, however, refers to the uncertainty associated with the profit potential of the property or business, while financial risk relates to the capital structure that is used to finance the assets of the firm. For example, the business risk associated with drilling for oil is separate from the manner by which the venture is financed.

Interest rate (money rate) risk   relates to the impact of changes in future interest rates on investment value. When interest rates fall, the market price of existing mortgages increases; conversely, when interest rates rise, the value of existing mortgages fall. Even the most secure investments from the standpoint of financial risk (U.S. Government Bonds) are highly subject to changes in interest rates, as evidenced by the significant drop in long-term government bond prices in the early 1980s when interest rates hit new highs. In general, the greater the financial safety of the investment, the lower the investment rate risk. For example, high grade bonds suffer most from changes in interest rates.

Risk and Return by Type of Investment

It is generally accepted that risk and return on the investment have a direct relationship to each other. That is, the higher the expected return, the greater the risk. In contrast, risk is low when guaranteed (or practically guaranteed) returns are involved.[2] Thus, the risk factor is low for savings accounts, life insurance and annuities and relatively low for corporate and municipal bonds. The effective interest rate (not necessarily the rate called for by the bond but the effective rate determined by the combination of the interest rate called for by the bond, the price at which the bond is selling and the time left to maturity of the bond) will reflect the relative risk attributed to the bond.

Corporate stock is more difficult to classify with respect to risk since it may have widely varying degrees of risk. Stock of a regulated public utility is generally considered less risky than the stock of a new, unproven company just entering the field. The latter may have more "action" among stockholders looking for dramatic increases, but the risk is more substantial.

Partnerships, syndicates and other forms of ownership in business ventures also have varying degrees of risk. Again, the risk and rate of return are directly related. Investments in speculative oil drilling, for example, may be very risky in terms of the percentage of wells that do strike oil, but the return may be substantial. The cost of an investment in a proven well will be much higher than in a wildcat venture because the risk is much less.

Real estate investments also run the gamut of degrees of risk. A property with a long-term lease from a national tenant is considered far less risky than one with a lease with only three years remaining. Some other factors that affect the degree of risk in a real estate investment may be unknown at the time the investment is undertaken. Changes in the economic viability of the neighborhood, changes in zoning, increases in real estate taxes, possible condemnation of the property and increases in interest rates are all examples of factors that affect risk.

Liquidity

Another factor important to many investors is the ability to convert an investment into cash or its equivalent rapidly and with little, if any, loss of principal. This attribute is called "liquidity." An example of a highly liquid investment would be a savings account that has no penalty for withdrawal before a specified date. Thus, not only can conversion take place quickly and easily, but also there is no loss whatsoever in the amount of principal invested at the time the investment is terminated.

Liquidity is important to both individual and institutional investors since liquid assets may be needed to meet unexpected expenses or in order to take advantage of unforeseen opportunities that are particularly favorable. A closely related attribute that may meet these requirements is "marketability," or the capability of the investment to find a ready market where the asset may be sold even at a possible loss of principal. Under this definition, an asset that is liquid must also be marketable, but assets that are marketable are not necessarily liquid.

Money in a savings bank, investment bonds, life insurance and annuities all are considered to be relatively liquid. They are already in the form of cash or may be converted into cash very quickly and generally with little or no loss of principal. This is in contrast to the characteristic of marketability where there is a ready and active market for the quick sale of the investment, although the sale price may be well below the original amount invested. Investments in common stocks listed on the New York Stock Exchange may be highly marketable but the price at which they are traded may fluctuate widely from week to week. Such securities would therefore be considered marketable but not liquid.

Investments in oil, cattle and other business ventures may be neither liquid nor marketable. An interest, especially a minority interest, in a closely held business (one held by only a few owners) may be difficult to sell at any price.

Real estate is generally not considered to be liquid and is often not marketable compared with other investment alternatives. Certainly it is not as readily salable as is stock trading on the New York Stock Exchange. However, cash is often available from a real estate investment without the necessity of a sale. Real estate, traditionally, is among the best types of security for a loan; mortgages on real estate are generally readily available. If property has increased in value, the immediate availability of this increase to the owner may be realized without the actual sale of the property; the owner can usually borrow against it by refinancing the property.

Return: Dollar and Rate

Not surprisingly, the *periodic income* from and the *appreciation* of the investment are two of its most important attributes. Generally, income and appreciation are combined into a measure of return that can be expressed as a periodic dollar amount or as a periodic rate measured as a percentage of amount invested. Investors are pressured to seek the highest return on their investment possible, commensurate with the risk they are willing to assume and other important attributes they desire.

Fixed income investments, while relatively free of risk, generally have no appreciation factor. The return on the investment is there (in the form of interest or dividends), but the dollar value of the capital investment remains unchanged. If a person deposits $10,000 in a savings bank and receives five percent interest per year, the original $10,000 investment grows only by the amount of the interest earned. If a person buys an annuity that pays $100 a month for life, that is exactly what will be received (except in the case of variable annuities whose periodic payouts are geared to the value of the equity securities in which the annuity company invests). The amount payable at the maturity of a bond is generally its face amount. So unless the bonds are purchased at a discount there is no capital appreciation. Interest is paid during the life of the bond, but when it matures, the investor receives only the face value of the bond.

Stocks may have a substantial appreciation factor. This will vary according to the nature of the stock, the industry involved, the expectations of investors for that particular industry, the position of the company in that industry, the inflation factor in the economy and many other intangibles that continue to baffle students of the stock market. Many stocks have been known to double, triple and quadruple in value in comparatively short period of time; others have nose-dived in similarly short periods.

Investments in oil, gas, cattle and the like may have some appreciation, especially if the price of the end products is influenced by inflation and other market conditions. Each of these specialized forms of investment has its own combination of periodic income and appreciation potential, and generalizations here would be hazardous.

Real estate, especially during the past 25 years, has shown remarkable increases in value because of a variety of factors such as increasing population and wealth, limitations on the quantity of land available, availability of mortgage money, inflation, and the special tax advantages available to real estate investors. As with other forms of investments, there is no point in generalizing, but the basic economic characteristics of real estate provide persuasive rationale for an expectation of long-term appreciation.

Manageability

The manageability of an investment is the extent to which it requires monitoring and periodic change. As a rule, real estate investments require much more management than, for example, a savings account or even common stocks. It is possible, however, to acquire the services of professional management and thereby reduce the burdens and risk of management.

In the context of this discussion "management" refers to the management of the investment as a segment of an investment portfolio, and not management of the operation of the business entity or property that may represent the investment. Probably every investment has a charge for management built into it when it does not require direct management by the investor. An investment in a savings bank does not seem to require management by the investor at all. However, the bank has to select the properties on which it will grant mortgage loans and determine what other investments and loans it may make. The cost of this management reduces the net return of the bank and, therefore, to the investor. Admittedly, this management cost is almost negligible as far as each individual depositor in the bank is concerned.

Stocks and bonds require careful and constant management regarding both the selection of individual stocks or securities and the timing of purchase and sale. The management may be supplied by the investors themselves, by professional management available from brokers or by professional managers hired for a fee. Investors may try to avoid the management problem and, in effect, hire professional management by investing in mutual funds. But here, too, professional management must be paid since each mutual fund has a professional management advisor who is paid a fee from the assets of the fund based upon the size of the fund's portfolio.

Other types of investments, such as those in oil, gas and cattle, require management, and the investors are often not experienced in these roles. Hence, included in the fees they pay for their investments is a charge for management.

For small properties, the investors may be their own managers. For large properties, they will generally need professional management help and should take this fact into consideration when analyzing the returns they can expect from their investments.

Taxability

The effect of income tax is well known, for it is only the after-tax dollar that is spendable by the investor. The federal government (and many states) takes its share of income via income tax, and the investor gets what remains. Not all sources of income are taxed alike. The tax on some types of profit may even be deferred, as in the case of exchanges. Some investments have certain built-in tax advantages which reduce the tax impact on the income produced. Finally, certain investments deemed desirable from a public policy standpoint are encouraged through tax credits.

In general, dividends, rents and interest are taxable as ordinary income, with the exception of the interest on municipal bonds. However, the accounting measure of taxable rental income is reduced by depreciation deductions (requiring no cash outlay) which, in turn, can boost after-tax cash flows to the investor.

Annuity income is only partially taxed since part of the annuity is merely a return of the capital investment. However, the taxable portion is taxed as ordinary income.

Income from the participation in a business venture as a sole proprietor or partner is taxable as ordinary income. Income from the sale of oil, gas, or other minerals is subject to ordinary income tax, but a depletion allowance reduces the income subject to tax.

Gain from the sale (or exchange when applicable) of investment property is taxed as ordinary income. A tax advantage lies in the tax-deferred exchange. Real estate that has appreciated in value may be exchanged for other real estate with the tax on the appreciation deferred to a later time. Income tax on the appreciation may be avoided altogether if the property acquired in the exchange, or some other property acquired in still another exchange for this acquired property, is held until death.

NOTES

1. Keith V. Smith and David K. Eiteman, *Essentials of Investing* (Homewood, IL: Richard D. Irwin, Inc., 1974), p. 7.
2. Nearly the entire issue of *The Real Estate Appraiser and Analyst*, vol. 44, no. 6, November-December, 1978, is devoted to the issue of the relationship of real estate investment yields to other alternative investments in the money and capital markets.

2
Real Estate Investments

INTRODUCTION TO COMMERCIAL-INVESTMENT BROKERAGE

The previous chapter dealt with the characteristics found in all forms of investments. This chapter will focus specifically on the nature and scope of real estate investments. The real estate broker must deal with and therefore be aware of a number of investor and user needs and desires. These needs and desires may be satisfied by acquiring interests in a wide variety of investment properties, ranging from raw land to small duplex multifamily units to massive shopping center developments. The interests that may be acquired in this large array of alternative properties also may take many forms such as lessee, sublessor, equity owner, mortgagee, and so on. The overwhelmingly large number of combinations open to the broker in meeting the client's objectives makes this task both complex and challenging.

SPECTRUM OF INCOME-PRODUCING PROPERTY

The spectrum of real estate investments is quite broad, ranging from residential income properties to commercial and industrial properties and to farms and land. The following list is illustrative of the real estate investment spectrum. Any of these properties could be owned by users or held by investors for rental income.

Residential
    Apartment houses
        Garden
        High-rise
    Hotels
    Motels
    Rest homes

Commercial
    Professional buildings (doctors, lawyers, and other professionals)
    Office buildings
    Shopping centers
        Regional
        Community
        Local
    Single purpose buildings
        Theaters
        Bowling alleys
        Free-standing retail stores
        Service stations

Industrial
    Warehouses
    Industrial parks
    Manufacturing facilities
    Utility company buildings
        Power plants
        Steam generation plants

Farms and land
    Recreation land
    Lots for single-family residences
    Subdivision land
    Residential lots zoned for multiple dwellings
    Commercially zoned land
    Industrially zoned land
    Raw acreage
    Farms
    Ranches

Clients

Being knowledgeable about the types of properties in the market is only part of the real estate investment broker's responsibility. The broker must also be aware of the people in the market who might use the services of a broker and what motivates them to invest in real estate.

On one side of the market are the sellers, or disposers, of property. These people provide the basic inventory for the broker. In many cases, the disposition of the property is by sale or exchange, and usually the principal motivation is that the property no longer meets the investment goals of the owner.

In other cases, the owner of the property has a problem that can be solved by refinancing the property, by improving the management of the property or by taking some other action that improves property performance in terms of the owner's objectives.

On the other side of the real estate market equation are those persons or institutions who wish to acquire real estate. The motivations for acquisition generally focus on financial gain, but may also include a variety of other personal reasons such as the desire to be directly involved in the creation and management of a business enterprise, pride of ownership, and the like. The range of skills is from first-time, totally inexperienced buyers to highly sophisticated, well trained representatives of major corporations.

Thus, the professional commercial-investment broker must understand the needs, motivations and objectives of a wide variety of sellers and buyers of investment property. The broker must be able to assist clients, whether buyers or sellers, in selecting that strategy which has the highest probability of achieving the individual client's objectives.

Types of Interest in Real Estate

Real estate interests can be divided in a number of ways. One form is a fee ownership interest which is the outright ownership of the property (subject, in many instances, to encumbrances such as loans for which the property is security).

Parts or all of the fee, however, may be leased to lessees who, in turn, may sublease part or all of their leasehold interests. A lessee also may construct improvements on the leased property (for which the lessee may be entitled to deduct depreciation or amortization expenses). However, at the termination of the lease, the improvement reverts to the lessor unless otherwise provided for in the lease contract.

There is also the interest of the lender. The mortgagee may be entitled to foreclose on the mortgage loan, acquire the property and then sell it should there be a default on the loans on that property. In the case of mortgages, there may be several mortgagee positions, each with a different interest. The first loan on the property has the first lien. If a second lender has made a loan, the lender stands in line behind the first mortgagee and has no claim against the property until the first mortgagee's loans have been satisfied.

In addition, there may be other liens against a property. For example, if a judgment is placed against the owner, the judgment holder may have a lien against the property which means there is a claim against the proceeds of sale for the amount of the lien. There also may be a mechanic's lien against the property for unpaid amounts to those who have made repairs or have done other work on the property.

Finally, the property may be subject to easements—the rights of others to make certain use of the property. An example would be the right of a telephone company to string telephone lines across part of the land.

Forms of Ownership

The ownership of a fee or other interests may be by an individual or by several persons in the form of joint ownership, a partnership, a trust or a corporation. The manner in which real estate, or an interest in real estate, is owned often has great tax significance, as illustrated in Chapter 8.

Individual investors generally seek to have tax losses generated by the real estate investment available to offset their other taxable income. The corporation is a separate entity and pays its own tax on any income it earns. However, the income remaining after tax, if paid to the stockholders by the way of dividends, is taxable to the stockholders; as a result, income may be taxed twice.

Accumulating after-tax income in the corporation is not necessarily a long-term solution. The corporation may become subject to a penalty tax for unreasonably accumulating earnings and profits. There also are problems of disposing of corporate-owned property or getting that property back into the hands of the stockholders. Many of these problems can be solved, but astute planning prior to acquisition is preferable.

Both the tax problems and tax-saving opportunities that evolve from the proper form of ownership are mentioned here to alert the reader to the importance of the ownership form. Too often not enough attention is paid to this aspect of real estate investment; too often investors act without regard to all of the consequences, only to discover at some later date that they are faced with tax liabilities that otherwise could have been avoided.

FACTORS AFFECTING REAL ESTATE INVESTMENTS

The investment factors of risk, appreciation, marketability, liquidity and management were discussed in Chapter 1. They are discussed in more detail here with respect to how they affect real estate investments.

Risk

Risk is one of the most vital factors to consider in any investment. As previously indicated, in virtually all cases the greater the risk element the greater the expected return must be in order to attract investors. This element of risk is itself composed of component parts, namely the quantity, the quality and the durability of the future income stream produced by the property.

Quantity.   If all other factors are equal, a property that is estimated to produce $6,000 of income will be less valuable than a similar property estimated to produce $10,000 of income over the same period of time, assuming equal probability of attainment.

Quality. A rooming house for transients and a small industrial warehouse, both producing the same amount of net income, are not necessarily worth the same amount. The warehouse normally will be deemed more valuable because the quality of its income stream is more reliable than that of the rooming house.

Durability. A parcel of property having two years remaining on its lease may not be as valuable as one with 15 years still to run on its lease. The concept of durability also may be related to the economic life of the property.

In essence, then, risk is the chance an investor takes that the amount earned will not be as much as anticipated. Return from investment will vary directly with the degree of risk. High risk tends to yield high income and low risk tends to produce low income.

Appreciation

Another characteristic inherent in real estate investments is that of increment or appreciation. Part of the reason for the importance of appreciation is inflation, the decrease in the value of money. In the case of land, however, much of this appreciation is caused by the law of supply and demand. Even though land is occasionally reclaimed from the sea, there is a limited amount of land on earth; this cannot be increased. At the same time, the population of the earth is increasing steadily. There is, therefore, an increased need or demand for whatever land is available. As the ratio of supply and demand changes, so does the value of the commodity—in this case land. Because of these factors, it is often true that the value of land and buildings can appreciate even though there is physical deterioration to the improvement occurring at the same time.

Liquidity and Marketability

Liquidity is another basic characteristic of real estate investment property. This characteristic includes two elements: the loan potential and the sale potential. Real estate is particularly well suited to financing. The property is virtually immovable in the case of buildings and virtually indestructible in the case of land. Traditionally, lending sources have been willing to make loans secured by real estate. After the income from a land parcel has enabled its owner to pay off mortgage loans, a new mortgage can be placed on the property. Proceeds of this new loan will be tax-free at that time.

Often, with real estate, there is no instant market and the owner desiring to sell must wait a considerable period of time before the property can be sold at the desired price. This differs markedly from the case of an owner of a stock who can merely telephone a broker and have the sale completed within minutes. But, perhaps because of the slowness of the real estate market, real estate usually is not subject to short cycles of upward and downward trends in prices, as is the securities market.

Sources of financing are as varied as one's imagination. Conventional sources are the commercial banks, savings and loan associations and insurance companies. In addition, there are union welfare funds, pension programs, profit-sharing and other kinds of employee-benefit and retirement funds (both public and private) and some charitable and educational institutions that may be interested in placing such loans for their investment portfolios. Not to be overlooked is the seller of the property who may be willing to take a purchase-money mortgage that will provide sufficient financing to complete a transaction. In some cases, the necessary financing can come from the brokers handling the transaction.

Property Management

A sometimes neglected characteristic of a real estate investment is the requirement of property management, which may be necessary in varying degrees, from the mere receipting of one check a month to the full-time responsibility for a large building. In some cases, the investor may be buying a full-time job if suitable local property management is not available.

In computing return on investment, the investor should remember to charge a cost for management (even if the investment is self-managed and has no cash outlay) in order to determine true return on the capital invested. Often professional management is worth the out-of-pocket cash outlay. Professional management usually knows when to increase or decrease rents and provides protection, such as tax escalator and cost-of-living index clauses, that the lessor might not ordinarily think of. Professionals have the ability to guide and counsel the investor on proper timing for selling or exchanging. On the other hand, sometimes the personal attention of an owner-manager can counteract the forces of a depressed market. This largely depends on the management skills of the professional or the owner.

SPECIAL FACTORS AFFECTING REAL ESTATE

Three special factors particularly applicable to real estate investments should be noted. They are tax shelter through cost recovery, leverage and exchange or installment sale potential.

Cost Recovery

Under the Tax Reform Act of 1986, improvements on real estate are depreciated on a straight-line basis. The amount is amortized over 27.5 years for residential property and 31.5 years for commercial property.

The importance of the cost recovery deduction is that it requires no cash outlay, yet it reduces the income from the property that is subject to tax. Further, such deductions taken can exceed real depreciation in the property, thereby creating tax-free dollars because of income tax savings. (If the deduction exceeds the income from the property, the excess deduction may be applied to reduce other taxable income the property owner may have.) Since a dollar of tax that does not have to be paid is, in essence, a form of income, the deduction helps to produce more after-tax dollars from a real estate investment than would be available were the same amount of income earned from another form of investment which does not allow for such deductions.

The relationship between the tax accounting concept of *income* and the investment concept of *cash flows* is shown in Figure 1 for a single year. Assume that the property improvement cited above produced a net operating income (NOI) of $10,000.

As shown in Figure 1, the shelter of income from the real estate that otherwise would be taxed immediately may be seen as a three-step process, depending upon how large the cost recovery deduction is.

1. Cost recovery shelters the principal portion of the Annual Debt Service (ADS), since this is a cash outflow that is not deductible as an expense.
2. If the amount of cost recovery exceeds principal reduction (as in the example above), the next portion of income that is sheltered is the Cash Flow Before Tax (CFBT).
3. To the extent that total cost recovery exceeds the sum of principal reduction and CFBT, other income unrelated to the property may be sheltered. (See the discussion in Chapter 7 on passive losses.)

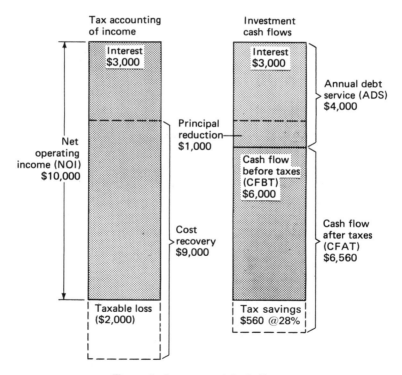

Figure 1　Income and Cash Flows

Leverage

As was previously mentioned, real estate is well suited to financing. Traditionally it has been very good security for loans. As such, real estate can be acquired or carried with a smaller percentage of cash outlay by the owner than most other investments.

The ability to finance the purchase or carrying of real estate gives rise to leverage. Leverage arises because all appreciation of the property belongs to the property holder even though there may be substantial loans against the property. Similarly, all of the income belongs to the property holder, regardless of the amounts of the loan.

Examples

      1. Assume a property available today for $100,000 will sell for $150,000 five years from now. If the property is bought for $100,000 cash, the buyer will subsequently realize a $50,000 profit or a 50 percent increase on the initial investment. Suppose, however, the buyer is able to obtain a $90,000 mortgage, committing only $10,000 of personal funds. When the property is sold for $150,000 and the $90,000 mortgage is paid off, the remaining $60,000 is a 500 percent increase over the initial investment. (The cost of the transaction and the loan for the five-year period have been ignored to simplify the example.)

      2. Leverage has its negative side, too. If the investor puts up $10,000 of personal funds and borrows $90,000, and if the value of the property then falls to $90,000, the entire $10,000 investment will be lost.

      3. Leverage is also present in terms of the current income from the property. Suppose the net operating income from the property in the previous example amounts to $5,000. If the investor puts up $100,000 in cash, there will be a 5 percent return on the initial investment. If the investor puts up only $10,000 in cash, there will be a 50 percent return on investment. (Again, we are ignoring the cost of the loan and the effect of income taxes to avoid complicating this illustration.)

Exchange or Installment Sale of Property

Investment real estate can be exchanged on a tax-deferred basis, a possibility not available with many other popular investment alternatives (see Chapter 11). Even if the property is sold, the gain on sale may be prorated over several tax periods through the vehicle of the installment sale (see Chapter 10). In either case, these options provide owners additional factors to consider before they dispose of property.

3
Fundamentals of Discounted
Cash Flow Analysis

VALUATION OF INCOME-PRODUCING PROPERTIES

Meaning of Value

Of central importance in the analysis of any investment is the determination of value. Real estate brokers, appraisers, investors and users are concerned with estimates of value for existing or proposed property developments. Those desiring an estimate of value have a variety of purposes; thus there is also a variety of definitions for value. In essence, the definition of value is a function of the purpose for which an estimate of value is sought.

For example, the well-known real estate appraiser, Alfred Ring, lists the following as representing only *a few* of the many types of value in common use today.[1]

Economic value	Sale value
Stable value	Salvage value
Appraised value	Intrinsic value
Potential value	Extrinsic value
Book value	Tax value
Sound value	Use value
Fair value	Rental value

Real value	Speculative value
Real value	Speculative value
True value	Reproduction value
Depreciated value	Nuisance value
Warranted value	Liquidation value
Free value	Mortgage value
Cash value	Improved value
Capital value	Insurance value
Exchange value	Leasehold value

The economist typically views value as the point of intersection on a supply and demand curve. The residential broker may consider the value of a certain property as the price the property will bring from an informed buyer after the property has had reasonable exposure in an active and competitive market. The appraiser may view the value of a property (1) as having the same value as a comparable property already in existence and sold in the marketplace; (2) as having a value equal to the cost of reproducing a given property with equivalent utility; and (3) as having the same value as an investment with a similar income stream. These all are related concepts of *market value*. To the user of the property, value is related to the specific purpose for which a property is used and the productivity achieved in this use. To the typical investor, however, value is the present worth of the anticipated future income stream or cash benefits that will accrue from the investment. The primary focus of this book is *investment value*. To the extent that a buyer is typical of investors in the market who are most likely to purchase an income-producing property, investment value may equal market value.

Amenity Properties versus Income-Producing Properties

For amenity properties, such as owner-occupied homes, the value of the property most often derives from the right to use the realty. Payment for the property typically comes from income and/or wealth totally unrelated to the property itself. The approval of a mortgage loan on such a property is generally based on the owner's ability to meet mortgage payments, not on the property's ability to generate income.

In contrast, income-producing properties provide a stream of payments from the rental of the property that may be used as the basis of its purchase price and as the security for mortgage financing. Typically, the investor collects rents and pays the necessary expenses of operation, such as property taxes and maintenance. What remains is available to pay financing charges. The balance provides a return to the investor for assuming the risk of ownership. In the case of real estate investments, like all other forms of investments, the investor is concerned with *cash* received in the future in return for cash or its equivalent invested in the present. Tax benefits from the ownership of real estate, the impact of financing and financial leverage, depreciation, and the like are factors that influence the after-tax cash flows accruing from a property. Once the after-tax cash flows are determined or estimated, it is still necessary to decide which alternative stream of future income is most valuable to a specific investor.

Even if the investor chooses to use the property rather than rent it, the rental payments that would have been paid to obtain a comparable property represent a savings to the investor-user-owner. The savings, in turn, may be used to support the purchase and financing of the property. In either case, whether the investor rents the income property to another or uses the property personally, the value of the property may be derived as the present worth of the estimated income from rents to be received by the investor (actual or imputed rent) plus the present worth of the estimated proceeds from selling the property.

Capitalization of Income

The basis used to estimate the value of income-producing real estate is the potential income it can produce in the future. The process of converting future income into a single present value is called capitalization. Value is a direct function of income. Therefore, any change in anticipated future income affects the capitalized value (present value) of the income.

Future income streams are capitalized into single values so the investors may have a consistent basis to compare investment alternatives. The primary selection criterion of the investor should be based upon some measure of the stream of income from rental payments plus proceeds from the eventual sale of the property compared with the initial cash (down payment) invested to receive this future income. Reduced to its simplest terms, the cash that a buyer is willing to invest for an income-producing property is directly related to the income that is estimated to be received and the rate of return that is desired.

Example

If $100,000 were invested today at an annual interest rate of 10 percent, the investment would accrue to a value of $110,000 by the end of the first year. If this total amount is considered to represent both return *of* the original investment ($100,000) and return *on* the investment ($10,000), the "return on" portion is indeed 10 percent and the earnings may be withdrawn and enjoyed with no effect on the original investment. This process of earning and withdrawal can take place endlessly as long as (1) only the "return on" portion is withdrawn and (2) the original investment amount ($100,000) can be reinvested each and every year at 10 percent. Stated another way, an income of $10,000 per year capitalized at 10 percent suggests that the investment value is $100,000.

This example represents the most simplistic form of income capitalization, perpetuity capitalization. The stream of equal payments are received at the end of each period (usually one year) for infinity. The capitalization rate must be consistent with the periods. In the example, the cash flows of $10,000 were received at the end of each year. The capitalization rate was 10 percent per year. Symbolically this may be stated as

$$V = \frac{I}{R}$$

V = value or present worth of the future rights to periodic income
I = periodic net income
R = rate of capitalization

This formula represents the most basic building block to an understanding of the investment process. However, the preceding illustration deals with the very simple case of capitalization in perpetuity where the principal is assumed to remain unchanged over an indefinite period. Although raw land may provide an excellent example of realty that could produce such a regular income stream, the more common investment situation involves capitalization of uneven cash flows over a term. To better understand the process whereby income received for a finite term is capitalized into a single present value, it is necessary to introduce the concept and technique of compound interest and discounting.

COMPOUND INTEREST AND DISCOUNTING

Every financial investment produces a stream of cash flows, or spendable dollars. The cash flows created by alternative investments are rarely equal in size or duration. Compound interest and discounting techniques are used to adjust cash flows for comparison on a par basis. These techniques are widely used in many financial fields, including investment real estate, mortgage lending, banking, corporate finance and securities investment. Compound interest and discounting methods are used to (1) compare investment alternatives, (2) compare anticipated investment performance to the investor's financial objectives and (3) compare investment performance under alternative assumptions that affect the cash flows.

Investor Motivation

When comparing investment alternatives with comparable risks associated with the return *on* and return *of* capital, the rational investor is motivated by two basic preferences. They are simply summarized as

more is better than less

and

sooner is better than later.

More Is Better than Less

This investor preference has two basic aspects. First, when given alternative investment opportunities of comparable risk that require an equal capital investment and have the same timing of cash flows, the investor will prefer the investment that produces the most cash. Consider the two comparisons of four investments below.

Example

The initial investment in each case is $1,000. The parentheses indicate that the cash flow is paid by the investor or that it is a negative cash flow. Time period 0 is the time the initial investment is made. Other cash flows are assumed to be received at the end of period (EOP) unless otherwise indicated.

Time Period (EOP)	Investment A	Investment B
0	($1,000)	($1,000)
1	–0–	–0–
2	–0–	–0–
3	$1,800	$1,500

Investment A is superior because the same investment of $1,000 will produce more return of funds at the end of the investment holding period.

Time Period (EOP)	Investment C	Investment D
0	($1,000)	($1,000)
1	600	500
2	600	500
3	600	500

Investment C is superior because each cash flow is more than those of investment D.

The second aspect of the assumption that more is better than less is that an investor will prefer to invest less to acquire the same cash benefits. In the preceding example, investment A was better than investment B. Investment A would be even more desirable if it were acquired for $800 instead of $1,000. The same reasoning is applicable to investment C compared with investment D. Compound interest and discounting techniques could be used to determine how much less would have to be paid for investment B or D, respectively, to produce the better return to the investor.

Sooner Is Better than Later

Among investment alternatives with comparable risk and which produce equal cash flows, the investor will prefer the alternative that produces cash flows sooner.

Example

Investment A is more desirable than investment E below since the cash flow is received one period sooner. There is no compensation for waiting the additional period; therefore, receiving the cash flow sooner is better.

Time Period (EOP)	Investment A	Investment E
0	($1,000)	($1,000)
1	–0–	–0–
2	–0–	–0–
3	$1,800	–0–
4	–0–	$1,800

Investment E would be more appealing if it cost less at time period 0 and/or produced more income at end of period (EOP) 4.

Compare investment A with investment C to determine which is preferable. The cost of each alternative is $1,000. The holding period is the same for each alternative. The total cash flows are $1,800 for both investments.

Time Period (EOP)	Investment A	Investment C
0	($1,000)	($1,000)
1	–0–	600
2	–0–	600
3	$1,800	600
Total Positive Cash Flows	$1,800	$1,800

The rational investor would prefer investment C because a portion of the total cash flows are received sooner. There is no compensation from investment A for forgoing the earlier payments available from investment C. Investment A might be better if it cost less or produced a larger cash flow at EOP 3.

Time Value (or Cost) of Money

The time value of money is the preference to have money now rather than receive the same amount in the future. It is exemplified by the interest charged on borrowed funds. A lender makes a loan as an investment. In return for extending funds to a borrower, the lender will receive the original funds loaned (return *of* capital) plus interest (return *on* capital). The interest rate represents the time value of money to the lender. The lender can invest the funds with any credit-worthy borrower at the going interest rate. The interest rate, in this case, would be the lender's *opportunity cost* of capital. That is, the lender would forgo the interest charge by not seizing a suitable investment opportunity (a loan to a credit-worthy borrower).

Cash flows can be converted to a present value—capitalized—with a specified interest rate as shown in the example below.

Example

A lender will loan $1,000 for one year at 12 percent interest. The loan plus interest will be paid in full at the end of the year (EOY) 1. The lender therefore will receive $1,000 plus $120 (12 percent of $1,000) or $1,120 at EOY 1. The ratio of the amount invested now ($1,000) to the lump sum amount to be received at EOY 1 ($1,120) is

$$\frac{\$1,000}{\$1,120} = 0.892857 \text{ or } 89.29\%$$

Given this ratio, a lender or other investor who requires a 12 percent return on money could compute the percent value of a lump sum of money to be received at the end of one year. The process of computing the present value of cash flows is called discounting. For example, the present value of $10,000 to be received at the end of one year to an investor requiring a 12 percent return on capital is

$$\begin{array}{r} \$10,000.00 \\ \times \ 0.892857 \\ \hline \$8,928.57 \end{array}$$

An investor requiring a 12 percent return on capital would be indifferent to receiving $8,928.57 now or receiving $10,000 one year from now.

In summary, there are two basic aspects to time value of money calculations. First, cash flows can be *compounded* to determine an amount to be received in the future, or a future value $\boxed{FV}$.[2] Second, anticipated cash flows to be received in the future can be *discounted* to determine the present value $\boxed{PV}$ at the beginning of the first relevant time period. A specific interest rate $\boxed{i}$ is required for both compound interest and discount calculations as well as the number of compounding periods $\boxed{n}$.

CONCEPT OF COMPOUND INTEREST

In the preceding example, the time period used to illustrate the time value of money was one year, with interest paid only once during the one-year period. This is generally referred to as simple interest since interest was earned only on the original investment. However, investment opportunities with compound interest are generally available. Compounding occurs when periodic earnings are reinvested each period along with the original investment. It is difficult to compare alternative investments with different investment compounding periods.

Example

Suppose that the following two investment alternatives were presented: (1) an investment of $100 that returns $160 at the end of five years and (2) an investment of $100 that returns $112 at the end of one year. One simple means of comparing these two alternatives is to convert the five-year investment to an annual simple rate. Since the investment returns 60 percent per five-year period, the average annual rate is 60 percent divided by five—12 percent per annum. Since the one-year investment also returns 12 percent per annum, it would appear that the two investments produce the same return.

This comparison precludes the possibility of reinvesting both principal and interest at the end of each year for five years when selecting the one-year investment. This is exactly the same investment amount and duration as the five-year investment since annual interest earned is not withdrawn but reinvested. Both investments would then involve the commitment of $100 for a duration of five years with no cash returns to the investor until the end of the fifth year. In the case of reinvestment each year, the following would occur.

Year	Investment Beginning of Year (BOY)	Interest Rate	Interest Earned During Year	Investment Amount Plus Interest Earned EOY
1	$100.00	.12	$12.00	$112.00
2	112.00	.12	13.44	125.44
3	124.44	.12	15.05	140.49
4	140.49	.12	16.86	157.35
5	157.35	.12	18.88	176.23

Thus, if the one-year investment is selected *and* the investor is able to reinvest the annual proceeds at the 12 percent rate over the five-year term, the $100 investment would grow to an amount of $176.23, or $16.23 more than the simple five-year investment that returns only $160.

Comparing Alternative Investments

The rate of return for nearly all investments may be measured in terms of *annual return* on invested capital, with compounding assumed when the capital invested is not returned within one year. Thus, the concept of compound interest and discounting is fundamental to evaluating investments in general and real estate investments specifically. Compound discounting not only reflects the investor's preference for returns sooner rather than later but also includes in the cost of waiting the assumption that the investor has the opportunity to reinvest both principal and earnings each period.

If the investment choice is simple, such as the choice of investing $1,000 today and receiving either $1,100 one year from today or $1,100 two years from today, no measurement is actually needed. However, investment alternatives are seldom that simple. For example, consider the problem of measuring the annual rate of return for the following investment alternatives, each of which cost $10,000.

CASH RECEIPTS FROM ALTERNATIVE INVESTMENTS

End of Year	Discounted Mortgage	Five-Year Note	Stock	Insurance Annuity	Land
1	$ 1,627.45	–0–	$ 1,000	$1,000	–0–
2	1,627.45	–0–	1,000	each	–0–
3	1,627.45	–0–	1,000	year	–0–
4	1,627.45	–0–	1,000	to	–0–
5	1,627.45	$16,105.10	1,000	perpetuity	–0–
6	1,627.45	–0–	1,000		–0–
7	1,627.45	–0–	1,000		–0–
8	1,627.45	–0–	1,000		–0–
9	1,627.45	–0–	1,000		–0–
10	1,627.45	–0–	11,000		$25,937.42
Total Receipts	$16,274.50	$16,105.10	$20,000	∞	$25,937.42

The problem here is to convert each of these cash flows to a common base so that they may be compared. In order to deal with this type of measurement problem, compound interest and discount techniques must be used. The calculation required may be performed with a wide variety of preprogrammed, hand-held, financial calculators. However, the following explanations use compound interest and discount tables to illustrate the concepts associated with the calculations.

Compound Interest and Discount Calculations

Proper use and understanding of compound interest and discount tables is a prerequisite to grasping the measurement of investment rates of return, present value and a number of other calculations commonly used in real estate investment analysis. Today, most calculations are made using an electronic financial calculator. However, the compound interest and discount tables present a complex picture that is not possible with the typical single line display of a hand-held calculator. For this reason a rather detailed presentation will be made of such tables, their construction and their real estate applications.

Appendix A to this book contains selected compound interest tables from Part II of the fourth edition of Ellwood's *Tables for Real Estate Appraising and Financing.*[3] The sample tables shown are 5 percent and 10 percent (monthly, quarterly, semiannual and annual factors) and are used for purposes of illustration. You also may use them to follow the examples in this chapter. The full set of tables contained in Ellwood has monthly, quarterly, semiannual and annual factors for rates of interest in .25 percent increments from 3 percent to 12 percent. In addition, factor tables in 1 percent increments are available from 13 percent through 30 percent. Each table contains six columns as follows.

Column	Function of the Dollar (Factor)
1	Amount of 1 at compound interest
2	Accumulation of 1 per period
3	Sinking fund factor
4	Present value, reversion of 1
5	Present value, ordinary annuity of 1 per period
6	Installment to amortize 1

1. Amount of 1 at compound interest (column 1). The fundamental building block of all compounding and discounting calculations is the future value of a sum compounded at a specific interest rate per period. A time deposit or savings account is a common example. Consider a savings account deposit of $10,000 at 10-percent interest per annum, compounded annually, which is left on deposit for two years. Since the interest is compounded annually, the interest earned EOY 1 will also earn interest during Year 2.

The balance EOY 1 will be

$$\$10,000 + (\$10,000 \times .10) = \$10,000 + \$1,000 = \$11,000$$

This equation may be restated as

$$\$10,000\ (1\ +\ .10)\ =\ \$11,000$$

Interest will be earned on the total balance of \$11,000 during year 2. The balance EOY 2 will be

$$\$11,000\ (1\ +\ .10)\ =\ \$12,100$$

This equation may be restated as

$$\underbrace{\$10,000\ (1\ +\ .10)}\ \times\ (1\ +\ .10)\ =\ \$12,100$$

Calculation of balance
EOY 1 from above

This is equal to

$$\$10,000\ (1\ +\ .10)^2\ =\ \$12,100$$

The general formula for this calculation is

$$\boxed{FV}\ =\ \boxed{PV}\ (1\ +\ i)^n$$

where:

$\boxed{PV}$ = amount invested at the present

$\boxed{i}$ = interest rate per period (effective rate)

$\boxed{n}$ = number of compounding periods

$\boxed{FV}$ = future value at the end of n compounding periods.

The expression $(1\ +\ i)$ is called the base. The base with the exponent n is part of all six functions of the dollar (listed on page 29). The base is the mathematical translation that expresses the *return of* capital (1) and the *return on* capital (i). Note that if the interest rate is 0, the base would equal 1, just the return of capital.

$$\boxed{FV}\ =\ \boxed{PV} \qquad (1 \qquad + \qquad i)^n$$
$$\qquad\qquad\qquad\quad \uparrow \qquad\qquad\qquad \uparrow$$
$$\qquad\qquad \text{return } of\ \boxed{PV} \qquad \text{return } on\ \boxed{PV}$$

Rates of return (e.g., interest rates, bond yields) usually are stated as annual rates. However, the compounding periods frequently are less than one year. For example, savings accounts may be compounded quarterly, monthly or daily. The *effective* rate (i) or interest rate per period must be consistent with the length of the compounding period. Therefore, the annual interest rate is divided by the number of compounding periods per year. The effective rate is the rate actually applied to the investment balance *each* period. In the case of the investment in the preceding example, here are the effective rates for some alternative compounding periods.

Compounding Period	Annual Rate		Compounding Periods Per Year		Effective Rate (*i*)
Annual	10%	÷	1	=	10%
Semiannual	10%	÷	2	=	5%
Quarterly	10%	÷	4	=	2.5%
Monthly	10%	÷	12	=	0.8333%

The number of compounding periods (*n*) during the investment horizon (holding period) must be consistent with the effective rate (*i*). Therefore, the total number of compounding periods is equal to the number of compounding periods per year multiplied by the number of years (*N*) during the investment horizon. Continuing with the same example, the number of compounding periods in the two-year investment horizon are summarized below.

Compounding Period	Investment Horizon (Years)		Compounding Periods Per Year		Total Compounding Periods (*n*)
Annual	2	×	1	=	2
Semiannual	2	×	2	=	4
Quarterly	2	×	4	=	8
Monthly	2	×	12	=	24

The effect of different compounding periods is illustrated in the following table. It is a summary of the future value $\boxed{FV}$ of the $10,000 invested for two years at 10-percent interest per year with different compounding periods. The effective rates and total compounding periods were calculated in the preceding tables.

Compounding Periods (EOP)	Amount of 1 at Compound Interest		Period in Time	
	Calculation	Factor	$\boxed{PV}$	$\boxed{FV}$
Annual	$(1 + .10)^2$	1.210000	× $10,000	= $12,100.00
Semiannual	$(1 + .05)^4$	1.215506	× $10,000	= $12,155.06
Quarterly	$(1 + .025)^8$	1.218403	× $10,000	= $12,184.03
Monthly	$(1 + .00833)^{24}$	1.220390	× $10,000	= $12,203.90

Note that the future value increases as the number of compounding periods per year increases. This could be expected because the return *on* investment is added to the balance sooner and therefore earns interest for a longer time.

The compound interest formula for compounding periods may be generalized as

$$\boxed{FV} = \boxed{PV} \, (1 + I/p)^{N \times p}$$

where

$$I = \text{annual interest rate}$$
$$N = \text{number of years}$$
$$p = \text{number of compounding periods per year}$$

Therefore,

$$\frac{I}{p} = i = \text{effective rate of interest earned per period}$$

$$N \times p = n = \text{total number of compounding periods}$$

From the example, the $10,000 invested at 10 percent interest per year, compounded monthly, is

$$\$10,000 \times \left(1 + \frac{.10}{12}\right)^{2 \times 12} = \$10,000 \times (1 + .008333)^{24} = \$12,203.90$$

This is a restatement of the results from the table above.

The facts in the summary above can be found in column 1 of the tables in Appendix A of this book. Refer to the pages showing 10 percent for this example. Then turn to the 10 percent table with the appropriate compounding periods per year (e.g., monthly). The factors are listed for each period during the first year, then each year for at least 25 years, depending on the interest rate. The number of years is found in the left-hand column. The total number of compounding periods (*n*) for each year is found in the right-hand column. The amount of 1 at compound interest for two years at 10 percent interest per year, compounded monthly, will be found on the 10-percent monthly compound interest table, in column 1, next to year 2. There you will find the calculated factor of 1.220390.

The factors are computed for $1.00. Simply multiply by the number of dollars of the investment to determine the appropriate quantity. Our example, thus far, has used an investment of $10,000. Using the appropriate table, the future value $\boxed{\text{FV}}$ of $10,000 invested at 10 percent, compounded monthly for seven years, would be

$$\$10,000 \times 2.007920 = \$20,079.20$$

⌐factor from column 1 of 10 percent monthly table

Indeed, the calculated value is

$$\$10,000 \times \left(1 + \frac{.10}{12}\right)^{7 \times 12} = \$20,079.20$$

The $\boxed{\text{FV}}$ for seven years, $20,079.20, is greater than the $\boxed{\text{FV}}$ for two years, $12,203.90. This would be expected since the investor waited longer to receive the money. One interpretation of the forgoing is that an investor with an opportunity cost of capital of 10 percent that could be compounded monthly would be indifferent to having $10,000 today, $12,203.90 at the end of two years or $20,079.20 at the end of seven years.

The amount required by an investor in the future will increase as the interest rate (or opportunity cost of capital) increases. If an investor could earn 12 percent compounded monthly on the $10,000, instead of 10 percent, the $12,203.90 would not be sufficient compensation EOY 2. The investor would require the $\boxed{\text{FV}}$ of $10,000 compounded monthly at 12 percent for two years. That amount is

$$\$10,000 \times \left(1 + \frac{.12}{12}\right)^{2 \times 12} = \$12,697.35$$

$\boxed{\text{FV}}$ of $10,000 @ 10%, compounded monthly $= \underline{\$12,203.90}$

Difference $= \quad \$493.45$

The investor would require an additional $493.45 EOY 2 if the required interest rate were 12 percent instead of 10 percent.

The characteristics of any amount at compound interest are the same. Many investments produce cash flows with more than one amount to be received in the future. If the income stream has equal payments received at the end of equal time periods it is easy to calculate the future value based on the mathematics of the amount of 1 at compound interest.

2. Accumulation of 1 per period (column 2) is used to calculate the future value of *equal* payments invested at the *end* of each period for a total of n compounding periods at i interest rate per period. To illustrate, the $\boxed{\text{FV}}$ of five equal payments of $1,200 invested at the end of each year for five years, compounded annually at 10 percent, could be calculated as five separate investments, as follows.

Year	Time Invested (years)	Column 1 factor	Amount Invested	$\boxed{\text{FV}}$
1	4	1.464100	× $1,200.00 =	$1,756.92
2	3	1.331000	× $1,200.00 =	$1,597.20
3	2	1.210000	× $1,200.00 =	$1,452.00
4	1	1.100000	× $1,200.00 =	$1,320.00
5	0	1.000000	× $1,200.00 =	$1,200.00
Totals		6.105100		$7,326.12

Payments are made at the end of each period. Therefore, no interest is earned during the first period. It is as if the first payment were made at the beginning of year (BOY) 2. The last payment is made at the end of the investment term; accordingly, no interest is earned on the last payment. The total balance EOY 5 will be $7,326.12 which is equal to the sum of the column 1 factors multiplied by the amount of the payment:

$$\$1,200 \times 6.105100 = \$7,326.12$$

The sum of amount of 1 at compound interest (column 1 factor) for each period at a specific interest rate is equal to the accumulation of 1 per period in column 2. Compare the factors above with those found in the 10 percent annual compound interest table. This is most apparent on the annual tables. The column 1 factors for each compounding period less than one year are listed for the first year only (the column factor for an amount invested at compound interest for 13 months is not listed).

The formula to calculate the factor for the accumulation of one per period is

$$\boxed{\text{FV}} = \left[\frac{(1 + i)^n - 1}{i} \right]$$

The effective rate (i) must be consistent with the total number of compounding periods (n). The factor for the preceding example is

$$\left[\frac{(1 + .10)^5 - 1}{.10} \right] = 6.105100$$

The future value of n equal payments made at the end of each period, compounded at i interest rate, is

$$\boxed{\text{FV}} = \boxed{\text{PMT}} \left[\frac{(1 + i)^n - 1}{i} \right]$$

Compare \$1,200 invested at the end of each year for five years compounded annually at 10 percent with monthly investments of \$100 compounded monthly at 10 percent per year for five years. The $\boxed{\text{FV}}$ of the latter is

$$\$100 \left[\frac{(1 + .10/12)^{5 \times 12} - 1}{.10/12} \right] = \$7,743.71$$

As we saw above, the $\boxed{\text{FV}}$ of the annual compounding is \$7,326.12.

The same total funds are invested each year (\$100 × 12 months = \$1,200); however, the investor begins to earn interest at the end of the first month and the interest is compounded more frequently. Therefore, shorter compounding periods with comparable payments will produce a greater future value.

Two generalizations are consistent with the characteristics of an amount invested at compound interest. First, an increase in the number of compounding periods and, consequently, the number of periodic payments will increase the future value. This is because more payments will earn more interest for more compounding periods. Second, as the periodic effective rate increases, the future value of the accumulated equal investments per period also increases. Each payment will then earn more interest.

3. Sinking fund factor (column 3) is used to calculate the equal payments required to be invested at i interest rate per period at the end of each period for n periods that will grow to a specified future value. This is similar to the accumulation of 1 per period, except that the future value is known and the payment is unknown. Thus the accumulation of 1 per period (column 2) and the sinking fund factor (column 3) are reciprocals.

Suppose that an investor required \$7,743.71 at the end of five years. In order to achieve this financial goal, equal payments will be invested monthly at 10 percent per year compounded monthly. It has been determined that $100 invested each month at 10 percent per year, compounded monthly, will grow to $7,743.71. Recall that the formula for the accumulation of 1 per period is

$$\boxed{FV} = \boxed{PMT}\left[\frac{(1+i)^n - 1}{i}\right]$$

The reciprocal formula to calculate the sinking fund factor is:

$$\boxed{PMT} = \frac{\boxed{FV}}{\left[\frac{(1+i)^n - 1}{i}\right]} = \boxed{FV}\left[\frac{i}{(1+i)^n - 1}\right]$$

The computation to determine the equal monthly payment that will grow to $7,743.71 in the five years, compounded at 10 percent per month, is

$$\$7,743.71\left[\frac{.10/12}{(1+.10/12)^{5\times12} - 1}\right] = \$7,743.71 \times 0.012913 = \$100$$

Note that i is the effective rate per month, which is 10 percent divided by 12 months per year. There are five years multiplied by 12 months per year, or 60 monthly investments. That is, n equals 60. The factor (0.012913) for $1 may be found under column 3 in the 10-percent monthly table.

The periodic payment will decrease if periodic investment earns more interest during the investment horizon. Compare the $100 per month in the example to the monthly payment required to grow to the same future value of $7,743.71 at 12 percent per year.

$$\$7,743.71\left[\frac{.12/12}{(1+.12/12)^{5\times12} - 1)}\right] = \$94.82$$

The periodic payment declines as the number of payment periods (n) increases. For example, compare the annual payment, compounded at 10 percent, required to grow to $10,000 in five years and ten years.

For five years,

$$\$10,000\left[\frac{.10}{(1+.10)^5 - 1}\right] = \$1,637.97$$

For ten years,

$$\$10,000\left[\frac{.10}{(1+.10)^{10} - 1}\right] = \$627.45$$

This relationship is apparent from the factors listed in the tables. For any effective rate, the sinking fund factor is 1.000000 for the first period since one payment made at the end of one period does not earn any interest. The factors decline as the number of periods increase.

4. Present value reversion of 1 (column 4)   shows the amounts that must be invested at present to grow to a specific value at the end of n periods at i effective rate. This is the reciprocal of the amount of 1 at compound interest (column 1). For example, an investor wishes to know how much should be invested now, at 10-percent interest compounded annually, to have $10,000 EOY 2. The formula for the present value reversion of 1 is

$$\boxed{PV} = \boxed{FV} \left[\frac{1}{(1 + i)^n} \right]$$

The solution to the problem is then

$$10,000 \left[\frac{1}{(1 + .10)^2} \right] = 10,000 \times 0.826446 = \$8,264.46$$

The investor would have to invest $8,264.46 at 10 percent compounded annually to grow to $10,000 EOY 2. Stated another way, an investor with an opportunity to invest money at 10 percent compounded annually would be indifferent to having $8,264.46 today or receiving $10,000 EOY 2. The factor of 0.826446 will be found in column 4 of the 10 percent annual table.

Determining the present value of money to be received in the future is called discounting. The opportunity cost of capital, 10 percent in the example above, is the discount rate. As demonstrated in Chapter 4, the present value of cash flows is a valuable measure to determine the relative benefits of investment alternatives.

The impact of effective rates and investment duration on the present value reversion of 1 is inversely related to the amount of 1 at compound interest. The present value of a sum to be received in the future is less if the investor must wait longer to receive the money. That is, the present value of $10,000 to be received EOY 10 is less than if it were to be received EOY 2. Remember that sooner is better than later.

The present value of a future lump sum of money is less if the number of compounding periods per year is greater. Compare $8,264.46, the present value of $10,000 to be received EOY 2, *discounted* at 10 percent and compounded annually, to the same terms except for monthly compounding:

$$\$10,000 \left[\frac{1}{(1 + .10/12)^{2 \times 12}} \right] = \$8,194.10$$

The present value is less for the monthly compounding.

The present value of a future cash flow decreases as the discount rate increases. Compare $8,264.46 from above with the present value of $10,000, discounted at 12 percent with annual compounding for two years:

$$\$10,000 \left[\frac{1}{(1 + .12)^2} \right] = 7,971.94$$

5. Present value of an ordinary annuity (column 5)   shows the present value of an ordinary annuity—a stream of equal payments made at the end of equal time periods—as the sum of the present value of each individual payment (column 4). For example, the present value of $1,000 to be received at the end of each year for five years and discounted at 10 percent annually is

Year	$\boxed{\text{PMT}}$	$\boxed{\text{PV}}$ of 1 Factor	$\boxed{\text{PV}}$
1	$1,000.00 ×	0.909091	= $ 909.09
2	$1,000.00 ×	0.826446	= 826.45
3	$1,000.00 ×	0.751315	= 751.31
4	$1,000.00 ×	0.683013	= 683.01
5	$1,000.00 ×	0.620921	= 620.92
Total		3.790786	$3,790.79*

*Rounding error results from alternative methods of computation.

An investor with a 10 percent cost of capital would be indifferent to receiving an ordinary annuity of $1,000 at the end of each year for five years or the lump sum of $3,790.79 today.

The formula to calculate the present value of an ordinary annuity is

$$\boxed{\text{PV}} = \boxed{\text{PMT}} \left[\frac{1 - \frac{1}{(1 + i)^n}}{i} \right]$$

Using the same example, the present value would be calculated as

$$\$1,000 \left[\frac{1 - \frac{1}{(1 + .10)^5}}{.10} \right] = \$1,000 \times 3.790787 = \$3,790.79$$

The factor 3.790787 will be found in column 5 of the 10 percent annual table.

As with all compound interest and discount problems, the number of periods, n, and the effective periodic rate, i, must be consistent. For example, the present value of $250 received at the end of each calendar quarter and discounted at 10 percent per year for five years is

$$\$250 \left[\frac{1 - \frac{1}{(1 + .10/4)^{4 \times 5}}}{.10/4} \right] = \$250 \times 15.589162 = \$3,897.29$$

Notice that the present value of the four quarterly payments per year for five years of $250 discounted at 10 percent quarterly is greater than the $\boxed{\text{PV}}$ of five annual installments of $1,000 discounted at the same rate. That is because the cash flow starts at the end of one calendar quarter compared to one calendar year.

The $\boxed{\text{PV}}$ of an ordinary annuity decreases as the discount rate increases. Compare $3,897.29, the $\boxed{\text{PV}}$ of $250 received at the end of each calendar quarter for five years and discounted at 10 percent per year, to the same cash flow discounted at 12 percent.

$$\$250 \left[\frac{1 - \dfrac{1}{(1 + .12/4)^{4 \times 5}}}{.12/4} \right] = \$250 \times 14.877475 = \$3,719.37$$

The $\boxed{PV}$ of an ordinary annuity increases as the number of payments increases. However, since the payments to be received in the distant future have a smaller $\boxed{PV}$ than do earlier payments, the $\boxed{PV}$ increases by smaller and smaller increments as the term increases.

Ordinary annuity payments are assumed to be received at the end of each period. The $\boxed{PV}$ of an *annuity due*, an equal stream of period payments received at the beginning of each period, is the $\boxed{PV}$ of an ordinary annuity times the base $(1 + i)$. Using the previous example, the present value of $250 received at the beginning of each calendar quarter discounted at 12 percent is

$$\$250 \left[\frac{1 - \dfrac{1}{(1 + .12/4)^{4 \times 5}}}{.12/4} \right] (1 + .12/4) = \$3,830.95$$

6. Installment to amortize 1 (column 6)   shows the equal periodic payment required to provide the return of and return on capital invested at present for a specified number of periods, n, at the effective rate, i. This is the reciprocal of the present value of an annuity. Recall from the first example in the preceding section that the present value of $1,000 received at the end of each year for five years, discounted at 10 percent, is

$$\$1,000 \times 3.790786 = \$3,790.79$$

The installment to amortize $3,790.79 with five equal installments including interest of 10 percent per year could be calculated from the above as

$$\$3,790.79 \left[\frac{1}{3.790786} \right] = \$1,000$$

The general formula for the installment to amortize is

$$\boxed{PMT} = \boxed{PV} \left[\frac{i}{1 - \dfrac{1}{(1 + i)^n}} \right]$$

Using this formula for the example above, the installment to amortize is

$$\$3,790.79 \left[\frac{.10}{1 - \dfrac{1}{(1 + .10)^5}} \right] = \$3,790.79 \times 0.263797 = \$1,000$$

The payment will decrease as the number of payments per year increases. Compare $1,000, the annual installment to amortize $3,790.79 at 10 percent in five years, to the monthly installment required for the same investment.

$$\$3,790.79 \left[\cfrac{.10/12}{1 - \cfrac{1}{(1 + .10/12)^{5 \times 12}}} \right] = \$3,790.79 \times 0.021247 = \$80.54$$

The payment also will decrease if the number of years to amortize is increased. Compare the monthly payment above to a monthly payment for the same investment to be amortized in ten years.

$$\$3,790.79 \left[\cfrac{.10/12}{1 - \cfrac{1}{(1 + .10/12)^{10 \times 12}}} \right] = \$3,790.79 \times 0.013215 = \$50.10$$

The payment increases as the effective rate increases. Using the example above, the monthly payment to amortize \$3,790.79 in ten years at 12 percent per year is

$$\$3,790.79 \left[\cfrac{.12/12}{1 - \cfrac{1}{(1 + .12/12)^{10 \times 12}}} \right] = \$3,790.79 \times .014347 = \$54.39$$

The installment to amortize presumes payments are made at the end of each period. The same investment would be amortized with a smaller payment if each installment were received at the beginning of the period. The payment made at the beginning of the period is equal to the payment made at the end of the period divided by the base. Using the first example, the installment at the beginning of each year (including the first year) required to amortize \$3,790.79 in five years at 10-percent interest per year is

$$\frac{\$1,000}{(1 + .10)} = \$909.09$$

FINANCIAL CALCULATORS AND COMPUTERS

The preceding discussion on compound interest and discounting problems is intended to present the conceptual framework for all quantitative financial analysis. The formulas are presented to enable the reader to become familiar with the impact of rate and term on unknown values. The time value of money calculations can be performed on a wide variety of financial calculators and computers. Modern technology has produced inexpensive, preprogrammed calculators with a wide range of financial functions. Even the most simple can perform the calculations we have explored in this chapter. More sophisticated equipment combines the same basic calculations to save steps for the user.

It is important to understand the conceptual framework of time-value of money calculations in order to use financial calculators effectively. Skill with compound interest and discounting concepts will enable the analyst to comprehend the nature of any cash flow problem and, therefore, establish a valid approach to the solution. The results of *appropriate* calculations will be reasonable to the analyst. In contrast, the potential applications of these tools will be substantially limited for those who attempt to solve compound interest and discounting problems mechanically, with a few keystroke sequences on their particular calculators.

In general, financial calculators have five financial keys identified by the same symbols used in the preceding section ([n], [i], [PV], [PMT], [FV]). Most financial calculators will solve for any one unknown value when given three specified values. The number of periods, [n], and the effective rate, [i], always must be consistent with regard to compounding periods. The present value of a sum, [PV], is always assumed to be invested or available at the immediate beginning of the time horizon of the cash flows (now); henceforth in this book, [PV] will be paid or received at time period zero. Payments, [PMT], are always assumed to be equal and occur at the end of each equal compounding period *including* the last period. Many financial calculators have some simple adjustment or procedure to convert computations for payments made at the beginning of each period, as with an annuity due. In this book, the reader will always be informed when payments are received at the beginning of each period. Otherwise it can be assumed that payments are made at the end of the period. The future value, [FV], of a sum will be received at the end of the period. When cash *flows* include an ordinary annuity and a future value, [FV] and [PMT] are *not* added together.

As we have seen, the compound interest tables list factors for any combination of compounding periods, effective rates and number of years. Financial calculators can compute factors and subsequent values for terms and effective rates that are not included in the tables. To calculate any of the six factors, refer to the summary table on page 41. Use the value of $1 in place of the known dollar amount [PV], [PMT], or [FV] and solve for the unknown value.

Example

To calculate the column 6 factor, the installment to amortize 1, for a loan at 12 percent interest per year with payments every five months for ten years, input $1 for [PV] and solve for [PMT]. The known values for this problem are

$$[PV] = \$1$$
$$[n] = 10 \text{ years} \times (12 \div 5) = 24 \text{ periods}$$
$$[i] = 12\% \div (12 \div 5) = 5\% \text{ per period}$$

The calculated factor for the installment to amortize 1 is

$$[PMT] = 0.072471$$

The quantity (12 ÷ 5) is the number of five-month periods per year. Notice that this need not be an integer value. There are indeed 24 five-month periods in ten years (24 × 5 = 120 months; 120 months ÷ 12 months per year = 10 years).

Many financial calculators compute values to several decimal places. Some calculators round results if the next significant digit is greater than or equal to five; some do not. The use of rounded or unrounded intermediate values can easily cause a slight rounding error in the final result. The reader is urged not to become distressed by minor discrepancies between values caused by rounding.

Figure 2. Summary of Compound Interest and Discount Factors

Function of the Dollar (Factor)	Column	Known Values	Unknown Value	Result of Increasing	
				n	i
Amount of 1 at compound interest	1	$\boxed{PV}$, i, n	$\boxed{FV}$	↑	↑
Accumulation of 1 per period	2	$\boxed{PMT}$, i, n	$\boxed{FV}$	↑	↑
Sinking fund factor	3	$\boxed{FV}$, i, n	$\boxed{PMT}$	↓	↓
Present value reversion of 1	4	$\boxed{FV}$, i, n	$\boxed{PV}$	↓	↓
Present value of an ordinary annuity	5	$\boxed{PMT}$, i, n	$\boxed{PV}$	↑	↓
Installment to amortize 1	6	$\boxed{PV}$, i, n	$\boxed{PMT}$	↓	↑

where

$\boxed{PV}$ = Present value of a single sum available immediately

$\boxed{FV}$ = Future value of a single sum to be received in the future

$\boxed{PMT}$ = Payment to be received at the end of each period

i = effective periodic interest rate

n = number of periods

↑ = increase

↓ = decrease

Examples (compounding)

1. Future value at compound interest.   A survey of land sales over the past 15 years indicates that comparable land to the subject site has increased in value at a rate of 5 percent per year. If this trend continues, what would the estimated sales price be in five years for a property worth $15,000 today?

The known values are

$\boxed{PV}$ = $15,000

$\boxed{n}$ = 5 periods

$\boxed{i}$ = 5% per period

$\boxed{FV}$ is unknown. It is computed to be

$\boxed{FV}$ of $15,000, five years at 5% per year = $19,144.22

2. Future value at compound interest.   An investor pays $100,000 for a vacant site in January, 1980. In January, 1990, the site is sold for $250,000. At what annual compound rate of interest did the value of the land increase?

The known values are

$$\boxed{PV} = \$100,000$$
$$\boxed{FV} = \$250,000$$
$$\boxed{n} = 10 \text{ years}$$

The effective rate is unknown. It is computed to be

$$\boxed{i} = 9.60\%$$

Determine the annual interest rate for the problem above if semiannual compounding were assumed. Now the number of periods is

$$\boxed{n} = 10 \times 2 = 20 \text{ periods}$$

Recall that i is the effective rate *per period*. The periodic effective rate is calculated to be

$$\boxed{i} = 4.69\%$$

The annualized rate is two times the semiannual effective rate since there are two compounding periods per year.

$$2 \times 4.69\% = 9.38\%$$

Notice that this rate is less than the rate with annual compounding of 9.60 percent. This could be expected since there are more compounding periods for the semiannual rate.

3. Accumulation of 1 per period.   An investor has leased a site for use as a parking lot. The lessee agreed to pay all expenses, including property tax, in the net lease contract. The lessor is to receive a ground rent of $250 per month for nine years with the first payment to begin one month after signing the lease. If the lessor were to invest the monthly rental proceeds at an annual rate of 12 percent compounded monthly, how much would be in the investment account at the end of the lease?

The known values are

$$\boxed{PMT} = \$250 \text{ per month}$$
$$\boxed{n} = 9 \text{ years} \times 12 = 108 \text{ periods}$$
$$\boxed{i} = 12\% \div 12 = 1\% \text{ per period}$$

The $\boxed{FV}$ is unknown. It is calculated to be

$$\boxed{FV} = \$48,223.14$$

4. Sinking fund factor.   An investor purchases an apartment building that is projected to need a new roof which will cost $15,000 in five years. How much must be invested at the end of each calendar quarter, at 10 percent interest per year, so that the necessary capital for the roof will be accumulated?

The known values are

$$\boxed{FV} = \$15,000$$

$$\boxed{n} = 5 \text{ years} \times 4 = 20 \text{ periods}$$

$$\boxed{i} = 10\% \div 4 = 2.5\% \text{ per period}$$

The $\boxed{PMT}$ is the unknown value. It is calculated to be

$$\boxed{PMT} = \$587.21$$

Note that 20 investments multiplied by \$587.21 is \$11,744.20; thus \$15,000 less \$11,744.20, or \$3,255.80, is the amount of interest earned over the five-year period.

Examples (discounting)

1. Present value at compound interest.   An investor is considering the purchase of a ''remainder'' (the interest in a property which matures at the end of another estate). The property is under lease for the next seven years. The investor estimates that the value of the fee interest at the end of the lease will be \$50,000. What should the investor be willing to pay for the remainder interest today if the required rate of return on invested capital is 15 percent?

The known values are

$$\boxed{FV} = \$50,000$$

$$\boxed{n} = 7 \text{ periods}$$

$$\boxed{i} = 15\% \text{ per period}$$

The $\boxed{PV}$ is unknown. It is calculated to be

$$\boxed{PV} = \$18,796.85$$

If an investor were to invest \$18,796.85 today at 15 percent compounded annually, the investment would grow to the amount of \$50,000 by the end of seven years.

It is often helpful to identify each known factor and determine which value is unknown when solving compound interest or discounting problems. When using the compound interest tables or a financial calculator, it may be useful to refer to Figure 2 which summarizes the compound interest and discount factors in the preceding section.

All discounted cash flow analyses can be reduced to four simple questions.

1. How much money does the investment cost?
2. When is each payment made?
3. How much money does the investment produce?
4. When does the investor receive each cash flow?

The numerical answers to these questions may be summarized on a **t-chart** as follows:

EOY	$
0	PV
1	PMT
2	PMT
3	PMT
↓	↓
n	PMT + FV

The left-hand column indicates the time period each payment is made or cash flow received. The end of time period 0 is, by definition, the present or the time at which the investment term begins. The periods, n, are consistent with the cash flows (monthly or annual). The heading in the example above indicates annual periods; EOY is End of Year. Cash flows are listed in the right-hand column. In this case, each periodic payment is equal— an ordinary annuity. Thus PMT is used. Unequal cash flows may replace the equal cash flows. An algebraic sign convention is used to distinguish cash payments from cash receipts. Payments are negative, indicated by the negative sign or parentheses. Cash receipts are positive. To illustrate, the t-chart for an investment that costs $10,000 and produces $1,000 at the end of each quarter (EOQ) for eight quarters plus a reversion of $12,000 at the end of the last period would be as follows:

EOQ	$	
0	($10,000)	amount *paid* for the investment
1	$1,000	
2	$1,000	
3	$1,000	
↓	↓	
(2 years × 4 quarters per year) 8	$1,000 + $12,000	

2. Present value of an ordinary annuity.   What is the present value of a leasehold interest of $2,650 per year for four years when discounted at 10 percent per year? The known values are

$$\text{PMT} = \$2,650$$

$$n = 4 \text{ periods}$$

$$i = 10\% \text{ per period}$$

The PV is unknown. It is calculated to be

$$\text{PV} = \$8,400.14$$

Now, suppose that the same stream of income were available in an investment ($2,650 per year for four years) but that the first payment would begin three years from today rather than one year from today. This is sometimes called a deferred annuity. In essence, this problem could be solved in three different ways, as follows:

	Method 1 Addition of Reversion Factors		
EOY	Column Factor (10%)	Cash Flows	Present Value
2	—	0	0
3	.751315	$2,650	$1,990.98
4	.683013	2,650	1,809.98
5	.620921	2,650	1,645.44
6	.564474	2,650	1,495.86
Total	2.619723	—	$6,942.26

2.619723 × $2,650 = $6,942.27

The known values are

$$\boxed{FV} = \$2,650 \text{ received four times}$$

$$\boxed{n} = 3, 4, 5 \text{ and } 6$$

$$\boxed{i} = 10\%$$

The sum of the four $\boxed{PV}$s is unknown. It is calculated to be

$$\boxed{PV}_{n=3} \quad = \$1,990.98$$

$$\boxed{PV}_{n=4} \quad = 1,809.99*$$

$$\boxed{PV}_{n=5} \quad = 1,645.44$$

$$\boxed{PV}_{n=6} \quad = \underline{1,495.86}$$

$$\text{Total} = \$6,942.27$$

*Differs from above due to rounding.

	Method 2 Subtraction of Annuity Factors
This approach may be viewed as removing or subtracting out those periods for which no cash flows are received.	

Column 5 Factor 10%, $n = 6$ 4.355261

Column 5 Factor 10%, $n = 2$ − 1.735537

2.619724

× $2,650

$6,942.27

Note that the factor calculated by subtracting annuity factors is the same as that arrived at in method 1 by adding reversion factors.

For a financial calculator, this method is a three-step process: (1) calculate the present value of a six-year annuity; (2) calculate the present value of a two-year annuity; (3) subtract the $\boxed{\text{PV}}$ of the six-year annuity from the $\boxed{\text{PV}}$ of the two-year annuity.

For Steps 1 and 2 the known values are

$$\boxed{\text{PMT}} = \$2,650$$
$$\boxed{\text{n}} = 6 \text{ (for step 1) and 2 (for step 2)}$$
$$\boxed{\text{i}} = 10\%$$

The solution is

Step 1 $\boxed{\text{PV}}$ of 6 year annuity		\$11,541.44
Step 2 $\boxed{\text{PV}}$ of 2 year annuity		−4,599.17
Step 3 $\boxed{\text{PV}}$ of deferred annuity		\$6,942.27

Method 3
Calculating Deferred Annuity

The logic employed in this method is that at a 10% discount rate:

EOY	\$		EOY	\$
1	0		1	0
2	0		2	\$8,400.14
3	2,650	equals		
4	2,650			
5	2,650			
6	2,650			

Column 5 Factor 10%, $n = 4$	3.169865
Column 4 Factor 10%, $n = 2$	× .826446
	2.619722
	× \$2,650
	\$6,942.26

Method 3 may be accomplished with two steps on a calculator. First, calculate the $\boxed{\text{PV}}$ of the four-year annuity as though it were not deferred. In essence, this $\boxed{\text{PV}}$ occurs *one year prior* to the first future payment $\boxed{\text{PMT}}$ to be received; in this example, the time period of the $\boxed{\text{PV}}$ would be EOY 2 as seen above.

The known values for step 1 are

$$\boxed{\text{PMT}} = \$2,650$$
$$\boxed{\text{n}} = 4 \text{ periods}$$
$$\boxed{\text{i}} = 10\%$$

The $\boxed{\text{PV}}$ of the regular annuity is calculated to be

$$\boxed{\text{PV}} = \$8,400.14$$

Since the above $\boxed{PV}$ is equivalent to the annuity to be received EOY 2, the $8,400.14 becomes the $\boxed{FV}$ for step 2. Thus, the known values for step 2 are

$$\boxed{FV} = \$8,400.14$$

$$\boxed{n} = 2 \text{ periods}$$

$$\boxed{i} = 10\% \text{ per period}$$

The $\boxed{PV}$ of the deferred annuity is calculated to be

$$\boxed{PV} = \$6,942.26$$

3. Installment to amortize. What is the monthly payment for a $100,000 mortgage loan at 12 percent for a term of 30 years?

The known values are

$$\boxed{PV} = \$100,000$$

$$\boxed{n} = 30 \times 12 = 360 \text{ periods}$$

$$\boxed{i} = 12\% \div 12 = 1\% \text{ per period}$$

The $\boxed{PMT}$ is unknown. It is calculated to be

$$\boxed{PMT} = \$1,028,61$$

Another example of the use of the installment to amortize would be a situation where a portion of a real estate investment must be recovered over a finite time period. Assume a situation where an investor pays $10,000 for a site and builds a $90,000 warehouse on it. Assume that the land value remains stable to perpetuity and that the warehouse has an economic life of 25 years. What would be the proper *annual net rental* on a 25 year contract if the investor requires a 10-percent return before taxes?

This may *seem* much more complex than the previous problem but it is not. The $90,000 structure in this problem is treated as though it were a loan to be repaid with interest over its economic life. Thus, the annual rent must include the following:

Rental of land

(10% of $10,000) $ 1,000.00

Rental of structure

The known values are

$$\boxed{PV} = \$90,000$$

$$\boxed{n} = 25 \text{ periods}$$

$$\boxed{i} = 10\% \text{ per period}$$

The $\boxed{PMT}$ is calculated to be

$$\boxed{PMT} = \$9,915.13 \qquad +9,915.13$$

Required annual net rental $10,915.13

4. Perpetuity. In the previous problem it was presumed that the site would produce $1,000 net rental each year to perpetuity. Thus, at a 10 percent discount rate, the present value of the site is $10,000 ($1,000 ÷ .10). But what if the stream of income to perpetuity is deferred? For example, what is the present value of a perpetual income stream of $1,000 which begins at EOY 5 instead of EOY 1 when discounted at 10 percent?

Method 1 Subtraction of an Annuity				
EOY	$		EOY	$
1	1,000 received *each year* to perpetuity	minus	1	1,000
			2	1,000
			3	1,000
			4	1,000

This is the same three-step process used in the preceding deferred annuity example. First, calculate the PV of the perpetuity. Second, calculate the PV of a four-year annuity. Third, the PV of the deferred perpetuity is the PV of the perpetuity less the PV of the four-year annuity.

Step 1: The PV of the perpetuity is

$$\boxed{PV} = \frac{\boxed{PMT}}{\boxed{i}} = \frac{\$1,000}{.10} = \$10,000$$

Step 2: The known values for the annuity are

$$\boxed{PMT} = \$1,000$$
$$\boxed{n} = 4$$
$$\boxed{i} = 10\%$$

The PV of the annuity is

$$\boxed{PV} = \$3,169.87$$

Step 3: The PV of the deferred annuity is

PV of perpetuity (from Step 1)	$10,000.00
PV of annuity (from Step 2)	$-3,169.87$
PV of deferred perpetuity	$ 6,830.13

The logic employed is that the present value of an ordinary perpetuity assumes that the income stream begins at EOY 1. If it begins at a later time, the present value of the amounts not received must be subtracted from the present value of an ordinary perpetuity.

Method 2 Calculating Deferred Perpetuity				
EOY	$		EOY	$
1	0		1	0
2	0		2	0
3	0	equals	3	0
4	0		4	10,000
5	1,000—received *each year* to perpetuity			

Thus, the calculation becomes that of a simple single sum reversion of $10,000 to be received at EOY 4.

The known values are

$$\boxed{FV} = \$10{,}000$$

$$\boxed{n} = 4$$

$$\boxed{i} = 10\%$$

The $\boxed{PV}$ of the deferred perpetuity is

$$\boxed{PV} = \$6{,}830.13$$

5. Combinations of cash flows.   Calculate the present value of the following annual cash flows for an investor with an opportunity cost of capital of 15 percent.

EOY	$
0	0
1	$10,000
2	10,000
3	10,000
4	10,000
5	10,000 + 150,000

The unknown value is $\boxed{PV}$. This problem may be solved by adding the present value of two cash flows, the five-year annuity and the future sum received EOY 5:

EOY	$		EOY	$		EOY	$
0	0		0	0		0	0
1	$10,000		1	$10,000		1	0
2	10,000		2	10,000		2	0
3	10,000	equals	3	10,000	plus	3	0
4	10,000		4	10,000		4	0
5	10,000 + 150,000		5	10,000		5	$150,000

The known values for the annuity are

$$\boxed{PMT} = \$10{,}000$$

$$\boxed{n} = 5 \text{ periods}$$

$$\boxed{i} = 15\% \text{ per period}$$

The $\boxed{PV}$ is calculated to be

$$\boxed{PV} \text{ annuity} = \$33{,}521.55$$

The known values for the reversion are

$$\boxed{FV} = \$150{,}000$$

$$\boxed{n} = 5 \text{ periods}$$

$$\boxed{i} = 15\% \text{ per period}$$

The $\boxed{\text{PV}}$ is calculated to be

$$\boxed{\text{PV}} \text{ reversion} = \$74,576.51$$

The $\boxed{\text{PV}}$ of all the cash flows is the sum of the calculated present values of each component of the cash flows. The $\boxed{\text{PV}}$ is then

$\boxed{\text{PV}}$ annuity	$ 33,521.55
$\boxed{\text{PV}}$ reversion	+74,576.51
$\boxed{\text{PV}}$ of all cash flows	$108,098.06

An investor who requires a 15 percent return on invested capital would pay $108,098.06 for an investment that would produce these cash flows.

MORTGAGE CALCULATIONS

Calculation of the *size* of periodic (generally monthly) payments, over a given term, necessary to fully amortize a mortgage loan has already been illustrated. Another very useful application of the compound interest tables is the calculation of mortgage *balances* over the term of the loan.

The typical mortgage loan contract can be considered from the standpoint of both the lender and the borrower. To the borrower, the mortgage loan represents a loan amount received in the present in return for level payments in the future over a specified term. In contrast, the lender views the loan as an investment outlay in the present in return for a series of equal cash flows over a specific term in the future.

Example

In the previous section, we worked with an example of a mortgage loan of $100,000 at 12 percent with monthly payments for a term of 30 years. The monthly payment necessary to amortize this loan was found to be $1,028.61. From the standpoint of the investor (lender) in this example, the initial mortgage loan amount represents the *present value* of the 30 year stream of monthly payments of $1,028.61, discounted at their opportunity cost of capital, 12 percent. Therefore, the known values are

$$\boxed{\text{PMT}} = \$1,028.61$$
$$\boxed{\text{n}} = 30 \times 12 = 360 \text{ periods}$$
$$\boxed{\text{i}} = 12\% \div 12 = 1\% \text{ per period}$$

The $\boxed{\text{PV}}$ is calculated to be

$$\boxed{\text{PV}} = \$100,000$$

(Actual calculation is $99,999.75 because of rounding cents in the payment.)

Since the periodic payments on a mortgage loan can be viewed as an ordinary annuity, it is very simple to calculate the balance of the mortgage loan to any point in time over the life of the mortgage. This is the present value of the remaining stream of payments when discounted at the mortgage lending rate. For example, after ten years of payments (120 payments of $1,028.61) have been made, 20 years (240 payments) remain. Therefore, the known values for calculating the balance of the mortgage loan at EOY 10 are

$$\boxed{\text{PMT}} \ = \ \$1{,}028.61$$

$$\boxed{\text{n}} \ = \ 240 \text{ periods (the remaining payments)}$$

$$\boxed{\text{i}} \ = \ 1\% \text{ per period}$$

The loan balance EOY 10 is calculated to be

$$\boxed{\text{PV}} \ = \ \$93{,}417.76$$

The lender would be indifferent to receiving either the remaining loan payments or the present value of those payments discounted at the mortgage lending rate. The forgoing presumes there are no prepayment penalties or **lock-in** clauses.

In the analysis of real estate investments, it is often necessary to calculate both future mortgage balances and annual accumulated interest. This may be done for the same loan as shown in the table below.

The procedure used to construct the preceding table was (1) calculate the mortgage balances for each of the ten subsequent periods using the remaining terms of 29 years through 20 years respectively; (2) subtract from each year the balance from the previous year-end balance to obtain the second column, principal reduction; (3) calculate amount of annual payment by multiplying 12 times the monthly payment; and (4) find interest expense by subtracting the principal reduction from the annual payment.

Year	EOY Mortgage Balance	Principal Reduction	Annual Payments	Interest Expense
0	$100,000.00	0	0	0
1	99,636.87	$ 363.13	$12,343.32	$11,980.19
2	99,227.97	408.90	12,343.32	11,934.42
3	98,767.21	460.76	12,343.32	11,882.56
4	98,248.01	519.20	12,343.32	11,824.12
5	97,662.97	585.04	12,343.32	11,758.28
6	97,003.73	659.24	12,343.32	11,684.08
7	96,260.88	742.85	12,343.32	11,600.47
8	95,423.82	837.06	12,343.32	11,506.26
9	94,480.60	943.22	12,343.32	11,400.10
10	93,417.76	1,062.84	12,343.32	11,280.48

SUMMARY

This chapter has been devoted to a systematic presentation of the concepts and techniques of compound interest and discounting. The tools and applications presented here can serve as a useful reference and guide to the real estate investment broker.

It simply is not possible to understand the ever-changing world of real estate finance and investment without a thorough working knowledge of the compound interest and discount tables and their many applications. There is no doubt that the investment problems and instruments of tomorrow will be different from those of today; however, the tools discussed in this chapter will be used to create the many innovations of the future. The time spent now in mastering these tools should be considered a sound *investment* which will pay great dividends in the future.

NOTES

1. Alfred A. Ring, *The Valuation of Real Estate* (Englewood Cliffs, NJ: Prentice-Hall, Inc., 1970), p. 6.
2. All abbreviations in boxes, such as $\boxed{\text{FV}}$ and $\boxed{\text{PV}}$ relate both to the compounding and discounting variables and to the financial keys on the typical financial calculator. This is done in an attempt to link together the concepts and the mechanical calculations.
3. L. W. Ellwood, *Ellwood Tables for Real Estate Appraising and Financing*, 4th ed. (Chicago: American Institute of Real Estate Appraisers, 1977).

4
Measuring Investment Returns

One of the most critical considerations in the analysis of real estate investments is the measure of investment desirability. Over the years, many measures have been used to indicate the relative profitability of alternative real estate investments. The interesting dilemma is that different approaches or methods of measuring relative investment desirability produced both different relative rankings and different indicators of investment returns. It is not the purpose of this chapter to critique all past practices and techniques of analysis since this topic has already been discussed in various publications.[1] It is worthwhile noting, however, some of the principal weaknesses of traditional techniques.[2]

Investment in real estate involves making choices among many other investment alternatives. These choices must be made within the context of investment objectives. Real estate investors, like all investors, are concerned with providing for future consumption for themselves and/or others by limiting present consumption. Their selection of a particular investment to meet this end takes into account several investment characteristics such as risk, return on investment, timing and duration of cash flows. Most traditional measures of return are ill-equipped to provide a clear and unequivocal indication of investment desirability in view of the variety of investment characteristics that may be important to a single investor.

A general shortcoming of traditional methods of measuring investment returns from real estate is the failure to account for the realities of the marketplace. There are several instances of this weakness. For example, it is common to measure the return on a real estate investment on a before-tax basis. This may be extremely misleading since each real estate transaction has unique income tax effects. Although most investors are aware that the federal income tax is a significant expense item of most investments, it is often ignored in selecting an investment. This may be because small, middle-income investors assume that they are not really tax sensitive or believe that all investments are affected proportionally by the income tax. Also, the returns of the most common investment alternatives to real estate are stated in before-tax terms. Many investors considering savings accounts or certificates of deposit as investment alternatives tend to forget that the annual interest on those investments will be treated as ordinary income for tax purposes. Even common stocks and corporate bonds are evaluated by many investors on the basis of before-tax yields.

In addition, some techniques ignore the timing of cash flows from the investment while others stabilize a single-year income and thus distort the importance of timing. Still other techniques utilize nonmarket rates as ''opportunity costs'' in a practical world where markets exist. Finally, other approaches omit consideration of the impact of financing when measuring returns to the equity investor.

PRESENT VALUE AND INTERNAL RATE OF RETURN

Because of the many shortcomings related to those techniques which distort or disregard the timing of cash flows, there has been a significant move toward the use of the Internal Rate of Return (IRR) as the standard measure of return on equity investments in real estate. This widespread acceptance can be explained by the advantages offered by this measure of return.

1. It is simple to understand and compute.
2. It is the ''standard'' among most financial institutions and has been widely used for mortgage loan rates, bond rates, and the like.
3. It is provided in a convenient form—a rate—which can readily be used as the criterion of comparison for alternative investments.

In Chapter 3, several investment alternatives were presented.

CASH RECEIPTS FROM ALTERNATIVE INVESTMENTS

End of Year	Discounted Mortgage	Five-Year Note	Stock	Insurance Annuity	Land
1	$1,627.45	–0–	$ 1,000	$1,000	–0–
2	1,627.45	–0–	1,000	each	–0–
3	1,627.45	–0–	1,000	year	–0–
4	1,627.45	–0–	1,000	to	–0–
5	1,627.45	$16,105.10	1,000	perpetuity	–0–
6	1,627.45	–0–	1,000		–0–
7	1,627.45	–0–	1,000		–0–
8	1,627.45	–0–	1,000		–0–
9	1,627.45	–0–	1,000		–0–
10	1,627.45	–0–	11,000		$25,937.42
Total Receipts	$16,274.50	$16,105.10	$20,000	∞	$25,937.42

By now, with the use of the compound interest and discount tables, it should be clear that each of the alternative investments above has a present value of $10,000 when discounted at an annual rate of 10 percent. Since the cost of purchasing each alternative is exactly $10,000, the rate of return to the investor is 10 percent, that discount rate which reduces the sum of all future amounts to be received to exactly the amount of the initial investment.

Cash Flow as the Focus of Analysis

All real estate investments may be viewed as cash flows. Subsequent chapters of this text are devoted to methods of determining or estimating the cash flows from real properties with particular emphasis on the effect of depreciation method, form of ownership, age and type of property and various other factors that influence the after-tax cash flows. It is the function of the compound interest and discount factors to determine both investment value and/or rate of return on the various investment alternatives available to the investor.

Within the context of the present value tables, estimated cash flows from real estate investments are treated as though they are *sums certain to be received*. That is, when future cash flows are discounted to the present, the discounting process makes no specific allowance for risk. Even the use of relatively higher discount rates, while having the effect of producing relatively lower present values, does not actually take into account the element of risk associated with the specific property. When comparisons are made among the present values and/or rates of return among investment alternatives, the alternatives should represent cash flows of similar risk and duration.

Future cash flows are also treated as though they represent dollars with the same purchasing power as those of the present. Since future cash flows are discounted to the present and compared with present dollar outlays, such comparisons are valid only when constant dollars are assumed.

Present Value

The present value or present worth of an interest in a real property investment may be defined as the sum of all future benefits accruing to the owner of the interest when such benefits are discounted to the present by an appropriate discount rate. In the case of investment real estate, future benefits are expressed as *cash flows* which may be both receipts and outlays. As a general proposition, the present value of any interest in real estate may be estimated if the *amount* and *timing* of cash flows and the appropriate *discount rate* are known.

Any form of cash flow, whether level, increasing or variable, may be converted to a simple present value figure. Negative cash flows are discounted in the same manner as positive cash flows, with the sum of such flows subtracted from the sum of positive flows.

Example

Compare the following present value calculations of different cash flows discounted at 15 percent, all of which total $100,000, to be computed over a six-year period.

PRESENT VALUE OF CASH FLOWS

	Investment A		Investment B		Investment C	
EOY	CF	PV	CF	PV	CF	PV
1	$ 85,000	$73,913	$ 1,000	$ 870	$ 25,000	$21,739
2	5,000	3,781	2,000	1,512	25,000	18,904
3	4,000	2,630	3,000	1,973	25,000	16,438
4	3,000	1,715	4,000	2,287	(25,000)	(14,294)
5	2,000	994	5,000	2,486	25,000	12,429
6	1,000	432	85,000	36,748	25,000	10,808
	$100,000	$83,465	$100,000	$45,876	$100,000	$66,024

One interpretation of the forgoing is that an investor who requires a 15 percent return on investment would pay $83,465 for investment A, $45,876 for investment B and $66,024 for investment C. The *investment value* of each group of cash flows depends upon the discount rate and is the worth of a forecast stream of cash flows to a specific investor. Recall from Chapter 3 that the present value of cash flows to be received in the future decreases as the discount rate increases. Thus, investors who have different yield requirements will employ different discount rates in estimating the investment value of a property.

Net Present Value

The net present value (NPV) of an investment is the sum of the present value of all future cash flows less the initial investment. The cash flows are discounted at the investor's *opportunity cost of capital*, the rate of discount that represents the yield the investor could obtain from the next best alternative investment of similar size, duration and risk.

Example

Suppose that each of the investments above are available at a cost of $50,000. The NPV of each of the three alternatives to an investor who has $50,000 to invest and requires a 15 percent return on investment are shown in the following table.

Investment	PV of Cash Flows @ 15% (from above)	minus	Initial Investment	equals	NPV
A	$83,465	−	$50,000	=	$33,465
B	45,876	−	50,000	=	(4,124)
C	66,024	−	50,000	=	16,024

Assuming that the risk associated with each alternative investment is comparable, investment A is the best financial choice because it has the greatest NPV. We said above that an investor who required a 15 percent return on investment could pay $83,465 for investment A. In that case, it would certainly be a higher yielding investment at a price of $50,000. Investment B, however, is unsuitable because the NPV is less than zero; therefore, the investor would not achieve the required rate of return of 15 percent on invested capital. Recall that it was only worth $45,876 to the investor; at that price it would yield exactly 15 percent.

The NPV of cash flows is affected by the discount rate because the present value of cash flows depends on the discount rate. The NPV increases as the discount rate decreases. For example, the NPV of the same three investment alternatives with a 12 percent opportunity cost of capital is summarized below.

Investment	PV of Cash Flows @ 12%	minus	Initial Investment	equals	NPV
A	$86,274	–	$50,000	=	$36,274
B	53,065	–	50,000	=	3,065
C	71,009	–	50,000	=	21,009

The ordinal ranking of the investment alternatives is the same as before. However, at the lower required return on investment of 12 percent, investment B becomes acceptable.

Internal Rate of Return

The typical investor is concerned with the complete return *of* invested capital and an adequate return *on* investment. In general, this return *on* invested capital is expressed as an annual rate. The calculation of *rate of return* or *yield* of a real estate investment is an important measure of investment worth because it provides one basis for selecting among alternative investments. Since it is calculated from cash flows internal to a specific investment (the initial investment outlay and the future cash flows), it is frequently called the Internal Rate of Return (IRR).

The IRR of an investment may be defined as *that rate of discount at which the present value of all future cash flows is exactly equal to the initial capital investment.* Also, the IRR is the discount rate at which the NPV equals zero.

Three forms of IRR calculations are common in the analysis of real estate investment. The first represents the most simple form of investment return: a single sum returned for an initial investment. The second is a level annuity and the third is a stream of variable cash flows.

Examples

1. Single sum received.   Find the IRR of an investment of $15,000 that returns $39,900 in seven years. This may be done with a financial calculator by solving for the unknown value of $\boxed{i}$ with the known values of

$$\boxed{PV} = \$15,000$$
$$\boxed{FV} = \$39,900$$
$$\boxed{n} = 7 \text{ periods}$$

The IRR is calculated to be 15 percent.

The same result could be derived by using the compound interest tables (see Appendix A). Recall that the amount of 1 at compound interest, column 1 factor (F_1), times the $\boxed{PV}$ equals the $\boxed{FV}$. In this case,

$$\boxed{PV} \times F_1 = \boxed{FV}$$
$$\$15,000 \times F_1 = \$39,900$$

Solving for the column 1 factor,

$$F_1 = \frac{\$39,900}{\$15,000} = 2.66000$$

Thus, the solution will be found by looking for a column 1 factor for seven years with annual compounding which equals 2.66000. This is found at an annual rate of approximately 15 percent. Thus, the IRR of this investment is 15 percent because at this discount rate the present worth of the future amount to be received is equal to the initial investment. The present value reversion of 1, column 4 factor (F_4), could have been used in a similar fashion to solve for IRR since it is the reciprocal of column 1.

2. Level annuity received.   Another common form of investment return is a level stream of income (ordinary annuity) in return for an initial investment. For example, find the IRR of an investment of $15,000 that returns $3,600 each year for seven years.

This may be done with a financial calculator by solving for the unknown value of $\boxed{\text{i}}$ with the known values of

$$\boxed{\text{PV}} = \$15,000$$
$$\boxed{\text{PMT}} = \$3,600$$
$$\boxed{\text{n}} = 7 \text{ periods}$$

The IRR is calculated to be 14.95 percent.

Use of the tables would indicate the same approximate yield. Since both $\boxed{\text{PV}}$ and $\boxed{\text{PMT}}$ are known, the factor for either the present value of an ordinary annuity of 1 per period, column 5 (F_5), or the installment to amortize 1, column 6 (F_6), could be used. Solving for the column 6 factor,

$$\boxed{\text{PV}} \times F_6 = \boxed{\text{PMT}}$$
$$\$15,000 \times F_6 = \$3,600$$

$$\frac{\$3,600}{\$15,000} = 0.24000$$

This is very close to the column 6 factor for seven years of 0.240360 found in the 15 percent annual table. The actual IRR is slightly less than 15 percent because the installment to amortize 1 decreases as the interest rate decreases.

3. Variable cash flows.   Calculation of the IRR of the investment forms illustrated above may be accomplished directly because the basic solution equation involves only one unknown. Variable cash flows, however, cannot be solved quite as readily from the tables; a trial-and-error process must be used to find that rate which discounts the future cash flows such that their sum equals the initial investment. Of course, IRR calculations with financial calculators are greatly simplified.

Consider the investments discussed in the earlier section called Net Present Value. They were ranked for an investor who has a required yield of 15 percent. Since the NPV is 0 for an investment discounted at the IRR, the IRR on an investment with a positive NPV is always greater than the discount rate used to calculate the present value of the cash flows. This is because NPV declines as the discount rate increases.

For example, look at investment B.

Investment B

EOY	$
0	($50,000)
1	1,000
2	2,000
3	3,000
4	4,000
5	5,000
6	85,000

NPV @ 12% = $3,065
NPV @ 15% = ($4,124)

Therefore, the yield to the investor who pays $50,000 for investment B is less than 15 percent and greater than 12 percent. One way to estimate the IRR within a narrower range is to interpolate between the two rates.[3]

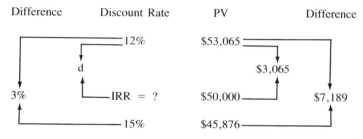

Difference	Discount Rate	PV	Difference
	12%	$53,065	
d		$3,065	
3%	IRR = ?	$50,000	$7,189
	15%	$45,876	

INTERPOLATION

Percentage Rate			Present Value Amount			
Smaller	.12	$53,065		$53,065		
Larger	.15	$45,876	Initial Investment	$50,000		
Absolute Difference	[.03	÷ 7,189]	×	3,065	=	.01279

Smaller Rate .12 + Interpolation Amount .01279 = .13279

The IRR to an investor will increase if the initial investment is decreased. At a cost of $50,000, the IRR of investment B is 13.28 percent. The investor's IRR would be 15 percent if it were acquired for $45,876. This is consistent with the time value of money concepts. The present value of cash flows decreases as the discount rate increases. Recall that the IRR is the discount rate at which the present value of cash flows is equal to the initial investment. Therefore, in order for the present value of cash flows to equal a lower initial investment, the discount rate must be increased.

Periodic and annualized IRRs.   The rate of return on an investment is usually stated as an annualized rate. The annualized IRR is merely the effective periodic IRR multiplied by the number of periods per year. This is the reverse of the process used to compute the effective periodic rate from an annual rate for compound interest and discounting problems.

Example

To compute the annualized IRR to a lender for a $100,000 loan with monthly payments of $1,028.61 to be received for the next 30 years, we must first find the monthly effective rate. The known values are

$$\boxed{PV} = \$100,000$$
$$\boxed{PMT} = \$1,028.61$$
$$\boxed{n} = 30 \times 12 = 360 \text{ periods}$$

The monthly rate is computed to be 1 percent. The annualized rate is

$$12 \times 1\% = 12\%$$

Proof of IRR.   The IRR is the return *on* each dollar each year that the dollar remains invested. It is *not* the rate earned by the total initial investment throughout the entire term of the investment.

Example

Consider a borrower with a bank line of credit. The IRR to the lender, or the cost of borrowing, is the interest rate on the *outstanding annual balance*. The annual cash flows are listed below. Negative cash flows are loan proceeds paid to the borrower. Positive cash flows represent payments of interest and principal reduction by the borrower.

EOY	$
0	($10,000)
1	2,000
2	(5,000)
3	–0–
4	18,029

The IRR is calculated to be 10 percent. The loan schedule is summarized below.

Year	Investment Balance BOY	10% Interest Due EOY	Principal Plus Interest	Cash Flows of Lender	Balance EOY
1	($10,000)	$1,000	$11,000	$2,000	$ 9,000
2	(9,000)	900	9,900	(5,000)	14,900
3	(14,900)	1,490	16,390	–0–	16,390
4	(16,390)	1,639	18,029	18,029	–0–

The original loan balance of $10,000 earns $1,000 interest EOY 1. The borrower's $2,000 payment is allocated to $1,000 interest and $1,000 principal reduction. The new balance EOY 1 of $9,000 earns $900 interest and the lender advances an additional $5,000 to the borrower EOY 2; so the new balance is $14,900 ($9,000 + $900 + $5,000). Interest of $1,490 is added to the new balance of $14,900 EOY 3. The borrower does not make a payment at EOY 3. The interest earned during year 4 on the new balance of $16,390 is

$1,639. The total loan balance, including interest, is $18,029 ($16,390 + $1,639), which is paid in full EOY 4. The investor (lender) earned 10 percent on each dollar that was invested each year.

This example is intended to demonstrate that the IRR is calculated like, and is directly comparable to, the typical loan in which interest charges are based upon the outstanding balance each payment period. Thus, the IRR is directly comparable to all compound interest (yield) measures.

Applications of IRR.   The IRR is useful to measure the yield on capital remaining at risk in an investment. The impact on yield of alternative investment assumptions with respect to financing or taxation can be measured with IRR. The effective cost of borrowing—the lender's yield—for creative financing can also be measured with IRR to compare alternative financing. In general, the IRR is useful for measuring the *internal* performance of a particular investment.

SELECTING AMONG ALTERNATIVE INVESTMENTS

Problems with the Use of IRR

Although IRR is widely used as a measure of investment return, there are a variety of problems connected with relying on IRR as the exclusive criterion of investment desirability. Before critiquing some of the procedural problems inherent in quantifying the relative yield advantage of one real estate investment alternative over another, let us weigh again at least two other considerations that should be taken into account when selecting (or guiding the selection of) investments: risk and nonfinancial elements. The following discussion is based upon the assumption that investments being compared are of *similar risk* so that an explicit measure of risk is not necessary. As indicated earlier in this text, present value discount factors are not an acceptable means of adjusting for the risk inherent in an investment.

Turning to the particular weaknesses of the IRR as a measure of investment desirability, five problems are apparent.

1. Lack of unique yield.   Conventional investments involve an initial outlay of capital with future receipts. For such investments, there can be one and only one IRR. For nonconventional investments, where the future net cash flow stream contains both receipts and outlays, the calculation may become more complex. Under certain circumstances, a given investment may have multiple IRRs or no IRR within the realm of real numbers.[4] Whenever this occurs, it is clear that the use of the IRR as the criterion of investment selection can be misleading.

Example

The IRR of the following cash flows is either 0 percent, 100 percent or 200 percent.

EOY	$
0	(25,000)
1	150,000
2	(275,000)
3	150,000

2. Discounting negative cash flows. In the standard approach to the calculation of IRR, negative cash flows are discounted at the same internal rate as are positive cash flows. However sound this approach may be from a mathematical standpoint, it generally makes little financial sense. The discount rate for negative cash flows should be that rate at which funds could be invested in the present so as to be available to meet future outlay requirements. It seems most reasonable to discount future negative cash flows by that rate which represents the best estimate of the investor's after-tax yield on relatively safe investments so that the amount set aside in the present would have a reasonable guarantee of increasing in value to the amount needed as an outlay in the future.[5]

3. Initial investment. Directly related to the procedure of discounting future outlays is the problem of improperly identifying the true initial investment. In the typical IRR approach, the outlay in the present is the measure of the initial investment. However, this does not take into account outlays (investments) in the future that may be necessary to continue the investment. The typical real estate investor is concerned not only with the initial capital investment needed to acquire an interest in the real estate, but also in the capital requirements occurring prior to the future obligations that may not be met either by borrowing and/or by positive cash flows.

Example

Suppose that a developer is considering a project that offers the following cash flows after taxes and after borrowing.[6]

EOY	$	
0	($230,000)	Initial investment
1	($500,000)	Future outlays
2	($500,000)	
3	$2,000,000	Future receipt

The IRR on this investment is approximately 30 percent. However, note that the investor is, in effect, discounting $1 million of future outlays at 30 percent so that it represents a present "cost" of only $680,000. The key question here is could the developer reasonably expect to invest $680,000 in the present in order to meet solid obligations of $500,000 in one year and $500,000 at the end of the second year? The answer is yes only if the $680,000 could be invested in some form of investment that is relatively liquid and has an after-tax yield of 30 percent. Without belaboring the argument, it would seem clear that an *after-tax* rate of between 5 and 7 percent would be more realistic. If 5 percent were used, the adjusted rate could be calculated as follows.

EOY	$
0	($230,000)+ ($929,705) = ($1,159,705) Adjusted initial investment
1	–0–
2	–0–
3	$2,000,000
Adjusted IRR = 20%	

The substantial drop in IRR took place because of the different manner in which negative cash flows in the future were discounted. In addition, the initial investment is increased by $929,705. It is the contention here that these adjustments represent a significant improvement over the simple IRR procedure.

4. Reinvestment of cash proceeds.   When the IRR is used to choose between mutually exclusive investment alternatives, the user (not the IRR) makes the implicit assumption that the cash proceeds from the investments can be reinvested at the calculated IRR. If the timing of the cash flows differs among the investments being compared, the IRR may provide an invalid indicator of investment desirability.

Example

Consider the following choice between two investments.

EOY	Investments	
	A	B
0	($10,000)	($10,000)
1	–0–	$11,000
2	–0–	–0–
3	–0–	–0–
4	–0–	–0–
5	$20,114	$ 2,074

If the IRR is calculated for each of the above investments, the yield of investment A is 15 percent, while the yield of investment B is 20 percent. The investments look quite similar; they both require the same initial investment and they are both for a duration of five years. Using IRR as the basis for investment selection, B is preferable to A. However, this presumes that the investor's goal is to maximize rate of return or at least choose that investment alternative among several which has the highest IRR. What this approach does not consider are the *reinvestment* opportunities that should be taken into account in most investment decisions. Investment A involves only one cash flow received in the future while investment B involves two. The question that should be asked when making investment comparisons of this type is at what rate can the investor invest the intermediate cash flows? Suppose that the investor could hope to achieve a yield of only 10 percent on the EOY 1 cash flow from investment B. A direct comparison of the result would be as follows.

EOY	Investments	
	A	B
0	($10,000)	($10,000)
1	–0–	$11,000
2	–0–	–0– Reinvested
3	–0–	–0– at 10%
4	–0–	–0–
5	$20,114	$ 2,074 + $16,105 = $18,179

Clearly, the investor's future wealth position would have increased by a substantially greater amount if investment A were selected rather than investment B if the immediate cash flows could be reinvested at a rate of only 10 percent. So, to make investment choices that reflect true market conditions, the reinvestment rate should be explicitly considered in the analysis of alternatives, and it should not be assumed that the rate to be earned on reinvested funds is exactly equal to the IRR.

5. Size differences in investments.   The size of an investment can influence the return in a number of ways. Implicit in the use of IRR is that investments being compared are both *divisible* and *replicable*. That is, the use of IRR to select among alternative investments carries with it the assumption that any size cash flow can be reinvested at the constant IRR and that a given investment may be undertaken or replicated at any time and on any size scale. Obviously, this is seldom possible in the real world.

Example

Assume the following mutually exclusive investment alternatives.

EOY	Investments	
	A	B
0	($10,000)	($15,000)
1	–0–	–0–
2	–0–	–0–
3	–0–	–0–
4	–0–	–0–
5	$30,518	$40,541

If the IRR is calculated for each of the alternative investments, the yield of investment A is 25 percent and the yield of B is 22 percent. If we rely exclusively upon IRR in the selection of one of these investments, A would be selected because it has the higher IRR. However, the real issue here is what the investor would do with the incremental investment (the $5,000 difference between the two initial investments) if investment A is selected. If we assume that either A or B could be selected, we must assume that the investor has the larger of the two investment amounts available to invest. Under these circumstances, it is critical to the investment decision to make an explicit estimate of the rate of return that the differential investment might earn, and then incorporate that rate in the decision. For example, if the investor could earn only 10 percent on the differential $5,000 initial investment, the following case would result.

EOY	Investments			B
	A			
	Original (25%) + Differential (10%) = Total			
0	($10,000) +	($5,000) =	($15,000)	($15,000)
1	–0–	–0–	–0–	–0–
2	–0–	–0–	–0–	–0–
3	–0–	–0–	–0–	–0–
4	–0–	–0–	–0–	–0–
5	$30,518 +	$8,053 =	$38,571	$40,541

Thus, the investor would have been better off selecting investment B with the lower IRR than selecting investment A and investing the remaining $5,000 at 10 percent. The key question again is what is the *actual* market rate that the investor can expect to invest the differential cash flows?

Another size-related issue occurs when a decision maker uses the IRR as the sole investment criterion for mutually exclusive investment alternatives. That is, the user of the IRR makes the implicit assumption that any future cash flow (negative or positive), *regardless of size*, can be reinvested at the IRR. Within the realm of real world investment opportunities it is clear that the dollar size (as well as the duration) of an investment is related to the yield. This market phenomenon is well known and widely observed, yet is ignored by the IRR measure.

Introduction to the Financial Management Rate of Return

In view of the shortcomings and deficiencies of the use of IRR in many investment decisions, an alternative model called the Financial Management Rate of Return (FMRR) was developed.[7] This model was specifically developed around the assumption that the primary goal of the investor is to maximize long-run wealth. Although this may not be the only goal, it is generally consistent with other goals the investor may have. This model is based upon the terminal value rate of return concept which has existed in economics and finance literature for some time.[8]

In particular, the FMRR is a specialized version of the geometric mean rate of return and is thus directly consistent with the goal of long-run wealth maximization.[9] It is described as specialized because the structure of the model has been modified to include as many of the unique characteristics of the real estate market as possible. FMRR makes the following assumptions.

1. *Only cash flows after financing and taxes from the property under evaluation are considered.* The fact is ignored that other sources of cash (such as other properties

owned by the investor) may be available in future years to meet cash outflow requirements on the given property, as is the possibility of the investor meeting such payments through the use of unsecured credit.

2. *Funds can be invested at any time in any amount at a safe after-tax rate (i_L) and withdrawn when needed.* This would represent highly liquid holdings at modest after-tax yields, comparable to a savings account. The key points here are safety to principal and stability of interest with the ability to make any size investment, however small.

3. *Funds can also be invested in "run of the mill" real estate projects of comparable risk at after-tax rates (i_R) above the safe rate.* The stipulation here is that such investments must be in minimum quantities of R dollars and such investments may not be liquidated to meet other cash requirements during the period under analysis.

These assumptions allow the model to recognize market realities and to simulate the actions of a rational financial manager. Real investments are *not* completely divisible; they require a certain minimum level of investment and typically cannot be liquidated without significant loss. At the same time, returns are higher than those of the safe rate. The variables are defined in terms of "run of the mill" projects so that i_R will represent the minimum acceptable return at the given level of risk for an investment of R. Defined in this manner, i_R also represents the minimum return which could be earned by reinvesting cash thrown off early in a project's life. Hence, the main test of the appropriateness of i_R used in a given application of the model is whether the analyst is confident that numerous investment projects would be available yielding at least that rate; if not, i_R should be lowered until such confidence is achieved.

Derivation of the Basic FMRR Model

The FMRR was designed to overcome the deficiencies of the IRR outlined previously. More specifically, it is designed to do the following:

1. Avoid the possibility of a nonunique or ambiguous solution by converting the cash flows into a conventional investment format and
2. Make explicit those assumptions implicit in the use of IRR regarding the discounting of outflows and the reinvestment of inflows. In essence, this eliminates the problems associated with cash flow reinvestment assumptions, variations of rate with size of investment and reinvestment and recognition of true initial investment.

Example

A simple example can be used to demonstrate the calculation and use of the FMRR model, using only after-financing and after-tax cash flows to show how they are treated within this model.

EOY	$
0	($10,000)
1	($50,000)
2	($50,000)
3	$30,000
4	($20,000)
5	$30,000
6	$250,000

IRR = 25.2%

Step 1. Remove all future outflows by utilizing prior inflows where possible. In this example, if $19,048 of the $30,000 received at EOY 3 were invested at a safe rate (i_L) of 5 percent, it would grow to $20,000 by EOY 4 and be available to meet the $20,000 outflow requirement at that point in time.

The cash flows, therefore, are changed as follows.

EOY	$	Modified Cash Flows
0	($10,000)	($10,000)
1	($50,000)	($50,000)
2	($50,000)	($50,000)
3	$30,000 + ($19,048)	$10,952
4	($20,000) ─── 5%	–0–
5	$30,000	$30,000
6	$250,000	$250,000

Step 2. Discount all remaining outflows to the present at the safe rate. In this example, the $50,000 payments at EOYs 1 and 2 are discounted to the present at a rate of 5 percent. The cash flows are changed as follows.

EOY	$	Modified Cash Flows
0	($10,000) + ($47,619) + ($45,352)	($102,971)
1	($50,000) ─── 5%	–0–
2	($50,000) ─── 5%	–0–
3	$10,952	$10,952
4	–0–	–0–
5	$30,000	$30,000
6	$250,000	$250,000

Note that this reflects the fact that the actual investment amount to be made or assumed by the investor is $102,971, not $10,000.

Step 3. Compound forward those positive cash flows remaining at the appropriate rate. In this example, assume R is equal to $10,000 and i_R is 10 percent. Thus, cash flows received at EOYs 3 and 5 will be compounded forward at $i_R = 10$ percent. The cash flows are again changed as follows.

EOY	$	Modified Cash Flows
0	($102,971)	($102,971)
1	–0–	–0–
2	–0–	–0–
3	$10,952 ———— 10%	–0–
4	–0–	–0–
5	$30,000 ———— 10%	–0–
6	$250,000 + $33,000 + $14,577	$297,577

Therefore,

FMRR = 19.4% (the rate at which $102,971 grows to $297,577 in six years)
IRR = 25.2% (the rate which discounts all future cash flows such that the sum of the present values is equal to $10,000)

The difference between these two measures of yield is entirely explained by the explicit estimates made for the various rates utilized within the FMRR calculation as compared with the assumption of the IRR approach, in which all relevant rates (safe rates and reinvestment rates) are exactly equal to the calculated IRR. Alternately stated, FMRR is the forecast compound rate of growth of the investor's wealth, measured in dollars, with reinvestment assumptions consistent with the particular investor's financial management strategy, including consideration of cash flows external to the investment under consideration. In contrast, recall that IRR is the return on each dollar each year that the dollar remains at risk in an investment.

Use of FMRR to Compare Investment Alternatives

Real estate investment alternatives often require different initial investments and have different anticipated holding periods. It is appropriate, therefore, to adjust cash flows for time and size disparities among investment alternatives under consideration for comparison on a par basis. As with all preceding examples, the investment alternatives below are assumed to have comparable risk and all cash flows shown are after-tax. Usually, investments will have intermediate periodic cash flows. They are adjusted independently, as demonstrated above. The adjusted cash flows are then compared.

Example

To illustrate the final adjustment process, compare the cash flows from the previous example (henceforth investment A) to investment B, an investment in raw land that costs $130,000. Assume that holding costs are $1,000 per year and that sale proceeds EOY 5 are projected at $331,000. The cash flows and adjusted cash flows for investment B are shown on the following page.

EOY	Investment B	
	$	Modified Cash Flows
0	($130,000) + ($3,546)*	($133,546)
1	($1,000)	–0–
2	($1,000)	–0–
3	($1,000) 5%	–0–
4	($1,000)	—0—
5	($1,000) + $331,000	$330,000

*PV of an ordinary annuity of $1,000 per year for four years discounted at 5 percent.

The IRR of investment B is 20 percent compared to 25.2 percent for investment A. Note that the initial investments are not equal for A and B, nor are the holding periods. If investment B is indeed an alternative, the investor must have $133,546 to invest. If A were acquired, it is assumed that the balance of investment capital would be invested at 10 percent for the longest holding period, six years. The holding period of A is six years compared to five years for investment B. The cash available at EOY 5 for investment B will be reinvested at a forecast 10 percent. The adjustments to cash flows for comparison of the two investment alternatives are summarized in the following two tables.

EOY	Investment A	
	Modified CF	Adjusted for Comparison
0	($102,971) + ($30,575)	($133,546)
1	–0–	–0–
2	–0–	–0–
3	–0– 10%	–0–
4	–0–	–0–
5	–0–	–0–
6	$297,577 + $54,165	$351,742

EOY	Investment B	
	Modified CF	Adjusted for Comparison
0	($133,546)	($133,546)
1	–0–	–0–
2	–0–	–0–
3	–0–	–0–
4	–0–	–0–
5	$330,000 ——— 10%	–0–
6	–0– $363,000	$363,000

The alternative investments can now be compared on a par basis. The table below summarizes the cash flows and investment measures. Note that the IRR alone would not have indicated the investment alternative which would produce the maximum amount of future wealth with the forgoing financial management assumptions.

EOY	Investment A		Investment B	
	$	Adjusted for Comparison	$	Adjusted for Comparison
0	($10,000)	($133,546)	($130,000)	($133,546)
1	($50,000)	–0–	($1,000)	–0–
2	($50,000)	–0–	($1,000)	–0–
3	$30,000	–0–	$1,000)	–0–
4	($20,000)	–0–	($1,000)	–0–
5	$30,000	–0–	($1,000) + $331,000	–0–
6	$250,000	$351,742	–0–	$363,000
IRR	25.2%		20.0%	
FMRR		17.5%		18.1%

Investment B will produce the greatest future wealth EOY 6. Calculation of the actual FMRR is not even required for this decision once the cash flows have been adjusted. The appropriate financial choice is simply that alternative which will provide the most dollars at the end of the investment time horizon.

It should be noted here that the 10 percent rate for reinvestment of the sale proceeds from investment B may be understated. The $330,000 available EOY 5 may very well have been reinvested in another property that would produce a higher yield. This assumption could have been imputed into the analysis easily by compounding the future wealth EOY 5 from investment B at a greater rate of perhaps 20 percent since this was the yield on the last investment. The safe rate(s) and reinvestment rate(s) must be consistent, after-tax rates. Do not use a *before*-tax bond yield for a safe rate with an analysis of cash flows *after* tax.

Other Applications of the FMRR

One of the more interesting and useful applications of the FMRR is in determining the optimal holding period of an investment. The holding period of a real estate investment has traditionally been determined by the IRR, which is especially ill-suited to the task. In addition, the FMRR can be used in selecting among mutually exclusive alternative investments and in selecting from a mix of alternatives when investment funds are rationed.

There are several other applications of the FMRR that can be most helpful in real estate investment decision-making. It is not within the scope of this chapter to detail such applications, but the concerned reader is referred to the Messner-Findlay article for some extensions or modifications of the basic FMRR model.[10]

DETERMINATION OF INVESTMENT BASE

Investment Base Concept

Different properties usually require different cash investments. As discussed earlier, there are limitations in using a rate of return measure, such as IRR, to choose among investments if the initial investments (cash or cash equivalent) differ in size. The suggested method of circumventing this problem is to use the FMRR process. When applying the FMRR process, the *investment base concept* allows the analyst to establish the appropriate *opportunity cost* for existing properties so that adjustments can be made to compare alternatives by starting with a *common initial investment*. Further, when calculating the IRR of an investment or group of investments, it may be necessary to apply the investment base concept to determine an appropriate initial investment. In this section, the investment base concept and related topics will be discussed.

Types of choices. Investors are faced with investment choices. With mutually exclusive choices, the investor can choose one and only one of a group of investments or investment-related alternatives.

Example

Jack inherited $100,000. The $100,000 is all of the cash that Jack has available to invest. He has the following choices.

A Shopping Center		B Apartment	
Cost	$500,000	Cost	$700,000
Financing	400,000	Financing	600,000
Cash	100,000	Cash	100,000

These investments are mutually exclusive since each one requires $100,000, and Jack has no more than $100,000.

Example

Fran purchased an office building for $1,600,000. Fran must obtain financing of $1,200,000. Her choices are the following.

Loan A	Loan B
$1,200,000	$1,200,000
10%, 25 years	11%, 30 years
3 points	1.5 points

These choices are also mutually exclusive, since Fran can obtain one loan or the other, but not both.

However, the investor can choose one or more or all of a group of possible investments.

Example

You have inherited $100,000 and must choose among the following.

A 4 Unit Apartment		B 3 Unit Apartment		C Office	
Cost	$250,000	Cost	$220,000	Cost	$200,000
Financing	200,000	Financing	170,000	Financing	150,000
Cash	50,000	Cash	50,000	Cash	50,000

You may choose A and B, B and C, or A and C. Choosing any two of the investments is
possible. You cannot, however, choose A, B, and C since that choice would require more
cash than you have. In the above example, $100,000 is the investment base of your portfolio,
or the total amount of money that you have available for investment.

Procedure.   There are several procedures available. One can create mutually
exclusive portfolios. To obtain a common initial investment (which equals the investment
base of your portfolio), an investor must combine investments into alternative portfolios
that are mutually exclusive. (The investment base concept will be discussed shortly.)

Example

Sue has $200,000 in cash to invest. The following investments and their cash requirements
are available to her.

Property	Abbreviation	Cash Down Payment
Apartment	A	$ 70,000
Shopping Center	S	160,000
Office	O	120,000
T-Bills	T	Any Amount

These can be combined into the following alternative portfolios.

	1		2		3	
A	$ 70,000	A	$ 70,000	S	$ 160,000
O	120,000	T	130,000	T	40,000
T	10,000		–0–		–0–
	$ 200,000		$ 200,000		$ 200,000

	4		5	
O	$ 120,000	T	$ 200,000
T	80,000		–0–
	–0–		–0–
	$ 200,000		$ 200,000

Sue has five mutually exclusive choices, each of which uses the entire $200,000 investment base.

An alternative is to determine the cash flows produced by each choice.

To continue the example, the following are the cash flows produced by the investments. Assume a five-year holding period (the period was chosen arbitrarily for this investment analysis).

A		S		O		T
n	$	n	$	n	$	
0	$70,000	0	($160,000)	0	($120,000)	6% after tax
1	$ 6,000	1	$ 19,000	1	–0–	
2	$ 7,000	2	$ 20,000	2	–0–	
3	$ 8,000	3	$ 21,000	3	$ 4,000	
4	$ 9,000	4	$ 24,000	4	$ 10,000	
5	$85,000	5	$ 200,000	5	$ 211,000	
IRR = 12.22%		14.75%		13.65%		6%

Note that, based solely on IRR, the investor would choose the shopping center, S. The cash flows produced by each portfolio are as follows.

	1		2		3	
Investments	A + O + T		A + T		S + T	
n	$	n	$	n	$
0	($200,000)	0	($200,000)	0	($200,000)
1	$ 6,600	1	$ 13,800	1	$ 21,400
2	$ 7,600	2	$ 14,800	2	$ 22,400
3	$ 12,600	3	$ 15,800	3	$ 23,400
4	$ 19,600	4	$ 16,800	4	$ 26,400
5	$ 306,600	5	$ 222,800	5	$ 242,400
IRR =	12.43%		8.25%		13.06%

	4		5	
Investments	O + T		T	
n	$	n	$
0	($200,000)	0	($200,000)
1	$ 4,800	1	$ 12,000
2	$ 4,800	2	$ 12,000
3	$ 8,800	3	$ 12,000
4	$ 14,800	4	$ 12,000
5	$ 295,800	5	$ 212,000
IRR =	10.99%		6.00%

The following t-charts assume that cash flows have been reinvested at an appropriate rate. For this example, assume an after-tax reinvestment rate of 6%.

	1		2		3
n	$	n	$	n	$
0	($200,000)	0	($200,000)	0	($200,000)
1	–0–	1	–0–	1	–0–
2	–0–	2	–0–	2	–0–
3	–0–	3	–0–	3	–0–
4	–0–	4	–0–	4	–0–
5	$ 358,917	5	$ 293,410	5	$ 350,372
FMRR =	12.41%		7.97%		11.87%

	4		5
n	$	n	$
0	($200,000)	0	($200,000)
1	–0–	1	–0–
2	–0–	2	–0–
3	–0–	3	–0–
4	–0–	4	–0–
5	$ 333,152	5	$ 267,645
FMRR =	10.74%		6.00%

The relative measure of desirability of alternative portfolios changes when FMRR is used as the selection device rather than IRR. The change is a result of (1) the pattern of the cash flows for each investment portfolio and (2) the reinvestment assumption. Key points to note about the application of the FMRR process and the portfolio approach are

The initial investment is the same for each alternative portfolio and
the holding period is the same for each alternative portfolio.

The initial investment and the holding period must be uniform for each alternative, even if this is contrived by using T-Bills or some unknown future real estate investment. Mutually exclusive alternatives require us to compare "apples to apples," and if the investment bases or holding periods differ, this direct comparison is not possible.

Investment base concept.   The investment base concept was developed so that investors could determine the amount that is invested in a given investment or group of investments. Unless an investor can determine the amount that is invested, the IRR and

FMRR measures cannot be calculated. Therefore, it is necessary to apply the investment base concept to (1) properly determine the IRR of an investment or investment portfolio and (2) properly apply the FMRR process to an investment or investment portfolio.

1. When calculating the IRR of an investment or investment portfolio, the initial investment will be calculated by applying the investment base concept.
2. When applying the FMRR process to mutually exclusive investments or mutually exclusive investment portfolios, the common initial investment (the adjusted initial investment) will be calculated by using the investment base concept. Note that it is not necessary to have a common initial investment to calculate the IRR.

The investment base concept encompasses two steps, the identification of the investment base of an investment or of each investment in a portfolio of investments and the measurement of the investment base of an investment or of each investment in a portfolio of investments. It is important to note that there is an investment base for every investment. The investment base of a portfolio is the sum of the investment bases of the investments that comprise that portfolio.

Identifying and measuring the investment base.   The investment base in any investment or group of investments equals the after-tax amount that must be given up to acquire that investment or group of investments. Suppose that Sue decides to use her $200,000 to acquire portfolio 1, described above.

PORTFOLIO 1	
Property	Cash Down Payment
Apartment	$ 70,000
Office	$ 120,000
T-Bills	$ 10,000
	$ 200,000

In this case, the investment base of the entire portfolio and of each of the component investments is easy to identify and measure. The investment bases are simply the amounts of cash given up to acquire the investments. Sue must give up (1) $200,000 after taxes to acquire the entire portfolio, (2) $70,000 after taxes to acquire the apartment building, (3) $120,000 after taxes to acquire the office building and (4) $10,000 after taxes to acquire the T-bills. Therefore, Sue's investment base in the decision to acquire the portfolio is $200,000; her investment base in the decision to acquire the apartment building is $70,000, and so on.

After Sue actually acquires the portfolio, however, the various investment bases are less easy to identify and measure. Assume that one year has passed and that Sue would like to explore the following investment decisions which would be implemented one year after she acquired her portfolio of investments:

- Do nothing with the apartment building
- Sell the office building under an installment sale agreement and use the proceeds to buy stock
- Sell the T-bills
- Use the proceeds from the sale of the T-bills and add $50,000 of cash to acquire a small strip shopping center

The Do-Nothing Decision. Sue's investment base in the decision to do nothing with the apartment building is simply the amount that she must give up to acquire (actually, to continue holding) the apartment building. In this case, identifying the investment base in the apartment building is less easy than it was before. Instead of cash given up, the investment base in the do-nothing alternative (continue holding) one year hence will equal some cash equivalent given up. Specifically, the investment base in the decision to do nothing with the apartment building will equal the amount of after-tax cash proceeds that would be received if Sue were to sell the apartment building.

Up to this point, the investment base has been identified. In order to measure the investment base in the do-nothing decision, the proceeds-from-sale portion of the cash flow model must be employed.

$$\boxed{\text{Sale Price}}$$

Less

$$\boxed{\text{Sale Costs}}$$

Less

$$\boxed{\text{Mortgage Balance}}$$

Less

$$\boxed{\text{Tax Liability on Sale}}$$

Equals

$$\boxed{\text{PROCEEDS AFTER TAXES}}$$

or

$$\boxed{\text{INVESTMENT BASE IN DO-NOTHING ALTERNATIVE}}$$

At this time, it is important to note the role that decisions play in identifying the investment base. In this example, Sue explored the do-nothing decision. That is, she sought to determine her investment base in the apartment building. This is true because she decided to retain the apartment building. Therefore, after she implements her decision, her investment will still be defined as the apartment building.

Suppose, instead, that Sue decided to dispose of the apartment building under terms of an outright sale and to then use the proceeds to purchase some other investment(s). In this case the numerical value of the investment base throughout the process would remain the same. However, Sue's investment would be defined differently. That is, she would reinvest the amount of her investment base in some other investment(s). Therefore, the investment base in the other investments (after the sell or reinvest decision is implemented) would equal the investment base that existed in the apartment building prior to implementation.

Given the assumptions above, it can be said that Sue's investment base in her sell or reinvest decision (which is actually two decisions: sell then reinvest) has the same value as the investment bases in the apartment building and the new investments. Although the distinction between the investment base in a decision (action) and the investment base in an investment (thing) may seem like nothing more than an academic exercise, this is not the case. A comprehension of this distinction is necessary to enable an investor to identify the investment base (what is given up). That is, by applying the logic that a given decision (action) will transform a given investment (or investments) into some other investment(s), the investor can identify what is being given up and, of equal importance, what is being acquired. The application of this decision-yields-investment process will be further described below.

The Installment-Sale Decision. As before, Sue's investment base in the installment-sale decision is simply the after-tax amount that she must give up to acquire a new investment. However, identification of the investment base will be more complex than it was under the do-nothing alternative.

To identify the investment base, the investor must consider the outcome of the installment-sale decision. If Sue disposes of the office building under an installment sale contract, the outcome will be as follows:

- Sue will have a new investment in the form of the installment-sale note. (Although Sue may secure this note with the office building, she essentially has a new investment with risks that are distinctly different than those encountered while the office building was held.)
- Sue will have a new investment in the form of cash proceeds. These proceeds will, in turn, be transformed into some other investments like T-bills, savings account, stock, real estate, and so on.

Under the installment sale alternative, Sue must give up the entire office building to acquire her new investments. Therefore, her investment base in the installment sale decision equals the after-tax proceeds from sale that would be received if she were to sell the office building for cash. Sue's investment base in her new investment (she will use the proceeds to acquire stock) would be measured as follows.

Investment Base In Installment Sale Note:

> Sales Proceeds After Tax from Outright Sale

Less

> CFAT (EOY 0) from Installment Sale

Equals

> Investment Base in Installment Sale Note

Investment Base In Stock:

> Amount of CFAT from Installment Sale Used to Acquire Stock

It is important to note that Sue's investment base in the installment sale note will not likely equal the face value of that note. The investment base will depend on her tax bracket, the amount of any depreciation recapture, the extent of any mortgage-over-basis, the market value of the office building, and so on.

Decision to Sell T-Bills and Acquire Shopping Center. Under this alternative, Sue would give up the T-bills and use the proceeds to acquire some other investments. Specifically, she will use the proceeds to acquire a shopping center. The investment base in the disposition decision, then, will equal the after-tax proceeds from the sale of T-bills.

Sue's investment base in her new investment, the shopping center, will equal the after-tax proceeds from the sale of the T-bills plus any cash (or after-tax cash equivalent) added to acquire the new investment. In this case, $50,000 in cash will be added. (This disposition-reinvestment scenario will be further discussed below.)

Investment Base: Decisions, Investments and Time. Implicit in the concept of investment bases in decisions and in investments is the element of time. Suppose an investor decides to sell investment A to acquire investment B. The investor's investment bases over time would be as follows.

Investor acquires investment A. The investment base in investment A, at the time of acquisition, is equal to the after-tax cash or cash equivalent used (given up) to acquire A.

Investor decides to dispose of investment A. The investment base in investment A, before the decision is implemented, equals the after-tax proceeds that would be received from the sale of A. After the decision is implemented, this investment base is transferred to some other investment(s) and the investment base in A is reduced to zero.

Exhibit 1

Investments, Decisions, and Time

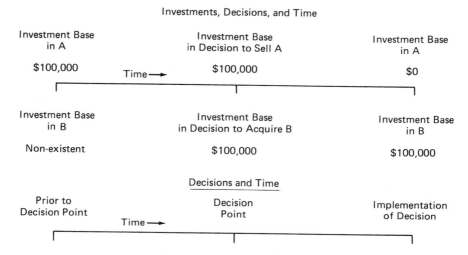

Investment Base in A	Investment Base in Decision to Sell A	Investment Base in A
$100,000	Time → $100,000	$0

Investment Base in B	Investment Base in Decision to Acquire B	Investment Base in B
Non-existent	$100,000	$100,000

Decisions and Time

Prior to Decision Point	Decision Point	Implementation of Decision
Time →		

Investor decides to acquire investment B. This decision occurs at the same point in time as the decision to sell investment A. Assuming that the investor adds nothing more than the after-tax proceeds from the sale of investment A, the investment base in the decision to acquire will equal that of the decision to sell. Prior to the implementation of the decision to acquire investment B, investment B has no investment base (it does not exist yet). After the decision is implemented, given the assumption that only the proceeds from A are given up, the investment base in investment B will take on the same numerical value as that of investment A prior to implementation. Graphically, the transformation in investment bases is illustrated in Exhibit 1 (assume the after-tax proceeds from the sale of A equals $100,000).

Decision to Sell T-Bills and Acquire Shopping Center Revisited. Recall that Sue wished to explore the decision to sell her T-bills. Further, she wished to explore the decision to acquire a shopping center. This disposition-reinvestment decision requires the addition of $50,000 in cash.

Graphically, the disposition and reinvestment decisions described in the previous paragraph can be combined as shown in Exhibit 2, p. 80 (assume Sue's after-tax proceeds from the sale of the T-bills equals $10,200).

Investment Base in Decisions. As mentioned above, the discussion of investment base in decisions was not developed as an academic exercise. The purpose of this discussion was to emphasize the fact that decisions, when implemented, can transform one investment into some other investment. (Even the do-nothing decision should be viewed as a disposition-reinvestment process). After this section, the discussion of investment base in a decision will be dropped. However, before moving on, the key elements that should be retained from this discussion will be summarized.

Exhibit 2

Investments, Decisions, and Time

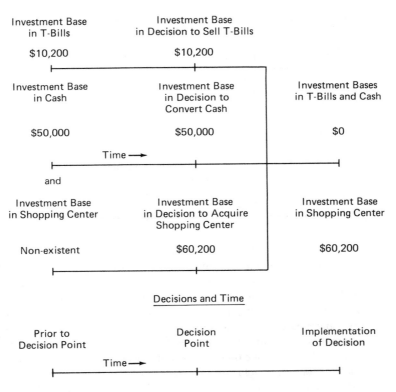

Decisions and Time

1. Decisions, when implemented, transform a given investment into some other investment.
2. As the investment cycle continues, the investment base in any given investment is subject to change. At each decision point (see the diagram following and the discussion at the beginning of this module), the proposed disposition and acquisition decisions will dictate how the investment bases in investments before and after the decision point will be identified and measured.
3. The investment cycle progresses through time with multiple decision points and many decision alternatives.

The decision alternatives are the same as those listed under the previous Decision Alternatives column. That is, the investment cycle can be viewed as something that progresses through time and something that contains many decision cycles.

Decision Alternatives

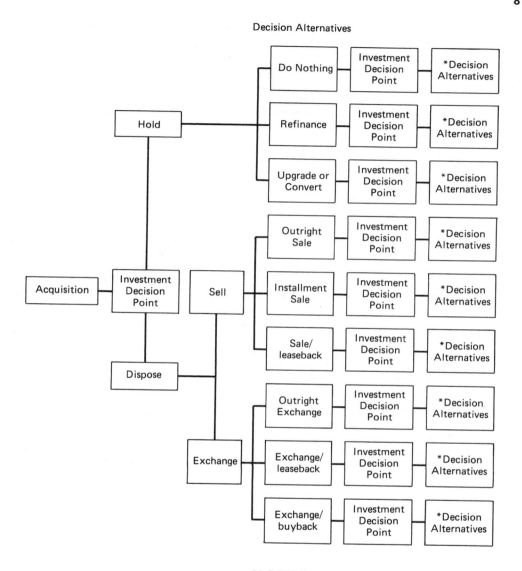

NOTES

1. For an exposition of some of the traditional and conventional methods of measuring the return on real estate investments and their respective shortcomings, see James R. Cooper, *Real Estate Investment Analysis* (Lexington, MA: Lexington Books, 1974), Ch. 1; Stephen E. Roulac, "Truth in Real Estate Reporting," *Real Estate Review*, Spring, 1974, pp. 90–95; and Victor Lyon, "ABC's of Investment Analysis," *real estate today*, February, 1980, pp. 20–25.

2. Much of the following discussion is based on Stephen D. Messner and M. Chapman Findlay, "Real Estate Investment Analysis: IRR Versus FMRR," *The Real Estate Appraiser*, July–August, 1975, pp. 5–20.

3. See Appendix B for a further discussion of interpolation.

4. See Messner and Findlay, pp. 8–9, for numerical examples of nonconventional investments and the phenomenon of multiple yields. See also Donald J. Valachi, "More on the Arithmetic of Multiple and Imaginary Rates of Return," *The Real Estate Appraiser and Analyst*, Vol. 46, No. 5, September–October, 1980, pp. 19–22.

5. Messner and Findlay, pp. 9–11.

6. Messner and Findlay, pp. 10–11.

7. The FMRR was developed by M. Chapman Findlay and Stephen D. Messner of the School of Business Administration, the University of Connecticut, Storrs, Connecticut, in 1973. Jay W. Levine, working with Realtron Corporation, assisted the originators to relate and adapt their model to problems found in the real estate investment market. An explanation of this model was first published as *Determination and Usage of FM Rate of Return*, 1973, by Realtron Corporation, Detroit. An expanded version was presented by Findlay and Messner at the Eastern Finance Association meetings in April, 1975, at the University of South Carolina. Subsequently, the model has been refined and much discussed in real estate literature. For example, see Guilford C. Babcock, M. Chapman Findlay and Stephen D. Messner, "FMRR and Duration: Implications for Real Estate Investment Analysis," *AREUEA Journal*, Vol. 4, No. 3, Winter, 1976, pp. 49–67; M. Chapman Findlay, Stephen D. Messner and R. Tarantello, "Risk Analysis in Real Estate," *The Real Estate Appraiser and Analyst*, Vol. 45, No. 4, July–August, 1979, pp. 27–38; M. Chapman Findlay, Carl W. Hamilton, Stephen D. Messner and Jonathan S. Yormark, "Optimal Real Estate Portfolios," *AREUEA Journal*, Vol. 7, No. 3, Fall, 1979, pp. 298–317; and M. Chapman Findlay, Stephen D. Messner and R. Tarantello, *FMRR Simulation Model and User Manual* (Storrs, CT: Center for Real Estate and Urban Economic Studies, 1980).

8. Gene Dilmore, *The New Approach to Real Estate Appraising* (Englewood Cliffs, NJ: Prentice-Hall, Inc., 1971), pp. 122–23.

9. H. Latane, "Criteria for Choice Among Risky Ventures," *Journal of Political Economy*, April, 1959, pp. 144–55.

10. Messner and Findlay, pp. 18–20. See also Note 7 of this chapter.

5
Estimation of Real Estate
Cash Flows (Forecasting)

INTRODUCTION TO FORECASTING

Thus far the major emphasis of this text has been on the process of converting forecast future cash flows (income receipts) into present value estimates by using the mathematical process of compound discounting. The mathematical logic employed in discounting future cash flows is essential in analyzing real estate investments. Of equal importance, however, is the process by which the future cash flows of a specific property (or group of properties) are estimated. Generally, this process stands in marked contrast to the inexorable precision of the discounting process. Since estimates of cash flows generated by real estate necessarily involve estimates of the future, they are more often than not significantly less precise than the mathematical technique used to discount them to the present.

The estimation of future cash flows for income-producing real estate requires a variety of judgments and assumptions concerning the future. Among these are judgments concerning the property itself, the future of the neighborhood in which it is located, the general market conditions that will prevail in the future and their impact on the specific property, future developments in the federal income tax laws that may influence the after-tax cash flows of the property and myriad other factors which may affect the cash flows of the specific property over time. The point is that the task of income estimation typically requires both experience in and knowledge of the operation of the real estate market. It is not simply an extrapolation of the known market behavior of preceding years, nor can the estimation problem be refined completely to objective statistical probabilities. In its final form, the estimate of future benefits from an investment in real estate must relate to the *amount, timing, duration* (or term) and *stability* of after-tax cash flows to be received by the investor.

This process may be viewed as more an art than a science because of the variety of types of real estate income. The income from a long-term net lease is simplest to define because the lease itself usually states the rental stream. This estimation could become more complicated if a percentage rent is also required. At the other extreme, the income from a vacant portion of land, encumbered with debt, can account for a negative income stream created by real estate taxes and loan payments, until the land is sold.

Between these extremes is the apartment building, the store building or other improved real estate with short-term leases where the owner pays all or most of the expenses. Other examples include vacant buildings as well as properties to be developed where all income and expense items must be estimated and projected.

INCOME ESTIMATION AS A BROKERAGE TOOL

Distinctions between Residential and Investment Property

At the outset, it is important to recognize the differences between marketing investment property and residential property. By understanding the differences, the broker presenting an investment property can readily see the most effective means of making such a presentation.

Residential properties that are owner-occupied are paid for from income unrelated to the property and are purchased to satisfy the functional and structural arrangement needed by the purchaser. These properties must have the floor plan and amenities that are of personal importance to the buyer. The buyer is interested in the size of the home, the number of bedrooms and the room arrangement. Neighborhoods, the local school system, available transportation, churches, shopping, social and recreational facilities and, perhaps, the view from the living room window are important considerations. Real estate brokers stress these items in showing a home intended for owner occupancy.

In selling residential properties, a market data approach is typically used in determining market value and/or price. Market value is determined by the sale prices of similar properties. In some cases, replacement costs and the amount of actual depreciation that the property has already undergone might be considerations influencing residential property buyers.

When income-producing property is involved, the amenities, churches, neighborhood and view all are secondary considerations. Income-producing properties are purchased for their ability to produce an income stream, whether that income is operating income or potential capital gain on resale, or both, and are paid for with the income generated. The amenities and other factors that are so important with residential properties have importance for income-producing property only if they influence the stream of cash flows. Do they add to the quantity of that income; do they make the quality or the durability of that income any better?

Many brokers make the mistake of stressing only the physical characteristics of an investment property and/or its replacement cost when the purchaser is really interested in the future income benefits. The fact that the present owner has invested considerable sums in the property does not necessarily influence the potential buyer of investment property. If the income produced by the property will only justify a sale price of $175,000, the buyer does not care that the owner has actually invested $300,000 in the property and is willing to let it go for $250,000.

If buyers purchase investment property for future income, it is absolutely imperative that the broker have all of the financial information about a property prior to marketing it. Just as a stock broker cannot market stock without a prospectus (operating history), a real estate broker cannot intelligently present a property if the owner will not produce an operating statement until a qualified buyer is found.

Appraiser versus Investment Broker

The task of the real estate appraiser is most often that of estimating the *market value* of a property, that is, the most probable selling price of the property under "normal" exposure to the market and under financing terms generally available for similar properties. Under the somewhat rigid definition utilized for market value, particularly in the legal context imposed by institutional mortgage lenders, property tax authorities and others, there is a single value at any point in time. Obviously, different opinions of market value among appraisers may prevail, but in concept there is only one correct market value for a given property at any one time.

In contrast, the investment broker is generally concerned with the value of a property to a specific potential investor or class of investors. Under these conditions, the analysis of value takes into account the estimated after-tax cash flows, the desired or required rate of return on the equity investment and the financing terms available on the property to the specific investor. This value estimate is *investment value*; it may be less than, equal to or greater than market value. For example, *if* the potential investor is also typical in terms of the group of investors most likely to purchase the property under the competitive market conditions required by the definition of market value, investment value will be exactly equal to market value.

COLLECTION OF PROPERTY DATA

The first step in estimating the future cash flows that will be generated by a specific property is to collect the most recent operating data from the present owner. Obtaining financial information about previous years' operations, however, is not the broker's only responsibility. The broker must also be able to analyze and evaluate the information, process the data in an operating statement, convert the income stream to an estimate of value and, finally, interpret to the owner or client the consequences of owning the property under present and alternate financing arrangements.

Interview with Owner

In an interview with the owner the broker must be adamant in the quest for information. Many owners only reluctantly divulge financial information about their property. Most agree to supply the information when a qualified buyer is found.

It is only when the broker truly understands that buyers are buying the future income rather than the structure that the broker can insist on obtaining proper information from the owner *before* any potential purchaser is contracted. When owners understand what truly motivates a buyer, they will usually supply the necessary information. No one buys securities without a prospectus. In the same way, the public cannot be expected to purchase income property without a past history of its operations.

The broker cannot always depend on the owner's memory and should insist on statements from previous years. The best information is usually obtained when the broker gets written authority from the owner's accountant for all the data needed. The owner's records will have validity but income tax statements will provide the best information. It is rare for income tax records to overstate income or understate expenses.

Property Inspection

Although the property will be sold mainly on the basis of the financial data, it is necessary that the broker also obtain physical data on the property. This will include type of construction, condition of the property, the size and area of the land and improvements. This information will be used as an aid in verifying incomes and expenses and for estimating value.

It is also important for the broker to inspect the neighborhood to observe if it is economically stable, dying or growing.

Depending on the type of property involved, the broker should also investigate all or some of the following facilities with respect to the property:

Public transportation
Highways and expressways
Interchanges
Power
Utilities
Railroad transportation
Schools
Taxation procedures

Revision of Property Data

The information the broker obtains from the owner may be 100 percent truthful and still not be valid. The owner, even if truthful, can only report what the property took in for the previous year or years and what expenses were incurred during the same years. The owner is not in a position to *evaluate* the data. This is the task of the broker who is interested in developing an operating statement that will closely reflect what the property might be expected to do under average management conditions during future years. Buyers, after all, are paying for future potential, not for past income.

It is possible that the indicated previous year's rents were unusually low or high. It is the broker's job to find out what rents *should be* for this type of property. It is also possible that last year's maintenance costs or taxes or any other particular expense might have been unusually high or low; the broker must then determine typical costs. Possibly, when all adjustments and revisions have been completed, not a single item of expense or income may be the same as indicated by the owner for previous years. However, such a revised operating statement supplied by the broker will more closely reflect what the property can be expected to do in the future, which is of utmost importance to any potential buyer.

The first step in revising property data is to analyze the information obtained from the owner and make certain obvious adjustments. For example, if the owner is occupying the building, it is necessary to determine what rent would be paid if someone other than the owner occupied the building. If the broker is unable to evaluate what the rent should be, a notation should be made that the owner is not paying rent to occupy the space. The key point is that any items on the owner's income statement that fail to reflect the market should be modified.

The expenses should be evaluated to determine if they include any of the owner's personal expenses. It is possible that they could be legitimate tax deductions for the present owner yet not be true expenses involved in obtaining rent for the building.

Obtaining Relevant Market Data

In order to make the necessary adjustments to the operating information supplied by the owner, the broker must investigate and/or be familiar with a variety of market data.

Rental information must be obtained. What do similar properties rent for per square unit per month or per year? Is a percentage rent applicable and, if so, how much? What are typical rent terms and provisions? How valid are the owner's stated rents as to quantity, quality and durability? What vacancy and credit loss factor should be applied? Are utilities included in the rent or are they paid for by the tenant? Do rent schedules of comparable buildings include comparable services or furnishings?

Expenses must be analyzed both individually and totally. Are the expenses indicated by the owner valid or should they be adjusted upward or downward? Are sufficient amounts allowed for taxes in districts that need new schools and other facilities? Are there proper amounts allowed as maintenance and repair expenses? Is the total expense-to-income ratio adequate?

The broker should also obtain reconstruction costs for the type of building under study and should search the market for recent sales of similar properties and land. These figures will be needed for estimating market value.

Financial data provided by the owner must be verified for accuracy and thoroughness. The broker should find out whether existing financial arrangements are by mortgage, trust deed, or contract and determine the order of the liens. Exact encumbrances, payments, interest rates, and due dates should be determined. The broker should also determine if the existing loans may be assumed by a prospective purchaser and whether the seller will carry back any financing and on what terms.

Other important items of information the broker should include on the statement are assessed values of land, improvements and personal property, as well as the present owner's basis and depreciation schedule.

ORGANIZATION OF PROPERTY DATA

For purposes of investment analysis, *cash flows* are used rather than accrual accounting concepts to measure benefits. Thus, non-cash flow expenses such as cost recovery are *not* included in the measure of cash flows (although the impact of cost recovery may be reflected through reduced tax outlays) while the cash outflow of debt repayment through mortgage amortization is not recorded as an accounting expense.

The typical cash flow statement for real estate is divided into the major categories of potential rental income, effective rental income, operating expenses, net operating income, cash flow before tax and cash flow after tax.

Potential Rental Income

This is generally defined as the *rent roll* or annual market rental for the entire capacity of rentable space in the property. If the property is owner-occupied, a market rental would be imputed; if the property is under long-term lease, the contract rent would be the most appropriate measure of rent receipts. Present rents for the property may be higher, lower or approximately equal to market rents. It is important to determine (estimate) the *most probable* rent levels for the future; this is a critical first step in determining the future cash flows that the potential investor might expect to receive.

Effective Rental Income

As indicated, potential rental income is the annual amount that the property would produce *if* all rentable space were rented. In most cases, it is not reasonable to assume 100 percent occupancy of the property. In any case, the vacancy and credit losses of similar and competitive properties must be compared with those of the subject property so that reasonable expectations of the future rate can be made. In general, the rate is measured as the annual percentage of total rentable space that is vacant. This rate is then converted into an annual dollar amount and subtracted from potential rental income to obtain effective rental income.

Gross Operating Income

To obtain the figure for gross operating income, "other income" is added to the effective rental income. Other income is income related to the property but not derived directly from the rental of building space. Examples would be income from the rent of parking space or income from concessions.

Operating Expenses

Gross operating income, as defined, represents the total cash inflows to the property that are available to pay operating expenses, to cover annual debt service, to pay income taxes, and to provide for a return on investment as well as a complete return *of* the investment over time. Operating expenses typically include the following.

Taxes.   The major tax paid on real estate is property tax. This is a fixed expense in that it does not vary with occupancy but does (or can) change over time. Factors such as trends in the local or state property tax law and the frequency of reassessment can help in estimating likely future tax payments.

Insurance.   Current quotations or estimates are needed on multiperil insurance for the property.

Utilities.   Today utility costs often increase so rapidly that actual costs for the past year may significantly understate probable future costs. Utility companies may be able to provide some reliable estimates for the future based on past levels of consumption.

Licenses, permits and advertising.   A check should be made to determine what licenses and/or permits are needed, if any, to operate the property and their annual costs. Local property management companies and other owners can provide some comparable information on the annual cost of advertising utilizing signs, newspapers and other publications.

Management.   There are two kinds of property management: professional and resident. Professional management firms generally charge a percentage of gross operating income. The use of a resident manager is required in many areas and is generally done in conjunction with a professional management firm when a large number of units is involved and/or when day-to-day requirements call for constant supervision. Market data are usually available on the cost of such management. The real problem is the tendency to omit consideration of this experience when the owner acts as manager and/or the prospective buyer is planning to do so.

Payroll and payroll taxes.   In addition to the payroll expense of regular employees used in operating the property, there is also the cost of payroll taxes, such as social security tax and workers' compensation insurance.

Supplies.   This category of expense will vary significantly from one type of property to another, but similar properties should have relatively similar supply expenses.

Services.   Special services required by the property such as rubbish collection and pool service must be included as operating expenses. Typically this category of expense is relatively small but, as in the case of supplies, can vary greatly from one type of property to another.

Maintenance.   Actual maintenance and repair expenses for the subject property for the past few years can be used as a starting point for estimating future expenses. However, current trends in the market should be compared with recent costs. Market data can generally be obtained from local management firms; in addition, there is published data on several types of income-producing properties which provide average annual maintenance costs per unit of space.

Replacements.   Equipment and building parts with relatively short lives must be replaced periodically over the term of investment. Typical appraisal practice calls for prorating or stabilizing such outlays on an annual basis. This is accomplished by dividing the replacement cost by the forecast economic life to obtain the annual amount needed to cover replacement. However, this appraisal treatment is technically incorrect for two reasons. From the standpoint of income tax calculations, the cost of replacements is a capital expenditure, *not* an expense, and must be depreciated over the economic life of the asset. Also, the practice of prorating the cash outlay over several annual periods distorts the actual cash flows used to measure investment value and return. Thus, the proper practice for investment analysis is to forecast *actual* cash flows for each year.

Net Operating Income

Net operating income is obtained by subtracting operating expenses from gross operating income. This is *the* key measure of income used by appraisers and mortgage lenders when market value is sought because it is the measure of return *before* financing, taxes and capital recovery.

Cash Flow before Taxes (CFBT)

As indicated, net operating income (NOI) represents an estimate of the typical year's income return to the *entire* property. When the property is financed with a mortgage loan, the NOI must provide for the annual debt service associated with the loan. Thus, cash flow before taxes is obtained by subtracting the annual debt service from the NOI.

Cash Flow after Taxes (CFAT)

This is the true "bottom line" of the annual return of the investment. Each year's income tax liability is subtracted from CFBT to obtain cash flow after taxes. The calculation of income tax liability will be considered in subsequent chapters, but it is important to note that this may be a negative figure. That is, accounting losses (because of the non-cash depreciation expense) may be used to reduce taxes that would be paid on other income.

Example

The following illustration is intended to show how data collected from both the present owner of an apartment property and from the marketplace may be used to develop cash flow estimates.

Owner's Property Data

The accounting records of a 28 unit apartment building for the past year showed the following:

Rental receipts		$51,000
Operating expenses		
Real estate taxes	$7,956	
Property insurance	4,203	
Utilities	2,669	
Supplies	1,173	
Contract services	1,511	
Other expenses		
Cost recovery	5,000	
Interest	9,076	
		$31,588
Taxable income (accounting income)		$19,412

A physical inspection of the property indicated the following information:

The apartment building contained	26,500 sq. feet
garages	6,900 sq. feet
land (270 × 200)	54,000 sq. feet
apartment rooms	100

All this information was listed on an Annual Property Operating Data form showing the Owner's Statement, an example of which can be seen as Figure 35 in Chapter 12.

The owner's mortgage loan record indicates that the original mortgage loan of $200,000 is now eight years old. The interest rate of the loan is 6 percent, payable monthly, and the term of the loan is 20 years. Monthly payments on the loan are $1,432.86 and the present balance of the loan is $146,832.17.

Based upon this accounting record of the past year's income, NOI for the past year for the owner would be as follows:

Taxable income		$19,412
Plus:		
Depreciation	$5,000	
Interest	9,076	
		+ 14,076
Owner's net operating income		$33,488

Broker's Cash Flow Estimate (Forecast of Cash Flows)

Up to this point the only thing that has been accomplished is the organization of the owner's accounting data relating to the building in a form that will allow comparison with market data. The next step is to compare the past year's performance with the performance of other similar apartment properties in the same market area.

The information submitted by the owner reflects the results of last year's operations. Last year's results may or may not be an indication of results in the future. Consequently, an analysis must be made of what the *potential* income of the property is because the purchaser is really buying the future potential benefits of the property.

To test the validity of the income information submitted by the owner, the broker reconstructs a new operating statement based upon both the owner's statement and the market area. An example of a Broker's Forecast is shown on an Annual Property Operating Data form in Figure 37 in Chapter 12.

The first item needed is the Potential Rental Income. This is the income that the property would produce if rented at market or economic rents 100 percent of the time. To estimate Potential Rental Income, it is necessary to know what the typical rentals in the area are for this type of apartment. Studies may have to be made to determine unit rents on a square- or cubic-foot basis or per-room or per-apartment basis. In this case the broker's study indicates rents as $2.40 per square foot annually. Thus, Potential Rental Income would be $63,600 (26,500 square feet × $2.40).

The broker's studies also indicate that Vacancies and Credit Losses are to be estimated at 6 percent or $3,816 ($3,800 rounded). This amount is subtracted from Potential Rental Income, resulting in Effective Rental Income of $59,800.

The broker finds that garage space rents at $96 per year and, because the property has only 14 garages, they have historically been fully rented in spite of changes in the building's occupancy rate. This source of Other Income is likely to provide $1,344 (14 garages × $96) per year. When this amount is added to the Effective Rental Income, Gross Operating Income becomes $61,144.

Next, an analysis of expenses is in order. The taxes submitted on the Owner's Statement were $8,000. An analysis of the tax situation must be made to determine whether that figure will hold for the next few years. (For example, are the schools in the neighborhood adequate? Are there other improvements planned?) In this case, the broker estimates an annual tax cost of $8,400.

The broker asks the insurance agent to check the owner's reported premium of $4,500. It was determined that this amount was for a three-year policy, the average annual cost being $1,500.

A check with the utilities companies indicated an increase in utilities costs over those submitted by the owner. Therefore, the broker increases the utility cost figure to $2,700.

The broker determined that the present owner managed the property, collected the rents, did minor repairs and kept the lawn and garden. Investigation in the market area indicated that typical management costs were a 5 percent management fee plus an on-site manager rental allowance of $50 per month. Thus, total estimated management costs were approximately $3,700 per year.

Supplies were estimated at $120 per month, or $1,400 per year. Services were estimated to be $175 per month, or $2,100 per year. Maintenance costs were estimated at $140 per year per unit and miscellaneous costs at $50 per month.

It is now possible for the broker to calculate net operating income for this property for a typical investor.

Potential Rental Income		$63,600
Less Vacancy and Credit Losses		− 3,800
Effective Rental Income		$59,800
Plus Other Income		+ 1,344
Gross Operating Income		$61,144
Less Operating Expenses		
Taxes	$ 8,400	
Insurance	1,500	
Utilities	2,700	
Management	3,700	
Services	2,100	
Supplies	1,400	
Maintenance	3,920	
Other	600	− 24,320
	$24,320	
Net Operating Income		$36,824

Obviously, the broker's cash flow estimate for the property is significantly different from the owner's accounting of the past year's income for the property. It must be noted that the broker's estimate is based primarily on current market conditions. Thus, the estimate of cash flow is essentially a one-year estimate for the property. Whether or not this may be safely extrapolated into the future beyond the first year depends on specific circumstances. In later chapters, we will examine further examples of the process whereby future income streams of properties can be estimated.

6
Real Estate Financing

INTRODUCTION

Financing is often the most important element of a real estate transaction. Indeed, the finalization of many transactions can be contingent upon available financing. Even the market value of income-producing real estate is affected by current market financing availability and terms. Real estate purchase and sales agreements usually include at least one clause regarding the amount, term and rate of the financing to be acquired by the buyer. It is essential to understand the implications of the terms of financing in order to choose the most appropriate alternative for a specific borrower-investor.

Real estate, like most other forms of economic goods, may serve as collateral for loans. A key difference, however, is that real estate provides unique advantages to both lender and borrower which tend to make borrowing the rule of the real estate investment market rather than the exception. Of key importance to the lender is the fact that as security for a loan, most real estate has a long life (both physical and economic) and a fixed location.

Debt financing may be used for a variety of reasons. The borrower may diversify risk by investing limited equity capital in several properties rather than in only one property. Equity funds may be retained for alternative uses that may provide a greater return or more financial security. Since debt financing is most often required to supplement the purchase price of the property, equity yield may be increased as a result of financial leverage—which is the primary topic of this chapter.

94

GENERAL FINANCING CHARACTERISTICS

As one views the financing of real estate, certain outstanding characteristics that tend to set it apart from other types of financing become obvious. The relatively *long-term* nature of loans on real estate is unique. Of course, short-term construction loans are typical for development projects, but this is only a form of interim financing until the permanent loan is made. The durability of the property and its fixed location have made such long-term loans a standard of the industry. Long term means relatively small principal returned per annum and increased cash flows for the investor in real estate.

Related to the long-term nature of real estate loans are the special risks associated with such long-term commitments. A wide variety of factors in the neighborhood where the property is located, the urban area that provides the demand for the property's services and the national economy which is responsible for changes in purchasing power, federal government spending and monetary policy all affect the income-producing potential of a specific property. These must be taken into account by both the lender and the borrower-investor in making real estate finance decisions.

Also important to an understanding of real estate financing is the predominant instrument used in the market—the mortgage. The legal complexities surrounding the mortgage contract have tended to make real estate transactions relatively cumbersome and costly. In addition, mortgage terms, rates and conditions may vary significantly from location to location and time to time.

Real estate may be financed in a variety of ways other than simply through mortgage loans. Partnerships, syndicates and trusts may be created to accumulate the necessary equity funds. In addition, leasing is a popular alternative means of financing real estate.

SOURCES OF REAL ESTATE FUNDS

The major sources of mortgage loans for real estate investments are life insurance companies, commercial banks, mutual savings banks and savings and loan associations. Other important financial operatives in the market are mortgage brokers and companies, real estate investment trusts and individual lenders.

Life Insurance Companies

Life insurance companies specialize in large long-term loans on major real estate development projects and represent the most important source of debt financing for major shopping center developments, office buildings and large multifamily projects. They have been the leaders in innovative financing techniques in this country: in the early 1980s, they helped revive lender participation as a means of coping with double-digit inflation.

Commercial Banks

Commercial banks also play a highly specialized role in real estate financing and have extended the scope of their activities in recent years. Although commercial banks do make mortgage loans, this has not been the area where they have had the greatest impact on the market. They are closely regulated with respect to their mortgage lending practices and by policy have not been as aggressive in mortgage lending as some other financial institutions even though their mortgage portfolios have increased in recent years. Their primary significance in the real estate market is in the area of short-term lending where they supply the vast majority of interim financing for real estate. They lend not only to developers during the construction phase of the project but also to other real estate lenders and investors such as mortgage brokers and companies.

Mutual Savings Banks

Most mutual savings banks are found on the east coast where they invest a major portion of their total portfolios in real estate. They are quite active in home mortgages and are also important local lenders for commercial and investment real estate. Like insurance companies, they have been somewhat innovative and creative in their lending procedures and are aided by being somewhat less regulated than are other mortgage lenders.

Savings and Loan Associations

Savings and loan associations are home loan specialists which originate most of their mortgage portfolios locally. They are by far the most important sources of single family mortgage loans in this country and have historically restricted the majority of their loan portfolios to this type of financing. In recent years, however, they have moved to diversify into other types of real estate investments including an emphasis on financing multifamily housing projects. By granting broader lending powers to savings and loans, the 1980 ''deregulation act'' passed by Congress added further stimulus to this move by savings and loan associations to finance investment properties.

Deregulation

The stimulus from deregulation has led a number of thrift institutions astray. Aggressive thrifts can become involved in excessive risk taking which can create heavy losses or, in extreme cases, failures.

Mortgage Banking

The primary function of mortgage brokers and companies is to channel mortgage funds from large institutional investors to developers and other real estate owners and users. The broker serves as an intermediary between borrower and lender and receives a fee for these services. Mortgage bankers, on the other hand, use their own funds (or warehoused funds borrowed from commercial banks) to make mortgage loans.

Real Estate Investment Trusts

REITs pool funds from investors to invest in real estate. Special conduit tax treatment allows earnings to "pass through" to shareholders without tax to the trust. Individual REIT investment portfolios may include one investment or any combination of the full spectrum of real estate investments, including long-term mortgages, short-term construction and development loans and equity investments in one or more types of real estate (shopping centers, apartment buildings, office buildings).[1]

ANALYZING THE IMPACT OF DEBT FINANCING

The typical informed purchaser (user and/or investor) of income-producing property uses mortgage financing primarily to take advantage of leverage. In addition, the purchaser may also borrow to supplement equity capital to meet the relatively large initial investment amount usually required in the real estate market. The knowledgeable investor with the necessary funds to buy a real estate investment on a "free and clear" basis generally would *not* do so, even in the face of the apparently high interest rate charges of the early 1980s.

Small investors, both individuals and syndicated groups formed to buy real estate investments, may require mortgage financing because they lack the necessary cash to buy on a completely equity basis. Businesses that acquire income properties for their own use frequently can pay for the properties from cash available within the firm. They usually elect not to do so, however, because of their need for working capital for the business and because they feel that their funds are more profitable when used in the business. Investors, whether users of the property or not, recognize that the *interest rates* on mortgages are usually lower than the overall rate of return (sometimes called the capitalization rate) on the property (the "cap" rate is the NOI divided by the selling price). Maximum borrowing can accomplish two objectives: (1) enhance equity yield (the annual rate of return on each dollar of equity funds invested) over what it would be without the use of borrowed funds and (2) extend available funds into other leveraged investments which can produce higher yields on those funds.

Nature of Leverage

The term "leverage" refers to the use of borrowed funds which have a fixed cost to the borrower (or at least which have a portion of the borrowing cost fixed, as in equity participations) to complete the purchase of an investment property. Generally, the larger the percentage or ratio of borrowed funds to total value (or purchase price), the greater the amount of leverage.

Leverage may be represented visually by a diagram of a lever. The length of the lever is 100 percent of the cost of the investment. The portion financed with mortgage

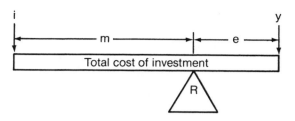

Figure 3 Leverage

proceeds (*m*) plus the percentage equity investment (*e*) is equal to the total cost. To continue the analogy, the interest rate on borrowed funds (*i*) is the force applied to the end of the debt side of the lever and the yield to equity (*y*) is applied to the equity side. The force of the fulcrum is equal to the overall rate of return (*R*). The balanced lever would look like Figure 3.

The following mathematical statement is true of the lever:

$$R = (m \times i) + (e \times y)$$

Example

To illustrate, a property that costs $100,000 with an NOI of $12,000 will be used throughout this chapter. Assume that the overall rate of return (*R*) is 12 percent ($12,000 ÷ $100,000). Assume that income and value will remain constant indefinitely. In this first instance, a buyer finances 75 percent of the purchase price with a 10-percent interest-only loan. Therefore, the equity investment is 25 percent of the price, or $25,000. Each year the equity investor will receive the NOI of $12,000 less the interest on the loan of $7,500 (10 percent of $75,000), or $4,500. The equity yield is

$$\frac{\text{Cash flow to equity}}{\text{Equity investment}} \qquad \frac{\$4,500}{\$25,000} = 18\%$$

Notice that the equity yield exceeds the overall rate.
The leverage formula is valid.

$$12\% = (.75 \times 10\%) + (.25 \times 18\%)$$

$$12\% = 7.5\% + 4.5\%$$

This formula may be formatted as

$$
\begin{array}{ll}
.75 \times 10\% = & 7.5\% \\
.25 \times 18\% = & 4.5 \\
\hline
1.00 & 12.0\%
\end{array}
$$

This format, common in real estate, is called the *band of investment*. It is a useful guide in determining the impact of changes in the financing structure of an investment. Notice that all of the rates in the preceding example represent the return *on* capital since the property value is constant and the loan is not amortized. The return *of* all capital will occur upon disposition of the property. The equity yield will be affected by either a change in value or a change in NOI.

The leverage diagram and the band of investment formula identify several factors that affect the benefit of leverage. The overall rate is the maximum rate on debt financing available from property income. Net cash flow to the equity investor is a function of the interest rate on borrowed funds and the amount borrowed. The amount of equity funds required to buy a property decreases as the portion of borrowed funds increases. Band of investment analysis will indicate the impact on investment performance from a change in any of the previous factors.

Recall, from the lever analogy, that the force, or weight, on the ends of the lever are the rate on borrowed funds (i) and the equity yield (y), respectively. The diagrams in Figure 4 (page 100) show a variety of combinations of loan amounts and resulting equity yields. The band of investment formulae are also shown. The interest rate is 10 percent in each case.

As with a real lever, the same force—interest rate—on one side of the fulcrum will be balanced with more force—equity yield—as leverage is increased. These numerical relationships are true only for this special case where income and value are assumed to remain constant.

Forms of Leverage

Leverage may affect the equity yield in one of three ways. Financing may increase, decrease or have no effect on the investor's return. The equity yield was increased in each of the examples above. However, some interest rate and repayment terms may not benefit the investor financially.

Positive leverage is the term associated with financing that increases the equity yield. It will occur when the cost of debt financing—interest rate on borrowed funds—is *less* than the yield on the property without debt financing.

Example

In the preceding example, the yield on the property without financing is 12 percent. The cash flow is like an interest-only loan where the investor pays $100,000 for the property to receive $12,000 at the end of each year until all capital is returned when the property is sold. The cash flow for a five-year holding period would be

EOY	$
0	($100,000)
1	12,000
2	12,000
3	12,000
4	12,000
5	12,000 + $100,000

It was demonstrated earlier that the investor's yield was increased to 18 percent when a 75 percent interest-only loan at 10 percent interest was taken to purchase the investment. After financing, the equity investment to the investor is

Examples

1.

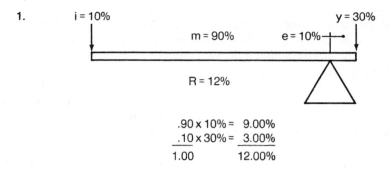

$$
\begin{array}{ll}
.90 \times 10\% = & 9.00\% \\
\underline{.10 \times 30\%} = & \underline{3.00\%} \\
1.00 & 12.00\%
\end{array}
$$

2.

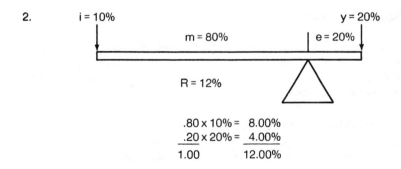

$$
\begin{array}{ll}
.80 \times 10\% = & 8.00\% \\
\underline{.20 \times 20\%} = & \underline{4.00\%} \\
1.00 & 12.00\%
\end{array}
$$

3.

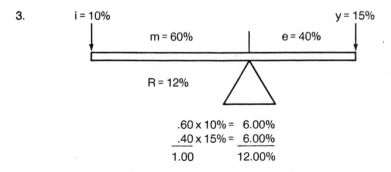

$$
\begin{array}{ll}
.60 \times 10\% = & 6.00\% \\
\underline{.40 \times 15\%} = & \underline{6.00\%} \\
1.00 & 12.00\%
\end{array}
$$

Figure 4 Loan Amounts and Equity Yields

100

Total purchase price	$100,000
Less loan proceeds	− 75,000
Equity investment	$25,000

Annual cash flows are

NOI	$12,000	
Less interest on loan*	7,500	(10% of $75,000)
Cash flows to equity	$4,500	

*Interest-only loan, no principal reduction

The investor's equity reversion is

Sale price EOY 5	$100,000
Less loan balance	− 75,000
Equity reversion	$25,000

Thus, the equity cash flows are

EOY	$
0	($25,000)
1	4,500
2	4,500
3	4,500
4	4,500
5	4,500 + $25,000

The equity yield is 18 percent (IRR of the cash flows to equity) which is greater than the 12 percent return on the whole investment in the property. Therefore, this financing produces positive leverage.

Neutral leverage   occurs when there is no change in equity yield as a result of using debt financing. It is the result of financing a property at the interest rate equal to the yield on the property had it not been financed.

Example

Using the same example as above, with an interest rate of 12 percent, the equity investment and reversion are the same, but the annual cash flows are

NOI	$12,000	
Less interest on loan	− 9,000	(12% of $75,000)
Cash flows to equity	$3,000	

The equity cash flows are

EOY	$
0	($25,000)
1	3,000
2	3,000
3	3,000
4	3,000
5	3,000 + 25,000

The equity yield is 12 percent, equal to the return on the property without financing.

Negative leverage occurs when the equity yield is decreased as a result of debt financing at a cost *greater* than the yield to the property. When debt financing causes negative leverage, the equity yield will be maximized by minimizing the amount borrowed.

Example

Consider the same example with a loan at 14 percent. The annual equity cash flows are

NOI	$12,000
Less interest on loan	− 10,500
Equity cash flows	$ 1,500

The equity cash flows are

EOY	$
0	($25,000)
1	1,500
2	1,500
3	1,500
4	1,500
5	1,500 + 25,000

The equity yield is 6 percent which is less than the 12 percent yield on the property without financing.

Sources of Financial Benefit from Leverage

Equity yield is influenced by either periodic cash flows or a lump sum received in the future, or a combination of both. The examples so far have illustrated the impact of periodic cash flows and financing on equity yield. The return *on* equity was produced solely by the annual cash flows to equity. All of the equity investment was returned upon disposition. But consider an investment that appreciates in value but has no periodic cash flows.

Example

A vacant site is acquired for $125,000. Two years later it is sold for $156,800. Assume all holding costs are equal to the rental income for a billboard on the property; therefore, NOI is 0. The overall rate of return is also 0. The net cash flows without financing are

EOY	$
0	($125,000)
1	–0–
2	156,800

The yield (IRR) on this investment is 12 percent. Consider the same site financed with three alternative loans of $100,000. Interest is compounded annually and payable upon disposition for each loan. The interest rates are 10 percent for loan A, 12 percent for loan B and 14 percent for loan C. The equity investment in each case is $25,000 ($125,000 less $100,000 loan). The equity reversions for each financing alternative are summarized below.

	Loan A	Loan B	Loan C
Interest Rate	10%	12%	14%
Sale Price of Land EOY 2	$156,800	$156,800	$156,800
Less loan balance (principal + accrued interest)	121,000	125,440	129,960
Equity Reversion	$35,800	$31,360	$26,840

The cash flows to equity for each financing alternative are

EOY	Loan A	Loan B	Loan C
0	($25,000)	($25,000)	($25,000)
1	–0–	–0–	–0–
2	35,800	31,360	26,840
IRR	19.7%	12.0%	3.6%
Leverage	Positive	Neutral	Negative

Loan A would produce the greatest return to equity. Note that band of investment analysis would not have been appropriate here since the overall rate is zero. The benefit of leverage is consistent with the comparisons of interest rates on the loans and the return from the property without financing, 12 percent. The interest rate below 12 percent produced positive leverage, the 12 percent loan produced neutral leverage and the 14-percent loan resulted in negative leverage.

MAJOR FINANCING VARIABLES

When borrowing is undertaken to finance the purchase of a real estate investment, several variable items are crucial:

1. Effective rate of interest on debt financing
2. Ratio of loan to value
3. Term of the loan (period over which the loan is made) and method of amortization
4. Ratio of annual debt service to net operating income (see section on Determination of Maximum Loan Amount, p. 119)

Each of the variables listed above is included in every financing alternative for income-producing properties. In the following sections, we will isolate each to illustrate the impact on equity yield. In each example, property value and income are constant in order to isolate the impact of financing on equity yield.

Effective Rate of Interest

The interest rate paid for the use of money is one of the key variables in analyzing financing alternatives. The idea of increasing equity yield through borrowing is based upon the expectation that money can be borrowed at a rate of interest lower than the overall rate of return produced by the property. If this expectation is realized, that proportion of the total investment financed by the mortgage produces an additional amount that is available to the equity investor. This was demonstrated in the preceding discussion on positive, neutral and negative leverage.

Loan-to-Value Ratio (Leverage Factor)

The percentage of the property value or purchase price that the loan represents can also influence equity yield. The higher the proportion of total investment represented by borrowed funds, the *greater* the leverage. The leverage factor (*L*) is another means of expressing this and is simply the reciprocal of 1 minus the loan-to-value percentage.

Example

In the examples for positive, negative and neutral leverage, all loans were 75 percent of value; therefore, they each have the following leverage factor.

$$\frac{1}{1 - 0.75} = 4$$

In other words, the equity investment goes into the total investment four times. If an equity investor had $10,000 to invest and could borrow 75 percent of value, the leverage factor times equity available for investment determines the size of total investments.

$$4 \times \$10,000 = \$40,000$$

Viewed another way, if the investor can borrow 75 percent of the property value, the equity portion must be 25 percent (or, 1 − 0.75). Thus, the leverage factor is simply the number of times the *equity* investment goes into the *total* investment.

The following table shows loan-to-value ratios and the corresponding leverage factors.

Loan-to-Value	Leverage Factor (*L*)
95%	20
90	10
85	6.7
80	5
75	4
70	3.3
65	2.9
60	2.5
55	2.2
50	2

Note that the leverage factor changes in geometric terms as the loan-to-value changes by increments of five percentage points (see Figure 5). This demonstrates the power of leverage and also provides an alternative means of measuring the impact of leverage on equity yield.

Rather than the form

$$R = (m \times i) + (e \times y)$$

we could define e as $1 - m$ since $m + e = 1$. Alternatively,

$$R = (m \times i) + [(1 - m)y]$$

$$R - (m \times i) = (1 - m)y$$

$$y = \frac{R - (m \times i)}{1 - m}$$

Add and subtract i in the numerator.

$$y = \frac{R - (m \times i) + i - i}{1 - m} \quad \text{or} \quad \frac{R - i + i - (m \times i)}{1 - m}$$

Factor the numerator.

$$y = \frac{(R - i) + i(1 - m)}{1 - m} = \left[\frac{R - i}{1 - m} \right] + i$$

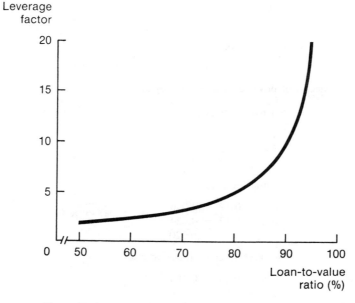

Figure 5 Loan-to-Value Ratio and Leverage Factor

Thus, an alternative means of solving for y is

$$y = i + \left[\left(\frac{1}{1-m}\right)(R - i)\right]$$

Note that

$$\text{Leverage factor } (L) = \frac{1}{1-m}$$

$$\text{Borrowing differential } (D) = R - i$$

Therefore,

$$y = i + (L \times D)$$

Thus, the equity impact of borrowing can be thought of as the product of two variables—the leverage factor (L) and the borrowing differential (D). Equity yield is determined by adding the cost of borrowing (i) to the equity impact.

Example

A property that sells for $80,000 has an NOI of $10,400, with a 90 percent loan at 11.5 percent interest. The impact of financing in this instance may be seen as

$$R = 13\% \qquad [\$10,400 \div \$80,000 = 13\%]$$
$$D = 1.5\% \qquad [13\% - 11.5\% = 1.5\%]$$
$$L = 10 \qquad [1 \div (1 - 0.9) = 10]$$

Where

$$y = 11.5 + (10 \times 1.5) = 26.5\%$$

If the loan were only 80 percent, then

$$y = 11.5 + (5 \times 1.5) = 19\%$$

The concepts of positive, neutral and negative leverage also may be demonstrated.

1. Positive leverage $\qquad\qquad i + (L \times D) = y$

$$\begin{array}{l} 0.8 \times 0.11 = 0.088 \\ 0.2 \times 0.16 = \underline{0.032} \\ \hphantom{0.2 \times 0.16 = }\overline{0.120} \end{array} \quad \text{or} \quad 11 + (5 \times 1) = 16\%$$

2. Neutral leverage

$$\begin{array}{l} 0.8 \times 0.12 = 0.096 \\ 0.2 \times 0.12 = \underline{0.024} \\ \hphantom{0.2 \times 0.12 = }\overline{0.120} \end{array} \quad \text{or} \quad 12 + (5 \times 0) = 12\%$$

3. Negative leverage (positive return)

$$\begin{array}{l} 0.8 \times 0.13 = 0.104 \\ 0.2 \times 0.08 = \underline{0.016} \\ \hphantom{0.2 \times 0.08 = }\overline{0.120} \end{array} \quad \text{or} \quad 13 + [5(-1)] = 8\%$$

4. Negative leverage (zero return)

$$\begin{array}{r} 0.8 \times 0.15 = 0.12 \\ 0.2 \times 0.0 = 0 \\ \hline 0.12 \end{array} \quad \text{or} \quad 15 + [5(-3)] = 0$$

5. Negative leverage (negative return)

$$\begin{array}{r} 0.8 \times 0.16 = 0.128 \\ 0.2 \times -0.04 = -0.008 \\ \hline 0.120 \end{array} \quad \text{or} \quad 16 + [5(-4)] = -4$$

Based upon the foregoing, certain generalizations can be made.

1. Under conditions of positive leverage ($D > 0$), the larger the leverage factor, the higher the equity yield.
2. Under conditions of neutral leverage ($D = 0$), the leverage factor has no impact on the equity yield, and the equity yield equals the overall rate ($y = R$).
3. Under conditions of negative leverage ($D < 0$), the larger the leverage factor, the lower the equity yield.

These equity yield generalizations are only valid with the assumptions that NOI and property value are constant and the loans are not amortized. However, this is an excellent preliminary step to a detailed analysis.

It should be obvious at this point that there is an infinite variety of interest rate/loan-to-value combinations that could be produced at any given equity yield.

Example

As in the case of an interest-only loan and a constant 20 percent equity yield, there are *many* other combinations that can produce the same equity yield.

$$\begin{array}{r} 90\% - 0.1111 = 10.00\% \\ 10\% \times 0.20 = 2.00 \\ \hline 12.00\% \end{array} \qquad\qquad \begin{array}{r} 85\% \times 0.1059 = 9.00\% \\ 15\% \times 0.20 = 3.00 \\ \hline 12.00\% \end{array}$$

$$\begin{array}{r} 80\% \times 0.1000 = 8.00\% \\ 20\% \times 0.20 = 4.00 \\ \hline 12.00\% \end{array}$$

$$\begin{array}{r} 75\% \times 0.0933 = 7.00\% \\ 25\% \times 0.20 = 5.00 \\ \hline 12.00\% \end{array} \qquad\qquad \begin{array}{r} 70\% \times 0.0857 = 6.00\% \\ 30\% \times 0.20 = 6.00 \\ \hline 12.00\% \end{array}$$

Property value and income are constant, as above, for these relationships. Notice that the interest rate declines as the loan-to-value ratio declines with the constant equity yield.

Amortization Method and Term

The *term* of the loan is the length of time over which there will remain some outstanding balance. The amortization of the loan is the periodic repayment of the principal plus interest. Three general types of amortization are common in the market.

1. *Straight mortgage loan.* Only interest is paid during the term, and the entire amount of the original mortgage amount is paid at maturity.

2. *Fully amortized mortgage loan.* This is the typical loan payment method whereby periodic (most often monthly) equal payments are made so that the loan is completely paid back at maturity.

3. *Partially amortized mortgage loan.* The periodic payments of debt service are not sufficient to amortize the loan completely by its maturity; a lump sum payment, generally called a balloon payment, must be made to complete the return of all principal. This is often done by establishing the maturity of the loan for one period and setting the debt service payments for a longer period.

The impact of loan-to-value ratio and interest rate on equity yield have been demonstrated with interest-only loans. Amortization is the lender's return *of* capital. It can be imputed into the band of investment formula by replacing the interest rate (return *on* lender's capital) with the *loan constant* which is the return *of* plus the return *on* the lender's capital.

Calculation of the loan constant.   The loan constant is defined as the ratio of annual debt service to loan proceeds.

Example

The loan constant for a $100,000 loan, at 10 percent interest with monthly payments of $877.57 for 30 years, is calculated as follows.
Annual debt service is

Monthly payment	$877.57
Annual debt service	× 12
	$10,530.84

The loan constant is

$$\frac{\text{Annual debt service}}{\text{Loan proceeds}} = \frac{\$10,530.84}{\$100,000.00} = 0.1053$$

Since the loan constant is a ratio, the Ellwood table column 6 compound interest table factor, installment to amortize 1 (see Appendix A) could be used. The factor for a 30-year loan at 10 percent interest with monthly payments is 0.008775. The loan constant would be

Monthly payment for $1	0.008775
	× 12
Annual loan constant	0.1053

Given a loan constant and annual debt service, the loan proceeds can be calculated. Using the 0.1053 loan constant and annual debt service of $10,530.84, the loan proceeds are

$$\frac{\$10,530.84}{0.1053} = \$100,000 \text{ (rounded)}$$

Likewise, given the loan constant and loan proceeds, annual debt service may be calculated. The $100,000 loan with a loan constant of 0.1053 would have annual debt service of:

$$\$100,000 \times 0.1053 = \$10,530$$

The loan constant depends on both the term and interest rate of a loan. Thus, a particular constant has an infinite variety of interest rate-term combinations. The following table is a summary of such combinations for an $80,000 loan with annual payments of $8,800 and the balance EOY 10. The loan constant is 0.1100 ($8,800 ÷ $80,000) in each case.

Interest Rate	Term in Years*	Mortgage Balance EOY 10
5%	12.4	$19,626
6	13.5	27,277
7	14.9	35,787
8	16.9	45,232
9	19.8	55,691
10	25.2	67,250
11	∞	80,000

*The term (n) is calculated with the known values of interest rate (i), loan amount ($\boxed{PV} = 1$) and the loan payment ($\boxed{PMT} = 0.1100$).

The term increases as the interest rate increases because more of the $8,800 payment is allocated to interest. At 11 percent interest, all of the payment is required for interest ($80,000 × 11% − $8,800). Thus, the constant for an interest-only loan is equal to the interest rate.

Loan constant and band of investment. The loan constant is used in the band of investment formula in place of the interest rate for amortizing loans. Thus, the lender's return *of* capital is imputed into the formula. However, band of investment analysis will indicate the exact equity yield only in the special situation where income and property value are constant and the loan is payable interest-only.

Example

In the case of the $100,000 subject property with a constant NOI of $12,000, the indicated equity yield with the $80,000 loan and the 0.1100 loan constant is

Total investment   100% × 0.1200 = 12.00%
Mortgage interest and
  principal $\dfrac{80\%}{20\%}$ × 0.1100 = $\dfrac{8.80}{3.20\%}$

Equity yield $\dfrac{3.20\%}{20\%}$ = 16.00%

The loan balance EOY 10 decreases as the interest rate decreases. Therefore, the equity reversion EOY 10 will increase as the interest rate decreases. The periodic cash flows will be the same since debt service is the same in each loan. The equity investment is $20,000

($100,000 − $80,000) for the subject property and annual cash flows to equity are $3,200. The following table summarizes the equity reversion EOY 10 for each loan shown in Figure 6. The IRR for equity yield is also calculated based on the $20,000 investment that produces $3,200 per year for ten years plus the reversion EOY 10.

Interest Rate	Sale Price EOY 10		Loan Balance EOY 10		Equity Reversion EOY 10	IRR
5%	$100,000	−	$19,626	=	$80,374	25.1%
6	100,000	−	27,277	=	72,723	24.2
7	100,000	−	35,787	=	64,213	23.3
8	100,000	−	45,232	=	54,768	22.1
9	100,000	−	55,691	=	44,309	20.6
10	100,000	−	67,250	=	32,750	18.6
11	100,000	−	80,000	=	20,000	16.0

Given equal loan constants and loan-to-value ratios, the yield to equity increases as the interest rate decreases as shown in Figure 6. The only difference in the cash flows for these financing alternatives is the equity reversion. As the loans are amortized, the equity in the property is increased. The loan balance is amortized faster with a lower interest rate. Therefore, both the equity reversion and equity yield increase as the interest decreases.

The loan constant, however, may not indicate which loan, among alternatives, will produce the greatest equity yield.

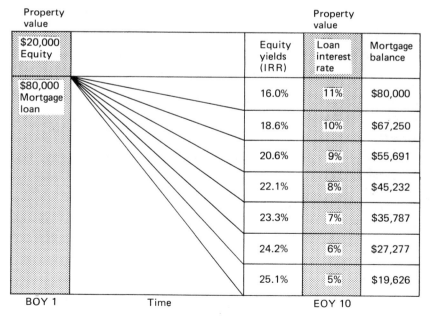

Figure 6 Alternative Equity Yields with the Same Annual Debt Service and Loan Amount

Example

An investor may finance the subject property with one of the two alternatives below. Each requires annual payments.

	Loan Amount	Interest Rate	Term	Loan Constant
Loan A	$80,000	11%	17 years	0.1325
Loan B	$80,000	12%	35 years	0.1223

The equity investment is $20,000 with either loan. The equity cash flows and equity yields for both loans for a ten-year holding period are:

	Loan A	*Loan B*
Loan amount	$80,000	$80,000
Loan constant	× 0.1325	× 0.1223
Annual payment	$10,600	$9,784
NOI	$12,000	$12,000
Less annual payment	10,600	9,784
Cash flows to equity each year	$1,400	$2,216
Sale price	$100,000	$100,000
Less loan balance EOY 10	49,900	76,771
Equity reversion	$50,100	$23,229
Equity yield (IRR) (rounded)	14.6%	12.0%

Loan A produced the higher yield, even though the loan constant was greater than the loan constant for loan B. Notice the yield of 12 percent with loan B, resulting from neutral leverage. Band of investment analysis would have indicated just the opposite result.

	Loan A	*Loan B*
Total investment	100% × 0.12000 = 12.00%	100% × 0.12000 = 12.00%
Mortgage interest and principal	80% × 0.1325 = 10.60%	80% × 0.1223 = 9.78%
Equity	20% 1.40%	20% 2.22%
Equity yield indicated by band of investment	$\frac{1.40\%}{20\%}$ = 7.00%	$\frac{2.22\%}{20\%}$ = 11.10%

The yield is understated because band of investment does not include provision for the increase in the equity resulting from loan amortization. Even though the constant (0.1325) is greater than the overall rate (0.1200) for loan A, the equity yield is still greater. The investor benefits from positive leverage because the interest rate is less than the overall rate of the investment.

Holding period.   Two loans of $80,000 at 11 percent interest were used in the foregoing discussion. The 11 percent interest-only loan produced an equity yield of 16 percent in contrast to only 14.6 percent when the same 11 percent loan was amortized in 17 years over a 10-year holding period. The yield to equity is less with the amortizing loan because the equity investment is increased with each loan payment. Recall that IRR is the return on each dollar *invested*. Principal amortization is additional equity investment. Each dollar of principal amortization invested during the holding period is returned *without* any additional return when the property is sold. Therefore, the same cash flows produce a lower return on more dollars invested, compared to an interest-only loan. In short, the benefit of positive leverage (or cost of negative leverage) diminishes as leverage declines from loan amortization.

Since leverage changes with each loan payment of an amortizing loan, equity yield will be different for alternative holding periods. If the interest rate on borrowed funds is constant and financing produces positive leverage, the equity yield will decrease over time for an amortizing loan.

Example

The equity yields for several possible holding periods of the subject property financed with an $80,000 loan at 10 percent interest with annual payments of $9,397 for 20 years are summarized below. The equity investment is $20,000 and the annual cash flows are $2,603 ($12,000 − $9,397).

Holding Period	Sale Price	Loan Balance EOY	Equity Reversion	IRR
5 years	$100,000 −	$71,473 =	$ 28,527	18.9%
10 years	100,000 −	57,739 =	42,261	17.8
15 years	100,000 −	35,621 =	64,379	17.0
20 years	100,000 −	–0– =	100,000	16.3

Notice that the equity reversion increases as the holding period increases. The equity yield decreases as the holding period increases because the benefit of positive leverage decreases as the loan is amortized. The equity yield is not affected by amortization for an interest-only loan. Since the outstanding loan balance for a loan at the same interest rate but longer amortization term will be greater with a shorter term, the equity yield for any holding period will be greater.

Below are five financing alternatives, each requiring annual payments, for our subject property.

Loan	Loan Amount	Rate	Term
A	$80,000	10%	Interest only
B	80,000	10%	30 years
C	80,000	10%	20 years
D	80,000	10.25%	30 years
E	95,000	10%	20 years

Recall that NOI and value are constant for the subject property. Therefore, the equity yield is not influenced by appreciation or increased income. Figure 7 plots the equity yields for loans A, B and C.

Figure 8 shows loan B compared to a new, higher-interest loan, loan D, under the same assumptions. In this case, the loan-to-value ratio and amortization term are the same for either alternative. Only the interest rates are different: 10 percent for loan B and 10.25 percent for loan D. As might be expected, the equity yield of loan B, with the lower interest rate, is always greater, regardless of holding period.

Loan-to-value ratio will also influence the volatility of equity yield over time. With positive leverage, the equity yield will decline faster over time as the loan-to-value ratio is increased if all else is the same. The converse is true for negative leverage. Figure 9

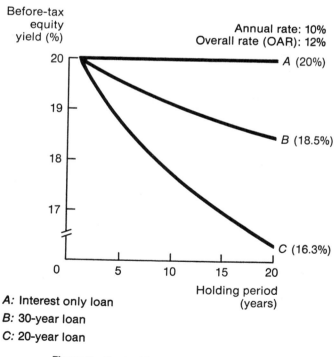

Figure 7   Equity Yield and Holding Period

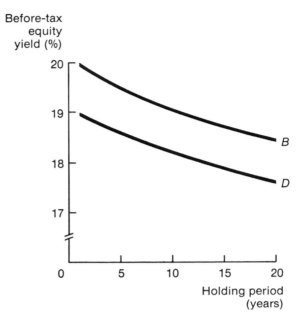

Figure 8 Equity Yield and Holding Period

compares loan C ($80,000, 10 percent, 20 years) with yet another loan, loan E, which represents a $95,000 loan at 10 percent fully amortized for 20 years.

Notice in Figure 7 that the equity yield is 20 percent for loans A, B and C up to the first payment EOY 1. The loan balance and interest due are the same until that time. The yield for loan A is constant at 20 percent because it is an interest-only loan. After the first year, the equity yield for any holding period will always be greater for the loan with the longer amortization term if all else is equal.

The interest rate will have an effect on the equity as well as the amortization term. Figure 10 compares the equity yield from loan C ($80,000, 10 percent interest, 20-year term) with that of loan D, an $80,000 loan at 10.25 percent interest, 30-year term. The loan-to-value ratio is the same. However, the equity yield for loan D exceeds that of loan C for any holding period over three years, even though the interest rate of loan D is higher. The reason is apparent from Figure 10. The equity yield curve associated with loan D does not decline as rapidly over time as it does with loan C. Therefore, if the investor intends to hold the property more than three years without refinancing, loan D would produce the higher yield.

Effective equity yield.   Thus far in this chapter, the analyses of equity yield over time have assumed annual compounding periods. The equity yields (IRR) have been calculated from annual cash flows. The yield from annualized cash flows may be overstated, however, and may lead to the incorrect decision. This distortion is more

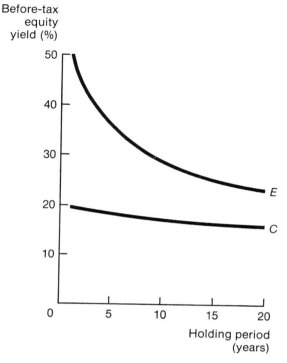

Figure 9 Equity Yield and Holding Period

apparent for short holding periods. The difference declines to a few basis points (a basis point is ½₁₀₀ of 1 percent, or 0.01 percent) for extended holding periods.

Example

Consider financing the subject property with either of the following loans. Assume equity investment of $20,000 and monthly NOI of $1,000 for the subject property.

> Loan A $80,000 loan at 10 percent interest, with monthly payments of $1,057.21 for 10 years. Balance EOY 1 is $75,092.65.
>
> Loan B $80,000 loan at 10 percent interest, with monthly payments of $702.06 for 30 years. Balance EOY 1 is $79,555.30.

The following table summarizes the *annualized* cash flows to the equity and the IRR for each loan assuming a sale price of $100,000 at EOY 1.

EOY	Loan A	Loan B
0	($20,000)	($20,000)
1	(686.52) + 24,907.35	3,575.28 + 20,444.70
IRR	21.10%	20.10%

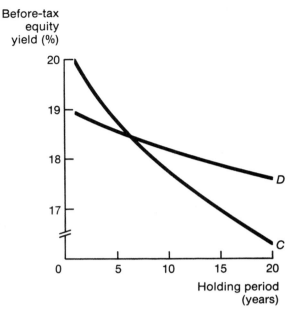

Figure 10   Equity Yield and Holding Period

Loan A would seem the appropriate choice from the annualized analysis. The next table is a summary of the *monthly* cash flows and IRR for each loan.

EOM	Loan A	Loan B
0	($20,000)	($20,000)
1	(57.21)	293.94
↓	↓	↓
12	(57.21) + 24,907.35	293.94 + 20,444.70
IRR (monthly)	1.59%	1.64%
	× 12	× 12
IRR (annualized)	19.08%	19.68%

It is apparent that loan B would be the better choice, based on IRR. The IRR with loan A was distorted by more than two percentage points for the one-year holding period. The difference between the equity yields for annualized cash flows and monthly cash flows EOY 30 for loan B declines to 15 basis points (18.35 percent − 18.20 percent) from 42 basis points EOY 1 (20.10 percent − 19.68 percent). The analyst should be aware of this potential source of error. It should also be noted that the *range* of distortion declines as the term of the loan is extended.

Notice that loan A produced positive leverage even though monthly cash flows are negative.

Conclusions

Certain observations and generalizations can be made from our analysis of debt financing.

1. Simple band-of-investment analysis is only valid for an interest-only loan with an interest rate *equal* to the annual mortgage constant.
2. The equity yield of the investment is greater than the overall rate of the investment if the interest rate on the loan is less than the overall rate.
3. As the interest rate on the loan goes down relative to the overall rate, the equity yield rises.
4. Even though the mortgage constant is greater than the overall rate, there are still loan terms that can result in equity yields which exceed the overall rate of returns on the property.
5. Even lower debt service (mortgage constant) may not result in higher equity yields.
6. The equity yield declines over time for investments financed with loans that are amortized.
7. Loan constants are affected by both the interest rate and the amortization term. If the interest rate is constant, the loan constant decreases as the term increases. If the term is constant, the loan constant increases as the interest rate increases.
8. The benefit of positive leverage (or cost of negative leverage) increases as the loan-to-value ratio increases.
9. The benefit of positive leverage (or cost of negative leverage) increases as the loan term is increased.

Although some generalization can be made, the specific alternative terms and conditions of the mortgage contract should be compared on the basis of cash flows in order to test for relative yield.

MORTGAGE UNDERWRITING

Fundamental to a discussion of the impact of debt financing on commercial and investment real estate is mortgage underwriting—the analysis and evaluation of a loan from the standpoint of the lender to determine the risk of making the loan using the real estate as collateral. Although this text will make no attempt at comprehensive coverage of this topic, certain key elements are critical to the broker/analyst who is involved in the process of acquiring funds to finance investment real estate.[2]

Risk Aversion

Although the real estate serves as collateral for the mortgage loan, it is not the primary defense against loss to the lender. The typical lender does not want to obtain ownership of the property through foreclosure because of default. This is really an extreme line of defense against the loss of investment position, one which can be very costly and time consuming and detrimental to good public relations. Basically, such lenders are not in the business of operating and/or selling commercial/investment real estate and usually like to avoid the necessity of doing so through the vehicle of foreclosure. This points to the first line of defense, reducing the probability of default in payment of loan obligations in the first place.

The most direct means of ensuring prompt and continuous payment of a mortgage loan on an income-producing property is to accurately forecast the income flow from which the annual debt service will be paid. This is a principle applied widely in bond securities repayment as well as being a fundamental underwriting tenet.

Debt Coverage Ratio

Most lenders who finance investment real estate projects are concerned more with the relationship between net operating income and annual debt service than they are with the loan-to-value ratio. The reason for this is the general lack of agreement concerning the value of the property and/or the overall rate used to capitalize NOI.

The foundation of the market value or investment value of income-producing real estate is the future stream of income. The key to estimating the present value of this future income rests in estimates of the *size, timing, duration* and *stability* of future income flows. The process of converting these future income flows to a present value is a simple matter of capitalization at the appropriate rate. In the area of mortgage lending, the appropriate rate can sometimes present quite a problem, particularly when the overall rate on the property combines such factors as the tax situation of the typical investor, typical financing terms, appreciation and holding period. As indicated above, the lender is not interested in acquiring the property by default. That, in essence, is the *final* step in protecting loan capital. The first line of protection for the loan is the *income stream*, for it is from the income stream that the lender will be repaid. Loan payments include both interest on the loan and periodic principal payments. Thus, the lender is much more concerned with a careful examination and analysis of the validity of estimates of NOI than with estimates of the present market value of the property.

Lenders use a *debt coverage ratio* that compares ADS to NOI. The debt coverage ratio is the NOI divided by ADS:

$$\text{debt coverage ratio} = \frac{\text{NOI}}{\text{ADS}}$$

The lender's margin of safety—that debt payments can be met by property income—increases as the coverage ratio increases.

Example

A loan which requires ADS of $9,600, with an NOI of $12,000, would have a coverage ratio of

$$\frac{\$12,000}{\$9,600} = 1.25$$

In this case, NOI could decline 20 percent (from $12,000 to $9,600) before the lender would have to rely on the investor to contribute to debt service from other sources of funds.

Based upon experience, lenders may specify a maximum debt coverage ratio for particular types of property. In the case of an NOI that can be forecast with a high degree of accuracy with respect to size, timing and duration (such as a long-term completely net lease with a AAA tenant), the lender should require relatively less margin between NOI and ADS—a lower debt coverage ratio. Accordingly the debt coverage ratio should increase with the risk (uncertainty) associated with the NOI.

Determination of Maximum Loan Amount

The analyst (lender, broker or investor) can determine the maximum loan available on an income property when the NOI, debt coverage ratio, loan term and interest rate are known. The loan amount will be the present value of the debt service discounted at the interest rate of the loan.

Example

A lender will make a 10 percent loan with monthly payments for 30 years. The required debt coverage ratio for the subject property by that lender is 1.25. NOI is $12,000. First determine the monthly payment.

$$\frac{NOI}{\text{debt coverage ratio}} = ADS$$

$$\frac{\$12,000}{1.25} = \$9,600$$

The monthly debt service or loan payment is

$$\frac{ADS}{12} = \frac{\$9,600}{12} = \$800 \text{ per month}$$

The maximum loan on the subject property is the present value of an annuity (the loan payments) at 10 percent per year with monthly compounding for 30 years. The known values are

$$\boxed{PMT} = \$800 \text{ per period}$$

$$\boxed{n} = 30 \text{ years} \times 12 = 360 \text{ periods}$$

$$\boxed{i} = 10\% \div 12 = 0.83\% \text{ per period}$$

$$\boxed{PV} = ?$$

The maximum loan is calculated to be $91,160.66, rounded to $91,000.

Alternately, the loan amount could be calculated by dividing ADS by the loan constant. This procedure is demonstrated in the following section.

Additional Underwriting Considerations

In a broader context, the loan underwriting process includes (1) an estimate of the property value, (2) an evaluation of the risk associated with the income stream, (3) an assessment of the credit-worthiness of the borrower, (4) an appraisal of real estate and financial market conditions and (5) determination of the interest rate, duration and size of the loan. The latter is the topic of this discussion.

A typical mortgage loan analysis might proceed in the following manner.

1. Analysis of NOI forecasts.   The lender examines the estimates of NOI in terms of size, timing, duration and stability. Based upon experience and knowledge of the market in which the property is (or is to be) located, forecasts of the future for the location and type of property and past experience in lending on this type of property in the same or similar locations, the lender will establish the required *safety margin* for the loan.

2. Determination of mortgage constant.   The previous analysis established the *duration* of the income stream of at least a range of years, perhaps between 30 and 35. The lender has also established, again within a range, the interest rate required on a current basis for long-term loans. Based upon this combination of term and interest rate an annual mortgage constant is estimated.

3. Mortgage loan amount.   The first approximation of the loan amount can be calculated by dividing the ADS by the mortgage constant.

Example

A numerical example of this process would be as follows.

$$\text{NOI} = \$12,000$$

Lender requires 20 percent margin (ADS must be at least 80 percent of NOI). Therefore, the debt coverage ratio is 1.25 (1 ÷ .80)
Interest rate must be at least 10 percent
Term cannot exceed 25 to 30 years (monthly payments)
ADS = $9,600 (80% × $12,000)
Mortgage constant = 0.109044 to 0.105309

Loan amount is $\dfrac{\$9,600}{0.109044} = \$88,038$ or $88,000

to $\dfrac{\$9,600}{0.105309} = \$91,160$ or $91,000

Thus, the preliminary loan amount indicates an approximate range between $88,000 and $91,000. The most likely area of negotiation would be with the *term* of the loan.

4. Relationship between loan-to-value and ADS-to-NOI.   It is immediately apparent that there is a direct relationship between the ratio of loan-to-value and the ratio of ADS to NOI. The direct link between these two is the overall rate of capitalization. When the mortgage constant and the overall rate are *equal,* the ratios of loan-to-value and ADS-to-NOI are exactly equal.

Example

$$\text{Loan} \quad 80\% \times .12 = 0.096\%$$
$$\text{Equity} \quad 20\% \times .12 = \underline{0.024}$$
$$0.120\%$$

$$\frac{\text{Loan}}{\text{Value}} = \frac{\$80,000}{\$100,000} = \frac{9,600}{12,000} = \frac{\text{ADS}}{\text{NOI}}$$

OTHER FINANCING CONSIDERATIONS

Balloon Payment Mortgages (Partially Amortized Mortgages)

Generally speaking, mortgage payments include both interest and principal payments such that the original mortgage amount is completely repaid over the full term of the loan. Sometimes, however, the amortization schedule agreed upon by the borrower and lender provides for only partial reduction of the principal amount, with a *balloon* payment of the remaining principal at the end of the term.

Calculating periodic payment. A popular and easy way of calculating the periodic payment under such a mortgage contract is to agree upon a rate and term but to calculate the mortgage payment based upon a somewhat longer term.

Example

Assume a 9 percent interest rate, a 15-year term, but monthly payments based on a 20-year amortization schedule. The annual mortgage constant would be as follows.
The monthly constant for a 9 percent loan, for 20 years is 0.008997.
The annual constant is

$$0.008997 \times 12 = 0.107964$$

This is somewhat less than the constant of 0.121716 for the same loan with a 15-year amortization schedule. The balloon payment due EOY 15 is equal to the present value $\boxed{\text{PV}}$ of payments for five years (20-year amortization term less 15-year loan term) discounted at the interest rate of 9 percent. For example, if $100,000 is loaned at the terms described above, the payment is calculated from the following known values:

$$\boxed{\text{PV}} = \$100,000$$
$$\boxed{\text{n}} = 20 \times 12 = 240 \text{ periods (amortization term)}$$
$$\boxed{\text{i}} = 9\% \div 12 = 0.75\% \text{ per period}$$

The monthly payment is $899.73. The balloon payment due EOY 15 is the $\boxed{\text{PV}}$ calculated from the following known values:

$\boxed{\text{PMT}}$ = $899.73

$\boxed{\text{n}}$ = 5 × 12 = 60 periods (remaining amortization term)

$\boxed{\text{i}}$ = 9% ÷ 12 = 0.75% per period

The balloon payment is $43,343.03.

Calculating the balloon payment. Often during loan negotiations for a balloon payment mortgage an amount that can be paid from NOI is specified by the borrower rather than utilizing a specific amortization schedule.

Example

Suppose that an $80,000 loan is desired by the mortgagor who can pay a maximum of $650 per month. The mortgagee is willing to lend at 9 percent for 15 years with monthly payments. If the loan were fully amortized over 15 years, the monthly payment would be $811.41. Thus it will be necessary to create a balloon payment loan if the mortgage is to be made. The size of the balloon payment at the end of 15 years can be calculated from the following data:

$\boxed{\text{PMT}}$ = $650

$\boxed{\text{n}}$ = 15 × 12 = 180 periods (the term of the loan)

$\boxed{\text{i}}$ = 9% ÷ 12 = 0.75% per period

The $\boxed{\text{PV}}$ is $64,085.72, the amount amortized by the monthly payments over 15 years. The difference of $15,914.28 ($80,000.00 − $64,085.72) will be compounded at the interest rate. The balloon payment is the future value $\boxed{\text{FV}}$ calculated from the following known values:

$\boxed{\text{PV}}$ = $15,914.28

$\boxed{\text{n}}$ = 15 × 12 = 180 periods

$\boxed{\text{i}}$ = 9% ÷ 12 = 0.75% per period

The balloon payment is $61,079.70.

Another way of viewing the process of partial amortization is to consider the total loan as two loans, an amortizing loan and an interest-only loan. In the case of the loan above, the payment would be calculated as follows:

Monthly payment to amortize $18,920.30 at	
9% in 15 years	$191.90
Plus monthly interest only on	
remaining $61,079.70 at 9%	+ 458.10
Total monthly payment	$650.00

Mortgage Participation Financing

In 1967, and again in 1980, a lender's market for mortgage funds was created by tight money market conditions which were part of a national effort to halt inflation.[3] Since lenders held the clear upper hand in their loan negotiations during these periods, they sought new ways to guard against inflation not only by increasing their yield through high fixed interest rates on the loans but also by participating in a part of the anticipated gain or profit which had heretofore been reserved for the equity investor. One of the more interesting aspects of this lending innovation was the uniqueness of each contract, with over 40 standard formulas in use by lending institutions.

Forms of lender participation.   Although there is a wide variety of contracts which provide the mortgage lender with some form or combination of forms of variable participation in the future benefits of the property, such interests can be classified in six basic forms, divided into two categories.

1. Income participations   This type of participation grants the lender the right to share in some part of the cash flow to the property for a specified period of time, generally the term of the loan. It takes on three major forms:

- Percentage of gross rental income provides the lender with a fixed percentage for a specified period.
- Percentage of net income provides for a fixed percentage of the net income of the property.
- Percentage of cash flow provides for a share of either before- or after-tax cash flow (NOI less ADS).

2. Equity participation   This type of participation grants rights to the lender that may endure beyond the term of the loan and may represent a true equity share of the property. The equity participation may or may not involve any direct investment by the lender beyond the amount of the loan.

- Percentage of equity reversion is the right to share in some future reversionary value such as that derived from refinancing or sale.
- Percentage of equity interest is a means by which the right to share in all of the equity benefits is transferred to the lender.
- Percentage of tax shelter is a means by which the lender acquires a right to use all or a part of the tax shelter associated with the mortgaged property.

Example

Assume a lending situation which involves a gross income participation where property has the following characteristics.[4]

Purchase price	$1,100,000
Gross income	$200,000
NOI	$112,000
Mortgage loan	Amount $840,000
	Interest rate, 9%
	Term, 25 years with annual payments
	Annual debt service, $85,520

Forecast reversion	EOY 10, $1,250,000
Lender participation	4% of gross income for 25 years
	Desired return on participation income, 10%
Equity investor	Desired yield, 12% to 15%
	Holding period of property, 10 years

In order to analyze the impact of the 4 percent gross income participation, find the respective yield for each of the interests in the property, in this case the mortgagee and the mortgagor.

Mortgagee's (Lender's) Interest

Initial mortgage loan (lender's investment)	$840,000
Lender's annual cash flows	
Annual debt service	85,520
Participation income (4% × $200,000)	8,000
Total annual cash flows to lender	$93,520
Lender's reversion EOY 10	
Loan balance EOY 10	$689,350
$\boxed{\text{PV}}$ of $8,000 per year participation for	
remaining 15 years (25 − 10) discounted	
at 10%	60,849
Total due lender EOY 10	$750,199

The lender's cash flows are summarized as

EOY	$
0	($840,000)
1	93,520
2	93,520
3	93,520
4	93,520
5	93,520
6	93,520
7	93,520
8	93,520
9	93,520
10	93,520 + 750,199

The lender's yield, before tax, on these cash flows is 10.48 percent.

Mortgagor's (Equity) Interest

Equity investment	
Purchase price	$1,100,000
Less mortgage proceeds	840,000
Equity investment	$260,000

Annual cash flows to equity

NOI	$112,000
Less total annual cash flows to lender	93,520
Annual cash flows to equity	$18,480

Equity reversion

Sale price EOY 10	$1,250,000
Less total due lender EOY 10	750,199
Equity reversion EOY 10	$499,801

The cash flows to equity are summarized as

EOY	$
0	($260,000)
1	18,480
2	18,480
3	18,480
4	18,480
5	18,480
6	18,480
7	18,480
8	18,480
9	18,480
10	18,480 + 499,801

The yield to equity, before tax, is 12.29 percent, at a purchase price of $1,100,000. The investment value of this property is equal to the sum of the present value $\boxed{PV}$ of cash flows to each interest discounted at the appropriate rate. In this case, the $\boxed{PV}$ of the lender's position is $840,000, the amount of the loan. If the equity investor requires a 15 percent before-tax yield, rather than 12 percent, the investment value of this property is

$\boxed{PV}$ of lender's position	$840,000
$\boxed{PV}$ of equity cash flows discounted at 15%	216,290
Investment value of the property	$1,056,290

If this property were acquired for $1,056,290 under the assumptions listed above, the lender would earn 10.48 percent (IRR on lender's cash flows). The equity yield before tax would be 15 percent.

Wraparound Mortgages

Calculation of yield.   The wraparound mortgage is simply a refinancing device in which one lender uses to advantage the relatively low interest rate on an existing mortgage balance of another lender by creating a new mortgage instrument which incorporates the original loan. The wraparound lender advances the difference of the total wraparound loan less the balance on the existing loan. The borrower makes one payment on the total loan to the wraparound lender. The lender assumes the existing, or underlying, loan and therefore makes the remaining payments. Often, the term of the wraparound loan will be less than or equal to the remaining term of the underlying loan. The lender utilizes financial leverage to increase the yield over the nominal rate of the new loan.

This form of loan also can be seen in the situation of a land contract in which the owner or seller retains title until all (or a specified number of) payments on the property have been made by the purchaser. In this situation, the seller may have or may acquire a mortgage loan on the property that is below the rate being paid by the purchaser.

Example

A lender is approached by a potential borrower who has a property with an existing mortgage loan. The original loan, now five years old, was for $150,000 with a 7.5 percent interest rate and monthly payments of $1,108.49 for 25 years. The borrower wishes to refinance; the new lender agrees to wrap the existing loan and advance a new wraparound loan for $160,000 at 8.5 percent with monthly payments of $1,288.36 for 25 years. What is the rate of return to the lender if the loan is paid in full in ten years?

The first step is to identify the cash flows to the lender.

The wraparound lender's investment is

New loan amount	$160,000.00
Less balance of underlying loan	
(after 5 years)	137,598.82
Lender's investment	$ 22,401.18

The *monthly* cash flows to the lender are

Payment on $160,000, 25-year amortization at 8.5%	$1,288.36
Less payment on underlying loan	1,108.49
Net monthly cash flow to lender	$179.87

The lender's cash flow from the loan repayment is

Balance of wraparound loan EOY 10	$130,832.90
Less balance of underlying loan EOY 10	
(15 years after the loan was made)	93,384.18
Net balance due lender	$ 37,448.72

The cash flows to each of the parties to this loan and the before-tax yields are summarized in the following table.

EOM	Total Wraparound Loan	Underlying Lender	Wraparound Lender
0	($160,000)	($137,598.82)	($22,401.18)
1	1,288.36	1,108.49	179.87
↓	↓	↓	↓
120	1,288.36 + 130,832.90	1,108.49 + 93,384.18	179.87 + 37,448.72
IRR (monthly)	0.708% × 12	0.625% × 12	1.08% × 12
IRR (annualized)	8.5%	7.5%	12.95%

The cost of the loan to the borrower is 8.5 percent, the nominal rate of the loan. The underlying lender's yield is the nominal rate of 7.5 percent. Since the yield on the wraparound loan exceeds the interest rate on the underlying loan, the wraparound lender enjoys positive leverage. The wraparound lender's yield is 12.95 percent.

Notice that the cash flow to the underlying lender plus the cash flow to the wraparound lender is equal to the cash flow to the total wraparound loan for every period.

The wraparound lender's IRR is equal to the cost of borrowing the additional $22,401.18. It would be advantageous for the borrower to acquire the same $22,401.18 with another type of loan if the cost were less than 12.95 percent.

Wraparound loan with specified yield to wraparound lender. In some situations, the wraparound lender may make funds available at a specified before-tax yield. The borrower would need to know the effective interest rate on the total wraparound loan. This rate is calculated from the total cash flows to the borrower.

Example

Suppose the wraparound lender in the previous illustration required a 15 percent before-tax yield on the $22,401.18. The wraparound lender would require a monthly payment of $286.92, to amortize $22,401.18 in 25 years at 15 percent. Treated as a separate loan, the wraparound lender's EOY 10 would be $20,500.42. Now the yield and cash flows are known for both lenders. The borrower's effective rate is calculated from the total of the cash flows (see following table).

EOM	Underlying Lender	+	Wraparound Lender	=	Total Wraparound Loan
0	($137,598.82)	+	($22,401.18)	=	($160,000.00)
1	1,108.49	+	286.92	=	1,395.41
↓	↓		↓		↓
120	1,108.49 +	+	286.92 +	=	1,395.41 +
	93,384.18		20,500.42		113,884.60
IRR (monthly)					0.720%
					× 12
IRR (annualized)	7%		15%		8.64%

The effective interest rate is 8.64 percent. The borrower would be better off only if a new first loan of $160,000 were available at less than 8.64 percent.

Mortgage Discount Points

It is common among mortgage lenders to require the payment of *discount points* on mortgage loans as a means of increasing yields. A discount point is, by definition, 1 percent of the face value of the mortgage at the time it is granted. Obviously, by requiring the payment of discount points at the time the loan is granted, the lender decreases the loan amount without changing the flow of future debt service and, thus, increases the IRR on the loan.

Calculating yield.   In order to determine the effective interest rate (rate paid by the borrower if the borrower pays the points *or* the yield received by the lender) on a discounted mortgage, one has only to relate the actual amount loaned with the periodic mortgage payments and loan balance at the end of the loan duration. These are the lender's cash flows.

Example

A lender charges four points on the following loan.

Loan amount	$125,000
Nominal interest rate	10%
Amortization term	25 years, monthly payments

The loan payment and balance at the end of the loan duration are based on the amount of the total loan, before discount points. The *nominal interest rate* (sometimes called coupon rate) is used to calculate the payment and balance. The *effective interest rate* is the actual cost of borrowing (nominal interest rate plus discount points). The monthly payment, computed from the data above, is $1,135.88. The lender's investment, net loan proceeds, is

Face amount of loan	$125,000
Less 4% discount	5,000
Net loan proceeds	$120,000

The effective interest rate of this loan, if it is paid in full EOY 25, is calculated on the following cash flows.

EOM	$	
0	($120,000)	Net loan proceeds
1	1,135.88	Monthly loan payment
↓	↓	
25 years × 12 = 300	$1,135.88	The balance is -0- EOY 25

The annualized effective interest rate is 10.53 percent. Note that this is the yield on the loan held to maturity. This calculation allocates the discount points over the total term of the loan. If the loan balance were paid before EOY 25, the effective interest rate would be greater since the same number of points would be amortized over a shorter term.

The effective yield on this loan, if it were paid in full after two years, would be computed from the debt service for 24 months and the loan balance EOY 2 of $122,508.89 (present value of $1,135.88 per month discounted at 10 percent for the remaining term of 23 years). The lender's cash flows are summarized as follows.

EOM	$
0	($120,000)
1	1,135.88
↓	↓
2 × 12 = 24	1,135.88 + 122,508.89

The annualized effective interest rate EOY 2 is 12.29 percent. As expected, it is greater than the nominal interest rate.

Figure 11 shows the effective interest rate for loan durations up to the full maturity of 25 years. The rate is very high for very short holding periods because the same number of discount points are paid for shorter periods as for long periods.

The effective interest rate is always greater than the nominal rate because of the discount points. Obviously, the effective interest rate is increased if the number of discount points is increased. Although caution should always be used with rules of thumb such as these, each point will increase the effective interest rate *about* ⅛ percent at maturity.

Calculating points to achieve a specified yield. The lender can calculate the discount for a loan, when the effective interest rate is specified, by subtracting the PV of cash flows to the lender discounted at the appropriate rate from the loan amount.

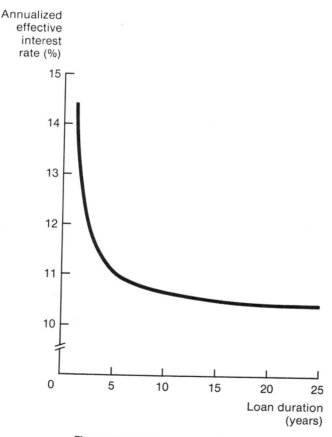

Figure 11 Effective Interest Rate

Example

Suppose the lender in the example above expected the loan to be paid in full EOY 10 and required an 11 percent yield.

The loan balance EOY is $105,702.08 ($\boxed{PV}$ of $1,135.88 per month discounted at 10 percent, the nominal rate, for the remaining term of 15 years).
The lender's cash flow is

EOM	$
0	PV = ?
1	$1,135.88
↓	↓
10 × 12 = 120	1,135.88 + 105,702.08

The $\boxed{PV}$ of these cash flows, discounted at 11 percent, the lender's required yield, is $117,821.45. The discount is

Loan amount	$125,000.00
Loan proceeds	− 117,821.45
Discount	$7,178.55

This translates to

$$\frac{\$7,178.55}{\$125,000.00} = 5.74 \text{ points}$$

Thus, the effective interest rate is 11 percent for a $125,000 loan at a nominal interest rate of 10 percent, with monthly payments based on a 25-year amortization term *if* the loan is paid in full EOY 10.

Impact of holding period.   When considering financing alternatives, it has been shown that the investor's anticipated holding period is an important variable. This is especially true with loans with discount points, since the effective interest rate changes over time. For a short holding period discounted loans may result in negative leverage on an investment. If the loan in the preceding example were used to finance a property which has a constant overall rate of return of 12 percent for any holding period, the investor would have negative leverage for a short holding period (recall that the effective interest rate was 12.29 percent EOY 2). For longer holding periods, this loan may become the higher yielding alternative.

Example

Suppose an investor used the loan in the example above to finance a property that cost $165,000 with NOI of $19,800 (12 percent of $165,000). Value and NOI are assumed to be constant over time. The equity investment is

Purchase price	$165,000
Less loan proceeds (net of discount)	120,000
Equity investment	$45,000

Monthly cash flows to equity are

NOI ($19,800 ÷ 12)	$1,650.00
Monthly loan payment	1,135.88
Monthly cash flows to equity	$514.12

The equity reversion EOY 2 is

Sale price	$165,000.00
Loan balance EOY 2	122,508.89
Equity reversion EOY 2	$42,491.11

The cash flows to equity are summarized below.

EOM	$
0	($45,000)
1	514.12
↓	↓
2 × 12 = 24	514.12 + 42,491.11

The annualized before-tax equity yield is 11.21 percent. As expected, the investor had negative leverage for the two-year holding period. The before-tax equity yield EOY 25 is 14.74 percent.

Figure 12 shows the before-tax equity yield for holding periods up to 25 years, the term of the loan. Equity yields on this graph are calculated assuming that the property is sold at the end of the holding period. For example, if the property were sold EOY 2, the before-tax yield would be 11.21 percent (point A).

Notice in Figure 12 that the equity yields for the shorter holding periods are very low, but increase rapidly year by year. This is the result of the very high effective interest rate on a loan with discount points for short holding periods.

The equity yield peaks during year 11 (point B). Two financing variables are affecting the yield. Leverage is declining over time which reduces the equity yield for longer holding periods, as discussed earlier in this chapter. The effective interest rate is also declining over time which in turn increases the equity yield. At holding period B, the impact of reduced leverage becomes greater than the impact of the decreased effective interest rates. Therefore, the equity yield will decline after 11 years. (Although the same principles apply to other similar financing situations, Figure 12 is unique to the assumptions described above.)

Prepayment Penalties

A prepayment penalty is an additional charge by a lender due only if the loan is paid in full before the end of the minimum period. The extra charge will increase the lender's yield.

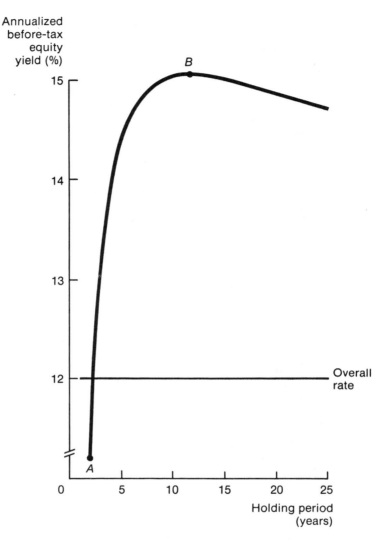

Figure 12 Equity Yields

Example

Consider a $100,000 loan at 10 percent interest per year with monthly payments of $897.90. The lender requires a prepayment penalty of 2 percent of the outstanding balance if the loan is repaid before the end of ten years. The borrower plans to repay the loan balance of $95,000 EOY 5. The lender's cash flows are summarized below.

	EOM		$
	0		($100,000)
	1		897.90
	↓		↓
5 × 12 =	60		897.90 + 95,000 + 1,900

The prepayment penalty EOY 5 is $1,900 (2 percent × $95,000). The annualized effective interest rate is the IRR of these cash flows, 10.3 percent. The effective interest rate will decline to 10 percent when the prepayment penalty no longer applies as the loan balance (therefore, the penalty) declines over time.

Alternative Mortgage Instruments

High interest rates and shortages of available mortgage funds have inspired many innovative financing techniques and alternative mortgage instruments.[5] Some of these instruments require debt service that changes during the investment holding period. Fluctuations in mortgage interest rates (as with variable rate mortgages or renegotiable rate mortgages) may change the periodic payment or the loan balance at the end of the cash flow projection. These characteristics add risk (uncertainty) to the analysis. Unfortunately, specific changes in interest rates are impossible to forecast accurately. The analyst should be aware of the implications of financing variables on yield for alternative holding periods in order to estimate the impact of changes in financing terms in the future.

NEW DEVELOPMENTS IN FINANCING

Securitization

Because commercial mortgages have been viewed as relatively nonliquid assets, real estate has been unable to compete with stocks and bonds for investors' attention. Now, investment houses and government agencies (FNMA, GNMA, and FHLMC) can purchase packages of similar mortgages from one or more lenders and issue securities backed by these mortgages. Instead of purchasing whole mortgage contracts, investors can purchase these mortgage-backed securities (MBSs) which provide more liquid pools of smaller debt pieces with reduced risks. Virtually nonexistent until 1984, the market for commercial mortgage securities has grown steadily, reaching about $10 billion by 1986.

There are primarily two types of MBSs: pass-through certificates, and bonds secured by a pool of mortgage loans. With the pass-through certificate, principal and interest payments on the underlying mortgage are paid to the originating institution which services the mortgage. These payments, which may or may not be guaranteed, are passed through to the buyer of the MBS. With bonds, the required amortization from the collateral pool is at all times at least as great as the coupon and principal payments on the bond. Bondholders receive additional payments of principal when prepayments are made on the collateral pool of mortgages.

To protect the investor against unpredictable prepayments made by owners in an attempt to refinance at lower rates, collateralized mortgage obligations (CMOs) have been developed. CMOs are collateral-backed bonds issued by single purpose business entities that purchase mortgages or mortgage securities as collateral. The cash flow from the collateral is redirected to service the CMOs. A CMO issue is divided into several offerings or tranches, each with a different maturity. Principal and interest payments from the mortgage pool go first to the shortest-maturity issue, then to the next-shortest-maturity issue once the first one is retired, and so on. By redirecting the cash flows of the underlying mortgage-related collateral, CMOs can offer investors various payment schedules, a wide range of maturities, fixed and variable rate coupons, and protection from risk associated with the unpredictable cash flow of the underlying collateral.[6]

Another refinement of the securitization process is the real estate mortgage investment conduit (REMIC) which went into effect January 1, 1987 as a result of the Tax Reform Act of 1986. The REMIC is a secondary mortgage market instrument that enhances previously securitized vehicles. It eliminates much of the uncertainty regarding the federal tax status of mortgage securities by enabling the related mortgage security to be taxed only once at the investor level without any taxation at the issuer level.

The securitization process abounds in other new developments as well. On July 11, 1986, the first public offering of stripped MBSs (strips formed by the separation of principal and interest distributions into various combinations) were sold for $400 million. Over the next year, nearly $10 billion of stripped MBSs were sold. Other new product enhancements include floating-rate CMOs, planned amortization classes (PACs) and targeted amortization classes (TACs) which reduce the maturity uncertainty of CMOs and provide for investors' special needs.

Lease Versus Buy

When a corporation or individual decides to acquire real estate for business use, the possibility of leasing the property rather than purchasing the property should be explored. The relevant comparison is the cost of purchasing the property (usually through borrowing) versus that of lease financing. The firm or individual will wish to use the least costly alternative as long as all of the relevant costs and benefits of the financing method are quantified.

Two approaches are available for analyzing the lease versus borrow decision: present value (cost) analysis of alternatives and internal-rate-of-return analysis of alternatives.

The present value analysis is a comparison of the present value of after-tax cash flows for each of the alternatives. For the leasing alternative, lease payments net of their tax benefits are determined for each year of the estimated holding period. These cash outflows are discounted back to the current year using an appropriate discount rate. For the borrowing alternative, the after-tax cash flows for each year of the holding period must also be determined. This requires knowing the amounts of annual interest and depreciation. Likewise, the after-tax proceeds (cash inflow) from the sale of the property at the end of the holding period must be determined. These cash flows are then discounted back to the current year and compared with the cash flows from the leasing alternative. The alternative that has the lowest cost expressed as a present value is the most desirable.

The internal-rate-of-return (IRR) approach avoids the problem of having to choose a discount rate. The IRR is calculated on the differential between cash flows from the present value analysis above. The resulting IRR must be compared with the firm's or individual's opportunity cost of using the funds for other purposes. For example, if a firm can generate a return greater than the IRR calculated on the differential cash flow analysis of the lease versus buy decision by purchasing capital equipment, the firm should lease the property and invest in the capital equipment.

SUMMARY

Debt financing of real estate investments is very common. The terms of mortgage loans have a great effect on the equity yield. The equity yield depends on the overall rate of return on the investment property and several financing variables including effective interest, loan-to-value ratio, terms of loan amortization and investment holding period.

The examples in this chapter have presumed constant property value and income to isolate the impact of debt financing to equity yield. In practice, income and property value are almost always expected to change in the future, and these changes can easily be imputed into the analysis. However, the ordinal ranking of alternative financing will be the same for any particular set of assumptions relevant to a specific property.

Equity yield, or lender's yield, is calculated from cash flows received. Typically, the process involves determining the initial investment, the periodic cash flows and the reversion at the end of the holding period. The yield is determined by calculating the IRR on the cash flows.

After-tax analysis of financing alternatives has been discussed briefly in this chapter. It is discussed in more detail later in this book.

NOTES

1. Gary Alan Brown, "Real Estate Investment Trusts," from *The Real Estate Handbook,* edited by Maury Seldin (Homewood, IL: Dow Jones-Irwin, 1980), pp. 686-87.
2. See Marshall Dennis, *Fundamentals of Mortgage Lending* (Reston, VA: Reston Publishing Co., 1978) for a much more complete discussion of this topic.
3. Much of the material and examples in this section are from Jerome J. Dasso, William N. Kinnard, Jr. and Stephen D. Messner, *Valuation and Analysis of Interests in Participation Financed Properties* (Chicago: Society of Real Estate Appraisers, 1972).

4. Dasso, Dinnard and Messner, pp. 21-22.
5. For more detailed discussion on this topic, see Arthur M. Weimer, Homer Hoyt and George F. Bloom, *Real Estate,* 7th ed. (New York: John Wiley & Sons, 1978), Ch. 15; and Donald R. Epley and James A. Miller, *Basic Real Estate Finance and Investments* (New York: John Wiley & Sons, 1980) Ch. 10-11.
6. For more detailed discussion on this topic, see Peter W. Badger, *Collateralized Mortgage Obligations,* a project of the Financial Managers' Statement Portfolio Management Committee, January/February 1989.

SECTION II
Impact of Federal Income Tax on Real Estate Investment

7
The Tax Process

While neither the investor nor the real estate broker is expected to be an income tax expert, familiarity with the general tax rules is essential for the purposes of determining motivation, comparison of alternatives or consequences of an investment program. Such familiarity also should enable the broker or investor to read a tax report and understand its makeup and consequences.

TAX LAW BACKGROUND

Tax legislation is combined into a single immense section of the federal statutory law called the Internal Revenue Code. This Code is revised from time to time by Congress; some of these revisions are extensive. In recent years, our national legislators have been extremely active in revising the Code. Extensive changes in the tax law have been made by the Installment Sales Revision Act of 1980, the Economic Recovery Tax Act of 1981 (ERTA), the Tax Equity and Fiscal Responsibility Act of 1982 (TEFRA), the Subchapter S Revision Act of 1982, the Tax Reform Act of 1984, the Tax Reform Act of 1986, the Revenue Act and Pension Protection Act of 1987, the Technical and Miscellaneous Revenue Act of 1988 and the Omnibus Budget Reconciliation Act of 1989. The Tax Reform Act of 1986 was so sweeping and comprehensive in its coverage that it replaced the 1954 Internal Revenue Code and was named the Internal Revenue Code of 1986.

Congress also has created an administrative agency to collect the tax and interpret the tax law, the Internal Revenue Service (IRS). IRS has issued elaborate regulations and rulings interpreting the Internal Revenue Code. The federal courts also constantly review the Code, the regulations and the rulings as applied to complaining taxpayers in literally thousands of cases and have upheld, upset or altered those rules by court opinions and decisions.

As a result of an accumulation of legislation, administrative rulings and court opinions, a continuing and ever-changing mass of tax law has been developed. Although it takes full-time professional experts to research and interpret specific, complex situations, because the income tax is an escalating major cost of living item, the tax law should be understood by every income-earning individual. All citizens have the legal right to minimize their tax bills by prudent management of their affairs within the framework of the rules.

NATURE OF TAXABLE INCOME

The income tax is not imposed on ALL income; it is imposed only on TAXABLE INCOME. Taxable income is an amount arrived at by making adjustments to gross income.

Gross Income

The tax law defines gross income as income from three types of activities: active, portfolio and passive.

Active income is income from one's principal business activity. Active income is income from salary, wages and activities in which the taxpayer materially participates. Portfolio income is income derived from stocks, bonds, etc. and includes such items as

Interest
Dividends
Royalties
Gain or loss attributable to disposition of portfolio property

Passive income is income derived from activity that is classified as passive and is described in detail later in this chapter.

Adjusted Gross Income

For individuals, gross income is reduced by certain adjustments to arrive at *adjusted gross income*. The individual must calculate adjusted gross income because certain deductions such as medical expenses, casualty losses, business expenses and charitable contributions are limited to a certain percentage of adjusted gross income. For taxpayers other than individuals, like corporations for example, the intermediate adjusted gross income calculation does not occur.

The following is a list of the most typical sources of gross income for the individual and the deductions that may be taken to reduce gross income to adjusted gross income.

Salary and wages. Among the deductions allowed are reimbursed transportation and travel expenses that were included in the employee's salary or wage, some contributions to IRAs and contributions to a Keogh retirement plan.

Pensions and annuities. Formulas are provided for excluding from gross income portions of pensions and annuities that are considered a recovery of the taxpayer's costs of acquiring the pension or annuity.

Rents and royalties. Cost recovery and other expenses incurred in earning rents and royalties are deducted.

Sole proprietor's business income. The cost of operation reduces the gross income.

Income from partnerships. The partnership calculates its gross income, reduces it by the cost of operations and allocates the appropriate portion of the net amount to each partner. Income from limited partnerships is generally considered *passive* income under the 1986 Code.

Unincorporated farm. The cost of operating reduces the gross income.

Sale and exchange of property. Gain or loss is computed as the difference between the sale price and the adjusted basis of the property sold or exchanged. Some exchanges are tax-free.

Alimony. A taxpayer may deduct alimony paid from gross income in arriving at adjusted gross income.

Taxable Income

To arrive at taxable income, the individual reduces adjusted gross income by personal deductions and exemptions and dependency deductions.

Personal Deductions

After arriving at adjusted gross income, the individual taxpayer may then take itemized deductions from the adjusted gross income. These include certain medical expenses, charitable contributions, interest expenses, money expenses, job expenses, taxes paid and other costs. If these deductions add up to less than a flat amount allowed by the tax law, the taxpayer is entitled to deduct this flat amount. This flat amount is called a standard deduction. It varies by type of taxpayer, year, age, and whether or not the taxpayer is considered legally blind. The standard deductions for 1988 and 1989 are as follows.

STANDARD DEDUCTION AMOUNTS

Taxpayer, not elderly or blind	1988	1989
Married, filing jointly	$5,000	$5,200
Single	3,000	3,100
Married, filing separately	2,500	2,600

In addition, each single taxpayer who is over 65, legally blind or both gets an additional $750 for each condition. Also, each married taxpayer who is over 65, legally blind or both gets an additional $600 for each condition.

Taxpayer	1988
Single, under 65	$3,000
Single, over 65 OR blind	3,750
Single, over 65 AND blind	4,500
Married, both under 65	5,000
Married, one over 65 OR blind	5,600
Married, one over 65 AND blind	6,200
Married, both over 65 OR blind	6,200
Married, both over 65 AND blind	7,400

Exemptions and Dependency Deductions

Finally, the individual taxpayer further reduces income (to arrive at taxable income) by exemptions and dependency deductions. There is a deduction for each exemption on the individual's tax return, including an exemption for the individual filing the tax return. If a joint return is filed, the couple filing will get two exemptions. In addition, there is a deduction for each dependent of the taxpayer. A dependent is someone who is closely related to the taxpayer (son, daughter, father, mother, and other enumerated relatives) who receives more than half of his or her support from the taxpayer and whose gross income is less than $1,950 in 1988 and $2,000 in 1989. Generally, individuals cannot qualify as dependents if they have gross incomes of at least the exemption amount ($1,950 for 1988). But the gross income limit does not apply to a child of the taxpayer who is either under 19 or a full-time student. After 1988, a son or daughter who is under 24 and a full-time student is permitted to have any amount of gross income and still be a dependent as long as the parent furnishes more than half of that child's support. In such a case, both parent and child may claim the exemption.

In 1988, each exemption and dependency deduction is $1,950. In 1989, each exemption will be $2,000. Under the previous tax code, an extra exemption was allowed for taxpayers over 65 or blind. These additional exemptions have been replaced by additional amounts allowed under the standard deduction (as noted above) for those taxpayers who do not itemize their deductions. Therefore, the additional allowances have been lost by blind taxpayers and taxpayers over 65 who itemize their deductions.

Types of Income

For federal income tax purposes, taxpayers may have two types of taxable income: ordinary income and capital gains.

Ordinary income.   Ordinary income typically arises from the individual's gainful occupation (salary or wages) and security income (dividends on stocks and interest on bonds, bank accounts, money market funds and the like). Real estate ownership can also create ordinary income. The ordinary income from real estate held for income-producing purposes is real estate taxable income, the gross income collected (rent) minus cost recovery, repairs, and other expenses.

Because cost recovery may exceed the total of otherwise taxable income and the principal payments on the loan, it is possible to receive cash flow from the real estate and still have a net loss for tax purposes.

Examples

1. Gross rents collected

Gross rents collected		$130,000
Less cost recovery	$40,000	
Repairs and maintenance	15,000	
Other expenses—interest, real estate taxes, management	85,000	140,000
Net loss		($10,000)

Although there was a tax loss, the owner of the property could still end up with cash in hand if, for example, the cash outlay for principal payments (not deductible for tax purposes) was less than the deduction for cost recovery (for which no cash outlay is required).

2. Assume in the preceding example that the owner paid $25,000 in mortgage principal payments during the year. The cash position would be as follows:

Gross rents collected		$130,000
Less cash outlays		
Repairs and maintenance	$15,000	
Principal payment on mortgage	25,000	
Other expenses	85,000	125,000
Cash available to investor		$ 5,000

Thus, while there was a tax loss of $10,000, there was also cash in hand of $5,000.

The tax loss of $10,000 may be fully deductible, partially deductible, or not currently deductible at all. Deductibility is based on passive loss rules, discussed below. If the owner's ordinary income from gainful employment, dividends, interest, and the like totals $35,000 after deductions and exemptions and the owner is allowed to deduct losses in full, the owner's ordinary income will be reduced to $25,000 by applying the $10,000 taxable loss from the real estate investment.

PASSIVE LOSSES

The 1986 Tax Reform Act radically changed the way losses from real estate ownership can be used to shelter income. Prior to this act, taxpayers could use tax losses from real estate ownership to shelter income from practically any source. This allowed high income taxpayers to greatly reduce their taxes. The government recognized that certain types of investments in which sophisticated taxpayers were investing were responsible for generating the tax losses. Taxpayers were buying tax losses rather than investing in economically sound investments. Buildings for which there was no need were being built if they could provide sufficient tax shelter to make them attractive investments. Congress believed the public had lost faith in the fairness of the tax code.

The passive loss provisions were enacted to prevent these abuses. The concept of *passive* loss is a concept that exists only in the tax world. When reference is made to either *passive income* or *passive loss*, it means *taxable income* or *tax loss* generated by a passive activity. The passive loss provisions of the 1986 Tax Reform Act apply to

Individuals, partnerships, and S-corporations

Estates

Trusts

Personal service corporations if the employee-owners own more than 10% of the stock

Closely held C-corporations (50% or more of the stock is held by not more than five individuals at any time during the last half of the tax year).

Regular C-corporations are not subject to these rules.

In order to implement these changes it became necessary to divide gross income into the three major segments defined earlier in this chapter: active income, portfolio income, and passive income.

Activities that are classified as passive are further broken down into three major categories:

Rental activities.   A rental activity is one which produces income consisting of payments for the use of tangible property, rather than for the performance of substantial services. Rental activities are divided into two levels of participation. Rental activities are divided into those in which the taxpayer is an active participant or is not an active participant.

Active participation requires that the taxpayer participate in the making of management decisions in a significant and bona fide sense *and own at least a 10% interest in the property*. This includes approving new tenants, rental rates and terms, capital or repair expenditures, and so on. The following factors apply.

Hiring a management company does not preclude active participation.

Services provided by a taxpayer's spouse are attributed to the taxpayer to determine active participation.

Limited partners do not meet the active test regardless of their activities.

If the taxpayer's interest is less than 10% or does not have any say in management decisions the taxpayer is not an active participant.

Activities in which the taxpayer is less than a material participant.   If a taxpayer is to be considered "less than" a material participant, a definition of material participation is required.

Material participation means involvement in the operations of an activity throughout the year on a regular, continuous, and substantial basis. This will usually mean the activity is the taxpayer's principal business. Some of the tests for material participation are

Is it your primary business?

Are you frequently on the premises?

Do you have a thorough knowledge of or experience in the activity?

In addition, in February 1988, Congress released temporary regulations setting forth what would be considered material participation. An individual will be considered to materially participate if at least one of the following seven tests is passed.

1. The person has more than 500 hours of participation during the year.
2. The person's yearly participation constitutes substantially all of the participation in the activity by individuals, including nonowners.
3. The person has more than 100 hours of participation and no other individual participates more.
4. The person's aggregate participation in all significant participation activities exceeds 500 hours for the year. A significant participation activity is one in which an individual participates for more than 100 hours, but does not meet any of the other material participation tests.
5. The person was able to qualify as a material participant in the activity for any 5 of the preceding 10 tax years.
6. The activity is a personal service activity in the field of health, law, engineering, architecture, accounting, actuarial science, performing arts, or consulting, and the individual materially participated for any 3 preceding tax years.
7. The facts and circumstances indicate participation in the activity on a regular, continuous, and substantial basis during the year, with at least 100 hours of participation.

The material participation standard is applied on a year by year basis. An individual's participation in an activity may change from passive to active during the life of an investment. When a taxpayer's participation in an activity becomes material, future losses become allowable against income from active and portfolio sources.

Limited business interests.   Limited business interests refer to investments such as limited partnerships in which the taxpayer's liability is limited. Limited partnership interests are by definition passive. If a taxpayer is both a general and a limited partner in the same activity, the lack of material participation presumption applies only to the limited interest.

The essence of the new passive income and loss rules is set forth in summary form in Figure 13.

The first two 3s have already been discussed. Much of the remainder of this section is devoted to discussing and diagramming the three basic rules and the three exceptions to these rules. The rules and exceptions are applicable to *net* passive losses. To arrive at these, income and losses from all categories of passive activities must be aggregated and netted.

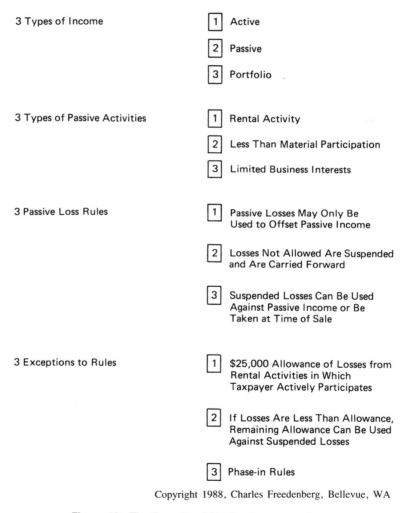

3 Types of Income

1 Active

2 Passive

3 Portfolio

3 Types of Passive Activities

1 Rental Activity

2 Less Than Material Participation

3 Limited Business Interests

3 Passive Loss Rules

1 Passive Losses May Only Be Used to Offset Passive Income

2 Losses Not Allowed Are Suspended and Are Carried Forward

3 Suspended Losses Can Be Used Against Passive Income or Be Taken at Time of Sale

3 Exceptions to Rules

1 $25,000 Allowance of Losses from Rental Activities in Which Taxpayer Actively Participates

2 If Losses Are Less Than Allowance, Remaining Allowance Can Be Used Against Suspended Losses

3 Phase-in Rules

Figure 13 The Four 3s of Passive Income and Loss

Rule 1. Tax losses from passive activities cannot be used to offset income from active and portfolio sources. Tax losses from passive activities may be used only to offset income from other passive activities.

Rule 2. Any passive losses which cannot be used in the year in which they arise are suspended and are carried forward indefinitely.

Rule 3. Suspended losses can be used against passive income in future years. Any suspended losses which remain unused at the time of a fully taxable disposition of the taxpayer's entire interest in the property may be deducted at time of sale. There are two other ways in which suspended losses may be used. These will be elaborated on later in this section.

These are general rules, and as such, they are subject to exceptions. The 1986 Tax Reform Act carved out three exceptions to these rules. These exceptions permit some, and in some cases all, of the losses from certain kinds of passive activities to be used to shelter active and/or portfolio income, but only if these losses qualify for the exceptions carved out by the 1986 Tax Reform Act. The first two exceptions are referred to as the small investor exceptions. The third exception is the grandfather phase-in provision for those activities that were owned prior to passage of the 1986 Act.

Figure 14 summarizes which passive activities are eligible for each of these exceptions.

The two small investor exceptions apply only to losses generated by rental activities

```
┌─────────────────────────┐        ┌─────────────────────────────────┐
│    Rental Activities     │        │ Activities in Which Taxpayer Is  │
│   in Which Taxpayer      │        │  Less Than a Material Participant │
│   Actively Participates  │        │                                  │
│                          │        │   Limited Business Interests     │
└─────────────────────────┘        │                                  │
                                    │  Rental Activities in Which      │
                                    │   Taxpayer Does Not              │
                                    │   Actively Participate           │
                                    └─────────────────────────────────┘


Exception #1
(Up to $25,000 Allowance)

Exception #2
(If Loss Is Less Than Allowance)

Exception #3                          Exception #3 Only
(Phase-in Rules)                      (Phase-in Rules)
```

Figure 14 Eligibility for Exceptions to Passive Loss Rules in which the taxpayer is an active participant. Therefore, it is necessary to segregate net passive losses from this type of activity from other types of passive activities.

If there are net losses from rental activities in which the taxpayer actively participates, these net losses must first be used to offset passive income, if any, from other passive activities. If there is a net loss remaining after offsetting income from other passive activities, this net loss qualifies for the small investor exceptions. Figure 15 fully illustrates the mechanics of the aggregation and netting of passive income and losses.

Qualification as a small investor requires the taxpayer's adjusted gross income to be

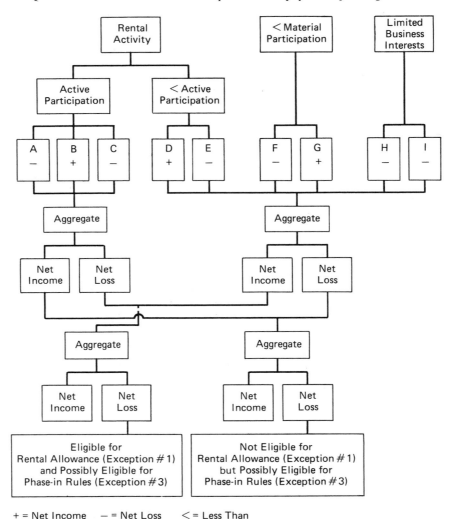

+ = Net Income   − = Net Loss   < = Less Than

Figure 15 Aggregation of Passive Income and Losses

less than $150,000. In computing the taxpayer's adjusted gross income for the purpose of this requirement *only*, certain items are not taken into account. These items are

1. Taxable social security benefits
2. IRA contributions
3. Losses from the operations phase of passive activities

The small investor is allowed to use up to $25,000 of passive losses from rental activities in which the taxpayer actively participates as an offset against active and/or portfolio income. In order to obtain the benefit of the full $25,000 allowance, the taxpayer's adjusted gross income must be $100,000 or less. The taxpayer whose adjusted gross income exceeds $100,000 starts to lose some of the $25,000 allowance at the rate of 50 cents for each dollar by which the adjusted gross income exceeds $100,000. The $25,000 allowance is per tax return, not per person. If a married couple files separately they cannot use this allowance.

Example

If a taxpayer's adjusted gross income is $120,000, the rental allowance for that year will be $15,000. It is arrived at in the following way. The taxpayer will lose $0.50 of the allowance for each dollar by which adjusted gross income exceeds $100,000. In this case the adjusted gross income exceeds $100,000 by $20,000. This $20,000 excess causes the taxpayer to lose $10,000 of the allowance resulting in a reduced allowance of $15,000.

Figure 16 illustrates that the amount of loss the taxpayer will be allowed to claim under the rental allowance will depend on the adjusted gross income. The actual loss incurred will be either less than, equal to, or greater than the rental allowance permitted in that year. In a year when the actual tax loss exceeds the rental allowance, the excess loss will have to be suspended if it does not qualify for phase-in treatment (exception 3).

In a year when the actual tax loss incurred is less than the permitted allowance, the taxpayer may use any remaining allowance against qualifying suspended losses. A qualifying suspended loss is one which arose in a prior year and was generated by a rental activity in which the taxpayer actively participated. The taxpayer must have been an active participant in the year in which the loss was suspended. This situation is covered by exception 2.

The $25,000 rental allowance is permitted each year. It is not scheduled to expire. However, it must be used in the year in which it arises or it will be lost. The $25,000 allowance is a "use it or lose it" allowance. If any part of it remains unused, the unused portion cannot be carried forward to the following year. Because the allowance must be used or lost, the Tax Reform Act of 1986 provides for two ways to use the allowance. The first way is against current year's tax losses from rental activities in which the taxpayer actively participates. The second way is against qualifying suspended losses.

The grandfather exception is better known as the phase-in rule. The phase-in rule for assets owned prior to the passage of the Tax Reform Act of 1986 applies to all forms of passive activities, not just rental real estate.

The phase-in rules were enacted in order to give some relief to those investors who had invested in properties prior to the passage of the law. A five year phase-in period

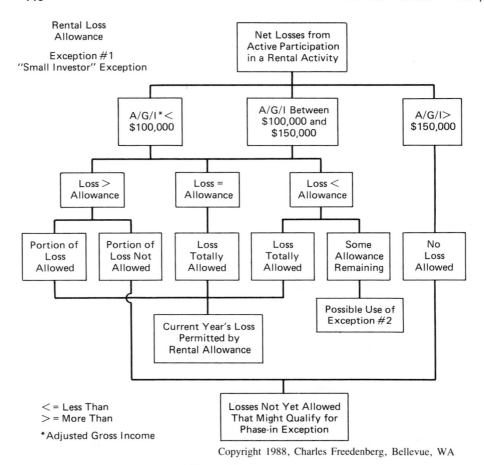

Figure 16

gives the investor sufficient time to adjust to the new law. Properties which generate losses will eventually generate taxable income instead of losses. The phase-in rules allow a percentage of the losses from properties owned prior to the passage of the 1986 Tax Reform Act to be used against active and portfolio income. The percentage of losses allowed for each respective tax year are as follows:

PHASE-IN TIMETABLE

Tax Years Beginning In	% Losses Allowed	% Losses Disallowed
1987	65%	35%
1988	40%	60%
1989	20%	80%
1990	10%	90%
1991	0%	100%

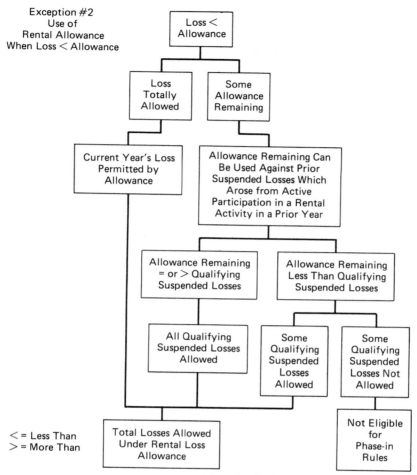

Figure 17

Phase-in rules apply to losses arising in the current tax year *only*. Suspended losses are not eligible for phase-in treatment.

The losses allowed by the above phase-in percentages are in addition to any losses allowed under the $25,000 exception discussed previously.

Any passive losses disallowed under the phase-in rules will be carried forward to subsequent years as *suspended losses*. They can be carried forward indefinitely until they can be used. Suspended losses may be used in the following ways:

1. To offset passive income (see rule 3)
2. To absorb unused rental allowance if the suspended loss arose from a *rental activity in which taxpayer actively participated* (see exception 2)

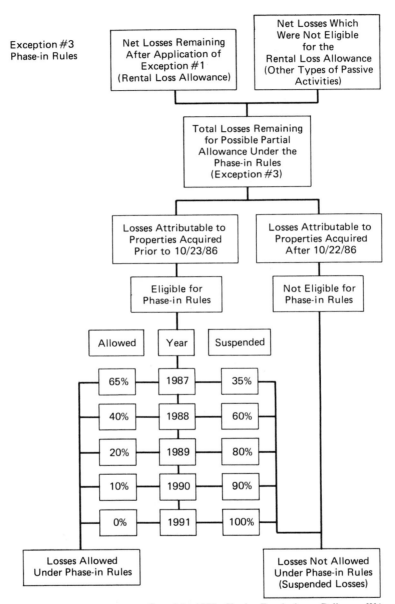

Copyright 1988, Charles Freedenberg, Bellevue, WA

Figure 18

3. To offset gain on the subject property when sold (see rule 3)
4. To offset gain on the sale of other passive activities

If, in any given year, the allowable losses are greater than the taxpayer's taxable income (if all active and portfolio income is offset and the taxpayer's taxable income has been reduced to zero), any remaining loss which would have been allowed but for lack of income to offset does not become suspended loss. Instead, it changes its character and becomes a net operating loss, which can be taken back 3 years and forward 15 years until it can be used up against any income source.

Property interests acquired after the Date of Enactment (October 22, 1986) are not eligible for phase-in treatment. To qualify as pre-enactment the property must have been placed in service by October 22, 1986.

Where a binding contract was entered into by August 16, 1986 to acquire the property interest the taxpayer will be deemed to have owned the interest even if there are contingencies (beyond the buyer's control).

If the taxpayer adds capital to the investment after enactment, the phase-in timetable is still applicable, so long as the added capital does not increase the taxpayer's ownership interest. If the taxpayer adds to the ownership interest after enactment, the new portion of the interest does not qualify.

Example

A homeowner owns a house *before enactment* but buys another and places the first in rental inventory *after enactment*. The homeowner is not eligible for the phase-in because the house was not available for rental prior to passage of the Tax Reform Act of 1986.

After 1990 the phase-in rules will no longer apply. After 1990, the only way to be able to use net passive losses against active and portfolio income will be the small investor exception. Figure 19 summarizes the key distinctions to remember between the exceptions to the passive loss rules.

Figure 20 provides an overall summary of the rules and exceptions discussed above. It is a generalized overview. The details of each portion of this chart have been set forth in the diagrams above.

Rental Allowance (Exceptions #1 and 2)	Phase-in Rules (Exception #3)
Depends on Adjusted Gross Income	Does Not Depend on Adjusted Gross Income
Does Not Depend on Date Placed in Service	Depends on Date Placed in Service
Is Not Scheduled to Phase Out	Will Phase Out by 1991
May Apply (Exception #2) to Prior Years' Suspended Losses	Applies to Current Year's Losses Only
On a Year by Year Basis, This Allowance Must Be Used or It Is Lost	

Figure 19 Summary of Passive Loss Exceptions

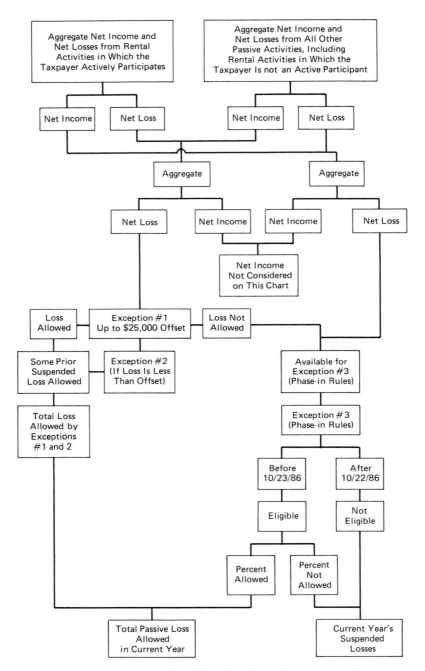

Copyright 1988, Charles Freedenberg, Bellevue, WA

Figure 20 Overview of Passive Loss Rules (Chart Considers Net Losses Only)

When analyzing a real estate investment the tax loss generated by the investment may not be allowed in the year in which the loss arises or may be only partially allowed. Remember, any loss that is not allowed is not lost. It may be allowed in a subsequent year. At the very least it will be allowed at time of sale.

The new tax law has placed a limitation on using certain tax losses as they currently arise. The use and resulting tax benefit of these losses may have to be deferred. When this occurs the taxpayer has effectively lost the time value of money from using losses in the current year to reduce taxes.

To conclude, however, that real estate investments no longer provide tax shelter is not correct. The tax losses generated by real estate continue to shelter all of the income and cash flow produced by the property itself. These losses may also be used to shelter income produced by other passive activities. They simply no longer provide unrestricted shelter against income produced from active and portfolio sources.

Furthermore, only losses from passive activities which are not sold during the year are considered in arriving at the net losses for the year. If a property is sold prior to the end of the calendar year, its losses, if any, will be applied directly against the gain on the sale and need not be aggregated with other operational losses incurred during the year. This relieves a taxpayer from using part of the "small investor" allowance on a loss which will be fully allowed anyway due to the sale of the property.

Allocating Specific Losses to Specific Properties

The $25,000 allowance and the phase-in percentages are taken against net passive losses. Only certain types of activities qualify for the $25,000 allowance. Only properties owned prior to October 23, 1986, qualify for phase-in treatment. Because of this an allocation must be made to each property of its pro rata share of the net losses.

Brokers will be dealing with investors whose properties will be subject to these new rules. A knowledgeable broker should be able to advise a client about the general provisions of this new law and tell the client when to seek competent accounting and legal advice. Brokers should know what impact these rules will have on the cash flows from operations and the cash flows from dispositions. A change in cash flows will have a significant impact on the yield of an investment.

Disposition of a Passive Activity

When the taxpayer's entire interest in a passive activity is sold or otherwise disposed of in a fully taxable transaction, all suspended losses related to that activity and any loss realized on the disposition will be allowed. If the disposition results in a gain, the gain may be offset by various types of passive losses. There are four types of passive losses that may be used to offset gain at time of sale. The four types of passive losses are listed in the order in which they may be applied to offset gain.

1. Losses from the operations of the subject property
2. Suspended losses from the subject property

3. Losses from the operations of other passive activities

4. Suspended losses from other passive activities

The first two types of losses are generated by the property being sold. These losses can be used in full. They are permitted to convert a gain into a loss. The third and fourth types of losses come from other passive activities. These losses can only be used to offset gain. They may not be used to convert a gain into a loss.

If the disposition is made to a related party in a fully taxable transaction, the taxpayer may not consider the suspended losses as being available until the activity is transferred to an unrelated party in fully taxable transaction or when the activity is abandoned. Abandonment is considered a disposition and will trigger suspended losses. Transfers to related parties do not trigger suspended losses.

Sham transactions that would not be recognized under general tax rules will not recognize suspended losses. Mere changes in the form of ownership do not trigger recognition of suspended losses.

Other Forms of Disposition

Death.   Suspended losses will be carried over to the decedent's final return to the extent the losses exceed the step up on basis.

Example

A's basis is $40,000 and she has suspended losses of $180,000 on a property whose fair market value is $200,000. A dies and leaves the property to B. The $160,000 step up in B's basis ($40,000 to $200,000) is subtracted from the $180,000 suspended losses, leaving the decedent's final return with $20,000 in deduction.

Gift.   Since the donor's basis flows through to the donee, the donor's basis is increased by the suspended losses just prior to the gift. The basis of the donee may not be increased beyond the basis of the donor or fair market value at the date of transfer.

Exchange.   A pure tax deferred exchange is not a taxable disposition and, therefore, does not trigger recognition of suspended losses. However, the taxpayer can trigger recognition of losses up to the amount of any net boot received.

Installment sales.   Remaining suspended losses are triggered in the same ratio that the gain recognized in each year bears to the total gain on the sale.

Record Keeping Requirements

The record keeping requirements under the new law are stringent. Because of all of the regulations imposed on the use of suspended losses, record keeping requirements will be increased.

Passive Credits

A passive credit can arise from purchasing, building or rehabilitating low income housing prior to 1990 or from rehabilitating older commercial or historic structures. The credit is considered a passive credit because the property against which it is claimed is a passive activity.

Passive credits are allowed on a ''deduction-equivalent'' basis. This means that a dollar for dollar credit against the tax *attributable to passive activity income* will be allowed to the extent the tax would be reduced by a $25,000 deduction against income. (For example, a $25,000 deduction would reduce tax liability by $7,000 if the taxpayer is in a 28% tax bracket.) Therefore, the maximum credit in any year would be $7,000.

However, to the extent permitted by the passive loss rental allowance, the $25,000 must first be applied to passive losses from operations and suspended losses which qualify under exception 2. Then, if any of the $25,000 remains, it may be offset by passive credits on a deduction-equivalent basis.

Under these rules, passive credits do no appear very attractive. To fully utilize their benefits one might consider incorporating the entity which will do the rehabilitation so as not to be subject to the passive loss rules.

There is no requirement that the taxpayer be an active participant in the rental activity to be eligible for this credit. The credit is subject to taxpayer income limits. The phase-out of the passive credit occurs for the rehabilitation of commercial or historic structures when the taxpayer's adjusted gross income is between $200,000 and $250,000.

At the time of sale, unused passive credits may *not* be deducted. They must be carried forward until they can be absorbed by passive income on a deduction-equivalent basis.

CAPITAL GAINS

Capital gains result from the sale or exchange of capital assets or assets which, for tax purposes, are treated as capital assets. For the most part, property held for investment by someone who is not a dealer in that type of property is a capital asset. Stocks, bonds, and vacant land may be capital assets. Similarly, other personal-use items not held for sale in business, like a personal residence or personal car, are capital assets. Section 1231 assets which are noninventory depreciable assets and land used in a business are also capital assets. To qualify as a Section 1231 asset, the property must have been held more than one year. In determining whether certain gains from the disposition of real estate are to be treated as capital gains or ordinary income, the status of the taxpayer relative to the property is a vital factor. If the taxpayer is deemed to be an investor, the gain will generally be a capital gain; however, if the taxpayer is a dealer in that property, the gain is ordinary income, or income derived from the operation of the business.

Capital gains can be either short-term (gains on assets held one year or less) or long-term (gains on assets held more than one year). Prior to the Tax Reform Act of 1986, short-term capital gains were taxed at ordinary income rates, but long-term capital gains received favorable tax treatment; only 40% of long-term capital gains were included in taxable income. The Tax Reform Act of 1986 eliminated this favorable treatment for long-term capital gains. Thus, all capital gains are now taxed at the same rates as ordinary income. Despite this change, the structure of capital gains treatment was left in the Internal Revenue Code because capital gains treatment may be reinstated at some time in the future. Therefore, taxpayers must continue to net short-term gains and losses and long-term gains and losses from the disposition of capital assets.

Calculating Long- and Short-Term Capital Gains and Losses

In the following paragraphs we will look at how net long-term and short-term capital gains and losses are determined by aggregating those gains and losses. However, keep in mind that the sale or exchange of property held for personal use (a personal residence, a car used for nonbusiness purposes, a ring, a boat, household furniture) gives rise to a long- or short-term capital gain when sold at a profit. But if such property is sold at a loss, the loss is *nondeductible*. Such losses *do not* enter into the aggregating procedures described in the following paragraphs.

The netting procedure begins with Section 1231 assets. All Section 1231 gains and losses that occur in one year are first aggregated to arrive at a *net* Section 1231 gain or loss. If the net figure is a gain, it is treated as a capital gain and aggregated with other long-term capital gains. If the net figure is a loss, it is deducted in full, without further netting.

In determining the net long- and short-term gains or losses for the year, short-term capital gains are aggregated with short-term losses and long-term gains are aggregated with long-term losses.

If both categories end up with gains, both are treated as ordinary income. If both categories end up with losses, however, the rules for capital losses (different rules for corporations and individuals) apply. These rules are spelled out later in this chapter.

If one category results in a gain and the other in a loss, the gain and loss must be aggregated to arrive at a net long-term or short-term gain or loss. The net figure is then given the treatment described in Figure 21 in the quadrant in which the gain or loss falls. Of course, if all the transactions fall into only one category, the net gain or loss in that category gets the treatment described for that category. Figure 21 summarizes all these rules in one easy-to-understand chart.

Treatment of Capital Gains

If, as a result of the calculations, the individual taxpayer ends up with a capital gain, short- or long-term, that gain is added to ordinary income. Capital gains are not added to ordinary income until *after* all of the aggregation of capital gains and losses are first made.

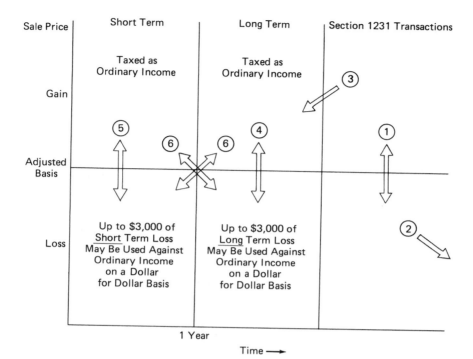

Figure 21   Net Gains and Losses

1. Net Section 1231 Gains Against Section 1231 Losses (Vertical Arrows).

2. If Section 1231 Transactions Net to a Loss, This Loss Is an Ordinary Business Loss and May Be Deducted in Full.

3. If Section 1231 Transactions Net to a Gain, the Gain Is Moved Over into the Column Labeled Long Term Gain and Is Aggregated with Other Long Term Capital Gain.

4. Long Term Gains Are Netted Against Long Term Losses (Vertical Arrows)..

5. Short Term Gains Are Netted Against Short Term Losses (Vertical Arrows).

6. If, After All Previous Netting, There Are Two Numbers on This Chart and They Are in Diagonally Opposite Quadrants, It Is Necessary to Net Numbers Located in Diagonally Opposite Quadrants Against Each Other (Diagonal Arrows).

After the Above Six Steps Have Been Completed, Apply the Rules in Each of the Quadrants to Any Numbers Contained in Those Quadrants.

Treatment of Capital Losses for Individuals

Net capital losses (both short- and long-term) may be used to offset ordinary income of up to $3,000. The losses remaining are then carried over to the following year and used as long- or short-term losses in that year. There is no limit on the number of years an individual may carry over a loss. Of course, if ordinary income is less than $3,000, the maximum amount that a capital loss may offset is the amount of the ordinary income.

In applying capital losses as offsets against ordinary income, both long-term and short-term losses offset ordinary income on a dollar-for-dollar basis. If a taxpayer has both short- and long-term losses, short-term losses are applied first in offsetting ordinary income. If the short-term losses are insufficient to offset $3,000 of ordinary income (or the total of ordinary income if that total does not exceed $3,000), then long-term losses are applied.

Examples

1. In 1988, Green has a long-term capital gain of $1,000 and a short-term capital loss of $6,000. After netting the two, he has a short-term loss of $5,000. His ordinary income is $12,000. He applies $3,000 of his short-term loss to reduce ordinary income to $9,000 and carries over $2,000 as a short-term capital loss to 1989.

2. In 1988, Black has $12,000 ordinary income but has a short-term gain of $1,000 and a long-term loss of $8,000. Now, she has a net long-term loss of $7,000. In this case, she has to use $3,000 of the $7,000 net long-term loss to offset $3,000 of ordinary income, reducing ordinary income to $9,000. She has $4,000 of long-term capital loss left which is carried over to 1989 as a long-term capital loss.

3. In 1988, Grey has ordinary income of $12,000, a short-term loss of $3,200 and a long-term loss of $400. She applies $3,000 of the short-term loss to reduce ordinary income to $9,000. And, she carries over to 1989 a short-term loss of $200 and a long-term loss of $400.

4. In 1988, Brown has ordinary income of $12,000, a short-term loss of $800 and a long-term loss of $4,800. He applies the $800 short-term loss to offset $800 of ordinary income. He has to use $2,200 of his long-term loss to offset $2,200 of ordinary income, thus offsetting a total of $3,000 of ordinary income. He has $2,600 of long-term capital loss to carry over to the next year.

Arithmetic of Capital Gains and Losses

Because of the limitations on applying net capital losses to offset ordinary income, good planning (when possible) is called for to keep taxes on these transactions to allowable minimums.

When year's end approaches, therefore, it is a good idea to take an inventory of capital gains and losses already realized that year and to survey the potential gains and losses that can still be realized in that year or postponed to the following year. The investor should then determine the desirability of realizing further capital gains and/or losses in the current year.

Of course, tax planning cannot be the only criterion for investment decisions. The reality of being able to postpone to next year a currently available gain or loss must be assessed. The market conditions may change, or a ready buyer may not be available later.

Sometimes postponement can be accomplished by entering into an installment sale. While the sale is made in the current year, the lion's share of the proceeds can be collected in the following year. The gain attributable to the proceeds collected in the following year would be taxable in that following year. Keep in mind, however, that installment sales can be used only to postpone gains, not losses. (The techniques and requirements for installment sale reporting are described in Chapter 10.)

Tax-Exempt Income

A taxpayer may also have tax-exempt income. This income is usually in the form of interest on bonds or other obligations of states, cities, and other subdivisions of a state (usually referred to as municipal bonds). It is also possible to have a gain or profit that is not recognized for tax purposes. While the gain is there, it is not taxable in the year in which it is realized. This often occurs when there is an exchange of like-kind property, usually real estate. (Exchanges are discussed in depth in Chapter 11.)

ACCOUNTING METHODS

As we have seen, taxable income is determined by reducing gross income by allowable deductions and exemptions. However, there is a timing factor to be considered, that is, *when* income or expense arises. The time when income is recognized or deductions are allowed depends on the accounting method used. There are two common, recognized methods of accounting, the accrual method and the cash method.

The Accrual Method

Considered the most accurate method, accrual accounting matches the income and expense attributable to a period of time, regardless of when the income is actually received or the expense paid. In other words, income is reported when everything that has to be done to entitle the recipient to the income has occurred. Similarly, an expense is deductible when everything has been done that requires the payment. The fact that the payment date is to occur prior to or after all the other events is disregarded.

Examples

1. Brown is a landlord and is entitled to receive $1,000 a month for the premises rented to Green. Rent is payable on the first day of the month for that month. Green is delinquent in the rent payment and pays the December, 1984, rent in January, 1985. If Brown is on the accrual basis, the December rent must be reported in 1984 even though payment was received in 1985. Even if (in the unusual event) the December rent were actually payable in 1985, Brown would still have to report the December rent as 1984 income.

2. Brown, the landlord in the previous example, has fuel oil delivered in 1984. He receives a bill for $950. Under the terms of his agreement with the vendor, payment is not due until 1985. Brown pays for the oil in 1985. On the accrual basis, Brown deducts the $950 in 1984.

The accrual method can only be used by certain taxpayers. It is, however, required if inventories are a substantial income-producing factor in a business.

For deductions claimed after July 18, 1984, a new concept, economic performance, has been added to the accrual method. Under this concept, an accrual basis taxpayer cannot accrue a deduction until economic performance has occurred. If, for example, the taxpayer's liability arises because the taxpayer is to receive property from another person, the economic performance occurs when the property is received. Thus, the new rule would not change the results in Example 2 above.

If the taxpayer's liability arises for services to be received from another person, economic performance occurs as the services are provided by the other person. Thus, if the services are provided over a period of more than one taxable year, the liability accruing in each year is limited to the amount of services received in that year. If the taxpayer's liability arises out of the use of property by the taxpayer (like rent for the use of the premises), economic performance occurs as the taxpayer uses the property. Therefore, the rent is deductible in one taxable year only to the extent that it covers the use of the property during that year.

The Cash Method

Cash accounting is a much simpler method to use although it is not considered as scientifically accurate. It also permits greater flexibility in moving income and deductions from one year to another. Under this method, income is recognized and deductions are allowable when the actual payment takes place.

Examples

1. Going back to our first example above, since Brown did not receive the December, 1984 rent until 1985, and is a cash-basis taxpayer, that rent is reported as income in 1985, when it was received.

2. In the second example, if Brown uses the cash method, deduction for the fuel payment is taken in 1985, when the bill was paid.

Section 467 Rental Agreements

Congress was disturbed by the fact that a cash-basis lessor included rent income only when payment was received and an accrual-basis lessee could deduct the rent on the basis of occupancy of the premises regardless of when payment was made. So, for rental agreements entered into after June 8, 1984, a new set of rules (applying to both lessor and lessee, regardless of their cash- or accrual-basis status) has been put into the law. This new set of rules applies if the rental agreement qualifies as a *Section 467 rental agreement*.

A rental agreement is a Section 467 rental agreement if *either* of the following two conditions exists:

1. Some amount of rent is payable in a future year for use of the property in a prior year. This rule applies if the future payment is made more than one year after the close of the taxable year in which the use of the property occurs.
2. The agreement calls for rent increases during the term of the lease.

Note, however, that if the total amount of the rents for the entire lease term is $250,000 or less, the agreement is *not* a Section 467 rental agreement.

If the rental agreement *is* a Section 467 rental agreement, the lessor and the lessee (regardless of the accounting method each uses) take into account each year the amount of rent allocable to that year by the rental agreement *plus* the present value of the rents to be paid in future years that are allocable to that year. IRS has issued regulations to explain how to compute the present value of the future rents.

In addition, interest is to be included for the amounts payable in future years that are allocable to the present year. In calculating the present value of future payments and of the interest, a rate equal to 110% of the applicable federal rate at the time the rental agreement was entered into (compounded semiannually) is used. The applicable federal rate, published by the IRS, is based on the rates paid on federal obligations.

Disqualified Leaseback or Long-Term Agreements

Special rules apply if a Section 467 rental agreement is a disqualified leaseback or long-term agreement, that is, if it has tax avoidance as a principal purpose and is either (1) part of a leaseback transaction or (2) for a term that is greater than 75% of the statutory recovery period of the property. For real estate, the statutory recovery period is 27.5 or 31.5 years. A leaseback transaction involves a leaseback to any person (or relative of that person) who had an interest in the property at any time within two years before the leaseback.

If the disqualified leaseback or long-term agreement does not provide for rent allocations that meet the requirements for Section 467 rental agreements, the rent allocable to each year is the portion of the *constant rent amount* allocable to each year. The constant rent amount is the amount that, were it paid at the end of each lease period, would add up to a present value equal to the present value of all the rent payments called for in the agreement. (Present value is computed as set forth above for Section 467 rental agreements.)

The IRS is authorized to issue regulations spelling out circumstances in which the agreement will not be treated as a disqualified leaseback or long-term agreement. These circumstances include (1) rent amounts geared to price indices, (2) rents based on fixed percentages of the lessee's receipts, (3) reasonable rent holidays and (4) changes in amounts paid by the lessor to third parties.

Recapture of prior understated income. If the transaction would have been a disqualified leaseback or long-term agreement but for the exceptions provided, the lessor may have ordinary income recapture on the disposition of the property. The recapture amount is calculated by first determining the amounts that would have been included as rent under the rules for Section 467 rental agreements. Subtracted from this amount is the actual amount of rents taken into account by the lessor during the period of the lease. The remaining amount is compared to the gain on the disposition. The lesser of these two amounts is the recapture amount.

Prepayments

The IRS has long taken a position (and it has been upheld by the courts) that prepayment of rent expense must be deducted over the period for which it was paid, *regardless of the accounting method used by the tenant.*

In addition, Congress has enacted legislation that now prevents a cash-basis taxpayer from deducting prepaid interest.

Constructive Receipt

When the cash method is used, income may not be avoided merely by turning one's back to available income. Once payment is tendered or is available for the asking, the income is deemed to have been realized even though the actual payment has not been received. For example, when interest is credited to a savings bank account, it becomes income even though the amount is not withdrawn.

Once payment is tendered, it becomes income. Asking the payor to hold up on payment at that point is too late. However, it is permissible to arrange in advance when payment is to be due. For example, even though title will close in December, 1988, a real estate broker can arrange in advance for the seller to pay the broker's commission in 1989. If this arrangement is made as a condition for the broker's representation of the seller prior to the sale, the income will become 1989 income if the broker is a cash-basis taxpayer. On the other hand, if the commission was to be paid at the closing and at that time the broker says, "hold onto the money until next year and then pay me," constructive receipt is in 1988.

Choosing and Changing Accounting Methods

A taxpayer may choose the accounting method (subject to the requirement that the accrual method be used when inventory is a substantial income-producing factor) on the first tax return for a business. Typically, individuals whose major (or sole) income is from wages and salaries use the cash method. Professionals (doctors, lawyers, accountants) and those in service businesses (real estate brokers, for example) use the cash method more often than not. Businesses that sell goods generally use the accrual method.

Once an accounting method has been chosen, the taxpayer must continue to use that method for that business unless permission is received from the IRS to change. (When permission for change is granted, the IRS generally requires certain adjustments and there may be additional tax to pay. Often, this additional tax is permitted to be paid ratably over a number of years.)

Installment Method

An exception to the cash and accrual method is the installment method. Under this method, gain on the sale of property is permitted to be reported ratably over the period of collection. This method applies when some portion (or all) of the sale price is to be paid in a year later than the year of sale. This is a very popular method for reporting gain on the sale of real estate. A complete discussion of the installment method is in Chapter 10.

TAXATION OF INDIVIDUAL'S TAXABLE INCOME

Tax Tables and Tax Rate Schedules

If the taxpayer's taxable income is less than $50,000, the taxpayer must use special tax tables provided by the IRS to determine the amount of tax. Taxpayers with taxable income greater than $50,000 must compute their tax using applicable tax rate schedules to compute their tax.

The tax rates applied to the amount on which the tax is computed (taxable income) depends on the taxpayer's marital status. The categories of taxpayers and their respective tax rates are shown in Figure 22. Figure 22 applies to 1988 only.

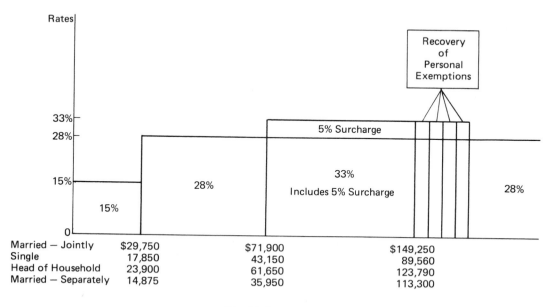

Married — Jointly	$29,750	$71,900	$149,250
Single	17,850	43,150	89,560
Head of Household	23,900	61,650	123,790
Married — Separately	14,875	35,950	113,300

Taxable Income

Figure 22 Tax Rates—1988

Example

Assume that for 1988, Mr. and Mrs. Jones, married individuals filing a joint return, have salary income of $60,000 and security income of $10,000. They have personal, itemized deductions of $7,000. To arrive at their taxable income, they reduce their $70,000 adjusted income (combined salary and security income) by the $7,000 of itemized deductions, to $63,000. They further reduce this figure by their $3,900 exemption, to $59,100. Then, to find their tax, the Joneses go to the tax rate schedule (Figure 22).

The first $29,750 of their taxable income is taxed at 15%. The excess over $29,750 ($59,100 − $29,750 = $29,350) is taxed at 28%. The total tax due is therefore $29,750 × 15% = $4,462.50 plus $29,350 × 28% = $8,218 or $12,680.50.

Marginal and Effective Rates

In the example above, Mr. and Mrs. Jones paid a tax of $12,680.50. Their total gross income before deductions and exemptions was $70,000. The Joneses' total tax was approximately 18 percent of their gross income. In effect, they kept 82 cents, after taxes, out of each dollar of gross income they acquired that year. Thus, it can be said that their overall tax rate was 18 percent.

On the other hand, because of the bracket system of imposing tax, the last $29,350 of the Joneses' taxable income was subject to a tax of 28 percent. This is their *marginal* tax rate, the rate at which the next dollar of additional income would be taxed. When you hear the expression, "they are in the 28-percent bracket" it is a reference to the marginal rate.

How, then, should a broker or investor look at tax rates?

Given a specific set of current facts, anyone who knows the tax rates can determine the exact tax. However, in most situations, we are dealing with comparisons and forecasts on income-producing properties. We are determining the type and amount of income a property is expected to produce. Exact tax computations reflect specious accuracy because all of the other figures with which we are dealing are estimates. Thus, we can rely on marginal rates to a degree.

Keep in mind, however, that future rates are always subject to change. Beginning in 1985, the tax brackets in the rate tables are adjusted for inflation; this is called indexing. This potential change in future tax rates must be taken into consideration in forecasting.

33 Percent Maximum Marginal Rate

The highest marginal rate applying to *any* taxable income is 33 percent. This maximum rate is an important consideration in planning for future years.

Sales of Personal Residences

A personal residence is a capital asset. Sale at a gain results in a taxable capital gain. If the sale results in a net loss, the loss is not deductible at all (it does not even offset other capital gains) because losses on disposition of personal items are not deductible.

Although a gain on the sale of a personal residence is a taxable capital gain, there are two exceptions to this rule.

1. Gain is deferred when the proceeds of the sale are reinvested in another personal residence within a prescribed time.
2. Once in a lifetime, $125,000 of gain on the sale of a personal residence is completely tax free if certain conditions are met.

Deferral of the gain. Under this provision of the tax law, on the sale of a principal residence, the taxpayer calculates the gain in the usual way (the excess of the net sale price—sale price minus cost of sale—over the basis). Then, if another principal residence is bought or built within a prescribed time, the cost of the new residence is compared to the *adjusted sale price* of the old residence. If the cost of the new residence is at least equal to the adjusted sale price of the old one, no part of the gain on the sale is taxable. If the cost of the new residence is less than the adjusted sale price of the old, that part of the gain on the sale which is equal to the *excess* of the adjusted sale price over the cost of the new residence is taxed.

The adjusted sale price of the old residence is the amount realized on its sale (sale price minus cost of sale) reduced by costs incurred in repairing or improving the residence to assist in its sale. These costs must be for work done within 90 days before the taxpayer enters into a contract of sale for the old residence. And these costs must be paid no later than 30 days after title to the old residence is passed.

Example

Here are some facts about such a transaction.

Sale price of old residence	$100,000
Sale commissions	−6,000
Amount realized	94,000
Basis of old residence	−60,000
Gain on sale of old residence	$ 34,000
Amount realized on sale of old residence	$ 94,000
Fix-up costs	−8,000
Adjusted sale price of old residence	$ 86,000
Cost of new residence	−81,000
Excess of adjusted sale price of old residence over cost of new residence	$ 5,000

Thus, of the $34,000 gain realized on the sale of the old residence, $5,000 is treated as a capital gain subject to tax. The balance of the gain is not taxed. Although $29,000 of the gain is not taxed, we referred to the gain as being deferred. The basis of the new residence is the cost of the new residence *minus* the gain that was not recognized on the sale of the old residence. Thus, while the new residence cost $81,000, its basis is only $52,000 ($81,000 minus the nontaxed $29,000 gain on the sale of the old residence). That $29,000 may be taxable in the future when the second residence is sold (unless the subsequent sale is also tax free because of another reinvestment in a residence or the once-in-a-lifetime exemption, discussed below).

There are a number of technical requirements that must be met in order to avoid gain under the rules just described.

1. The old residence and the new residence must be the taxpayer's *principal* residence. Thus, a summer home, used occasionally, will not qualify.
2. The purchase of the new residence must occur within a period that starts two years before the sale of the old residence and ends two years after that sale.

The purchase and sale of a cooperative or condominium apartment are treated the same as purchase and sale of a house under these rules.

Exclusion of gain once in a lifetime.   If a personal residence is sold at a gain, the taxpayer can elect to have that gain considered completely tax free. The maximum amount of gain that can escape tax is $125,000. *The election to avoid the tax on the gain can be made only once in a taxpayer's lifetime.* At the time the election is made, the taxpayer or spouse (if the property is held jointly and a joint return is filed) must be at least 55 years old and must have owned and used the property as a principal residence for a total of three years during the five-year period preceding the sale.

If a taxpayer sold a principal residence prior to July 26, 1978, and elected not to have part of the gain taxed (having qualified for exclusion available under the law prior to that date), the taxpayer is allowed to elect the exclusion of up to $125,000 on a subsequent sale if the tests of this new rule are met. However, once this up-to-$125,000 exclusion is used, it cannot be elected again.

This tax-free gain rule is not applied unless the taxpayer elects to take it. If the taxpayer intends to reinvest in another personal residence, the gain may be deferred under the rule discussed previously. If the amount reinvested in the new residence (within two years) is sufficient to wipe out the entire gain on the sale of the old residence, there is no point in electing the once-in-a-lifetime tax-free treatment, and thereby lose the opportunity of using the election in the future.

Alternative Minimum Tax

The alternative minimum tax is imposed in cases where a taxpayer has very high deductions (usually associated with tax shelters). When these items are so substantial as to reduce a very large gross income to a very small taxable income, the alternative minimum tax may be imposed.

As the word "alternative" implies, this tax is imposed *instead of* the regular tax. Therefore, the alternative minimum tax is imposed only if it is greater than the regular tax.

The alternative minimum tax is imposed on alternative minimum taxable income (AMTI). AMTI is calculated as follows:

The starting point is taxable income. If there is a net operating loss deduction involved in arriving at the taxable income, that loss (entered as a positive number) is added to taxable income. To this taxable income is added special adjustments to some of the tax items that were used to calculate taxable income. These include

1. Certain medical and dental expenses,

2. Taxes paid, including state and local income taxes, real estate taxes, and personal property taxes,
3. Personal interest paid and other interest adjustments,
4. Installment sales of certain properties.

The 1986 Act introduced some new adjustments which are added to taxable income. These include

1. Cost recovery on real property placed in service after 1986 to the extent it exceeds cost recovery computed over 40 years straight line,
2. Cost recovery on personal property placed in service after 1986 to the extent cost recovery taken exceeds what would be allowed using the 150% declining balance method switching to the straight line method,
3. Passive losses which have been permitted under the phase-in rules.

For long-term contracts entered into after February 28, 1986, the percentage of completion method must be used in calculating the alternative minimum tax.

After these adjustments are added to taxable income, the balance is added to the total of the taxpayer's tax preference items. Taxpayer preference items are those tax items singled out as potential sources of extraordinary tax savings. This is the major area of vulnerability to the alternative minimum tax. These items include

1. Depreciation (or accelerated cost recovery) exceeding the amount deductible under the straight line method that is deducted on real property placed in service before 1987,
2. Depreciation (or accelerated cost recovery) deducted on leased personal property placed in service prior to 1987, to the extent that it exceeds the deduction allowed under the straight line method,
3. Excess of fair market value of stock acquired under an incentive stock option over the exercise price of the option,
4. Intangible drilling costs in excess of 65% of net income from oil and gas properties,
5. Depletion in excess of basis of property at end of year and
6. Excess reserves for bad debts of financial institutions.

To arrive at the alternative minimum taxable income, the alternative tax net operating loss deduction is subtracted from the sum of taxable income, adjustments and tax preference items. The alternative tax net operating loss deduction is computed in the same manner as an ordinary net operating loss, except that it is reduced by tax preference items and tax items which must be adjusted for AMTI calculations.

The resulting total is then reduced by an exemption amount. The exemption amount is $40,000 on a joint return; $30,000 on a separate return of an unmarried individual; and $20,000 on a separate return of a married individual or on the return of a trust or estate. The amount remaining after the exemption is subtracted is the AMTI which is subject to a flat tax of 21 percent.

While the exemptions have remained the same under the Tax Reform Act of 1986, they are now subject to phase out, in whole or in part, for taxpayers with high alternative minimum taxable incomes. Under this Act, the exemption amounts will be reduced, but not below zero, by $0.25 for each dollar by which the taxpayer's alternative minimum taxable income exceeds

1. $150,000 for married persons filing a joint return
2. $112,500 for single taxpayers
3. $75,000 for married persons filing separately

The effect of this phase out is to increase the alternative minimum tax rate to an effective rate of over 26% for certain individuals.

The 1986 Act introduced some new tax preference items which are to be added to the alternative minimum tax base. These include

1. Tax exempt interest on private activity bonds issued after August 7, 1986, with several exemptions,
2. Untaxed appreciation on charitable contributions allowed as a deduction for regular tax purposes. This applies when the 30% limit on contributions to maximum donee organizations is elected.

The tax due is the greater of the regular tax or the alternative minimum tax. The regular tax does not include recapture of investment tax credits. Therefore, if the regular tax is less than the alternative minimum tax, the tax due will equal the AMT tax plus the amount of tax credit recapture.

A new Minimum Tax Credit (MTC) has been introduced by the 1986 Tax Act. A minimum tax credit will be allowed against the regular tax in future years for prior years' minimum tax liability attributable to the timing of tax preferences. This means that any items of tax preference which were included in computing the alternative minimum tax which were included to prevent the deferral of tax under the regular tax method will give rise to this credit.

Example

To illustrate how the alternative minimum tax works, assume the following financial data for 1988 for William Harrison, an unmarried individual.

Salary	$ 70,000
Net long-term capital gain	35,000
Dividends received	25,000
Interest received	35,000
Investment in real estate partnership	(70,000)
Medical expenses	14,800
Interest paid	20,000
Contributions made	5,000
Taxes paid	15,000
Other business-related expenses	10,000

During the year, Harrison exercised an incentive stock option. The fair market value of the stock exceeded the exercise price by $20,000. Also, included in the $70,000 loss in the real estate partnership was $25,000 of cost recovery in excess of the amount allowable under straight line.

Harrison calculates his regular tax as follows.

Salary		$ 70,000
Long-term capital gain		35,000
Dividends received		25,000
Interest received		35,000
Investment in real estate partnership		(70,000)
Adjusted gross income		$ 95,000
Itemized deductions		
Medical expenses ($14,800 minus 7.5% of $95,000, or $7,125)	$ 7,675	
Interest paid	20,000	
Contributions	5,000	
Taxes paid	15,000	
Other business related deductions*	8,100	
Total itemized deductions	55,775	
Adjusted gross income minus net itemized deductions		39,225
Exemption		1,950
Taxable income		$ 37,275
Regular tax on $37,275		$ 8,117

*$10,000 minus 2% of $95,000 or $1,900

He calculates the alternative minimum tax as follows.

Taxable income		$ 37,275
Adjustments		
Personal exemption	$ 1,950	
Medical expenses ($14,800 minus 10% of adjusted gross income of $95,000)	$ 5,300	
Interest paid	20,000	
Taxes paid	15,000	
Total adjustments		42,250
Taxable income plus adjustments		79,525
Tax preferences		
Excess depreciation		25,000
Fair market value of stock option in excess of exercise price		20,000
Total		45,000
Alternative minimum taxable income		124,525
Minus exemption		30,000
Alternative minimum taxable income (AMTI)		$ 94,525
Alternative minimum tax (21% of AMTI)		$ 19,850

Since Harrison's alternative minimum tax of $19,850 is greater than his regular tax of $8,117, he has to pay the alternative minimum tax instead of the regular tax.

TAXATION OF PARTNERSHIPS

Partnerships and other joint, unincorporated ownership forms (which, for tax purposes, are treated as partnerships) are not separate taxable entities. The partners, be they individuals, corporations or other entities, report their shares of the partnership's ordinary income or loss and capital gains and losses on their own tax returns.

Partnership income or loss passes directly to the partners. While most tax elections (like installment sale treatment) must be made by the partnership rather than by its partners, the partnership is not a tax-paying entity. Types of income and deductions which have a special tax significance retain their special characteristics as they pass through the partnership conduit. Consider the following illustration.

Example

David, Melissa, Michael and Anna form a real estate partnership. At the end of 1988 their partnership records disclose the following items of income and expenses.

Rental income	$25,000
Tax exempt interest income from municipal bonds	10,000
Operating expenses (before cost recovery)	17,000
Cost recovery	5,000
Complete write-off for personal property	2,000
Charitable contributions	1,000

On their personal income tax returns, the partners will report their share of the income and special items of the partnership. Actual distribution of funds is not required from the partnership to the partners; each partner is taxed on the *distributive* share of the profits or losses and special items for the partnership taxable year that ends within the taxable year. The partnership will file an income tax return (actually, an information return) and will pay no tax. The tax returns of the four individual partners will reflect the following items of taxable income and deduction.

			Partnership	Each 25% Partner	
Tax exempt income			$10,000	$2,500	
Rent income		$25,000			
Operating expense	$17,000				
Cost recovery	5,000				
		$22,000			
Net rent income			3,000	$750	income
Complete write-off for					
personal property			2,000	$500	deduction
Contributions			1,000	$250	deduction

Each partner shares in the profits and losses of the partnership as well as in certain special items. Thus, tax-free income passes through to each partner as tax-free income. Partners must report their individual share of the partnership's charitable contributions.

Since each partner picks up a share of the partnership's income or loss, the effect that the cost recovery deduction has on the profit picture is reflected on each partner's own tax return. If, for example, the partnership had cost recovery deductions of $10,000, it would have had a net loss from real estate operations of $2,000 and each partner would have reported a $500 loss on the individual tax return. Any cash flow that the partnership earned could be distributed to the partners without causing any additional tax to them.

A taxpayer may completely write off the cost of personal property up to $10,000 (see Chapter 9). A partnership may write off the cost of personal property up to the limit allowed for that year. Each partner has allocated a proportionate share of that write-off. The amount allocated is added to any other complete write-offs that may have been taken for that year on property acquired or to any other allocations received from other partnerships. The total deductible amount may not exceed the limit applicable to that year.

LIMITED PARTNERSHIPS

The discussion thus far has dealt with general partnerships. Tax rules for limited partnerships are similar to general partnership tax rules.

Under the Tax Reform Act of 1986, income and losses from limited partnerships are considered passive. If the limited partnership generates a tax loss, that loss will be subject to all the limits on the allowance of passive losses. See the section on passive losses for a complete discussion of these limits.

While a partner in a limited partnership is taxed on the portion of the gain from the partnership, the amount of loss which may be deducted is limited to the basis for the partnership interest. This is usually the total amount placed at risk in the business plus that partner's share of partnership earnings and minus partnership losses allocable and earnings withdrawn from the partnership.

In addition, each partner usually may add a share of the partnership liabilities to the basis. This, of course, increases the basis against which losses may be deducted.

For a general partner this rule presents no problem. Since the general partner has unlimited liability, the share of all partnership liabilities increases the general partner's basis. The limited partner, however, does not have unlimited liability; the liability is limited to the investment. Thus, conceptually, the limited partner has no share in the partnership's liabilities.

There is, however, a special rule dealing with nonrecourse liabilities (those liabilities on which the borrower is not personally liable); the creditor can only take the property mortgaged or other property which secures the loan if the loan is not repaid. These liabilities to which the investor is not at risk (has no personal liability) cannot be added to an investor's basis for the purpose of determining deductible loss. This at-risk rule applies to all investors, whether or not they are involved in a partnership.

The IRS has agreed that when a partnership has a nonrecourse loan outstanding, it is not a partnership liability but rather a liability of all the partners, including the limited partners. Hence, in a limited real estate partnership, the nonrecourse mortgage is allocated to both the general and the limited partners, thus increasing each limited partner's basis for the partnership interest. Losses generated by a real estate partnership can be allocated to the limited partnership investors. In determining how much of the allocated loss is deductible, a limited partner includes the share of the partnership's nonrecourse mortgage in the basis.

Major Reasons for Using the Limited Partnership

Before going into a detailed explanation of the limited partnership, it is appropriate to review the principal reasons for using this form of ownership in syndications.

1. The liability of the limited partners (the investors) is limited to the amount of the investment they agree to make. This is similar to the treatment of stockholders in a corporation.
2. There is no double taxation on operating income or gains from sales; the partnership is a mere conduit and is not a tax-paying entity. Profits and capital gains pass directly through to the partners without first being taxed.
3. Losses, as well as profits, pass through to the partners. These losses include tax losses generated by noncash outlays such as cost recovery. Thus, while the partnership may have an actual cash surplus over cash outlay for the year (and the cash may be distributed to the partners), a tax loss is available to the partners to offset their other personal income. The Tax Reform Act of 1986 may severely limit the current deductibility of these losses.

In this respect, the availability of increased basis to partners for their share of the partnership's liabilities becomes important because a partner may not deduct that part of the partnership losses which exceed the basis. While a limited partner's basis for a share of liabilities that are specifically those of the partnership many not be increased, a limited partner may increase the basis by a share of the liabilities that are of a nonrecourse nature (those liabilities secured by liens on the partnership property where the only recourse of the creditor in case of default is to foreclose on the property and where the creditor has no recourse to the other partnership assets or to the assets of any of the partners) but *only if the partnership is involved in investment in real estate.* In all other cases, neither the limited partners nor the general partners may increase their bases by the amounts of the nonrecourse liabilities when measuring the amount of losses they may deduct.

Comparison with Corporation

A corporation offers the shareholders limited liability but it presents the problem of double taxation. The corporation is a tax-paying entity so that income and gains realized by the corporation are subject to corporate income tax and there may be another tax on distribution to the shareholders. Further, because the corporation is a separate entity, losses and deductions of the corporation do not pass through to the shareholders.

The S corporation.   Some of the tax objections to a corporation can be avoided if the corporation elects Subchapter S status. In that case, the shareholders retain the benefits of limited liability, avoid the corporate income tax and obtain the benefit of a pass-through of losses and deductions. However, in an S corporation the liabilities of the corporation or the liens on the corporation's property do not enter into the calculation of the basis of the shareholder's stock as in the case of a limited partnership. Yet, as in the case of a partnership, S corporation shareholders may not deduct losses in excess of their basis.

Assuring Partnership Status

If the limited partnership is chosen as the vehicle for a real estate investment, it is essential that the partnership be classified by the tax law as a partnership rather than what the law calls an association which is taxed as a corporation. (As will be explained, even though a business form is a partnership under state law, it may still be treated as a corporation under the tax law if it has enough corporate attributes.)

Avoiding corporate status.   Treasury Regulations (Reg. Section 301.7701-2(a)(b)) provide four criteria for determining whether an association is a corporation or a partnership. These four criteria are (1) continuity of life, (2) centralized management, (3) transferability of interest and (4) limited liability. The regulations further say that the unincorporated organization will not be considered a corporation unless it has more corporate characteristics than partnership characteristics. Thus, if an organization resembles a corporation as to two of the tests and resembles a partnership as to the other two, the regulations say that the organization is to be classified as a partnership. Let's consider the four criteria in greater detail.

Continuity of life.   This means, that the death or resignation of a member does not cause the dissolution of the organization. In a partnership agreement, provision can be made for the continuation of the venture despite the death or resignation of a general partner. But the regulations say that the partnership agreement does not determine whether continuity exists. If under state law, death or resignation causes a technical dissolution of the partnership, it is dissolved; the partnership does not meet the continuity of life test. Under just about every state law, death or resignation of a general partner *does* create a technical dissolution.

Centralized management.   The regulations take the position that centralized management exists only if management is substantially divorced from ownership. So, in a limited partnership there is centralized management only if the general partner has a 20 percent or less investment interest. The 20 percent, of course, is only a rule of thumb. In any event, most limited partnerships meet the centralized management standard. Usually the limited partners supply the bulk of the investment and the general partners operate the partnership without any voice in management by the limited partners.

Transferability.   The regulations seem to indicate that if there is any substantial restriction on transfer of interest (if the approval of the general partner is needed before a limited partner may transfer interest or the general partner has a right of first refusal) the transferability-of-interest test may not be met. The regulations are not specific here; they simply indicate that a substantial restriction on transferability of the interest may prevent the organization from being considered a corporation.

Limited liability.   The last test is limited liability, a corporate characteristic. An organization has the characteristic of limited liability if there is *no* member who is personally liable for the debts of the organization. In a limited partnership, limited liability would exist if the general partner is a person without substantial assets other than the interest in the partnership and if the general partner is a mere dummy, an agent for the limited partners.

Example

In a major case (*Phillip G. Larson*, 66 TC 159 [1976]) over the status of a limited partnership, the tax court determined that a limited partnership qualified as a partnership because it did not have continuity of life nor did it have limited liability. Of major significance was the IRS announcement that it would follow this case (*Acq., 1979—12 IRB 6*).

There was some question about whether under the California law which applies in this case the partnership would be dissolved in the case of the general partner's bankruptcy. The court found that it would. California law, however, is somewhat different than the Uniform Limited Partnership Act, which most states have adopted. Under the Uniform Limited Partnership Act, death, resignation, bankruptcy, etc. of a general partner *does* dissolve the partnership.

More important, however, was the fact that the general partner in this case did not have substantial assets. As indicated above, the regulations require the general partner to have substantial assets *and* not be a mere dummy. The court pointed specifically to the word and in the regulations. While the condition for not having substantial assets was met, the general partner was *not* a mere dummy. He was not used by the general partners as a screen to conceal their own involvement in the limited partnership. Since *both* requirements of the regulations' definition were not met, the general partner was considered to have unlimited liability. Therefore, the partnership was considered to have unlimited liability.

Since the partnership did not have continuity of interest and did not have limited liability, it lacked two of the four corporate characteristics. Consequently, its status as a partnership was recognized. As indicated above, IRS agreed to follow this court opinion.

Partnership Tax Returns

Although partnerships do not pay income taxes, they are required to file information returns. A penalty is imposed for failure to file a timely partnership return (unless reasonable cause for such failure is shown). The penalty is $50 per month or fraction thereof (not to exceed five months' penalty) that the return is late. The penalty is then multiplied by the number of partners involved during the partnership's taxable year for which the return was due.

The statute of limitations for assessing tax deficiencies on partners and for claiming tax refunds by partners is lengthened beyond the regular limitation in some cases. This extension of the statute of limitations applies only to federally registered partnerships—

those partnerships in which interests were offered for sale in an offering requiring Securities and Exchange Commission (SEC) registration or which are or have been subject to annual reporting requirements of the SEC.

Under the regular statute of limitations, assessment and refund time limitations are generally three years from the time a partner's tax return was due. The due date of the partnership information return is irrelevant for this purpose. For federally registered partnerships, the statute of limitations applied to each partner is four years after the *partnership return* is filed. This longer statute of limitations applies only to partnership items on each partner's personal tax return that arose in taxable years of the partnership beginning after 1978. To repeat, this new statute of limitations rule applies only in the case of federally registered partnerships.

After 1984, if a partner exchanges all or part of the partnership interest and receives amounts attributable to the partnership's unrealized receivables or appreciated inventory, the partnership must file an information return with IRS before January 31 of the year following the transaction. There is a $50 penalty for failure to file each information return. The reason for the information return is to make sure that the partner picks up the amounts allocable to the unrealized receivables or appreciated inventory as ordinary income (other gains on disposition of a partnership interest are treated as capital gains). Additional harsh penalties have been added by the Tax Reform Act of 1986 with respect to tax-shelter partnerships.

INCOME TAX ASPECTS OF CORPORATE OWNERSHIP

The corporation is a separate *legal* and *taxpaying* entity. It has its own tax rate structure applying to ordinary income as follows.

1988 CORPORATE TAX RATES

Taxable Income	Tax Rates
$0 to $50,000	15%
Over $50,000 to $75,000	25%
Over $75,000	34%

If a corporation has taxable income of more than $100,000, it is subject to an additional tax. This additional tax is 5 percent of the taxable income over $100,000, to a maximum taxable income of $335,000. In Congress's view, the tax savings in the first two brackets should apply only to small businesses. So, if a corporation has income in excess of $100,000, Congress wants to deprive it of the tax-rate advantages of the first two brackets.

The effect of the additional 5 percent tax is to remove the benefits of the lower rates. In effect, once a corporation's taxable income exceeds $335,000 it will pay a flat tax of 34 percent on all of its taxable income.

If a real estate corporation has losses, created very often by virtue of large deductions for cost recovery, these tax losses may not be used by the individual owners of the corporation on their own income tax returns. If such property was owned directly by the individuals, however, they may be entitled to use the excess real estate deductions to reduce their taxable income from other sources.

Although the corporation's losses are not available to its stockholders, a corporation having an accumulated deficit and current income tax losses, but also having an available cash flow might be able to make cash distributions to its shareholders that would not be taxable to them. These distributions would not be taxable at all to the extent that they did not exceed the shareholders' bases for their corporate stock. The rule is that a corporation which has *neither* current nor accumulated earnings and profits (a tax concept related to but not exactly the same as taxable income) may make distributions to its shareholders which will not be taxed as dividends. Such distributions are treated as a return of capital and, therefore, are not taxable at all to the extent that they reimburse the corporate shareholder for his investment in the stock of the corporation. Distributions received which exceed the tax basis for the stock are taxable, but as capital gains.

In determining a corporation's earnings and profits, only straight-line cost recovery will be allowed. This does not mean that accelerated cost recovery will not be allowed in determining the taxable income of the corporation; it will be allowed to be used if the corporation is eligible to use it. But straight line will have to be used to find out how much earnings and profits the corporation has in order to determine how distributions to the stockholders are to be taxed. This means that while a corporation may have a loss due to accelerated cost recovery, it may still have earnings and profits for determining whether a distribution to its stockholders is to be taxed as a dividend rather than a return of capital investment (or capital gain where the basis for the stockholder's stock has already been recovered via prior distributions).

Should a real estate corporation realize taxable profits, however, any distribution of such after-tax profits to the shareholders as dividends will be taxed again. These earnings would be taxed first to the corporation and then again to the individuals.

Examples

1. In 1988, X Corporation has taxable income of $10,000. Its tax on that amount is $1,500. It distributes the remaining $8,500 to A, its sole shareholder, as a dividend. A must include the $8,500 as taxable income and pay a second tax.

To some extent this second tax can be avoided by the payment of salaries to the corporation's owners, provided such owners actually perform services and their compensation is reasonable. This payment reduces the income upon which the corporation pays taxes, thus removing these salaries from one layer of taxation and, to that extent, results in a single tax on that salary income.

2. In the preceding example, in which X Corporation had taxable income of $10,000, if A had performed services for the corporation and received a salary of $10,000 (or a salary increase of $10,000), the corporation would have no taxable income since it would get a $10,000 deduction for salaries paid. It would pay no tax but would distribute the entire $10,000 to A as salary. A would include the $10,000 as taxable income.

In this connection, it is important to recognize that if A's salary had been increased to a point at which it is deemed to be unreasonably high, the unreasonable portion would not be deductible. Hence, the unreasonable portion would be treated as if it were a dividend payment to A.

If, even after the deduction of reasonable salaries to the shareholder-employees, the corporation still has taxable profits which it desires to shelter from double taxation by refusing to pay dividends, it may face another corporate tax. Such excess accumulation of earnings, beyond the reasonable needs of the business and in excess of $250,000, which are accumulated to avoid the tax on the shareholders, is subject to an additional tax. This is an annual tax at the rate of 27½ percent of the first $100,000 and 38½ percent of any excess of earnings beyond $100,000 unreasonably accumulated during the year. It is called an accumulated earnings tax.

Example

X Corporation has accumulated earnings of $250,000 on January 1, 1988. During 1988 it earns $50,000 *after all taxes* including federal income taxes.

Unless it can show a reasonable business need for the $300,000 accumulation of earnings or the lack of a purpose to avoid income tax to shareholders, the corporation will be subject to an additional tax of $13,750, 27½ percent of $50,000. If X Corporation pays a dividend of $50,000 to its shareholders, this tax will not be imposed. (This is a simplified version of a very complicated subject. For purposes of illustration certain technical adjustments have been omitted.)

CORPORATE TAX ON TAX PREFERENCES

The 1986 Tax Reform Act made significant changes to the rules relating to alternative minimum tax as it applies to corporations. If a corporation is subject to this alternative tax, it must be added to the corporation's regular tax. Items which trigger this tax in corporations are not the same as for individuals. For corporations, the following preferences are carried over from pre-1987 law.

1. The excess of accelerated depreciation on real property over the useful life or over the holding period, whichever is shorter for pre-1987 property.
2. The excess of accelerated depreciation on personal property subject to a lease over what straight line depreciation would have been.
3. The excess of various types of quick amortization techniques (such as for child care facilities) over what depreciation deductions would have been. Special rules apply to pollution-control facilities installed in tax years beginning after 1982.
4. Depletion deductions in excess of the tax basis for cost depletion. Special rules apply to coal depletion expenses.

The following corporation tax items have been added effective January 1, 1987:

1. Accelerated depreciation on all property (other than transitional property) placed in service after 1986. For real property, the preference will be the excess of acceler-

ated depreciation over depreciation on a 40-year straight-line basis. For personal property, the preference will be the excess of accelerated depreciation over depreciation computed using the 150 percent declining method switching to straight-line;

2. The excess of expensed intangible drilling costs over ten-year amortization or cost depletion to the extent in excess of 65 percent of net oil and gas income (similar to the preference item for individuals);

3. The excess of expensed mining exploration and development costs over that allowable if the costs had been capitalized and amortized ratably over ten years;

4. Tax-exempt interest on nongovernmental purpose bonds issued August 7, 1986, with certain exceptions;

5. Corporations that use the completed contract method of accounting for regular tax purposes must use the percentage of completion method in determining AMTI;

6. Corporations were subject to the proportionate disallowance rule of the installment method in 1987. This rule was imposed by the Tax Reform Act of 1986. It was repealed at the end of 1987.

7. Capital construction funds for shipping companies;

8. The untaxed appreciation on charitable contributions allowed as a deduction for regular tax purposes;

9. One-half of the excess of pre-tax income of the taxpayer over other AMTI (business untaxed reported profits).

The following tax preference items under present law are modified.

1. Special net operating losses will be provided for AMT purposes. Generally, this computation will take into account the difference between the regular tax base and the AMT base and, in no event, will AMT-NOLS be permitted to offset more than 90 percent of AMTI.

2. Only credits generally allowable against the AMT will be refundable credits. The foreign tax credit will not be permitted to offset more than 90 percent of the tentative minimum tax liability.

3. Creates a new minimum tax credit that generally will be allowed as a credit only against the regular tax liability of the taxpayer in subsequent years. The minimum tax credit can be carried forward indefinitely.

Corporations will have to make estimated tax payments with respect to their AMT liability, in addition to their regular tax liability. The AMT rate will be 20 percent of AMTI that exceeds $40,000. The $40,000 exemption will be reduced (not below zero) by 25 percent of the amount by which AMTI exceeds $150,000 of AMTI.

Multiple Corporations

As indicated above, there are three tax brackets for a corporation (with tax rates ranging from 15 to 34 percent). Beyond $75,000 of income, all income is taxable at 34 percent. If taxable income exceeds $100,000 there is an additional 5 percent tax for up to $335,000 of taxable income. In addition, each corporation may accumulate up to $250,000 in earnings and profits without fear of being subject to the 27½ percent and 38½ percent penalty taxes explained above.

Consequently, if a corporate business can be divided into several corporations, each would have its own brackets and each would have its own $250,000 "safe" earnings and profits accumulation. For example, if one corporation had $200,000 in taxable income, $125,000 of its income would be subject to a 34 percent tax plus an additional 5 percent on $100,000 of income in excess of the $100,000 threshold that triggers the 5 percent surcharge. If the same business were divided into four corporations, each would have only $50,000 of taxable income. Each would pay 15 percent tax. Obviously, the total tax paid by the four corporations would be considerably less than the tax on $200,000 earned by one corporation.

To prevent this practice, Congress treats certain groups of corporations (controlled by the same five or fewer persons) as if they were one corporation. Their incomes are combined and they calculate the tax as if the entire income were earned by one corporation. Similarly, this group of corporations as a whole is entitled to a total of $250,000 of "safe" accumulations of earnings and profits.

The S Corporation

It was pointed out above that a corporation is a separate entity for tax purposes and its profits and losses do not pass through to its shareholders (except by way of dividends, which are first taxed on the corporate level). There is one form of corporation, however, that is treated much like a partnership. Its profits and losses *do* pass through to the shareholders without first being subject to a tax on the corporate level. This corporation is the S corporation.

Although the S corporation has been in the tax law since 1958, until 1982 it was not very useful for real estate operations. The reason? It could not have more than 20 percent of its gross receipts in the form of passive income. Passive income included rents (as well as dividends, interest, royalties and capital gains) so that ruled out most real estate businesses.

Under a revision to the S corporation rules enacted in 1982, the passive income restriction no longer applies to taxable years beginning after 1982—unless the corporation had accumulated earnings from years prior to 1983. Thus, new corporations (which automatically have no prior earnings and profits) can elect S corporation treatment and not worry about passive income. (Corporations with pre-1983 accumulated earnings may not have passive income in excess of 25 percent of gross receipts in more than three consecutive years. If they do, they lose their S corporation status. And in the years they do have excess passive income, the corporation itself is subject to a tax. But these corporations can distribute their accumulated earnings and avoid the passive income restriction in the future.)

Passive income in the paragraph above refers to a type of income. It does not discuss how that income is taxed. All income from an S corporation is passed through to its shareholders. This income and losses may or may not be subject to the passive loss rules on the individual shareholder's tax return. If the individual shareholder is not a material participant in the business, the income and losses may be considered passive.

The income and losses of an S corporation pass through to the stockholders in proportion to their holdings (calculated on a daily basis during the year); the corporation itself pays no tax. The losses that pass through to each shareholder are deductible only to the extent of the basis of stock held in the corporation and the basis of any debt owed to the shareholder by the corporation. If the loss allocated exceeds the shareholder's basis, the excess is deferred. It is deductible in a future year in which the shareholder acquires sufficient basis to cover the loss (as would occur with the allocation of profits in a future year).

Corporate capital gains and losses also pass through to the shareholders as capital gains or losses. Specific items that affect a shareholder's tax return, like charitable contributions and tax-exempt interest, pass through to the shareholder in that form.

An S corporation is a regular corporation (for state corporate law purposes) organized in the United States. To become an S corporation for tax purposes, the corporation must elect that status by filing a form with IRS. All the shareholders must consent to this election. An S corporation may not have more than 35 shareholders, none of whom may be a nonresident alien. It may have only one class of stock (but that class of stock may be divided into voting and nonvoting stock). All the shareholders must be individuals, estates, or certain classes of trusts. Furthermore, the corporation may not be part of an affiliated group eligible to file consolidated returns.

Taxation of Corporate Capital Gains

Short-term, long-term and Section 1231 gains and losses for corporations are determined in the same manner as for individuals (see section on individual capital gains earlier in this chapter).

Net Section 1231 gains are included in long-term capital gains and *net* Section 1231 losses are deducted from ordinary income. Long-term gains and losses are aggregated separately, short-term gains and losses are aggregated separately and the results in the two categories are aggregated if one is a gain and the other is a loss. The final results are net short-term and/or long-term gains and losses.

Corporate net short-term capital gains.   These are added to ordinary income in the same manner as for individuals.

Corporate net long-term capital gains.   These are treated in one of two ways (the corporation chooses the method that results in the lower tax).

1. The full amount of the net long-term capital gains is added to ordinary income and taxed at ordinary income rates.
2. The corporate alternative capital gains tax is used. A flat 28 percent rate is applied to the net long-term capital gains. This tax is then added to the corporate tax computed on the ordinary income alone.

The corporate alternative capital gains tax is not the same as the corporate alternative minimum tax. S corporations generally are not subject to the alternative minimum tax. The tax preferences are deemed to belong to the shareholders, and are thus passed through the shareholders. Where significant tax preferences are passed through to the shareholders, the individual shareholders may be subject to alternative minimum tax.

To understand the significance of the two methods, it must be remembered that the first $50,000 of corporate ordinary income is subject to a 15 percent tax and the next $25,000 to a 25 percent tax. The first $75,000 of corporate ordinary income is subject to lower tax rates than the 28 percent flat rate of the alternative tax for corporate capital gains. The alternative tax would not be used if the total corporate income did not exceed $75,000 *after* the capital gains were added.

If, by adding the capital gains to the ordinary income, the total exceeds $75,000, the excess would be taxable at 34 percent, which is greater than the alternative tax on capital gains. At that point, it is necessary to determine whether it is cheaper to use the alternative tax. When ordinary income is very small and the capital gain is relatively large, even though the total exceeds $75,000, it may still be cheaper to avoid the alternative tax because a great part of the capital gain would be subject to ordinary income rates of less than 28 percent.

It is not permissible to add part of the long-term capital gain to the corporation's ordinary income and apply the alternative tax to the other part. The *entire* long-term capital gain must either be added to ordinary income or be subjected to the alternative tax.

Examples

1. In 1988, White Corporation has $10,000 of ordinary income and a long-term capital gain of $5,000. Obviously, it will add the $5,000 to its ordinary income because that $5,000 will be subject to a tax of only 15 percent.

2. In 1988, Black Corporation has ordinary income of $80,000 and a long-term capital gain of $25,000. Again the choice is obvious. It will use the alternative tax of 28 percent for its $25,000 capital gain. Otherwise, $20,000 of the capital gain would be subject to a 34 percent tax and $5,000 to the 34 percent plus a 5 percent added tax.

3. In 1988, Gray Corporation has ordinary income of $15,000 and a long-term capital gain of $40,000. Although, by adding the capital gain to ordinary income, $5,000 of the $55,000 total is subject to a 25 percent tax, it is still cheaper to add the capital gain to the ordinary income.

Corporate net capital losses. Whether the corporation ends up with a net long-term loss, a net short-term loss or both, it cannot deduct any part of that loss against ordinary income of any year.

Net capital losses become carrybacks and carryovers in the form of *short-term* capital losses (regardless of whether they arose as long- or short-term). The loss may be carried back three years and forward five in the following manner.

If the loss arose in 1988, it would first be carried back to 1985. It is then determined whether, if that loss arose as a short-term capital loss in 1985 the corporation's taxable income would have been different. (If the corporation had net capital gains, long- or short-term in 1985, the short-term loss carried back to that year would affect that year's taxable income since part or all of those gains would be offset by the loss. If it had no net long- or short-term capital gains in 1985, the short-term capital loss carried back to 1985 would have no effect on 1985 taxable income.) If the loss carried back to 1985 *does* reduce the 1985 tax, the taxpayer corporation is entitled to a refund.

If the corporation is unable to use all of the carryback loss in 1985, the portion not used is then carried to 1986 and the procedure used for 1985 is repeated.

To the extent the loss is not used in 1986, it is carried to 1987 and again the procedure is repeated.

If there is still an unused capital loss carryback after applying it to the prior three years, it becomes a carryforward to the succeeding five years. Thus, continuing our example, the unused loss would be available as a short-term capital loss in 1989. If there were not enough capital gains in 1989 to absorb the entire carryforward loss, the balance would be carried to 1990 as a short-term capital loss and then to 1991, 1992, and 1993 if necessary. After 1993, if the loss had not been absorbed by offsetting capital gains, it would no longer be available to the corporation for any purpose.

Corporate Dispositions

Once the corporate form has been chosen as the form of ownership, not only are there tax problems during ownership (like nonavailability of corporate losses to offset individual income) but additional tax problems also arise at the time it is decided to dispose of the property.

If the corporation sells the property, the gain or loss will be taxed to the corporate entity. What happens to the after-tax profits on the sale that remain in the corporation? They could be subject to a second tax if distributed to the shareholders. However, some tax relief provisions are available to those who have taken the proper steps to qualify for special corporate liquidations. In other cases, by way of corporate reorganization, tax may be deferred (as is the case of an exchange of like-kind properties) and a shareholder's investment diversified. Again, it is necessary to know the rules and make preparations to qualify. It is important to seek competent counsel when working in the area of corporate taxation.

8
Acquisitions

When an investment in real estate is made, a major decision involves the form of ownership.

If the property is being acquired by a single investor, it may be put in his or her name or may be owned jointly with his or her spouse. Or, the investor may decide it would be better to have the property owned by a corporation even though all the corporate stock would be in the investor's name. Where more than one person will own the property, it may be held in partnership, joint tenancy, tenancy in common or in a corporation. It is also possible to hold property in a trust.

When more than one form of ownership is available, which one should an investor choose? The answer is not simple. It depends on the investor's immediate and long-term goals, current personal tax position, and expected tax position in the future (plus good guesses about the state of the tax law and the economy in the future). No intelligent decision can be made, however, without an understanding of the various forms of ownership and the tax consequences of each.

Another important factor in the acquisition of property is the establishment of *basis*. This is the starting point for the calculation of the important cost recovery (depreciation) deductions and the determination of gain or loss on ultimate disposition of property. Establishing basis depends on the application of the appropriate rule (drawn from a complex network of rules concerning different forms of acquisition). The second part of this chapter is an explanation of the rules of basis and their ramifications.

FORMS AND NATURE OF OWNERSHIP

The basic forms of ownership were discussed in Chapter 2. Following is a summary of the rights inherent in the various forms of ownership.

Individual Ownership

Individual ownership refers to a person owning property in his or her own name. The danger of unlimited liability is often a deterrent to the use of this form of ownership. Where feasible, insurance may reduce or eliminate this risk. The factors which often tip the scales in favor of individual ownership are the income tax rules and the freedom of action it allows in making decisions regarding acquisition, management and disposition of the investment. However, an individual may have only a limited amount of capital available for use in any particular venture. For this reason, a form of ownership, which makes greater sums of capital available, is often preferred.

From a tax viewpoint, an advantage of individual ownership of investment or income-producing real property is the availability of cost recovery deductions which may be available to offset the owner's taxable income from other sources.

Example

> A is unmarried and has net taxable income after deductions and exemptions of $55,300 in 1989. The income tax on this amount is $14,910. If A were to invest in a property which showed a tax loss of $25,000 due to large depreciation deductions, the taxable income would be reduced to $30,300 and the tax would be only $6,660, a savings (and thus an increase in available cash flow) of $8,250.
>
> It would be necessary for A to invest $25,000 in cash to produce a tax loss of that amount. Basis for real estate usually includes any mortgages on the property. So, if an investor could buy a building for $20,000 cash and $80,000 debt, the basis for depreciation of the building would still be $100,000.
>
> Of course, if A had created a corporation and the corporation had purchased the property, the tax loss would not be available for personal tax return use even if A were the sole owner of the corporation. There would be no personal income tax saved for that year. However, A might be able to use an S corporation and claim the loss. (The requirements for qualifying as an S corporation are discussed in Chapter 7.)

Joint Ownership

Joint ownership is a type of concurrent ownership of property by several persons in which each joint owner possesses an undivided interest in the whole property. The joint ownership may be set up with or without a right of survivorship.

There are several types of joint ownership. A tenancy in common is one which does not involve any rights of survivorship. Upon the death of one of the co-owners, the heirs or the estate becomes the owner of those shares.

In a joint tenancy there *is* the right of survivorship. Upon the death of one of the co-owners, those shares pass to the other co-owner or owners. Sometimes this is referred to as a *joint tenancy with right of survivorship*. Generally, no probate proceedings are required to effect the transfer to the surviving joint owners. Where a joint tenancy exists between spouses, it is often called a *tenancy by the entirety*.

Who is entitled to the income from property held in joint ownership depends upon the provisions of law in the state where the property is located. As in the case of individual ownership, the profits or losses of the jointly-owned property pass directly to the owners according to the state laws for picking up income or losses.

Tenancy in common is often preferable to a formal partnership because each owner picks up the income or loss directly, without regard to the co-owners. Each owner can make individual tax elections (accounting method, reinvestment of funds received as condemnation awards, fire insurance and other involuntary conversion proceeds). In a partnership, the partnership files an information return in which each partner's share of income and losses is revealed. Tax elections are made by the partnership and are binding on all partners. If one partner's tax return is examined (perhaps because of nonpartnership items on an individual return), the other partners may find that their returns will be examined too. With tenants in common, this result is less likely.

A problem arises, however, when the jointly-owned property is, in effect, a business (such as an active ownership of rental property where the co-owners also manage the property). In that case, although the legal form of ownership is a tenancy in common or a joint tenancy, for tax purposes the owners will be treated as partners and a partnership tax return will be required.

Since joint ownership is so similar to ownership by a partnership, many of the advantages and disadvantages are identical. However, those forms of joint ownership with rights of survivorship offer the additional advantage of avoiding probate on the death of one of the co-owners. At death, the decedent's interest passes automatically with no need for court proceedings.

If a joint tenancy is not between spouses, for estate tax purposes, the entire value of the joint property could be included in the gross estate of the first joint tenant to die. However, this amount is reduced by the percentage of consideration that was *not* supplied by the deceased joint tenant in acquiring the property.

For property acquired by husband and wife as joint tenants, only half the value of the joint property is included in the deceased spouse's estate regardless of which spouse paid for the property. No formal gift had to have been made.

Community Property

Under the laws of some states, property owned by married individuals is deemed to be property of both of them. Generally, property owned by them prior to their marriage is separate property and property acquired during the marriage is community property. Laws of states applying this type of ownership will vary and, therefore, will not be discussed in detail here. It is important, however, for the real estate broker to know and be able to explain to clients the effect of community property laws if they can be applied.

Federal income taxation of property held in this form of ownership, as in the case of other types of joint ownership, depends on state rules as to who is entitled to the income and who is liable for the expenses.

Partnerships

Partnerships are an important form of real estate ownership. The partnership form of ownership permits the passing through of losses and income directly to the partners. Furthermore, the use of a limited partnership limits the investors' liabilities much in the same manner as the liabilities of corporate shareholders are limited. In real estate limited partnerships nonrecourse loans to the partnership can increase the limited partners' bases for their investments far beyond the amounts of their actual cash investments. This is not true for limited partnerships other than real estate insofar as nonrecourse loans are concerned.

The rules pertaining to limited partnerships are very complex, especially in view of recent IRS actions taken to curb what the government sees as abuses in this area.

Partnerships include all sorts of *unincorporated* businesses owned by more than one individual or entity. In most states, corporations and other partnerships may also be partners in a partnership.

Among the reasons for using a partnership to own investments is the increased availability of capital and skills arising from an association of more than one individual. A group of investors may be able to purchase a larger piece of property than can a single investor and have available a wider range of business skills, including managerial and financial talent.

On the other hand, it may be difficult to arrive at a consensus in making decisions for the group investment. Unless one member is given authority to act, the group may be hamstrung in efforts to act quickly to take advantage of rapidly changing business or market conditions.

Partnerships terminate at the death of a partner in absence of special arrangement to the contrary. Heirs and successors are usually entitled to an accounting for profits, but have no claim on specific partnership assets.

Partner's capital contributions.   As a general rule, no gain or loss is recognized by either the partner or the partnership on contributions of either cash or property. The basis of the partner's interest in the partnership is the amount of money contributed plus that partner's adjusted basis in the property transferred. The partnership assumes the partner's basis in the property transferred.

If property is contributed to a partnership by a partner and no gain or loss is recognized and if the property is transferred to the partnership after March 31, 1984, special rules apply when the partnership disposes of that property.

1. If the partner contributed unrealized receivables, the partnership will realize ordinary income or loss on the disposition of these.

2. If the property was an inventory item in the hands of a partner (property held for sale in the ordinary course of business), the partnership will realize ordinary income or

loss if it disposes of the property during the five-year period beginning on the date the property was contributed to the partnership. This assumes, of course, that in the hands of the partnership, the property is not an inventory item. This could occur when a partner who is a developer transfers buildings to the partnership which the partnership holds for rental income purposes. If the partnership held the property as inventory, it would realize ordinary income in any event even without the new provision of the law.

3. If the contributed property had a built-in capital loss at the time of contribution (its fair market value was lower than the contributing partner's basis for that property), if the partnership realizes a loss on the disposition of the property, the loss will be a capital loss to the extent of the capital loss built into the contribution by the partner. This rule applies to losses occurring during the five-year period beginning on the date of the contribution of the property to the partnership.

In order to prevent inequities from arising between partners when appreciated property with a low tax basis is contributed to the partnership, the law permits the partnership agreement to provide for special allocations among the partners of depreciation, depletion or gain or loss with respect to the property.

However, if the partnership agreement did not make the special allocations, the contributed property was treated as having been purchased from the contributing partner. This meant that depreciation, depletion, gain, or loss arising from the contributed property was allocated among the partners in their general profit and loss-sharing ratios. Congress felt that there was room for abuse when the partnership agreement did not make the special allocations—gain might be allocated to a low-bracket partner, loss to a high-bracket partner. So, for the property transferred to a partnership after March 21, 1984, the special allocations that previously were permitted are now mandatory. IRS issued regulations explaining how these allocations for partnership after May 1, 1986, are to be made. These regulations are extremely comprehensive and should be reviewed before any disproportionate allocation is made. (See IRC Reg § 1.704-1 [b] et seq.)

In the formation of a real estate partnership a problem frequently arises when a promoter-developer receives a partnership capital interest in exchange for services. The IRS regulations take the position that the promoter-developer has received ordinary income to the extent of the fair market value for services. This result might be avoided if the promoter-developer receives a partnership profits interest (the right to share in future partnership income) rather than a capital interest. In this manner, the tax would be postponed until the promoter-developer actually shares in the partnership income. However, the tax court and the Seventh Circuit Court have held that the promoter-developer will be taxed on the value of the income interest *upon receipt* if the profit interest has an ascertainable market value. In the particular case the courts were considering, the promoter's interest was sold three weeks after it was received, so the value was easily established.

To the extent that an acquired interest in partnership capital results in taxable income, that partner's basis is increased by the amount of such income.

Partnership.   Limitation of liability and income tax consequences are determined by the nature of the partnership. A general partnership is one in which all partners share in profits or losses. There is no limitation of liability; partnership liabilities, to the extent they cannot be satisfied out of partnership assets, become claims against the individual partners. The partnership files an income tax return which is merely an information return. It pays no federal income tax. All of the income and deductions of a partnership flow through to the income tax returns of its partners.

A disadvantage of both the individual and general partnership form of ownership is the lack of limited liability. Each of the general partners places not only the investment in the partnership, but all other business investments and personal assets as well, at the risk of the partnership venture. Each partner may be legally responsible for the business actions of *all* of the other partners in their conduct of the partnership business.

Another form of partnership is the limited partnership which is composed of both limited and general partners. The limited partnership must have at least one general partner. It is the general partner or partners who usually conduct the business of the limited partnership. A limited partner may not participate in active management without risking limited partner status and may then incur liabilities as a general partner. Each limited partner's liability is restricted to the amount that has been personally invested. Claims against the partnership which exceed partnership assets may be collected only from the general partners.

Possibly the greatest advantage of the limited partnership is that it enables larger amounts of capital to be invested than a single investor could raise alone, while providing limited liability for the bulk of its investors without the formalities and often onerous tax burdens of the corporate form. Disadvantages of both the general and limited partnership may arise when their size becomes too great for efficient operation. Further, some complications may occur with respect to the transferability of the interests of retiring and deceased partners.

Syndicates

A syndicate is a combination of investors. It may be set up in the form of a corporation, a general partnership or a limited partnership.

Trusts

A trust is a legal arrangement sometimes used as a vehicle to hold property. It is not itself a legal entity; the trust *itself* does not own property. Rather, the trustee, sometimes called the fiduciary, is the legal owner of all trust property. The trustee holds it for the benefit of someone else, the beneficiary. The person who sets up the trust arrangement by giving the property to the trustee to hold in trust is the grantor, settlor or creator.

Every trust must have one or more beneficiaries. They may get income from the trust and sometimes deductions. A beneficiary can have an income interest or a remainder interest in the trust property. If it is an income interest, the beneficiary has a right to some or all of the trust's income as it is earned. If it is a remainder interest, the beneficiary has a right to receive trust property at the termination of the trust.

Trusts are often used to separate the burdens of management from the benefits of ownership. For example, if a person wants to make a gift of income-producing real estate to someone who would not be capable or qualified to manage it (or to hire competent management) and to decide if and when the property should be sold or exchanged, the gift might be made to someone whose business acumen is respected by the donor, *in trust*, for the benefit of the intended beneficiary. The trustee will manage, or hire someone to manage, the property and make decisions about changing investments, while the beneficiary will receive the net income after expenses.

Some trusts are created by will; others are created by written instruments or deeds during the lifetime of the grantor, as *inter vivos* (or lifetime) gifts. An advantage of the trust as a gift vehicle is that it can be used as an arrangement for testamentary disposition of assets to be set into operation during the life of the grantor. Thus, the operation of the testamentary plan can be viewed during the grantor's lifetime. If the right to revoke or to change the trust has been retained, the grantor may alter the testamentary plan if it does not work as anticipated.

Since the powers of the trustee are set forth in the trust instrument and in the law of a particular state, the trust form is sometimes a little cumbersome in its operation. As with a corporation which may act only through its authorized officers, persons dealing with a trust should always be sure that the trustee is authorized to perform whatever acts are claimed to be within the scope of the trustee's authority. Consequently, copies of the trust instrument may often be required.

Federal income taxation of trusts is a rather complex topic. The income of a trust is sometimes taxed to the trustee who pays the tax from the funds held in trust and not from personal funds. Sometimes it is taxed to the beneficiary and sometimes part of the trust income is taxed to the beneficiary and part to the trustee. In other instances trust income may even be taxed to the grantor. The determining factors are the terms of the trust instrument and sometimes local law. If the grantor gives property to a trustee but retains too much control over the property, then trust income will be taxed to the grantor.

When the trust instrument requires all the income to be distributed to the beneficiary, that beneficiary will usually be taxed on all the trust's income, even if it has not actually been received. If, however, the trustee has discretion to distribute income to the beneficiary or hold it in the trust, the beneficiary is taxed only on the amount actually received and the trustee pays the tax on the income that is retained. A subsequent distribution of the income on which the trust was taxed may require an additional tax to be paid by the beneficiary. This is called the throw-back rule. Under this rule, if the trust paid less tax on the income it retained than the beneficiary would have paid had the income been distributed instead of retained, the difference in tax is paid upon ultimate distribution of the retained income.

Cost recovery on property held by a trustee is generally allocated among the beneficiaries and the trustee in the same proportion in which the income is allocated. If local law or the trust instrument provides that the trustee must set aside a reserve for cost recovery, the cost recovery deduction is allocated to the trustee to the extent of trust income retained. These principles are illustrated as follows.

Examples

1. A sets up a trust with T as the trustee and B as the beneficiary. According to the trust instrument, all the trust income is required to be distributed to B each year. In 1989, trust income consists of rent income of $7,000. Deductible expenses before cost recovery amount to $4,000 and cost recovery amounts to $1,000.

Here, the net income before cost recovery is $3,000:$7,000 income minus $4,000 expenses. B is entitled to receive this $3,000. Were it not for the special rule allocating the cost recovery deduction to the person getting the income, B would have to pay tax on $3,000 and the deduction for cost recovery would go to the trustee, who is the legal owner of the property. Since the trustee has no income, the deduction would be wasted. Applying the special rule requires the allocation of all the cost recovery deduction to the person getting the income. Therefore, B is required to pay tax on only $2,000:$3,000 net income less $1,000 cost recovery deduction. T, as trustee, has zero taxable income and pays no tax.

2. If, using the facts above, T had been required by the trust instrument or by local law to set aside $1,000 as a reserve for cost recovery, then B would only be entitled to receive $2,000:$3,000 income less $1,000 set aside for cost recovery. B would pay tax on that $2,000. T, as trustee, would have been allowed $1,000 of income allocated to him and also $1,000 of cost recovery expense, for a net result of zero taxable income and no tax due.

3. If the tax instrument had given T the right to withhold or distribute income to B and local law imposed no requirement as to a reserve for cost recovery, the result for tax purposes would depend on how much, if any, of the trust income was actually distributed to B. If T distributed half of the net income to B, then B would be entitled to half the cost recovery deduction. The final result, using the same facts, would be that the $2,000 would be taxable, half ($1,000) to B and the other half ($1,000) to T.

Corporate Ownership

A corporation is a legal entity chartered by a state. (Each state has its own procedural rules that must be followed to create a corporation.) The corporation is a fictional person with certain unusual attributes such as unlimited life. It is a form of ownership particularly suited for use when large amounts of capital are required or desirable. A corporation enables centralized management to direct the investments of numerous owners called shareholders. The owners elect a board of directors which is responsible for the overall policy decisions of the corporation. It, in turn, appoints officers who are in charge of the corporation's everyday activities.

The corporate form is also available for small groups of owners—even one owner. Because it is a legal person, the corporation is often used to shield its owners from the dangers of business liabilities or reversals.

Example

X Corporation is owned solely by A, who buys an old house at 2 Main Street in her own name. X Corporation buys the house next door at 4 Main Street. Some children injure themselves on the broken steps leading up to each house.

The children who were injured on the step leading to 2 Main, owned by A, can sue for everything. This includes personal assets as well as investments in business, other corporations and the like. The children injured on the steps of 4 Main, owned by the corporation, can only sue the corporation for all of *its* assets. They cannot get any of A's other assets (unless there was personal negligence), neither personal assets nor other business assets, *even though A is the sole owner of X Corporation.*

This attribute of limited liability, the risking of only those assets held by the corporation and not the shareholders' other assets, is the most frequently cited reason for using a corporation to hold property. For example, should the income from a parcel of real estate diminish so that its expenses exceed its income, the mortgage holder may not recover from the individual stockholders of the corporation, unless, of course, they have given personal guarantees of payment.

The fact that the stockholders are often called upon to guarantee personally the debts of a corporation should not be overlooked. Many times, for example, a corporation is formed upon advice to limit liability. Yet, under practical circumstances, the stockholders must personally endorse the notes. As a result, the limitation of liability is not really available, and the formation of the corporation may have deprived the individuals of the tax losses that would have been available to them to offset their personal income or result in double taxation.

It should also be remembered that the limitation of liability may be accomplished by means others than incorporating. A person holding property as an individual may arrange for the mortgage debt to apply only to the mortgaged property and not to any personal or other business assets. Similarly, liability insurance may be taken out to cover possible injuries to people caused by defects in the premises. The cost of such insurance might be prohibitive, especially in a run-down or slum area.

Another aspect of the corporate form is its continuity. The life of a corporation may be set up as perpetual or for a fixed term. Death of one or more shareholders does not require that corporate activity be stilled. Corporate life goes on with the estate or beneficiaries of the deceased as shareholders.

Another advantage is that management can be vested in representatives of the owners who usually operate without unanimous consent, thus permitting widely split ownership (including minors) without making management decisions cumbersome or impractical.

S corporations.   Certain corporations may take on special status for tax purposes. Provisions for this special status are found in Subchapter S of the Internal Revenue Code. These corporations have all of the nontax aspects of regular corporations, but if certain requirements are met, their income may escape taxation at the corporate level. Instead, the profits and losses are passed through to the stockholders who then report their proportionate shares of the corporate profits or losses on their individual tax returns. The rules applying to S corporations are explained in Chapter 7.

S corporations versus limited partnerships.   Inasmuch as profits and losses of S corporations pass through to the shareholders in the same manner as from partnerships, might it not be preferable to use the S corporation rather than the limited partnership for real estate ventures? This might be especially true since passive income from rents no longer disqualifies an S corporation (see Chapter 7).

On the surface there may seem to be an advantage to using the S corporation since it has limited liability. (Of course, if there are more than 35 investors, the S corporation cannot be used because an S corporation may not have more than 35 shareholders.) However, there is one major difference between the S corporation and the limited partnership that makes the limited partnership more attractive for real estate ventures.

Losses that pass through from a real estate limited partnership to the limited partners are deductible by those partners to the extent of their bases for their partnership interests. In the real estate limited partnership (not any other kind), each partner has allocated to the basis for partnership interest the appropriate ratable share of the limited partnership's nonrecourse liabilities (generally the mortgages on the real estate held by the partnership). This allocation increases the partner's basis and allows the absorption of a larger loss than could be absorbed were the basis limited to the partner's cash investment. In an S corporation, on the other hand, the corporation's liabilities do *not* increase each shareholder's basis or the S corporation stock owned. The corporation's loss allocable to the shareholder is deductible only to the extent of the basis for stock and for any loans the stockholder has made to the corporation. Thus, all other things being equal, the limited partner can deduct a larger loss than the S corporation shareholder.

Summary of Ownership Forms

The preceding discussion has considered in some detail the various forms of entities which may be owners of real estate. Figure 23 is a summary of the types of ownership entities and their various legal and tax attributes.

DETERMINING BASIS OF PROPERTY

Basis is a tax term that describes a taxpayer's investment in property. It is an important term to the real estate investor and broker because, for income tax purposes, it is an essential ingredient in determining gain or loss on the sale or exchange of property and the amount of cost recovery deductions allowable.

The concept of basis is required for tax purposes because cost is not an adequate reflection of the owner's investment in the property. Cost is generally the starting point for determining basis, but subsequent events call for adjustments to that cost. The owner may have made improvements to the property, or may deduct cost recovery. Each of these actions adjusts the investment.

Even the concept of cost is not clear-cut. If an individual pays $100,000 cash for a property and the property is not subject to any liens, clearly the cost is $100,000. But suppose only $20,000 is paid and the balance of $80,000 is borrowed by mortgaging the property. What is the cost? Or suppose the property is acquired by inheritance, gift or exchange. What is the cost?

The term basis, therefore, is an all-encompassing term. It reflects the various possibilities of acquisition and the changing level of the investment during ownership as a result of improvements, cost recovery, partial disposition and any other pertinent events.

How the original basis, referred to as unadjusted basis, is subsequently altered to arrive at adjusted basis is explained below. The adjusted basis is used in determining gain or loss on the sale or exchange of property. How basis affects the calculation of cost recovery deductions is described in Chapter 9.

Owner	Limited Liability	Authorized to Act	Taxable Status	Ownership Transferability
Corporation	Yes	Officers, employees, and agents	Pays tax	Easily assigned, sold, or divided
S Corporation	Yes	Officers, employees, and agents	Conduit	Easily assigned, sold, or divided
Individual	No	The individual agents, and employees	Pays tax	Easily assigned or sold but less divisible (spouse may have to join)
General Partnership	No	Partners, agents, and employees	Conduit	Partners must join or authorize
Limited Partnership	No, for general partners	General partners, agents, and employees	Conduit	General partners must join or authorize; no inchoate interest in spouse
	Yes, for limited partners			Limited partnership interest may be assigned or sold; no inchoate interest in spouse
Trusts	Yes	Trustee, agents, and employees	May pay tax, be a conduit, or be a combination of both	Easy assignment or sale depends on powers granted to trustee
Joint Ownership	No	Joint owners, agents, and employees	Conduit (each owner pays tax on his share)	May be assigned or sold; may require spouse to join

Figure 23. Ownership Forms

Allocation of Basis

When property is acquired, it may consist of several elements like land, building (referred to as improvements), and personal property (furniture, fixtures). One overall basis for the entire property may be the starting point when a lump sum is paid for the entire property. This basis must then be allocated among the various items making up the entire property. Allocation is required because cost recovery cannot be taken on land, and the building's basis may be subject to one cost recovery schedule while the personal property may be subject to another schedule.

It is possible for a purchase contract to specify how much is being paid for the land and how much for each of the improvements and the personal property. These figures are usually accepted for income tax purposes if they were arrived at by unrelated parties in an "arm's length" transaction. If, however, the sale is between related parties, such an allocation in the contract may be given less credence.

In the absence of a bona fide allocation in the contract, an allocation must be made on the basis of relative market values. Land and improvement values may be determined through competent appraisals.

Example

A parcel consisting of land and building is purchased for a total of $100,000. An appraiser estimates the allocation of the purchase price in proportion to the relative market values of the land and building. The appraisal indicates that 80 percent of the value of the parcel is due to the value of the building. Therefore, $80,000 of the total $100,000 purchase price will be allocated to the building and will be subject to cost recovery. The remaining $20,000 will be allocated to the land and will not be subject to cost recovery.

In the absence of fair market value appraisals, it is possible to allocate between land and improvement based on the relative assessed values of land and building for real estate ad valorem tax purposes. This procedure is one of the methods frequently used, but might not be acceptable to IRS.

Example

An individual buys a parcel consisting of land and building and pays $100,000 for the parcel; the purchase contract contains no allocation of price between land and building. Assessed values on the real estate tax bills of the land and building are $10,000 and $40,000 respectively. The ratio of the value of the land to the entire value of the parcel is 20 percent— $10,000 on $50,000. Therefore, in allocating basis to the building for the purpose of computing cost recovery deductions, $80,000 (80 percent of $100,000) will be allocated to the building, and $20,000 of the $100,000 purchase price will be allocated to the land.

Basis of Purchased Property

It is clear that if property is purchased for $50,000, the basis of that property is $50,000. It makes no difference whether the buyer pays all cash or meets part of the purchase obligation by giving a mortgage or by assuming (or taking subject to) an existing mortgage. The basis is still $50,000.

Examples

     1. The purchase of a parcel is $50,000. There is an existing mortgage on the property of $20,000. The buyer pays $30,000 cash and assumes the existing mortgage. The buyer's basis is $50,000.

     2. Assume the same facts as above, but the buyer pays only $20,000 in cash and, in addition to assuming the $20,000 existing mortgage, gives the seller a second mortgage of $10,000. The basis is still $50,000.

     3. Again, the same facts, but there is no existing mortgage on the property. The buyer secures a $30,000 mortgage from a bank on the property purchased. The $30,000 received from the bank plus $20,000 of personal funds is used to make the purchase. Again, the basis is $50,000.

The previous examples deal with real estate; the same rules apply whether or not the buyer is personally liable on the mortgage obligation. However, if the property is other than real estate and the loan is a nonrecourse loan—the lender's only recourse on default is to the property (no recourse to the buyer)—the buyer's "at risk" basis does not include the amount of the nonrecourse loan for purposes of claiming losses. In 1986, the at risk rules were extended to include real estate. However, so many exceptions were carved out of the rules that the new at risk provisions essentially apply to seller-carried nonrecourse notes and institutional nonrecourse financing of the lending institution's own real estate properties. The nonrecourse nature of the debt has no effect on the basis of the property for cost recovery purposes. Cost recovery deductions on the property may be computed in accordance with a basis that includes the nonrecourse loan.

If the buyer pays a fee to secure the mortgage, that fee is not deductible for tax purposes. Nor can the buyer add the fee to the basis of the property being acquired according to the IRS. However, assuming that the property is either income-producing or business property, the buyer can deduct the fee by amortizing it over the life of the mortgage. For example, if a $300 fee was paid to secure a 15-year mortgage, $20 per year can be deducted.

Property can be purchased with commodities other than cash or mortgage. For example, other assets—a car, boat, diamond ring, stocks or bonds—might be use as part payment. The fair market value of the assets used to make the purchase are part of the purchase price. If, however, the basis of an asset the buyer uses as part of the purchase price is less than that asset's market value, the difference between basis and market value will be treated as a gain realized by the buyer.

Example

A buys land for $35,000 and pays for it by transferring AT&T stock which has a market value of $35,000 to the seller. The basis for the land is $35,000. However, if the basis for the AT&T stock was $20,000, A would have realized a $15,000 gain on the transaction.

Exchange

In the above example, A gave up stock in part payment for the property. Suppose, however, A exchanged *like-kind* property—for example, land held for investment or an apartment building held for investment. In that case, even though the basis of the land given up was less than the market value of the building A received, the gain would not be taxable if A received nothing else but the building.

When property is exchanged for other like-kind property, there may be no immediate tax consequences; that is, the transaction may be tax free. In such cases, the basis of the property received is computed by reference to the basis of the property given up. But because the net debt against the property may change (as in the case in which the mortgage on the property given up is larger or smaller than the mortgage on the property received) and because cash or other unlike-kind property may be given or received to equalize the equities of the properties given up and received in the exchange, the basis of the property acquired may be higher or lower than the basis of the property given up. Further, the allocation of the basis between land and building on the acquired property may be made in proportions other than the proportions applied to the property given up. A discussion of the effect of exchanges on basis is included in Chapter 11.

Basis of Inherited Property

The basis of the property to the person inheriting is the property's market value at the date of death of the person from whom it was inherited.

An estate required to file a Federal Estate Tax Return may, however, choose an alternate valuation date to value the property in the estate. Instead of using the date-of-death values, it may elect to use values six months after the date of death. If property is *sold* or *distributed* to the beneficiaries *during* the six months after death and the alternate valuation date option is chosen, the alternate valuation date for the property is the date of sale or distribution. If the alternate valuation date is used, the basis of the property inherited becomes the value on the alternate valuation date, the value at which it was included on the Federal Estate Tax Return.

At one time, it was permissible to use the alternative valuation date value whether that value was greater or smaller than the value at the date of death. Often the greater value was used to step up the basis to increase depreciation and reduce gains on the subsequent disposition of inherited property; the added estate tax stemming from the increased value of the property was far less than the income tax saved via the step-up in basis.

Now, however, for estates of decedents dying after July 18, 1984, the alternate valuation date value may be used *only if* that will *decrease* the value of the decedent's gross estate *and* decrease the amount of estate tax. Thus, the alternate valuation date value may not be used if the property increased in value after the decedent's death.

Basis of Jointly-Held Property

When two or more people hold property jointly, they may be holding the property as tenants in common or as joint tenants.

Tenants in common. If property was held by the parties involved as tenants in common, each has his or her own interest in the property and his or her own basis. If one of the tenants in common should die, the basis of that tenant's interest to whomever inherits it is determined by the basis rules concerning inherited property (discussed previously).

Joint tenancy. When property is held in joint tenancy, upon the death of one of the joint tenants his or her interest in the property automatically passes to the surviving joint tenant or tenants. For example, if property is held by husband and wife as joint tenants (in some states, this type of ownership is referred to as a tenancy by the entirety), when the wife dies her interest automatically passes to her husband.

How does the surviving joint tenant figure the basis following the death of the other tenant(s)? The answer depends upon several factors: who paid for the property, how state law allocates income among the joint tenants and whether the joint tenants were husband and wife.

Indeed, most joint tenancies are between husband and wife. Special rules apply in determining the basis of the property in the hands of the surviving spouse when the other spouse dies.

To understand the implications of the special rules for joint tenancies of husband and wife, we shall first look at the general rules applying to basis when one joint tenant dies and the surviving tenant was not the spouse of the decedent. These rules are best explained by a series of examples.

Examples

1. A brother and sister purchase a tract of land for $10,000 in 1972, each contributing $5,000. They took ownership as joint tenants. In 1974, they spent $60,000 for an improvement (again, sharing the cost equally). They added another improvement in 1979 at a total cost of $12,000. The brother died on January 1, 1984. Depreciation claimed on the $60,000 improvement totaled $7,500. Depreciation on the $12,000 improvement totaled $1,200. The market value of the property at the brother's death was $180,000.

The federal estate tax rules (with an exception discussed below) require that the full value of jointly-held property be included in the estate of the first joint tenant to die unless it can be shown that the surviving joint tenant contributed his or her own funds toward the acquisition of the property. To the extent that the survivor did contribute to the property's acquisition, the value of the property included in the deceased joint tenant's estate is reduced.

In this example, the sister actually contributed half of the funds used to acquire the property and make the two improvements. So, only half of the property's value—$90,000—is taxed in the brother's estate. The sister's basis for the entire property, after the brother's death, is computed on the premise that she owned half from the beginning and inherited the other half.

Cost of land	$10,000
Cost of 1974 improvement	60,000
Cost of 1979 improvement	12,000
Total cost	$82,000
Depreciation allowed	8,700
Adjusted basis of property at time of brother's death in 1984	$73,300

Sister's basis for half-interest (half of $73,300)	36,650
Value of brother's half-interest included in his estate	90,000
Basis of property to sister after brother's death on entire property	$126,650

2. Assume the same facts of Example 1 with one exception: the brother paid for everything with his own funds although he took title to the property jointly with his sister. Assume further that under state law income from the property would be allocated equally between joint tenants.

In these circumstances, when the brother dies, the *entire* $180,000 value of the property would be included in his estate. Hence, the sister's basis for the property would then become $180,000 less half the depreciation allowed on the property during the brother's lifetime. So, the sister's basis for the property after her brother's death becomes $175,650 ($180,000 minus $4,350, which is half the $8,700 depreciation previously deducted).

The date-of-death value has to be reduced by half the depreciation because the sister was entitled to half the income from the property during the brother's lifetime. Hence, she should be charged with half the depreciation deduction allowable in computing her basis.

3. Assume the same facts as in Example 2 except that under state law, during the brother's life all of the income was allocated to him. In that case, the entire $180,000 value at the death becomes the sister's basis for the property.

The general rules outlined in these examples must be modified in the case of a joint tenancy between husband and wife when one of them dies after 1982. In that case, only half the value of the joint property at the time of death (or applicable alternate valuation date) is included in the estate. Hence, the surviving spouse's basis of the property is the amount included in the estate plus half of the basis of the joint property at the time of death.

Example

Assume, in a husband-wife joint tenancy, the same figures as in the brother-sister examples. The husband died in April, 1984. Assume, too, that the husband paid for all the property and the improvements.

Under the rules applying to husband-wife joint tenancies, half the value of the property ($90,000) is included in the husband's estate. Assume that under state law all of the income was allocable to the husband. As a result, the wife's basis for the property after the husband's death is $126,650—$90,000 included in the husband's estate plus $36,650 (half the $73,300 basis of the property at the time of the husband's death).

Compare this result with the $180,000 basis the sister had in Example 3 (when the full $180,000 was included in the brother's estate). While, under the husband-wife rule, the estate tax is cut (since only $90,000 instead of $180,00 is included in the husband's estate), the wife's basis is also severely cut. On subsequent sale of the property, she may incur a substantial taxable gain. Since the estate tax law now allows for an unlimited marital deduction, estate tax could be avoided even if the entire $180,000 were included in the husband's estate.

Thus, although the special provision for property held jointly by husband and wife was intended to be a relief provision (for estate tax purposes), it may not turn out to be that valuable because it may impose a greater income tax cost to the surviving spouse. It is possible that many tax advisors may now question the advisability of spouses holding property as joint tenants.

Community property.   Suppose property is held by husband and wife in a community property state and constitutes community property so that each spouse is deemed to own half the property. When the husband dies, half the property will be included in his estate. Nevertheless, the date-of-death value of the entire property will become the wife's basis for the property after her husband's death (assuming, of course, that she inherits the husband's half of the property).

Example

Using the figures in our examples above, upon the husband's death and the wife's inheriting his half of the community property, her basis for the property will be $180,000.

Life Estates

Sometimes an individual acquires a life estate in a piece of property.

Example

When Brown died, he left an apartment house he owned to his wife for her life; at her death the property was to go to their son. During her life, Mrs. Brown has a life estate in the property. On her death the property automatically goes to the son.

During her life, Mrs. Brown is entitled to collect the rents from the property. In computing her net taxable income from the property she is, of course, entitled to take a deduction for depreciation. How does she compute her basis for depreciation?

The tax law provides that Mrs. Brown's basis is the basis she would use if she owned the property outright. For example, if the property, when included in Brown's estate, had a value of $100,000, that $100,000 becomes Mrs. Brown's basis. If $80,000 of that $100,000 is allocable to the building, she uses $80,000 as her basis for figuring her depreciation.

On Mrs. Brown's death, her son gets the property outright. What is his basis for the property? The son's basis is the basis remaining to Mrs. Brown after deducting the depreciation she took during her lifetime.

If Mrs. Brown sells her life interest, she has to use a zero basis for determining gain. Hence, everything she receives is gain. If, however, Mrs. Brown's son joins with Mrs. Brown in the sale so that the purchaser is acquiring the entire property and not only Mrs. Brown's life interest, the remaining basis of the property (the original basis to Mrs. Brown minus the depreciation deductions she took) is divided between Mrs. Brown and her son according to factors in an IRS table (based on Mrs. Brown's life expectancy). Mrs. Brown and her son figure their respective gain or loss by comparing the basis assigned to each by the table with the share of the total sale price received by each.

What about the purchaser? If Mrs. Brown's life estate is the only purchase, the purchaser is entitled to keep the property only as along as Mrs. Brown lives. In that case, the entire cost of the life estate can be deducted over the life expectancy of Mrs. Brown. In other words, the cost of the entire property is divided by the number of years Mrs. Brown is expected to live and he deducts that amount each year. (If $100,000 was paid for the property and Mrs. Brown's life expectancy is ten years, $10,000 a year is deducted for ten years. If Mrs. Brown dies before the $100,000 has been fully deducted, the remaining amount of the cost is deducted in the year Mrs. Brown dies. If she lives longer than ten years, no further deductions can be taken after the $100,000 cost is recovered.)

Basis of Property Received as a Gift

When property is received as a gift, the general rule is that the donee (the one who receives the gift) takes as the basis the adjusted basis to the donor of the property at the time of the gift. If the donor had to pay a gift tax on the gift, the donee adds to this basis the amount of the gift tax. However, in no case can the donee's basis be increased beyond the market value of the property at the time of the gift.

Example

A mother has an adjusted basis of $25,000 for a property. The market value of the property is $30,000. She makes a gift of the property to her son and pays a gift tax of $2,000. Her son's basis of the property is $25,000 (mother's adjusted basis) plus the $2,000 gift tax for a total of $27,000

If the gift tax had been $6,000, the son's basis would be $30,000. Although the total of the mother's basis plus the gift tax is $31,000, the son's basis cannot be increased above the market value at the time of the gift.

Property sold at a loss.   Special basis rules apply if the donee sells at a loss property received as a gift.

1. If at the time of the gift the market value of the property is higher than the donor's adjusted basis, the general rule explained above applies.

Example

Green makes a gift of land to his daughter. Green's basis was $10,000. The fair market value of the property at the time of the gift was $12,000. No gift tax was payable. Green's daughter subsequently sell the land for $8,000. Her basis is $10,000 (donor's basis, that is, the general rule) and her loss is $2,000.

2. If at the time of the gift the market value is less than the donor's basis, the donee's basis for the purpose of computing the loss is the property's market value.

Example

Brown makes a gift of land to his brother. Brown's basis is $20,000. Fair market value at the time of the gift is $18,000. No gift tax is due. Later, the brother sells the land for $15,000. Although the general rule is that the donee takes the donor's basis, the exception applies here. Since the market value was less than the value at the time of the gift and the property was subsequently sold at a loss, the donee takes as his basis the lower value. Hence, his loss on the sale of $15,000 is $3,000.

3. In some cases the special basis rule creates a situation in which neither gain nor loss can be computed on the subsequent sale; therefore, no gain or loss is reported.

Example

Smith makes a gift of land to her mother. The fair market value at the time of the gift is $5,000; Smith's basis is $10,000. No gift tax is due. Smith's mother later sells the land for $7,000. If Smith's mother uses the donor's basis ($10,000) as her basis, there would be a loss of $3,000. But when there is a loss and at the time of the gift the fair market value is less than the donor's basis, the donee is supposed to use the fair market value as her basis. However, if Smith's mother uses the fair market value of $5,000 as her basis, the subsequent sale results in a $2,000 gain. Since basis for gain is always the donor's basis, in a case like this neither gain nor loss can be computed; so, Smith's mother has no gain or loss to report.

Note that the rule dealing with gift property sold at a loss does not apply to gifts between spouses made after July 18, 1984. As to those gifts, the donee takes as basis for the gift property the basis it had in the hands of the donor immediately before the gift, regardless of whether the property is subsequently sold by the donee at a gain or a loss.

Basis of Property Received for Services Rendered

If the person who is rendering services is paid with property instead of with cash, the market value of the property received is ordinary income to the recipient since that is compensation for services. The fair market value of services becomes the basis for the property received.

Example

A real estate broker receives her fee in property rather than cash. She is entitled to a $5,000 commission but instead receives a parcel of land worth $5,000. She has commission income of $5,000 and the basis of the land to her is $5,000.

Suppose, instead of receiving land worth $5,000, she receives improved property worth $25,000 subject to a mortgage of $20,000. She still has $5,000 of income since her compensation is the net value of the property received. But her basis for the property is $25,000. The situation is the same as if the broker purchased the parcel for $25,000, using her $5,000 fee as down payment, and financed the balance with a mortgage.

Basis of Property Acquired through Foreclosure or Other Repossession

When the seller receives a purchase money mortgage as part of the purchase price, the property may be subsequently repossessed on default of the buyer. If that happens, the seller must determine whether a gain or loss has been realized on the repossession by applying special tax rules regarding repossessions. The tax rules differ, depending upon whether the property repossessed is real estate or personal property.

Repossession of real property. When the seller repossesses the property in full or partial satisfaction of the purchase money mortgage, the tax rules provide that no loss may be recognized for tax purposes on the transaction and that gain, if any, will be taxed only to a limited extent. (Losses are not recognized in these situations on the theory that the seller really has not lost anything since the property is back in the seller's possession.)

On the other hand, the seller may have a gain. This would be the case if the seller received some money (and possibly also some other property such as marketable securities) and then regained the property as well. For income tax purposes, the seller has realized a gain equal to the amount of the cash and the other property received less that portion of the gain on the original transaction already reported.

Note that in the examples that follow distinction is made between situations in which installment sale reporting was used and those in which it was not. Under the installment sale provisions of a tax law enacted in October, 1980, all sales calling for payments in a year subsequent to the year of sale qualify as installment sales, unless the taxpayer elects not to have a sale treated as an installment sale (see Chapter 10). Hence, there will be very few situations in which installment sale reporting will not have been used when the sale took place in 1980 or thereafter. Nevertheless, some repossessions may involve sales in which the installment method of reporting was not used, either because the taxpayer elected to avoid installment sale reporting or because the original sale occurred prior to the effective date of the 1980 tax law change. The distinctions between cases where installment reporting was used and those where it was not used are set forth in the following examples.

Example

Barton sold a parcel of real estate, which had a basis of $15,000, for $25,000. He received $5,000 cash and a purchase money mortgage for $20,000, bearing 12 percent interest, payable $4,000 annually commencing the next year. The following year he received the $4,000 payment (plus interest) but the year after that the buyer defaulted and Barton repossessed the property.

Assuming that Barton had treated the sale as an installment sale (discussed in Chapter 10), the tax treatment would be as follows.

Total cash received ($5,000 + $4,000)	$9,000
Reduced by gain previously reported	
Gross profit = $10,000 ($25,000 minus $15,000)	
Gross profit percentage = 40% ($10,000/$25,000)	
40% of $9,000 collected	3,600
Gain on repossession	$5,400

Had the installment method not been used and if the entire $10,000 gain had been reported in the year of sale, there would have been no gain on Barton's repossession.

But this is not the complete story. There is another tax rule, applied in some cases, which limits the gain on repossession. This limitation is the amount of gain on the original sale of the property reduced by the total of the gain already reported plus the cost of repossession.

Example

Using the same facts as above and assuming the costs of repossession amount to $1,200, the limitation on gain would be computed this way.

Original gain		$10,000
($25,000 sale price less $15,000 adjusted basis)		
Reduced by		
Gain previously reported	$3,600	
Repossession costs	1,200	4,800
Limitation		$ 5,200

The limitation would apply to reduce the gain of $5,400 to $5,200.

Tax basis of repossessed real estate. The basis of the repossessed property is the basis of the unpaid obligation plus the sum of any gain required to be recognized by the rules above and the costs (if any) of repossession. This rule applies even if there is no gain and even if there is a loss which cannot be deducted for tax purposes. Its effect in situations where there is a nonrecognized loss on repossession is to add that loss to basis.

Example

Continuing the above illustration to compute the basis of the property repossessed, we find the following.

Face value of the unpaid notes ($20,000 − $4,000)	$16,000
Less unreported gain (40% of $16,000)	6,400
Basis of unpaid notes	9,600
Plus gain on repossession	5,200
Repossession costs	1,200
Basis of repossessed property	$16,000

Had the installment method not been used and had the entire $10,000 gain been reported in the year of sale, the loss on repossession would have been $1,000 ($9,000 total cash received minus $10,000 gain already reported). While this $1,000 loss would not be deductible under the rules relating to repossessions of real estate, it would, in effect, be added to the basis of the property by the application of the previous rule. The computation would be as follows.

Face value of notes (same as basis of unpaid notes)	$16,000
Plus repossession costs	1,200
Basis of repossessed property	$17,200

Notice that the new basis of the property can be said to consist of the following items.

Original basis		$15,000
Loss on repossession (not recognized)		
Gain tax on sale	$10,000	
Less cash received	9,000	1,000
Repossession costs		1,200
New basis of repossessed property		$17,200

Situations involving principal residence.   The rules discussed above regarding repossessed real estate may not apply if the realty consists of the seller's principal residence. The law provides that when the principal residence is sold and all or part of the gain is not recognized either under the special rule for persons age 55 or older or the special rule involving reinvestment of the proceeds in a new residence within a prescribed time, then if the seller resells the repossessed residence within one year of repossession, all the rules discussed previously will not apply. In those cases, the resale is treated as part of the original sale, ignoring the repossession. However, if the resale is not made within the year following repossession, all of the rules with respect to gains on repossessions and new basis will apply.

Basis of repossessed personal property.   The seller of realty will often sell personal property such as furniture within the building. Rules regarding repossessions of such property differ from those involving the real estate.

The market value of the property repossessed becomes the basis of that property after repossession because gain or loss on the repossession is recognized at the time of the repossession.

Gain or loss is the difference between the market value of the property retaken and the seller's basis for the notes canceled or adjusted, when necessary, for other amounts realized or other costs incurred in connection with the repossession. As in the case of real property discussed above, the seller's basis of defaulted notes is their face minus any unreported profit with respect to them.

Examples

1. In connection with the sale of her hotel, Green also sells the furniture for $15,000. Her adjusted basis for the furniture at the time of the sale was $10,000. She received $3,000 in the year of the sale and a note for $12,000, payable $1,000 per month, with 10 percent interest, beginning in the year following the sale. Green reports the gain using the installment method. Since her profit on the sale is $5,000 or one-third of the selling price, she will report one-third of each collection of cash as gain at the time she collects it.

After making three payments, the buyer defaulted and Green repossessed the furniture. Fair market value of the furniture at the time of the repossession was $14,000 and expense of repossession was $1,000. Green computes her gain on the repossession as follows.

Market value of the repossessed furniture		$14,000
Basis of buyer's notes		
Original face amount	$12,000	
Less three payments made	3,000	
Face value of unpaid notes	$ 9,000	
Less unrealized profit (one-third of $9,000)	3,000	
Basis of unpaid notes		6,000
Gain on repossession		8,000
Less repossession costs		1,000
Taxable gain on repossession		$ 7,000

If the installment method of reporting had not been used and the entire gain or loss on the sale was reported in the year of the sale, the basis of the notes or other obligations would be their face amount.

2. Assume that in the previous example the entire gain was reported in the year of sale. That gain was $5,000 and the basis of the unpaid notes was $12,000, their face amount. Subsequently, $3,000 of notes were paid off. So, at the time of repossession, the remaining unpaid notes had a face amount (and a basis) of $9,000. Since the fair market value of the repossessed furniture was $14,000, there was a gain on the repossession of $4,000, computed as follows.

Market value of repossessed furniture		$14,000
Less basis of unpaid notes (equal to face)	$9,000	
Repossession costs	1,000	10,000
Gain on repossession		$ 4,000

In either of the two examples, the basis of the repossessed furniture would be $14,000, its market value at time of repossession.

Nature of the gain on repossession. If the original sale was reported as an installment sale, any gain or recognized loss on the repossession of either real property or personal property (under the rules spelled out above) is treated the same way as the gain on the installment sale. That means if the sale resulted in capital gain under the installment method, the gain on the repossession is also a capital gain. If part of the gain on a transaction reported as an installment sale constitutes cost recovery recapture (explained in Chapter 10), all of this cost recovery recapture is subject to tax in the year of sale.

Basis of Property Foreclosed by Third Party Mortgagees

When money is borrowed from someone other than the seller of property and a mortgage or other pledge is given, the creditor is sometimes called a third party mortgagee. Rules with respect to defaults on such obligations are similar to those applicable to repossessions of personal property.

When mortgaged or pledged property is sold and the net proceeds are less than the amount of the debt, the difference, to the extent it is uncollectible, is deductible as a bad debt loss by the mortgagee. Business bad debts are fully deductible as ordinary losses; however, nonbusiness bad debts are treated as short-term capital losses.

The buyer of such property at a foreclosure sale, if the buyer is not the creditor, has a basis for the property equal to the amount paid.

Example

Shaw holds a $25,000 mortgage note which is in default. A foreclosure sale is held at which Smith buys the property for $15,000. Expenses of the sale amount to $1,000. The results are as follows: Shaw had a bad debt loss of $11,000 because that is the difference between his basis for the note ($25,000) and the net proceeds ($15,000 less $1,000) he received. Smith has a basis of $15,000 for the property because that is what he paid for it.

When the person buying the property at the foreclosure sale is also the creditor, it is possible for another gain or loss to occur. That is so because the purchase of the property with the defaulted obligation is considered a taxable transaction. Therefore, if the value of the property differs from the creditor's basis, the creditor will have a gain or a loss. The basis for the property will be its market value at the time it was acquired.

Example

  If, in the preceding illustration, Shaw had bid in the foreclosure sale and had purchased the property for $10,000 (assuming that its fair market value was still $15,000) he would have had a loss on the note of $16,000 ($25,000 less net proceeds of $9,000). He also would have had a capital gain of $5,000 on the exchange of note for property (market value of the property less the $10,000 bid price).

  Conversely, if he had bid in the property at $20,000, $5,000 in excess of its fair market value, he would have had a loss on the note of $6,000 ($25,000 less net proceeds of $19,000) and a capital loss of the $5,000 excess on the exchange. Whether this is long- or short-term depends on the holding period of the mortgage note.

  Finally, if he bought the property at $15,000, its fair market value, his bad debt loss on the note, as in the case when the property was bought by Smith, would be $11,000 and he would have no gain on the exchange.

  His basis for the property would be $15,000, its fair market value, in all three cases.

Note that the bid price is generally deemed to be the fair market value. Treasury regulations make that assumption unless there is clear evidence to the contrary. Further, the Uniform Commercial Code, which applies in most states, requires that bids be made in good faith and presumes that the bid price is the fair market value. Hence, there would be very few situations where there could be a difference between the price at which the property was bid in and its fair market value. Consequently, the first two situations in the example above are not very likely to occur.

Basis of Property after Involuntary Conversions

Sometimes property is converted from one kind to another against the wishes of its owner. Such a conversion occurs when property is condemned by a governmental authority and replaced by cash or state bonds. Similarly, a fire, flood or a natural disaster such as a storm could destroy property which is subsequently replaced with cash by an insurance company. When such an event occurs, a gain may result; that is, the proceeds received exceed the basis of the property destroyed.

  When there is a gain as a result of an involuntary conversion, the taxpayer has the option of postponing the taxability of the gain. To achieve such a postponement, the taxpayer must (within a specified time) purchase replacement property which costs as much as or more than the net proceeds received from the conversion. Generally, the replacement has to occur by the end of the second year after the year in which any part of the gain is realized. For example, if any part of the gain is realized any time during 1988, the replacement has to occur by the end of 1990. However, if the real property is used in the taxpayer's trade or business, the taxpayer has until three years after the close of the taxable year in which the conversion occurred to acquire replacement property. If a longer period is needed to make the replacement, IRS, at the request of the taxpayer, has the authority to grant an extension.

If the replacement property costs less than the net proceeds received from the involuntary conversion, the gain is taxed to the extent of the unexpended portion.

Example

> Long's factory was condemned by the state and she was awarded $160,000 for the property for which she had a basis of $150,000. Therefore, she realized a $10,000 gain from the condemnation. If she purchases another factory for $160,000 or more within the specified replacement period, she may elect to postpone the tax on her gain. If her new factory costs only $158,000, she would be required to pay tax on $2,000, the part of the gain not reinvested in the new factory.

Note that the *cost* of the new property must equal the proceeds of the involuntary conversion to avoid the tax on the gain. However, cost does not necessarily mean cash. Hence, while a $150,000 cash award on condemnation might have been received, taxable gain is avoided if $150,000 is reinvested in the replacement property within the required time, even if, for example, $20,000 cash is paid and a mortgage of $130,000 is given.

The replacement property has to be property similar or related in service and use to the property which it replaces. That means, says IRS, that it must be functionally the same as the property it replaces; it must serve the same use.

There is an important exception to this rule for real estate, however. This exception applies when real property used in a trade or business or held for production of income or for investment is involuntarily converted as a result of its seizure, requisition or condemnation or is sold because the authorities have indicated their intention to seize the property. (This exception would therefore not apply where the involuntary conversion is a result of a fire loss.)

When the exception applies, the replacement property can be of like kind—that is, any other real property used in the taxpayer's trade or business or held for the production of income or for investment. In other words, it makes no difference that the replacement property is not similar or related in service or use to the property converted. And the property that was given up or the property that was acquired can be either improved or unimproved real property.

Basis of replacement property. When replacement property is acquired and an election is made to have the tax postponed on the gain on the involuntary conversion of the old property, the basis of the new (replacement) property must be reduced by the amount of gain which has not been taxed.

Example

> In the prior example, assume Long invests $162,000 in a new factory property within the required time. She elects not to report any part of the gain since she has reinvested at least the entire $160,000 proceeds. Her basis for the new factory is $152,000, computed as follows:

Amount paid for new factory	$162,000
Less gain realized on condemnation but not reported for tax purposes	10,000
Basis of new factory	$152,000

If Long had invested only $156,000 in the new factory, she would have been taxed on $4,000 of the $10,000 gain on the condemnation; $6,000 of the $10,000 gain would be nontaxable. She has to reduce the nontaxable portion of the gain by the $4,000 difference between the $160,000 proceeds from the condemnation and the $156,000 reinvested in the new factory. In that case, the basis of her new factory would be $150,000, computed as follows:

Amount paid for new factory	$156,000
Less gain realized on condemnation but not reported for tax purposes	6,000
Basis of new factory	$150,000

Basis of Property Acquired through Exercise of Options

Often, prior to the acquisition of real property, the buyer first obtains an option.

Example

Jones pays $1,000 for a three-month option to acquire a property at $15,000. Within the three months, he exercises his option, paying the $15,000 for the property. His basis of the property acquired is $16,000—the $15,000 purchase price plus the $1,000 he paid for the option.

If he lets the three-month period expire without exercising the option, he has a $1,000 loss. The nature of the loss is the same as the kind of loss he would have had if he had sold the property (on which he had the option) at a loss.

Basis of Property Converted from Personal Residence to Income-Producing Property

If property has not been used in a trade or business or has not been held for the production of income, such as a former residence which is being converted into rental property, a different rule applies for basis computation. In that case, the basis for computing depreciation is the lower of (1) the property's adjusted basis or (2) the market value of the property. Both of these factors should be determined at the date of the conversion to income-producing status.

Example

Debra bought her personal residence in 1984 for $39,000. In 1989, she moves to an apartment and rents her house to Finch. At the time of the rental, the house is worth only $30,000. Debra's basis for it is still the $39,000 she paid; there have been no adjustments (she was not permitted to deduct depreciation on a personal residence).

For the purpose of computing depreciation to reduce Debra's taxable rental income reportable on her 1989 income tax return, the basis to be used for the entire property is

$30,000, the lower figure. (An allocation must then be made between land and improvements.)

ADJUSTMENTS TO BASIS

After the initial, unadjusted basis is determined under the rules we have been discussing, certain adjustments must be made to arrive at *adjusted* basis. Adjustments can take the form of additions to as well as reductions of the initial, unadjusted basis.

Addition to Basis

The cost of improvements to the property increases the basis. As a rule of thumb (and this is IRS' position), improvements which have a useful life of more than one year are added to basis.

Capital improvements must be distinguished from repairs and operating expenses. Repairs and operating costs, as well as improvements with a useful life of one year or less, are current deductions and have no effect on the basis at all. (See Chapter 9 for a discussion of repairs versus capital improvements.)

Capitalized Carrying Charges, Interest and Taxes

The lax law give owners of real estate, in certain instances, the option to deduct or capitalize interest, taxes and carrying charges. If the owner elects to capitalize these items, they are added to the basis. If the owner elects to deduct them, these items have no effect on the basis.

In the case of unimproved and unproductive property, the owner can elect to capitalize annual real estate taxes, interest on a mortgage or other loan and other carrying charges. The election is effective only for the year for which it is made. A new election may be made each year as long as the property remains unimproved and unproductive.

Example

Smith owns land which is both unimproved and unproductive for two years. In the third year the land is leased to a department store which uses it as a parking lot. Smith could elect in either or both of the first two years to capitalize taxes, interest and carrying charges. However, in the third year, he could not elect to capitalize those expenses because the property was no longer unproductive in that year.

In the case of real property, whether improved or unimproved, productive or unproductive, the owner may elect to capitalize interest on a loan, taxes measured by the compensation paid for work on construction and development (Social Security taxes, for example), state sales and use taxes paid on materials used in construction or development and other necessary expenditures. These expenses may be capitalized whether the property is improved or unimproved or productive or unproductive but only for such expenses paid or incurred up to the time the development or improvement is completed. Any or all of the taxes or carrying charges for each development or construction project may be capitalized. But once an election is made to capitalize a particular type of tax or carrying charge for a particular project, that type of expenditure must continue to be capitalized until the project is completed.

There is one important exception in this area. Interest and real estate taxes incurred during the time a building or improvement is under construction *must* be capitalized; the owner does not have the option of deducting these expenditures. This rule applies to property other than low-income housing and property that is not to be held in a trade or business or in an activity conducted for profit (e.g., a personal residence). Corporations used to be exempt from this rule as to residential real estate. However, for construction begun after March 15, 1984, in taxable years beginning after 1984, corporations are subject to capitalization of construction period interest and taxes on residential real estate (other than low income housing). When interest and taxes are required to be capitalized, these items are written off (amortized) over the useful life of the property.

The Tax Reform Act of 1986 made changes in the treatment of construction period interest and other *soft costs* that will have a significant effect upon the rate of return on newly constructed property.

> Interest on a debt must be capitalized if the debt is incurred or continued to finance the construction, building, installation, manufacture, development, or improvement of real or tangible personal property that is produced by the taxpayer and that has
>
> 1. An estimated production period exceeding two years
> 2. An estimated production period exceeding one year and a cost exceeding $1 million
> 3. A long useful life.

> Note that a long life property includes any real estate or any other property that has a class life of 20 years or more under class-life guidelines.

> Interest on construction loans will be capitalized as part of the construction costs, and thus recovered over the economical life of the improvements (27.5 or 31.5 years).

> The new rules apply to individuals, partnerships, C and S corporations, estates and trusts. Flow-through entities like partnerships and S corporations will first apply the capitalization rules at the entity level and then at the beneficiary level.

> The uniform capitalization rules generally apply to costs and interest paid or incurred after December 31, 1986. Self-constructed assets where substantial construction occurred prior to March 1, 1986, are not subject to the new rules. Construction of an asset which began after February 28, 1986, comes under the transitional rule (in 1, above) if it is an integral part of an integrated facility on which construction began before March 1, 1986.

On the sale of property, real estate taxes for the current real property tax year are apportioned between seller and buyer. To the extent that the buyer pays taxes allocable to the seller and other prior years' taxes that had been assessed on the property while owned by the seller, they are added to the purchaser's basis of the property.

The costs of purchase commissions, legal fees for perfecting or defending title to the property and title insurance are all items added to the basis of the property.

When property is sold, the cost of selling it (such as broker's commissions) reduces the gain on the sale or increases the loss. The expenses of sale are not separate deductions against ordinary income (unless the seller is a dealer).

Reduction of Basis

Cost recovery.   The major item which reduces basis is the cost recovery allowed or allowable during the time the property was held. Thus, if for some reason the property owner deducts less cost recovery than the amount allowed, the basis must still be reduced by the amount of the cost recovery that was *allowable*. Conversely, if the owner deducted more cost recovery than the amount allowed, the basis is reduced by the actual cost recovery deducted (as long as the cost recovery deducted reduced the owner's tax liability in the year it was deducted).

Reduction of basis when there is a partial divestiture of property. When property is acquired, it is necessary to make an allocation of basis between land and building. But subsequently, suppose part of the land is sold. Or, perhaps, part is taken by condemnation. How is the basis of the land allocated between the part that is disposed of and the part that is retained? Treasury regulations are not too helpful in this area. They require only that an equitable apportionment be made.

If the property was bought on a square-foot basis to begin with or for a single purpose and each part of the land has the same value as each other part, a square-foot approach can be used in determining the basis of the portion disposed of and the portion retained.

Example

> A 20,000 square-foot parcel of land is bought for $20,000 and a building is erected on half of the land at a cost of $100,000. Immediately the other half of the land is sold. The basis of the sold land would be $10,000 (half the basis of the total land), and the basis of the other half of the property would be $110,000 (the $10,0000 basis of the remaining land plus the $100,000 cost of the building).

However, all things are not always equal and a portion of the property (due to favorable frontage, for example, or lack of access to the other portion of the land) may be worth more or less than another portion. In that case, allocation of the basis to the various portions of the land in relation to their relative market values would be in order.

Example

> In one tax case, a 10-acre tract of land was acquired for the purpose of developing a shopping center. Later the plans fell through and a portion of the land was sold. IRS argued that the basis should be allocated to the land on a square-foot basis because the entire land was

acquired for a single purpose, to erect a shopping center. However, the portion of the land sold, considerably less than 40 percent of the total acreage, was determined by the court to be the most valuable portion of the land because it fronted on two busy streets and was worth about 40 percent of the total value of the land. Hence, 40 percent of the basis was allocated to the portion of the land sold. Subsequently, the IRS announced that it would go along with that decision.

Undivided interests. If the owner of a tract of land sells an undivided interest in the entire land, rather than a specific portion of it, the same portion of the basis is allocated to the property sold as is allocated to the portion that the owner has given up in terms of the undivided interest.

Example

If land cost Smith $100,000 and he sells Jones a 25 percent undivided interest in the entire tract, Smith will allocate $25,000 (25 percent of the basis of the entire tract to him) to the interest he sold to Jones. Consequently, if Jones paid $40,000 for his 25 percent undivided interest, Smith would have a $15,000 gain.

Parcels acquired at different times. If several parcels of land are acquired at different times at different prices, although they are contiguous and thus form one tract of land, the basis for each parcel is considered separately. Upon subsequent disposition, gain or loss on the parcel disposed of is computed separately by comparing the basis for that parcel with the respective portion of the sale price allocated to that parcel.

Casualty losses. If property is partially destroyed by fire, storm or other casualty, the owner may be entitled to a casualty loss deduction. The casualty loss is the difference between the value of the property immediately before and immediately after the casualty (but not more than the adjusted basis at the time of the casualty) reduced by any insurance recovery. (For nonbusiness casualties, the first $100 of each casualty loss is not deductible. Furthermore, the total of all such casualty losses in one year (after reducing each loss by $100) is deductible only to the extent it exceeds 10 percent of adjusted gross income.) The amount of the insurance proceeds received plus any casualty loss deducted reduce the basis of the property.

Example

Horne owned land and building used in her business for which she had originally paid $40,000, having allocated $35,000 to the building and $5,000 to the land. After it was purchased, Horne built an addition to the building at a cost of $10,000. On October 1, 1988, the building was completely destroyed by fire. Up to the time of the fire Horne had been allowed cost recovery deductions totaling $23,000. Horne sold what salvage she could recover for $1,300 and collected $19,700 insurance. She also deducted a $1,000 casualty loss on her 1988 tax return. She spent $19,000 of the insurance proceeds to restore the building. The restoration was completed by the end of 1988. The adjusted basis of her property on January 1, 1989 is computed as follows:

	Land	Building
Original cost or property	$5,000	$35,000
Addition to building		10,000
		45,000
Less cost recovery		23,000
Basis before casualty	5,000	22,000
Less		
casualty loss deduction $ 1,000		
insurance proceeds 19,700		
salvage proceeds 1,300		22,000
Basis after casualty	5,000	none
Add cost of restoring building		$19,000
Basis on January 1, 1989	$5,000	$19,000

Easements. If the property owner receives payments for the grant of an easement on the property, the amount received for the easement reduces the basis of the property.

9
Operations

The investor's return from a real estate investment consists both of the income produced from operating the property and the profit on its ultimate disposition. In both instances, however, there are income tax consequences with which to reckon. These consequences, of course, affect the net return on the investment.

In this chapter, we will be concerned with the impact of the tax rules on the income from operations of real estate—basically, the investor's return in terms of rental income and the impact of the tax rules on the cash flow from the property.

NATURE OF INCOME FROM OPERATIONS

Typically, the real estate investor receives a current return from the property in the form of rent. This rent is ordinary income. However, since rental income is classified as income from a trade or business, only the net income (after deducting ordinary and necessary business expenses) is subject to taxation. It is possible that after deducting all ordinary and necessary business expenses from the gross rental income, the result will be a taxable loss. As explained earlier, such a loss may be used to reduce the investor's other taxable income.

Deductible Items

The ordinary and necessary business expenses that the real estate owner may deduct in reducing gross rental income to net taxable income (or loss) are utility costs, management and maintenance salaries and wages, real estate taxes, repair and maintenance costs, interest and cost recovery.

In some instances, interest, taxes and carrying charges may be capitalized (at the taxpayer's election). Thus, they are not deductible as current expense but, instead, become part of basis.

Cash Flow

Any examination of the tax aspects of real estate operations must necessarily include a consideration of the cash flow from the investment. At the end of this chapter there are several illustrations which show how the application of the tax laws to the income from operations affects the investor's cash flow.

Repairs or Improvements

Sometimes it is difficult to distinguish between a repair and a capital improvement. There are probably more than 1,000 tax cases on the subject. Typically, the courts and IRS say that each case must be decided on the basis of its own particular facts and circumstances, a statement that offers no practical guide to anyone trying to distinguish between a repair and an improvement.

As a general rule an improvement is either an *addition* to the property (with a useful life of more than one year) or something that *prolongs* the useful life of the property. A repair is something more in the way of maintenance, the effect of which merely maintains but does not increase the useful life of the property.

THE INTEREST DEDUCTION

A major item of deduction for most real estate investors is interest expense. The Tax Reform Act of 1986 changed the rules with respect to the deductibility of interest expense. It effectively created five categories of interest expense (see Figure 24). Two of these categories of interest are related to business interest expense. The remaining three categories relate to personal interest expense. Interest paid or incurred to acquire or carry securities yielding tax-exempt interest income (for example to buy or carry municipal bonds the interest income of which is exempt from federal income taxes), is not tax deductible.

There are two additional problem areas that affect the deductibility of interest. One concerns the prepayment of interest. The other involves the rules governing excess investment interest, under which a portion of the interest expense may not be deductible in the year paid or incurred.

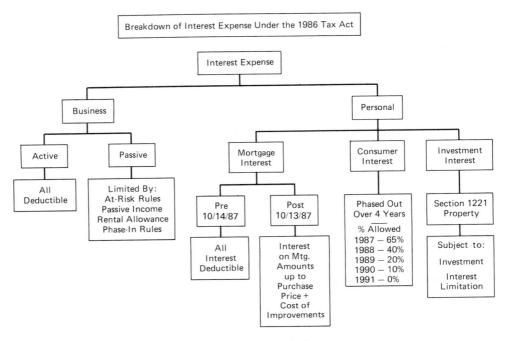

Figure 24

Prepaid Interest

There was a time when as much as five years' interest paid in advance by a cash basis taxpayer was deductible when paid. This is no longer the law. Interest paid or accrued is deductible only insofar as it covers a time period contained within the taxable year in question.

Example

> If Green, a cash basis taxpayer, pays $1,500 in interest on January 1, 1988, to cover the period from January 1, 1988 through March 31, 1989, he can deduct only $1,200 in 1988. (The $1,500 paid was for a 15-month period, or $100 a month.) So, Green can deduct the $1,200 covering the 12 months of 1988. The $300 balance would be deductible in 1989.

An exception to the above rule involves mortgage *points* paid in advance. They are deductible when paid, but only if the mortgage is on the taxpayer's principal residence and the amount paid is consistent with the points charged on similar transactions in that market area.

Excess Investment Interest

Part of an individual's interest expense (this rule does not apply to corporations) may be disallowed as a current interest deduction if it constitutes excess investment interest.

Excess investment interest is defined as the amount by which the individual's investment interest expense exceeds the net investment income.

Example

If investment interest expenses total $45,000 and investment income is $15,000 only $15,000 of the $45,000 would be deductible ($15,000 investment income). The $30,000 difference between the $45,000 investment interest expense and the $15,000 which was deductible is the amount of the excess investment interest not deductible in the current year. The full amount of the disallowed investment interest expense may be carried over and deducted in subsequent years (subject to the limitations on investment interest deductions in those years).

Investment interest expense must first be determined. The law says that investment interest expense means "interest paid or accrued on indebtedness incurred or continued to purchase or carry property *held for investment*" (emphasis added). For short sales of personal property made after July 18, 1984, deductible expenses in connection with the short sale are treated as investment interest paid. Specifically excluded from investment interest expense is interest on indebtedness incurred or continued in the construction of property to be used in a trade or business.

Net investment income.   Net investment income is investment income reduced by investment expenses. Investment income is made up of interest, dividends, rents, royalties and net short- and long-term capital gains from investment property.

Investment expenses are real and personal property taxes, bad debts, amortizable bond premiums, expenses for production of income on investment property, and depletion. Of course, these expenses have to be connected directly with the production of investment income.

SPECIAL DEDUCTION RULES FOR VACATION HOMES

It has become fairly common for owners of second homes and vacation homes to rent these facilities to others for part of the year. The question repeatedly has arisen concerning how much the owner may deduct as expenses because income is earned from the property. After many disputes arose between taxpayers and IRS, Congress enacted a special set of rules which set forth certain limitations on deductions relating to vacation homes.

Under these rules, a vacation home can be a house, apartment, condominium, house trailer, or boat. It also can be something like a garage that relates to the use of the dwelling unit. A vacation home is "personally used" if, for any part of the day, it is used by the taxpayer or a relative, an individual who uses it under a reciprocal arrangement or any other individual who is not charged a fair rental.

The rules enacted by Congress provide that

1. If the house is not rented at all during the year, the owner may deduct the interest on the mortgage, local property taxes and casualty losses in excess of $100 plus 10 percent of adjusted gross income.

2. If the house is rented for fewer than 15 days, and the owner personally uses the house sometime during the year, no deduction for rental-related expenses (cost recovery, maintenance, utilities) is permitted. However, mortgage interest, property taxes and casualty losses in excess of $100 plus 10 percent of adjusted gross income are still fully deductible. Any rental income the owner receives is *not* treated as taxable income.

3. If the owner's vacation home is rented for fewer than 15 days and is not personally used by the owner at all, or if it is rented for more than 14 days and the owner uses it personally for fewer than 15 days or 10 percent of the total rental days, whichever is greater, all or part of the rental-related expenses may be deductible.

To deduct these expenses in full, the owner must show that the rental of the vacation home is a profit-making activity. The intent to make a profit is presumed if, during any two years of a period of five consecutive years, the gross rental income exceeds the rental-related deductions. If the owner cannot satisfy this objective test, the intent to make a profit may still be demonstrated by other evidence. If the property owner cannot show the rental activity is for profit, the deductions allocable to the rental are deductible. However, they are deductible only to the extent that gross rental income exceeds the total of interest, property taxes and casualty losses in excess of $100 plus 10 percent of adjusted gross income.

Actually, there are three levels of deductions. First, mortgage interest, taxes and allowable casualty losses are deducted in full. Then, other rental-related expenses except cost recovery are allowed to the extent rental income exceeds the first category of expenses. Finally, cost recovery is allowed to the extent gross rental exceeds these two categories of deductions.

4. If the vacation home is rented for more than 14 days and the owner personally uses it for more than 14 days or more than 10 percent of the days it is rented, the following rules apply. Mortgage interest, property taxes and casualty losses in excess of $100 plus 10 percent of adjusted gross income are deductible in full. Other expenses attributable to the rental use of the home are deductible only to the extent rental income exceeds the interest, property taxes and allowable casualty losses *allocable* to rental use.

To determine the interest, property taxes and casualty losses allocable to rental use of the vacation home, multiply those expenses by a fraction, the numerator of which is the days of rental use, and the denominator of which is total days used.

Example

During the year, a taxpayer rents her vacation home for three months and personally uses it for one month. Her gross rental income is $2,000. She pays property taxes of $600 and $1,000 of interest on her mortgage. Her other expenses allocable to the rental of the house include $200 for utilities, $300 for maintenance, and $600 for cost recovery.

The deductions she may take on her vacation home are computed as follows.

Rental income	$2,000
Less taxes and interest allocable to rental period (¾ × $1,600)	1,200
Limit on rental expenses other than taxes and interest	800
Less utilities and maintenance	500
Limit on cost recovery deduction	$ 300

Summary

	Actual Expenses	Deductible Expenses
Taxes and interest	$1,600	
Allocable to rental period		$1,200
Balance deductible in any event		400
Utilities and maintenance allocable to rental period	500	500
Cost recovery allocable to rental period	600	300
Totals	$2,700	$2,400

The difference between the actual expenses incurred by the vacation homeowner and the expenses she is allowed to deduct stems from the $300 rental period cost recovery which the vacation home rules prohibit the taxpayer from deducting.

Some courts have disagreed with the IRS approach to allocating the fully deductible items (interest, taxes and casualty losses) to the rental period. According to these courts, the allocation should be made in terms of the percentage of the entire year in which the property was rented. Thus, in the example above, only one-fourth of the $1,600 property taxes and mortgage interest expense would be allocated to the rental period because the three-month rental period is equal to one-fourth of the entire year. The $2,000 rental income would be reduced by $400, leaving $1,600 to be offset by the $500 utilities and maintenance expense and the full $600 cost recovery. The remaining $1,200 of property taxes and mortgage interest are deductible in any event. Thus, under the courts' approach, the entire $2,700 of expenses would be deductible instead of only $2,400 under the approach required by IRS. (*See Bolton*, 77 TC 104 [1981], *aff'd*, 694 F.2d556, 9th Cir. 1982; *McKinney*, T.C. Memo 1981-377, *aff'd*, 10th Cir., 1983).

COST RECOVERY DEDUCTIONS FOR REAL PROPERTY

From a tax standpoint, cost recovery is a cost allocation concept. The cost or, more accurately, the adjusted basis of the property, is allocated over the years of its useful life. The allocation to each year constitutes a tax deduction for that year as a proper charge against the income earned by the property that year.

Put simply, if the basis allocable to a rent-producing property is $75,000 and the property is expected to last 25 years (after which time it is estimated the building will be worthless), it could seem reasonable that 1/25 of the basis, or $3,000, be allocated as an expense to each of the 25 years. As will be pointed out later in this chapter, while a portion of the adjusted basis is apportioned to each year, prior to the Tax Reform Act of 1986 it did not necessarily have to be done on a straight line basis. Both the Accelerated Cost Recovery System (ACRS) method of the 1981 tax law and the accelerated depreciation methods allowed under prior law permitted a greater portion of the basis to be allocated to earlier years of ownership and a lesser amount to later years.

The availability of the cost recovery deduction sets real estate apart from many other forms of investment. The deduction does not depend on a cash outlay. Yet it reduces the taxable income arising from the investment and thereby can generate a cash flow by reducing taxes which otherwise would have had to be paid. Examples of this cash flow application are set forth at the end of this chapter.

Cost Recovery Allowed or Allowable

During the period property is held for production of income or used in a trade or business, cost recovery reduces basis in an amount equal to the greater of the cost recovery allowed or the cost recovery allowable according to the cost recovery method used by the taxpayer.

Thus, if for some reason the property owner actually deducts less cost recovery than the allowable amount, the basis must still be reduced by the amount of the cost recovery that was allowable. Conversely, if a taxpayer has deducted more cost recovery than the allowable amount, the basis is reduced by the actual amount of cost recovery that was deducted as long as the cost recovery deducted reduced the tax liability in the year it was deducted.

MACRS: The New Cost Recovery

The Tax Reform Act of 1986 once again revised the cost recovery system. The computation of cost recovery for real estate is less complex that it was with ACRS (Accelerated Cost Recovery System). The ACRS which MACRS (Modified Accelerated Cost Recovery System) replaces had already gone a long way toward simplifying what had been a complex system of calculating depreciation deductions.

The ease of calculation under MACRS is mainly attributable to the lack of choices available. The taxpayer merely consults a government table to determine the amount of the cost recovery deduction. The only available methods and useful lives allowable under current law for real property placed in service after December 31, 1986, are

Residential income property: 27.5 or 40 years straight line and

Commercial Property: 31.5 or 40 years straight line.

No other cost recovery methods are currently available for real property placed in service after that date. Previously allowable cost recovery methods and useful lives may continue to be used on properties placed in service prior to 1987. It is generally the date a property is placed in service that determines the set of cost recovery rules for which the property will be eligible. A property uses the rules that were in existence at the time it was placed in service. It continues to use those rules as long as it is owned by the same owner or related parties.

For a comprehensive review of previously allowed methods of ACRS cost recovery and pre-ACRS depreciation, see previous editions of this text. The only useful life not covered in the third edition is the change to 19-year cost recovery which took effect on May 8, 1985. When that change took effect, the methods remained the same, but the useful life changed. Therefore, the discussion of 18-year cost recovery methods also applies to 19-year cost recovery. Only the government tables for use in computing the amount of the cost recovery deduction changed.

It is important to be aware of prior methods of cost recovery. Particularly important is the means by which the selection of the previously allowed *accelerated* method of cost recovery could cause an accumulation of excess cost recovery which would be subject to cost recovery recapture. This could occur when the amount of cost recovery taken on an accelerated basis over the holding period of the property exceeded what the cost recovery would have been if a straight-line method of cost recovery had been used. This difference is considered excess cost recovery. At time of sale, excess cost recovery is *recaptured* and taxed as ordinary income.

Since capital gain and ordinary income are currently taxed at the same tax rates, this may not appear to be an important consideration. It becomes quite important, however, if you are selling on an installment sale basis. Since June 6, 1984, all excess cost recovery is reportable and taxed in the year of sale *whether or not any money is received by the seller in that year*. Furthermore, excess cost recovery is reported and taxed *in addition to* any other taxable income the seller receives from the installment sale. So it can be seen that the concept of excess cost recovery is still quite important.

How MACRS Applies to Real Estate

The MACRS rules apply to properties acquired after 1986 if the property is used in a trade or business or is held for the production of income. An annual cost recovery deduction is determined from a government table for 27.5, 31.5, or 40 years. These are the only lives available for real property. All current MACRS methods are based on straight line cost recovery.

Under MACRS, manufactured homes now fall into a 27.5 year useful life classification instead of their prior 10-year life. Theme park structures now have 7-year lives. For properties placed in service between July 31, 1986, and January 1, 1987, the taxpayer can elect to take cost recovery under 1986 ACRS or 1987 MACRS. (See Figures 25 and 26.)

Built into the tables is the midmonth convention. The *midmonth* convention means that a property is considered to have been held for a half month in the month of acquisition regardless of when during the month the property was acquired. The midmonth convention applies to real property for both the month of acquisition and the month of disposition. The government tables only take into account the midmonth convention for the month of acquisition. The adjustment for the month of disposition must be done manually by the taxpayer in the year of sale.

To use the tables in determining the amount of the taxpayer's cost recovery deduction, consult the appropriate table for the type of property owned and life selected (27.5- or 40-year for residential income property and 31.5- or 40-year for commercial property). Only one column of numbers will be used. Choose the column representing the month in the tax year in which the property was placed in service. In that column the taxpayer will find the percentages that apply to each year of ownership. Each year the owner multiplies the original basis in the improvements by the appropriate percentage to determine the cost recovery deduction for the year.

If the Recovery Year is:	And the Month in the First Recovery Year the Property is Placed in Service is:											
	1	2	3	4	5	6	7	8	9	10	11	12
1	3.485	3.182	2.879	2.576	2.273	1.970	1.667	1.364	1.061	0.758	0.455	0.152
2	3.636	3.636	3.636	3.636	3.636	3.636	3.636	3.636	3.636	3.636	3.636	3.636
3	3.636	3.636	3.636	3.636	3.636	3.636	3.636	3.636	3.636	3.636	3.636	3.636
4	3.636	3.636	3.636	3.636	3.636	3.636	3.636	3.636	3.636	3.636	3.636	3.636
5	3.636	3.636	3.636	3.636	3.636	3.636	3.636	3.636	3.636	3.636	3.636	3.636
6	3.636	3.636	3.636	3.636	3.636	3.636	3.636	3.636	3.636	3.636	3.636	3.636
7	3.636	3.636	3.636	3.636	3.636	3.636	3.636	3.636	3.636	3.636	3.636	3.636
8	3.636	3.636	3.636	3.636	3.636	3.636	3.636	3.636	3.636	3.636	3.636	3.636
9	3.636	3.636	3.636	3.636	3.636	3.636	3.636	3.636	3.636	3.636	3.636	3.636
10	3.637	3.637	3.637	3.637	3.637	3.637	3.636	3.636	3.636	3.636	3.636	3.636
11	3.636	3.636	3.636	3.636	3.636	3.636	3.637	3.637	3.637	3.637	3.637	3.637
12	3.637	3.637	3.637	3.637	3.637	3.637	3.636	3.636	3.636	3.636	3.636	3.636
13	3.636	3.636	3.636	3.636	3.636	3.636	3.637	3.637	3.637	3.637	3.637	3.637
14	3.637	3.637	3.637	3.637	3.637	3.637	3.636	3.636	3.636	3.636	3.636	3.636
15	3.636	3.636	3.636	3.636	3.636	3.636	3.637	3.637	3.637	3.637	3.637	3.637
16	3.637	3.637	3.637	3.637	3.637	3.637	3.636	3.636	3.636	3.636	3.636	3.636
17	3.636	3.636	3.636	3.636	3.636	3.636	3.637	3.637	3.637	3.637	3.637	3.637
18	3.637	3.637	3.637	3.637	3.637	3.637	3.636	3.636	3.636	3.636	3.636	3.636
19	3.636	3.636	3.636	3.636	3.636	3.636	3.637	3.637	3.637	3.637	3.637	3.637
20	3.637	3.637	3.637	3.637	3.637	3.637	3.636	3.636	3.636	3.636	3.636	3.636
21	3.636	3.636	3.636	3.636	3.636	3.636	3.637	3.637	3.637	3.637	3.637	3.637
22	3.637	3.637	3.637	3.637	3.637	3.637	3.636	3.636	3.636	3.636	3.636	3.636
23	3.636	3.636	3.636	3.636	3.636	3.636	3.637	3.637	3.637	3.637	3.637	3.637
24	3.637	3.637	3.637	3.637	3.637	3.637	3.636	3.636	3.636	3.636	3.636	3.636
25	3.636	3.636	3.636	3.636	3.636	3.636	3.637	3.637	3.637	3.637	3.637	3.637
26	3.637	3.637	3.637	3.637	3.637	3.637	3.636	3.636	3.636	3.636	3.636	3.636
27	3.636	3.636	3.636	3.636	3.636	3.636	3.637	3.637	3.637	3.637	3.637	3.637
28	1.970	2.273	2.576	2.879	3.182	3.485	3.636	3.636	3.636	3.636	3.636	3.636
29	0.000	0.000	0.000	0.000	0.000	0.000	0.152	0.455	0.758	1.061	1.364	1.667

General Depreciation System
Applicable Depreciation Method: Straight-Line

Applicable Recovery Period: 27.5 years
Applicable Convention: Mid-month

Figure 25. Cost Recovery Tables Residential Real Property Mid-month Convention

If the Recovery Year is:	And the Month in the First Recovery Year the Property is Placed in Service is:											
	1	2	3	4	5	6	7	8	9	10	11	12
1	3.042	2.778	2.513	2.249	1.984	1.720	1.455	1.190	0.926	0.661	0.397	0.132
2	3.175	3.175	3.175	3.175	3.175	3.175	3.175	3.175	3.175	3.175	3.175	3.175
3	3.175	3.175	3.175	3.175	3.175	3.175	3.175	3.175	3.175	3.175	3.175	3.175
4	3.175	3.175	3.175	3.175	3.175	3.175	3.175	3.175	3.175	3.175	3.175	3.175
5	3.175	3.175	3.175	3.175	3.175	3.175	3.175	3.175	3.175	3.175	3.175	3.175
6	3.175	3.175	3.175	3.175	3.175	3.175	3.175	3.175	3.175	3.175	3.175	3.175
7	3.175	3.175	3.175	3.175	3.175	3.175	3.175	3.175	3.175	3.175	3.175	3.175
8	3.175	3.174	3.175	3.174	3.175	3.174	3.175	3.175	3.175	3.175	3.175	3.175
9	3.174	3.175	3.174	3.175	3.174	3.175	3.174	3.175	3.174	3.175	3.174	3.175
10	3.175	3.174	3.175	3.174	3.175	3.174	3.175	3.175	3.175	3.175	3.175	3.175
11	3.174	3.175	3.174	3.175	3.174	3.175	3.174	3.175	3.174	3.175	3.174	3.175
12	3.175	3.174	3.175	3.174	3.175	3.174	3.175	3.174	3.175	3.174	3.175	3.174
13	3.174	3.175	3.174	3.175	3.174	3.175	3.174	3.175	3.174	3.175	3.174	3.175
14	3.175	3.174	3.175	3.174	3.175	3.174	3.175	3.174	3.175	3.174	3.175	3.174
15	3.174	3.175	3.174	3.175	3.174	3.175	3.174	3.175	3.174	3.175	3.174	3.175
16	3.175	3.174	3.175	3.174	3.175	3.174	3.175	3.174	3.175	3.174	3.175	3.174
17	3.174	3.175	3.174	3.175	3.174	3.175	3.174	3.175	3.174	3.175	3.174	3.175
18	3.175	3.174	3.175	3.174	3.175	3.174	3.175	3.174	3.175	3.174	3.175	3.174
19	3.174	3.175	3.174	3.175	3.174	3.175	3.174	3.175	3.174	3.175	3.174	3.175
20	3.175	3.174	3.175	3.174	3.175	3.174	3.175	3.174	3.175	3.174	3.175	3.174
21	3.174	3.175	3.174	3.175	3.174	3.175	3.174	3.175	3.174	3.175	3.174	3.175
22	3.175	3.174	3.175	3.174	3.175	3.174	3.175	3.174	3.175	3.174	3.175	3.174
23	3.174	3.175	3.174	3.175	3.174	3.175	3.174	3.175	3.174	3.175	3.174	3.175
24	3.175	3.174	3.175	3.174	3.175	3.174	3.175	3.174	3.175	3.174	3.175	3.174
25	3.174	3.175	3.174	3.175	3.174	3.175	3.174	3.175	3.174	3.175	3.174	3.175
26	3.175	3.174	3.175	3.174	3.175	3.174	3.175	3.174	3.175	3.174	3.175	3.174
27	3.174	3.175	3.174	3.175	3.174	3.175	3.174	3.175	3.174	3.175	3.174	3.175
28	3.175	3.174	3.175	3.174	3.175	3.174	3.175	3.174	3.175	3.174	3.175	3.174
29	3.174	3.175	3.174	3.175	3.174	3.175	3.174	3.175	3.174	3.175	3.174	3.175
30	3.175	3.174	3.175	3.174	3.175	3.174	3.175	3.174	3.175	3.174	3.175	3.174
31	3.174	3.175	3.174	3.175	3.174	3.175	3.174	3.175	3.174	3.175	3.174	3.175
32	1.720	1.984	2.249	2.513	2.778	3.042	3.175	3.174	3.175	3.174	3.175	3.174
33	0.000	0.000	0.000	0.000	0.000	0.000	0.132	0.397	0.661	0.926	1.190	1.455

General Depreciation System
Applicable Depreciation Method: Straight-Line
Applicable Recovery Period: 31.5 years
Applicable Convention: Mid-month

Figure 26. Cost Recovery Tables Nonresidential Real Property Mid-month Convention

Example

On May 16, 1987, Marina acquires an apartment building for $1,125,000. Of this amount $125,000 is allocable to the value of the land. Hence, $1,000,000 is eligible for cost recovery. Assume that Marina is a calendar-year taxpayer. May is the fifth month of her taxable year. To determine her cost recovery deduction for 1987, Marina uses column 5 in Figure 25. For year 1, the percentage is 2.273. Therefore in 1987 Marina is entitled to deduct 2.273 percent of $1,000,000, or $22,730. In 1988, she will use the percentage in column 5, year 2, which is 3.636 percent. So, her 1988 deduction is $36,360. In 1989, she will use 3.636 percent (column 5, year 3), and so on.

The use of the cost recovery tables assumes that the property is acquired during a full 12-month taxable year. Suppose, however, that the property is acquired in the first year of the corporation's existence. Assume that in our previous example Marina organized a corporation on May 2, 1987, and that on May 25, 1987, the corporation acquired the apartment house. Assume, too, that the corporation is going to use the calendar year as its taxable year.

The corporation's first taxable year will run from May 2 through December 31, 1987. In using Figure 25 to determine its cost recovery deduction for 1987, the corporation will use column 5 and come up with the same deduction as Marina did. Although the property was acquired in the first month of the corporation's current taxable year, May is the fifth month of the full 12-month taxable year. So the corporation uses column 5 to calculate the deduction.

Substantial Improvements and Components

Under the MACRS rules, a substantial improvement is treated as a separate building. A substantial improvement requires at least a 25 percent addition to the building's capital account over a 24-month period. However, an improvement made within three years of the time that the building was placed in service will not qualify as a substantial improvement.

If the substantial improvement made after 1986 is treated as a separate structure, the owner will be required to use the appropriate MACRS rules for that improvement while otherwise using an ACRS method on the remaining improvements if the property was placed in service prior to 1987.

Cost Recovery Recapture on Disposition of Real Estate

Since cost recovery deductions reduce basis, gain on the subsequent sale of the property may be attributable to a great extent to the cost recovery that was previously deducted.

Example

If property is acquired for $100,000, cost recovery deductions of $40,000 are taken and the property is subsequently sold for $120,000, there will be a gain of $60,000. This is so because the $100,000 basis was reduced to $60,000 by the cost recovery deductions. Hence, the difference between the basis and the sale price is $60,000. Of that gain, $40,000 is attributable to the cost recovery deductions. (If no cost recovery deductions had been taken, the basis would have remained $100,000 and the gain would have been $20,000.)

Cost recovery deductions are ordinary deductions, reducing ordinary income. Gain on the sale is generally a capital gain. Thus, the $40,000 of ordinary deductions is subsequently recovered as capital gain. This used to be a benefit when tax on capital gain was much lower than tax on ordinary income. It was because of this disparity in treatment that the concept of cost recovery recapture was written into the tax law. That part of the gain which is equal to cost recovery deductions is treated as ordinary income under that concept. However, prior to 1981, there was a special rule for real estate. Only cost recovery deducted which exceeded the amount of cost recovery that *would have been deducted* had straight-line cost recovery been used was subject to recapture as ordinary income. (The rule is different for personal property as is explained later in this chapter.) Thus, for real estate, cost recovery recapture applied only if accelerated cost recovery was used.

From 1981 to 1987 the ACRS tables were based on accelerated cost recovery methods. Tax laws in effect during these years also provide for cost recovery recapture, although the rules are somewhat different than under the old law, with separate provisions for residential property and commercial property. For residential property, the old recapture rule applies. That is, if an ACRS table is used, the recapturable cost recovery deduction is the excess of the amounts actually deducted (via the use of the ACRS table) over the cost recovery that would have been deducted had a straight-line method been used.

For commercial property, however, if an accelerated method of cost recovery is used, the entire amount of the cost recovery deduction is subject to recapture (a sharp departure from the previous rule). When straight-line is used, there cannot be any cost recovery recapture. While the straight-line method may yield smaller deductions in the earlier years of ownership, there would have been a complete trade-off of ordinary deductions for capital gain on later sale of the property.

With the elimination of the 60 percent capital gains exclusion and with the taxation of capital gains at the same tax rates as ordinary income, the concept of cost recovery recapture appeared to become irrelevant. Such a conclusion is misleading.

While it is not possible to generate excess cost recovery for recapture purposes under the new MACRS law (because all cost recovery methods are now straight-line), it is still possible to have excess cost recovery generated by properties which were placed in service prior to 1987 and on which an accelerated method of cost recovery was used.

While excess cost recovery subject to recapture and capital gain are now taxed equally, in the event of an installment sale, all excess cost recovery is subject to tax *in the year of sale*. By taking accelerated cost recovery and selling by means of an installment sale the tax on a significant amount of money may be accelerated.

Special Rule for Subsidized Low-Income Housing

As indicated above, cost recovery recapture on residential property is limited to the excess of the ACRS deductions over the amount that would have been deducted as straight line cost recovery. However, if the property is subsidized low-income housing, this excess is further reduced before it becomes recapturable cost recovery. It is reduced by one percentage point per month for every month that this subsidized low-income housing property is held in excess of 100 months.

Example

> If excess cost recovery on subsidized low-income housing was $50,000 and the property was held for 120 months before it was sold, the $50,000 would be reduced by 20 percent (or $10,000). Thus, only $40,000 would be subject to cost recovery recapture.

Cost Recovery and Low Income Housing

The Tax Reform Act of 1986 made several changes with respect to cost recovery and low income housing. Under the current law, low income housing receives no special treatment. The cost of the improvements must be recovered over a 27.5 year useful life. Furthermore, the five-year *rapid write-off* for the rehabilitation expenditures incurred with respect to low income housing expired at the end of 1986. Apparently, expenditures in connection with the rehabilitation of low income housing will be treated like any other improvements. The issue will then become whether or not these are substantial improvements.

For information on pre-1987 low income housing rehabilitation expenditures, see the third edition of this book and other tax reference sources.

COST RECOVERY OF PERSONAL PROPERTY

Many acquisitions of real property include personal property as well. A hotel includes furniture, kitchen equipment, and other such property. An apartment building may include window air conditioners, movable refrigerators, and furniture. Generally, personal property is any property which is not real property, that is, not permanently attached to the building structure.

Prior to the enactment of ACRS in 1981, personal property was depreciable under the various accelerated methods or by straight-line depreciation. Useful life for each item had to be determined (although tables published by IRS, so-called ADR tables based on asset depreciation range, could be used to determine useful life). Salvage value had to be taken into account.

For personal property put into service between 1981 and 1987, ACRS rules apply. For personal property placed in service after 1986, MACRS rules apply. A discussion of ACRS rules can be found in the previous edition of this book.

How MACRS Applies to Personal Property

All personal property is divided into six classes:

Useful Life	Methods Allowed
3-year	200% declining-balance or straight-line
5-year	200% declining-balance or straight-line
7-year	200% declining-balance or straight-line
10-year	200% declining-balance or straight-line
15-year	150% declining-balance or straight-line
20-year	150% declining-balance or straight-line

Five-year property generally covers automobiles, light trucks, and computers. Most of the personal property with which real estate investors will be concerned is seven-year property.

Tables have been published which specify what percentage of the cost of the property is to be written off each year as cost recovery. The tables reflect the appropriate 150 or 200 percent declining-balance method with a switch to straight-line. Figure 27 reflects the use of the half year convention which applies to personal property. Figure 28 reflects the use of the midquarter convention as if the property were placed in service in the last quarter of the year.

The MACRS rules to not require that salvage value be taken into account. Nor is any distinction made between new and used property.

The MACRS tables for personal property are constructed to employ a half-year convention. Under this approach, the assumption is made that all property acquired during a year (regardless of when in the year it was acquired) was in service for one-half year. Thus, regardless of when in the year a piece of personal property was acquired, the cost recovery deduction for that property for that year will be the same. This is reflected in the table in Figure 27.

The Tax Reform Act of 1986 introduced the concept of the midquarter convention in the new MACRS rules. The midquarter convention provides that if 40 percent or more of any class of personal property is placed in service during the last quarter of the year, the taxpayer shall only be entitled to deduct one half of the cost recovery for that quarter. The purpose of this rule is to prevent taxpayers from placing most of their business personal property purchases in the final months of the year and still being able to claim cost recovery for them for half a year.

Example

In 1987, Brown buys two refrigerators to install in apartments in the building he owns. Each costs $600. One was bought on February 17, 1987, and the other on September 11, 1987. On February 9, 1987, he bought a light truck for $8,000 to use in his real estate business. To calculate his cost recovery deductions, he goes to the table in Figure 27.

The refrigerators are seven-year property. In the seven-year recovery column, he finds that he is entitled to recover 14.29 percent of his cost in the first year. Thus, he can deduct 14.29 percent of $1,200 (or $171.48) as cost recovery for the refrigerators in 1987. Note that although one refrigerator was purchased in February and the other in September, the amount of cost recovery for each is the same.

The light truck is five-year property. In the five-year column of the table he finds that in the first year he is entitled to a cost recovery deduction of 20 percent of the cost of the

If the Recovery Year is	and the Recovery Period is					
	3 Years	5 Years	7 Years	10 Years	15 Years	20 Years
1	33.33	20.00	14.29	10.00	5.00	3.750
2	41.15	32.00	24.49	18.00	9.50	7.219
3	14.81	19.20	17.49	14.40	8.55	6.677
4	7.41	11.52	12.49	11.52	7.70	6.177
5		11.52	8.93	9.22	6.93	5.713
6		5.76	8.92	7.37	6.23	5.285
7			8.93	6.55	5.90	4.888
8			4.46	6.55	5.90	4.522
9				6.56	5.91	4.462
10				6.55	5.90	4.461
11				3.28	5.91	4.462
12					5.90	4.461
13					5.91	4.462
14					5.90	4.461
15					5.91	4.462
16					2.95	4.461
17						4.462
18						4.461
19						4.462
20						4.461
21						2.231

General Depreciation System
Applicable Depreciation Method 200 or 150 Percent
Declining-Balance Switching to Straight-Line
Applicable Recovery Periods: 3, 5, 7, 10, 15, 20 years
Applicable Convention: Half-year

Figure 27. Cost Recovery Tables Personal Property Half-Year Convention

truck, or $1,600 (20 percent of $8,000). In 1988, he deducts 24.49 percent of the $1,200 cost of the refrigerators and 32.0 percent of the $8,000 cost of the truck.

Election to use straight line. As in the case of real estate, the taxpayer must either use the MACRS tables for personal property acquired in 1987 or thereafter or elect to use straight-line cost recovery. If straight-line is elected the useful life will be the same as the useful life used for accelerated cost recovery.

If the Recovery Year is	and the Recovery Period is					
	3 Years	5 Years	7 Years	10 Years	15 Years	20 Years
1	8.33	5.00	3.57	2.50	1.25	0.938
2	61.11	38.00	27.55	19.50	9.88	7.430
3	20.37	22.80	19.68	15.60	8.89	6.873
4	10.19	13.68	14.06	12.48	8.00	6.357
5		10.94	10.04	9.98	7.20	5.880
6		9.58	8.73	7.99	6.48	5.435
7			8.73	6.55	5.90	5.031
8			7.64	6.55	5.90	4.654
9				6.56	5.90	4.458
10				6.55	5.91	4.458
11				5.74	5.90	4.458
12					5.91	4.458
13					5.90	4.458
14					5.91	4.458
15					5.90	4.458
16					5.17	4.458
17						4.458
18						4.459
19						4.458
20						4.459
21						3.901

General Depreciation System
Applicable Depreciation Method 200 or 150 Percent
Declining-Balance Switching to Straight-Line
Applicable Recovery Periods: 3, 5, 7, 10, 15, 20 years
Applicable Convention: Midquarter (property placed in service in fourth quarter)

Figure 28. Cost Recovery Tables Personal Property Midquarter Convention

If straight-line cost recovery is used, the taxpayer must use the half-year convention or the midquarter convention (if applicable) to calculate the cost recovery deduction in the year the property is acquired. That is, one-half of a full year's depreciation is allowed in the year of acquisition unless 40 percent or more of any class of personal property was placed in service during the final quarter of the year. The straight-line life elected must be used for all property in that class acquired that year. This rule differs from the rule applying to real estate, which allows the straight-line lives to be elected on a property-by-property basis.

When personal property is disposed of, the half-year convention is applied in computing the final year's cost recovery. This, however, makes no different because, as explained later in this chapter, the application of the cost recovery recapture provisions would bring about the same result.

Cost recovery recapture.   The entire amount of cost recovery deductions claimed becomes cost recovery recapture on the sale of the property. Thus, that portion of the gain on the disposition of the property which is equal to the total amount of cost recovery deductions taken is treated as ordinary income. However, the amount subject to recapture is limited to the amount of gain.

Complete Write-Off of Cost of Personal Property

Beginning in 1982, taxpayers were permitted to write off the entire cost of some personal property up to a specific limit (see below) in the year it is acquired. This is known as the Section 179 limited expensing provision.

The limit under the complete write-off rules is $10,000. For a married individual filing a separate return, the above maximum amount is cut in half. To the extent that this expensing provision is used, it reduces the basis eligible for cost recovery.

The property eligible for this treatment is personal property used in a trade or business, not merely held for the production of income.

To get the complete write-off in the year of acquisition (up to $10,000) the taxpayer must make an election to take the write-off. This election must be signified on the tax return. Once the election is made, it cannot be revoked.

The property on which the complete write-off is taken must be purchased; it cannot be acquired from family members and related corporations, partnerships, trusts and estates. Inherited property also does not qualify.

Trusts and estates are not entitled to take this complete write-off. A partnership taking a complete write-off is limited to the dollar limitations listed above. The amount deducted is then allocated among the partners. Each partner adds the allocated amount of the write-off to any other complete write-offs that may have been acquired. The total write-off cannot exceed the dollar limits for that year.

The amount deducted as a complete write-off is treated as cost recovery recapture should the property be sold. Thus, for example, if the cost of the entire property was written off in the year of acquisition, the property's basis would be zero. Hence, whatever was received on the subsequent sale of that property would all be gain. And to the extent that the gain did not exceed the amount written off in the year of acquisition, the gain would be cost recovery recapture, taxable as ordinary income.

INVESTMENT CREDIT

The investment tax credit for personal property used in a trade or business was repealed by the Tax Reform Act of 1986. The repeal of this credit, while enacted on October 22, 1986, was retroactive to January 1, 1986.

For a discussion of this credit as it existed prior to 1986, see pages 251-255 of the third edition of this book.

Investment Credit for Rehabilitation of Real Estate

Buildings and structural components are normally not eligible for the investment credit. However, there is a special investment credit for qualified expenditures incurred in the rehabilitation of older *nonresidential* real estate. For expenditures incurred after 1986, there is a two-tier system of credits:

1. A 10 percent credit on qualified expenditures incurred in rehabilitating a building first placed in service before 1986 and
2. A 20 percent credit for rehabilitation of a certified historic structure.

The Senate Finance Committee report indicates that the credit for *non*historic structures is available only for nonresidential property, but this does not appear to be supported by the text of the act.

Qualified rehabilitation expenditure. The rehabilitation expenditure on which the investment credit may be claimed must involve a substantial expenditure. The expenditures during the 24-month period ending on the last day of the taxable year must exceed the *greater* of the basis of the improvements on the first day of the 24-month period, or exceed $5,000. If the rehabilitation is done in phases, a 60-month period may be used to apply this test. But if the 60-month period is used, there must be architectural plans and specifications for all phases of the rehabilitation and there must be a reasonable expectation that all phases of the plan will be completed.

Buildings other than historic structures must also meet three structural tests. Thus, under the Tax Reform Act of 1986, a building will not qualify for the 10 percent rehabilitation credit unless the following occurs.

At least 50 percent of the building's external walls are retained in place as external walls

At least 75 percent of the building's external walls are retained in place as either internal or external walls

At least 75 percent of the building's internal structural framework is retained in place.

The basis of the property has to be reduced by the full amount of the investment credit claimed for rehabilitation expenditures. If any part of the investment credit is recaptured, the increase in tax resulting from the recapture is added to the basis of the building.

Rehabilitation of certified historic structures. If the above qualified rehabilitation expenditure rules are met and the rehabilitation is certified by the Secretary of the Interior as a rehabilitation of an historic structure, a 20 percent investment credit applies.

Low Income Housing Credits under the Tax Reform Act of 1986

The 1986 Tax Reform Act introduced three new tax credits to the real estate industry. All three credits apply to the purchase, construction, or rehabilitation of low income housing. These credits were scheduled to expire at the end of 1989. The 1989 Revenue Reconciliation Act extended two of these three credits through 1990.

A credit of 4 percent per year for a period of 10 years used to be available for the purchase of existing low income housing and its maintenance for 15 years. This credit was not extended under the 1989 Act. It therefore expired at the end of 1989.

The credit for the construction and rehabilitation of low income housing, financed using governmental subsidies, is 4 percent per year for the next 10 years, while housing which is not financed using governmental subsidies is given a credit of 9 percent per year for the next 10 years.

In order to qualify as low income housing the project must meet a minimum set aside requirement, a rent restriction, special rules for already existing housing, state credit authorization and certification.

There are two possibilities for meeting the minimum set aside requirement. Either 20 percent or more of the units in the project must be occupied by tenants whose incomes are 50 percent or less of the area median gross incomes, adjusted for family size, or 40 percent must be occupied by tenants whose incomes are 60 percent or less of the area median gross incomes. The owner must irrevocably elect to come under either the 20–50 or 40–60 test. Once the test is elected, the minimum set aside must be met within 12 months of the date the project is placed in service. The second requirement involves rent restrictions. The gross rent charged to a tenant in a qualified low income housing unit may not exceed 30 percent of the qualifying income level for the tenant's family size. Gross rent is considered to include all utilities paid by the tenant other than telephone.

Special rules apply to already existing housing. Under the new law substantial rehabilitation must be done. The old law required an expenditure of at least $2,000 per dwelling unit. The new law requires an expenditure of the greater of $3,000 of qualified basis per low income unit or 10 percent of the unadjusted basis. The date of acquisition must be at least 10 years after the date the building was last placed in service or the date of the most recently non-qualified substantial improvement. Finally, the building must not have been previously placed in service by the taxpayer or any person related to the taxpayer.

Once the projects are authorized by the appropriate state or local agency, the owners are required to file a certification with the IRS before claiming the credit. This certification must be filed within 90 days after the end of the first tax year for which the low income housing credit is claimed.

The credit is available for a period of 10 years in an amount equal to the applicable credit percentage (4 or 9 percent) multiplied by the qualified basis allowable for low income units in each qualified low income building. The 1989 Act increases the maximum credit up to 91 percent (from 70 percent) of the present value for buildings in certain high cost areas. The new law also extends the credit to certain owner occupied buildings having four or fewer units.

The amount of credit available in a state depends on each state's housing credit ceiling. Under the law prior to 1990, a state's housing credit ceiling dollar allowance for any calendar year was equal to $1.25 multiplied by the population of the state. In 1990, the $1.25 amount was reduced by the new tax law to $0.9375—a 25 percent reduction.

The 1989 Act also removes the phase-out of the low income housing credit when the taxpayer's adjusted gross income exceeds $200,000. It does not however, remove the phase-out treatment for commercial and historic rehabilitation. In addition, developers acquiring low income property must agree to extend the low income use of the property for an additional 15 years beyond the end of the initial compliance period. After the end of the initial 15 year compliance period, an owner can petition the state agency to either buy the property or find a buyer who will continue the low income use of the property. If no buyer is found during a one year period, the property can be sold without any restrictions except that existing low income tenants must be allowed to remain in a project for a period of three years after the end of the 15 year compliance period.

CASH FLOW

Real estate investors commonly examine their investment results in terms of cash flow; how much actual cash (often referred to as spendable dollars) is available to them after taxes from their investment. They are not content merely with the bookkeeping result of net profit or loss from the operation.

The major reason for a difference between net operating income (or loss) and cash flow stems from the interaction of the cost-recovery deduction and the principal payments made on any mortgages on the property. Cost recovery reduces net taxable income from the property but requires no outlay of cash. On the other hand, principal payments require an outlay of cash but are not deductible for tax purposes. Further, a net taxable loss from operations may reduce the property owner's other taxable income and thereby reduces the cash outlay required for income taxes.

To illustrate the interaction of the factors discussed in this chapter and their impacts on cash flow, let us consider the following three examples. (The figures are arbitrary and are used merely to illustrate the principles involved.)

Examples

1. Assume that Brown, a single individual, has rental property which produces $100,000 in gross rents. There are operating expenses of $60,000; mortgage interest of $9,000, principal payments of $10,000, real estate taxes of $12,000 and a cost recovery deduction of $15,000.

The taxable income from the property would be computed as follows.

Rental Income		$100,000
Operating expenses	$60,000	
Mortgage interest	9,000	
Real estate taxes	12,000	
Cost recovery	15,000	96,000
Taxable income		$ 4,000

The cash flow from the property, however, would be computed as follows.

Rental income		$100,000
Operating expenses	$60,000	
Mortgage interest	9,000	
Real estate taxes	12,000	
Principal payments	10,000	91,000
Cash flow before taxes		9,000
Less tax on $4,000 taxable income (assuming a 28% marginal rate)		1,120
Cash flow after taxes		$ 7,880

2. Even though the result of operations is a taxable loss, it is still possible to have a positive cash flow from the property. Assume the same facts as in Example 1 except that the cost recovery deduction is $22,000 instead of $15,000. Taxable income (loss) would be computed as follows.

Rental income		$100,000
Operating expenses	$60,000	
Mortgage interest	9,000	
Real estate taxes	12,000	
Cost recovery	22,000	103,000
Taxable loss		($ 3,000)

Cash flow from the property would be as follows.

Rental income		$100,000
Operating expenses	$60,000	
Real estate taxes	12,000	
Mortgage interest	9,000	
Principal payments	10,000	91,000
Cash flow before taxes		9,000
Plus income taxes saved by applying $3,000 loss to owner's other income (assuming 28% marginal rate)		840
Cash flow after taxes		$ 9,840

3. It is of course possible to have a negative cash flow (the investor has to add personal funds to the operations). This will generally result when the amount of the principal payments during the year exceeds the cost recovery deductions. Assume the same facts as in the first example except that the cost recovery deduction is $10,000 while the principal payments are $20,000. Taxable income would be calculated as follows.

Rental income		$100,000
Operating expenses	$60,000	
Mortgage interest	9,000	
Real estate taxes	12,000	
Cost recovery	10,000	91,000
Taxable income		$ 9,000

Cash flow from the property would be calculated as follows.

Rental income		$100,000
Operating expenses	$60,000	
Mortgage interest	9,000	
Real estate taxes	12,000	
Principal payments	20,000	101,000
Cash outflow		(1,000)
Tax on taxable income (28% marginal rate)		(2,520)
Negative cash flow after taxes		($ 3,520)

10
Dispositions

Whenever property is sold or exchanged for cash, obligations or other property, gain or loss is realized.

Gain or loss is the difference between the basis of the property given up and the amount or value received. The gain is reduced or the loss increased by the cost of the transaction, including the brokers' commissions.

The gain or loss realized is not always immediately taxable or deductible. Like-kind-exchanges, for example, have the effect of deferring the gain or loss. (Tax-deferred exchanges are discussed in the next chapter.) In addition, it is possible, by using the installment method, to spread the taxation of the gain over the period during which the sale price is collected.

Unless the seller is a dealer, gain on the sale of real estate generally results in a capital gain. More accurately, it is usually a Section 1231 gain. (The tax treatment of these gains is explained in detail in Chapter 7.) Furthermore, even though conceptually the gain is considered capital gain, it is taxed as ordinary income since the Tax Reform Act of 1986 repealed the 60 percent long-term capital gain exclusion.

In this chapter the questions of who is a dealer, how to use installment and other deferred sales and when and how cost recovery recapture rules apply are explored in detail. In addition, other methods of disposition such as sales and leasebacks, involuntary conversions, demolition, charitable contributions and other gifts are examined for their tax consequences.

DEALER OR INVESTOR

Whether a seller is a dealer or investor makes no difference in the economic sense. However, in terms of taxation it can make a difference. That difference involves the treatment of gain on installment sales, the deductibility of investment interest, and eligibility for tax-deferred exhanges. The tax treatment of real estate gains and losses is as follows: A dealer can no longer use installment sales for tax purposes.

1. Non-income-producing investment property (such as nonproductive land) when sold at a gain will yield capital gain. When such property is sold at a loss, the result is capital loss, which, as explained in Chapter 7, is of limited value.

2. Property used in the trade or business of a taxpayer and held for more than one year is called Section 1231 property. Included in this category is property held for rental purposes. All gains other than those representing recapture of cost recovery and losses from such property for the taxable year are combined. If the net result is profit, it is taxed as a capital gain; if the net result is loss, it is taxed as an ordinary loss.

3. Property held for sale to customers in the ordinary course of trade or business yields ordinary income or ordinary loss. It is this type of property that is designated as dealer property. Under the current tax law, ordinary income and capital gains are taxed at the same rates. Therefore the distinction is somewhat less important than it used to be.

Factors Indicating Dealer Status

In some cases, the taxpayer is obviously a dealer—for example, a developer of a tract of residential properties that are sold to separate buyers. In other cases, the taxpayer is clearly an investor; one rental property is bought, held for a number of years for the investment return and subsequently sold, the taxpayer never previously having made a similar sale.

The difficulty arises in the "gray area" when someone who claims to be an investor is involved in numerous sales transactions.

The issue is considered to be a factual one and each case is considered on its own merits. However, there are certain factors which are usually examined in cases such as these to decide whether property is being held for sale in the ordinary course of business. No one of them is all-important and the relative degree of importance of each factor varies with the individual case. Of course, if a taxpayer claims (by advertising or some such means) to be in the business of buying and selling real estate and sells one of the parcels that is held as part of the inventory of properties available for sale, the taxpayer would be hard-pressed later to claim that the parcel was really held for investment purposes and to deny being a dealer in real estate. But that is the extreme case.

Quite often, the taxpayer is not in the real estate business on a full-time basis, but may be a doctor, a lawyer, or a police chief. In these cases it is often difficult to determine the principal purpose for holding the real estate.

Following are some of the factors that tend to cause a taxpayer to be classified as a dealer.

- The taxpayer has a real estate license and lists ''real estate dealer'' as the occupation on income tax returns.
- The taxpayer belongs to various real estate dealer organizations.
- The taxpayer makes frequent, quick turnover transactions.
- Business stationary, advertising and publicity releases all refer to the taxpayer as a real estate dealer.
- The taxpayer employs a staff of salespeople to solicit offers from purchasers.
- The taxpayer develops property by making substantial improvements and subdividing; then advertises the individual parcels for sale.
- The taxpayer receives a large part of total income from the sale of real estate.
- The taxpayer spends the majority of working time on real estate purchase and sale activities.
- The purpose at the time of acquisition and/or sale is quick resale.

All these factors and more must be examined in each case with respect to *each property* sold in order to determine the proper income tax treatment. Thus, if a taxpayer in the business of renting real property decides to liquidate, the sale of the rental property would be considered the sale of property used in trade or business. Hence, any gain would be a Section 1231 gain, taxable as a capital gain. However, if that taxpayer then engaged in a large degree of such activity, subdividing, improving, sales promotion and the like, the taxpayer's status might be converted to dealer status.

Dealer as an Investor

It is possible for a real estate dealer to hold some property for use in a trade or business or for investment purposes and not for sale to clients. A real estate dealer or broker who owns the building in which the real estate office is located is holding that building for use in a business and not for sale to customers in the ordinary course of business. If the dealer were to decide to move the office and sell the building, the gain would be treated as a Section 1231 gain.

Since a dealer may also be an investor, it is important that some designation be made, not only in the taxpayer's mind but also tangibly on paper and by action, to indicate which property is held for investment and which for use in a trade or business.

Example

Roberta is a real estate dealer. She buys and sells real estate in the ordinary course of business. When she buys real estate for her own investment and not for sale to customers, she segregates the purchase on her books. Her financial records have separate accounts for (1) inventory property, (2) investment property and (3) the building in which her office is located, her business property.

COST RECOVERY RECAPTURE

When depreciable property is sold at a gain the likelihood is that part of the gain is attributable to cost recovery deductions which reduced the basis of the property.

Example

> Depreciable property is purchased for $100,000; cost recovery deductions totaling $40,000 are taken over a period of years. The adjusted basis of the property becomes $60,000. A subsequent sale of the property at $100,000 (same as the original purchase price) results in a $40,000 gain. In this case, the entire gain arises from the fact that $40,000 of cost recovery was deducted. If the property were sold for $110,000, the resulting gain would be $50,000 of which $40,000 would be due to the cost recovery deductions taken.

The idea behind cost recovery recapture is to prevent converting an ordinary deduction (cost recovery deductions reduce ordinary income) into a capital gain when the amount of the previously deducted cost recovery is recovered in the sale price.

Consequently, the cost recovery recapture rules are designed to treat as ordinary income as much of the gain on the sale as is attributable to the recapture of cost recovery deductions by the seller. The rules accomplish this in the case of the sale of depreciable personal property (furniture, machinery, and the like). In the case of depreciable real property, usually the recapture is limited to the excess of the amount deducted as cost recovery over the amount which would have been deductible as straight-line cost recovery.

In spite of the provisions that cost recovery must now be straight-line and capital gain is treated as regular income, the explanation of cost-recovery recapture is presented here because cost recovery on properties placed in service prior to 1987 can still use accelerated cost recovery methods, and because capital gains treatment may be reinstated in the near future. If reinstated, the cost-recovery recapture provisions of Sections 1245 and 1250 of the Internal Revenue Code will most likely become operative again.

Under the cost recovery approach (MACRS rules are discussed in detail in Chapter 9), the cost-recovery recapture rules have been modified somewhat as is explained both in Chapter 9 and below.

Cost Recovery Recapture on Disposition of Personal Property

The rules governing the recapture of cost recovery deducted on personal property are found in Section 1245 of the Internal Revenue Code. Such property is commonly referred to as Section 1245 property.

The cost recovery recapture rules apply to cost recovery deducted after 1962 on any Section 1245 property. Elevators and escalators acquired after June 30, 1963, and before January 1, 1981, are included in the definition of Section 1245 property.

Section 1245 does not include elevators or escalators which have been acquired after 1980 (they are treated as 19-year real estate if they are put into service after May 8,

1985, 18-year real estate if they are put into service after March 15, 1984, and 15-year real estate if put into service before March 16, 1984). Section 1245 property *does* include nonresidential real estate acquired after 1980 if the 15-year cost recovery table is used (19-year, for property put into service after May 8, 1985, 18-year, for property put into service after March 15, 1984). If, however, the nonresidential real estate is being recovered under a straight-line method, the property is *not* Section 1245 property. The straight-line lives that are available are 15 years (19 for property put into service after May 8, 1985, and 18 for property put into service after March 15, 1984), 35 years, or 45 years.

It is to the taxpayer's advantage to have property treated as Section 1250 property (real estate) rather than Section 1245 property. The reason is that *all* cost recovery deducted on Section 1245 property is subject to recapture; only cost recovery in excess of straight line is subject to recapture under Section 1250.

How section 1245 cost recovery recapture works.   When the property is sold, the gain on the sale is compared with the amount of the cost recovery which has been deducted, whether it was depreciation deducted under the pre-1981 depreciation rules or as cost recovery deductions under the post-1980 ACRS rules. *All* cost recovery deducted is taken into account except depreciation deducted prior to 1962.

The amount of the gain is compared to the amount of the cost recovery deducted.

- If the gain is equal to or less than the amount of the cost recovery deducted, the entire gain is ordinary income.
- If the gain is greater than the cost recovery deducted, that portion of the gain equal to the cost recovery deducted is treated as ordinary income. The balance of the gain is treated as a Section 1231 gain, which usually translates into a capital gain.
- If the property is sold at a loss there is no cost recovery recapture.

Example

Smith sells furniture and fixtures used in his hotel. His adjusted basis for the items sold is $15,000. Cost recovery claimed on these items during the time he held the property (after 1961) totaled $4,000. Tax treatment of the gain or loss on the transaction, for each of the sale prices indicated, is as follows.

- Sale price is $17,000; gain is $2,000. Since the cost recovery total is $4,000, the entire gain of $2,000 is treated as ordinary income.
- Sale price is $19,000; gain is $4,000, exactly equal to the cost recovery deducted. Hence, the entire gain of $4,000 is treated as ordinary income.
- Sale price is $21,000; gain is $6,000, which is greater than the total cost recovery deducted. In this case, $4,000 of the gain is treated as ordinary income and $2,000 as a Section 1231 gain.
- Sale price is $12,000; since there is a loss of $3,000, cost recovery recapture rules do not apply. The loss is a Section 1231 loss.

Cost-recovery recapture is a component of gain. If there is no gain on a sale, there can be no recapture.

Cost Recovery Recapture on Disposition of Real Property Acquired after 1980 and before 1987

As indicated in Chapter 9, the ACRS rules divide real property acquired after 1980 and before 1987 into three categories.

1. Nonresidential real estate.   As indicated above, this real estate is treated as Section 1245 property. Hence, *all* cost recovery deductions are treated as recaptured depreciation. However, the taxpayer may elect not to use accelerated cost recovery and instead use straight line depreciation based on a useful life of 15 (19 years for property put in service after May 8, 1985, 18 for property put in service after March 15, 1984), 35 or 45 years. If the straight-line method is selected, there is no depreciation recapture at all.

2. Residential real estate.   Here, the excess of the depreciation deducted under the 18-year cost recovery table over the depreciation that would have been deductible under 18-year straight-line cost recovery is subject to treatment as recaptured depreciation. (For property put in service prior to March 16, 1984, use the 15-year cost recovery table and 15-year straight-line method; use the 19 year table if the property was placed in service after March 8, 1985.) Therefore, if straight line depreciation is used, there is no depreciation to be recaptured.

3. Subsidized low-income housing.   The excess depreciation deducted under the cost recovery table over the amount that would have been deductible under 15-year straight-line depreciation is first determined. This excess is then reduced by 1 percent for each month in excess of 100 months that the property was held. The excess depreciation remaining after the reduction under the more-than-100 month rule is the amount subject to depreciation recapture. Again, if straight-line depreciation was used, there is no recapture.

The above rules apply if the property was held for more than one year prior to disposition. If the property was held for one year or less, the full amount of the cost recovery (depreciation) deducted is subject to recapture even if the straight-line method was used.

Depreciation Recapture on Disposition of Real Property Acquired Prior to 1981

Prior to 1981, cost recovery was known as depreciation. In discussing pre-1981 activity, the use of the word depreciation is appropriate. The ACRS rules do not apply to property acquired prior to 1981. Taxpayers continue to deduct depreciation under the depreciation schedules established for the property prior to 1981. On disposition after 1981, the depreciation recapture rules which applied to pre-1981 holdings continue to apply. Therefore, it is important to understand the depreciation recapture rules which were in effect prior to the enactment of the 1981 tax law in order to apply them on the disposition of property acquired prior to 1981.

The old rules (applying to depreciation deducted on real estate after 1963) recaptured all or part of what is referred to as excess depreciation, the depreciation deduction in excess of the amount that was deductible under the straight-line method. The portion of the excess depreciation subject to recapture is called the *applicable amount.*

The applicable amount depends on a number of factors:

- The holding period of the property
- The depreciation method used
- How much depreciation was deducted
- When the depreciation was deducted
- Whether the property qualified for special uses

Straight line depreciation used.   If only straight line depreciation has been used for the property being sold or disposed of, there cannot be any depreciation recapture under Section 1250 as long as the property was held for more than one year.

Property held not more than one year.   If the property being sold or otherwise disposed of has been held for one year or less, all of the depreciation deducted, regardless of the depreciation method used, becomes subject to recapture. (This is essentially the same procedure as is used to recapture depreciation on personalty under Section 1245.) Of course, if the gain is less than the depreciation deducted, only the amount of the gain is treated as ordinary income.

Property held more than one year.   When the property has been held for more than one year, the *maximum* amount of depreciation which can be recaptured is the excess depreciation.

Except in the case of new residential rental property and special-purpose properties (discussed later in this chapter) depreciation claimed during two periods of time are considered in calculating depreciation recapture on real estate. It must be determined how much *excess* depreciation was deducted (1) after 1963 but before 1970, and (2) after 1969. Depreciation deducted before 1964 is never recaptured.

In practical terms, however, it is only necessary to determine the excess depreciation deducted after 1969. The reason is that only a portion of excess depreciation deducted after 1963 and before 1970 is recapturable. The longer the property is held, the smaller the portion subject to recapture. Once the property is held more than ten years, no part of the excess depreciation deducted during the years 1964 through 1969 is recapturable. Any sales made currently are more than ten years removed from 1969. Therefore, any depreciation deducted during the years 1964 through 1969 on property sold today would not be subject to recapture.

Consequently, except for the properties subject to the special rules, it is necessary to look only at the excess depreciation deducted after 1969. That portion of the depreciation deducted after 1969 which exceeds the depreciation which *would have been* deductible had straight line depreciation been used is the amount subject to recapture.

As in the case of personal property, the recapturable amount, (excess depreciation) is compared to the gain. That portion of the gain which is equal to the excess depreciation is "recaptured" as ordinary income. The portion of the gain which exceeds the excess depreciation is treated as a Section 1231 gain. Of course, if there is a loss, there is no depreciation recapture.

Examples

1. An office building acquired in 1968 is sold in 1984 for $1,000,000. The gain is $300,000. The amount of depreciation claimed after 1969 exceeds by $200,000 the amount of straight line depreciation which would be allowed for that period. Of the $300,000 gain, $200,000 is ordinary income; $100,000 is Section 1231 gain. While all depreciation deducted prior to 1970 and after 1969 is used in determining the basis of the property sold, only depreciation deducted after 1969 is used in the calculation of excess depreciation subject to recapture.

2. Assume the gain in Example 1 was $150,000. The entire gain would be subject to depreciation recapture.

3. Assume the sale in Example 1 resulted in a $50,000 loss. There is no depreciation recapture.

Residential rental property is defined as property from which 80 percent or more of the gross rental income comes from dwelling units. Dwelling units are living accommodations in houses or apartment buildings and do not include hotels, motels, inns or other establishments in which more than half of the units are used on a transient basis.

Additional Cost Recovery Recapture for Corporations

A corporation disposing of real estate after 1982 is subject to additional recapture. First it determines what the cost recovery recapture would have been had the property been personal (Section 1245) property and then subtracts the recapture calculated under the real property (Section 1250) rules.

If the property was disposed of before 1985, it calculates 15 percent of the excess of the Section 1245 recapture over the Section 1250 recapture. If the disposition occurs after 1984, it calculates 20 percent of that excess. (If straight-line cost recovery had been used, the amount of Section 1250 cost recovery is zero; so 15 or 20 percent, whichever is applicable, of the full amount of the Section 1245 cost recovery is used.)

The 15 or 20 percent of the excess is added to the cost recovery recapture calculated under the real estate (1250) method. This total then becomes the cost recovery recapture the corporation must apply.

Tax-Free Exchanges and Cost Recovery Recapture

It is possible to have a so-called tax-free exchange of property of a like-kind without *any* gain being recognized for tax purposes. In other cases, while the *entire* gain may not be recognized for tax purposes, *part* of the gain may be taxable. That occurs when property other than like-kind is received in the exchange. Often that other property is cash.

In the case of an exchange of Section 1245 property, the amount of the cost recovery deducted is compared to the portion of the gain taxable in the exchange. In other words, the recognized portion of the gain is treated as total gain.

The maximum amount of cost recovery recapture on real property which can be taxable as ordinary income is the larger of the two amounts:

1. The amount equal to the portion of the gain on the exchange table under exchange rules (see Chapter 11) or
2. The excess of the potential cost recovery recapture on the exchange (computed as though a sale were made for cash) over the fair market value of the depreciable real property received in the exchange. The purpose of this rule is to permit IRS to impose the real estate recapture rules when a good portion of the property being received in exchange is not depreciable real property and hence will not be subject to cost-recovery recapture in the future.

Similar rules are applied where property is replaced after an involuntary conversion (see Chapter 8).

INSTALLMENT SALES

It is quite common for real estate to be sold using an installment sale in which the buyer pays the purchase price over a number of years. Commonly, the purchaser will be paying part of the purchase price by mortgage principal payments. Of course, if the mortgage is being held by a bank or other lending institution, the seller will receive the entire amount in the year of the sale. This is *not* an installment sale, and the entire gain on the sale will be reportable by the seller for tax purposes in the year of the sale.

Examples

1. Seller has an adjusted basis for a property of $70,000 and sells it for $100,000, resulting in a $30,000 gain. The buyer pays the $100,000 price by paying $40,000 in cash and securing a mortgage on the property for $60,000 from a bank. In this case, the seller gets the full $100,000 at the time of the sale and the buyer ends up owing the bank the $60,000. So, the seller reports the full gain in the year of sale. As far as the seller is concerned the sale is not an installment sale. The buyer is paying installments by way of mortgage principal payments, but to the bank, not to the seller. In other cases, however, the installment payments are made to the seller

2. In the preceding case, if instead of borrowing $60,000 from the bank, the buyer pays $40,000 in cash and gives the seller a purchase money mortgage of $60,000, the seller will collect the $60,000 balance of the sale price over the term of the mortgage. Here, the seller considers the transaction an installment sale.

3. Seller sells for $100,000, but there is an existing mortgage of $25,000 on the property. The buyer pays the $100,000 by paying $40,000 cash, taking subject to the $25,000 mortgage and giving the seller a second mortgage of $35,000. Here, too, part of the sale price will be paid to the seller over a number of years, the term of the second mortgage. Again, an installment sale exists as far as the seller is concerned.

When a seller enters into an installment sale, the investment is no longer in real estate. The real estate investment has been converted into an investment in a note receivable. The inherent benefits of real estate ownership are not available to the holder of a note. Nevertheless, there are some similarities between the analysis of a note and the analysis of real estate. When analyzing a note, just as in analyzing property, two separate worlds must be dealt with simultaneously, the real world and the tax world. In the real world we are concerned with cash flows. How much money is coming in and how much money is going out? This concept is similar to checkbook accounting. In the tax world we are concerned with how many of the dollars will be subject to tax. Once the amount of tax can be computed, it becomes an additional amount due (cash flow out) in the real world. Figure 29 illustrates these two worlds side by side.

When there is an installment sale, the gain on the transaction is calculated in the usual way. The seller's adjusted basis is subtracted from the sale price to determine the gain. But since the seller will not get all the money in the year of sale, the seller would like to avoid paying the tax on the full gain in that year. The solution is to spread the tax burden over the period during which that portion of the selling price that has not been received in the year of sale will be collected. The tax law permits this spreadout via the installment method of reporting the gain. Losses on installment sales, however, must be reported in full in the year of the sale.

Electing Installment Sales

Any sale calling for payments in future years is automatically treated as an installment sale. This is so even if there is no payment at all in the year of sale and only one payment is called for (to be made in a future year). The taxpayer is not required to make an election. If the installment sale treatment is not wanted, the taxpayer must "elect out" by reporting the full gain on the tax return for the year of sale. If taxpayer has a large loss from another transaction, the taxpayer may prefer to forego installment sale treatment and use the loss to offset the entire gain—or most of it—by reporting the gain in full in the year of sale.

The seller may also "elect out" in a year in which there are large available passive losses. These losses can generally be used to offset gain from the sale of passive properties.

In an installment sale, the dollars paid to the seller can have one of the four following characteristics:

1. Interest,

2. Excess cost recovery recapture,

Installment Sale Process

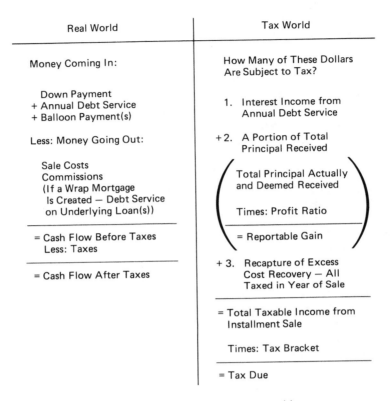

Real World	Tax World
Money Coming In:	How Many of These Dollars Are Subject to Tax?
Down Payment + Annual Debt Service + Balloon Payment(s)	1. Interest Income from Annual Debt Service
Less: Money Going Out:	+ 2. A Portion of Total Principal Received
Sale Costs Commissions (If a Wrap Mortgage Is Created — Debt Service on Underlying Loan(s))	Total Principal Actually and Deemed Received Times: Profit Ratio
= Cash Flow Before Taxes Less: Taxes	= Reportable Gain
= Cash Flow After Taxes	+ 3. Recapture of Excess Cost Recovery — All Taxed in Year of Sale
	= Total Taxable Income from Installment Sale
	Times: Tax Bracket
	= Tax Due

Figure 29. Real world and tax world.

3. Section 1231 gain or long term capital gain and
4. Recovery of the seller's remaining basis in the investment.

Recovery of remaining basis in an investment is not subject to tax. An investor is allowed to receive the remaining investment without paying a tax on that amount. If the sale price is greater than the adjusted (remaining) basis, there is a gain for tax purposes. The gain on the sale is subject to tax and is treated as passive income if improved property is sold. The interest income that is received on the note which the seller takes back is taxed as ordinary income. It is treated as portfolio income. The excess cost recovery recapture is also taxed as ordinary income. It, too, is passive income because it is a component of gain. If there is no gain, there can be no recapture of excess cost recovery.

The gain, if it is long term is taxed as long-term capital gain. The elimination of the 60 percent capital gain exclusion will have an impact on contracts entered into prior to 1987. Any long-term capital gain which is received on a contract that arose prior to 1987 will be taxed in full at the prevailing tax rate after 1986.

As mentioned above, a seller receives payments which, for tax purposes, can be separated into principal and interest payments. The principal payments are further broken down into (1) long- or short-term capital gain, (2) excess cost recovery recapture and (3) recovery of remaining basis.

There is one more very important category of principal the receipt of which will subject the seller to tax. This category is called *principal deemed received*. It consists of principal payments the receipt of which the government attributes to the seller even if the seller receives no money at all. There are a number of items which give rise to principal deemed received for tax purposes.

Principal Deemed Received from an Installment Sale

The amount of principal deemed to be received from an installment sale consists of the following:

1. Payment by the purchaser of any of the seller's matured obligations (back taxes, past due installments or other past due indebtedness),
2. The amount by which the mortgage assumed, or taken subject to, exceeds the seller's adjusted basis in the property (adjusted basis includes any capitalized costs of sale),
3. Buyer forgiveness of unrelated debt of the seller to the buyer,
4. Option money or earnest money deposited in previous years and included as part of the purchase price (option money is not reported until the option is exercised or is expired) and
5. Net loan proceeds if the note receivable is pledged as collateral for a loan.

Tax Treatment of the Various Parts of the Dollar
in an Installment Sale

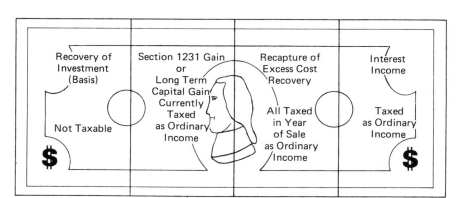

Figure 30

Payments on a loan assumed by the purchaser which are incurred in the ordinary course of business *do not* constitute payment to the seller for purposes of qualifying for installment reporting. Thus, the assumption of existing mortgages does not constitute payment received by seller.

In arriving at the gain on sale, the seller adds transaction costs and excess cost recovery recapture to the adjusted basis before comparing the basis to the sale price in order to determine the gain on sale. Because mortgage-over-basis represents principal deemed received in the year of sale, adding excess cost-recovery recapture and transaction costs to the basis narrows the gap between the mortgage and basis (reduces the excess) and thereby reduces tax liability at the time of sale.

At the time of sale, the broker must ensure that enough cash is generated (or is available) to pay existing, unassumed mortgages, commissions, closing costs, and income taxes. The broker must be able to determine the amount and timing of taxable gain in order to determine the amount and timing of income tax liability.

To the extent that there is a gain upon sale, the portion of the gain which is taxed during the year of sale includes the down payment, the mortgage over basis, principal payments on carryback financing, net loan proceeds if the note is pledged as collateral for a loan, and all excess cost recovery.

Income Recognized in Years Subsequent to Year of Sale

To the extent that there is a gain, the amount of the gain that will be taxed in years subsequent to the year of sale equals all or a portion of principal payments received on carryback financing and principal deemed received if the note is pledged as collateral for a loan. The way each dollar received by the seller is categorized and taxed is illustrated by Figure 31.

By examining Figure 29 which shows the differences between the tax world and the real world and Figure 31 which shows how the dollars to be taxed are categorized, it becomes apparent that a seller will need to know how to calculate

Interest income,

Principal actually received,

Principal deemed received,

Profit ratio and

Excess cost recovery subject to recapture.

A worksheet has been developed to facilitate calculation of these amounts. Figure 32 contains this worksheet. Chapter 13 contains fully filled out copies of this worksheet as used in making important real estate decisions.

The amount of the principal that is taxed, whether taxed in the year of sale or in years subsequent, is determined by the following formula:

principal received $\times$ gross profit ratio = reportable gain

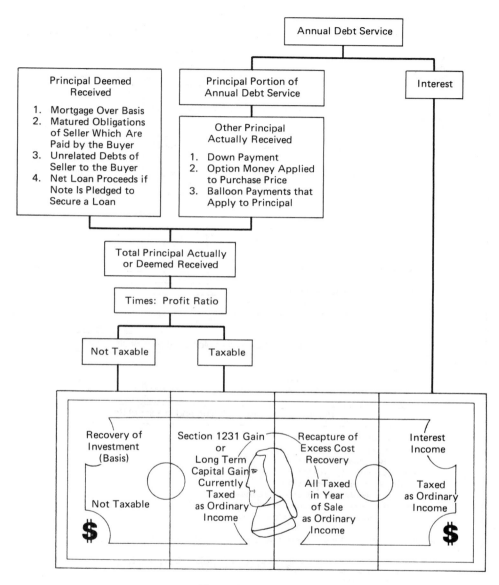

Figure 31

In the formula above, the principal received is made up of the principal actually received and the principal deemed received. The profit ratio equals the gain remaining to be reported divided by the contract price. The gain remaining to be reported equals the sale price less the sum of the adjusted basis of the property plus costs of sale and less any recapture of excess cost recovery (profit = total gain − recapture).

Installment Sale Worksheet

Pg _____ of _____

Date _____

Prepared for _____

Property _____

Sale Price _____
- Down Payment _____
- Existing Loan _____
= Purchase Money Note _____

Amortization of Purchase Money Note

Amount _____ Rate _____ Term _____ Pmt _____ A.D.S. _____

Year	Annual Debt Service	Interest	Principal	Remaining Balance
1				
2				
3				
4				
5				
6				

Calculation of Gain

1 Gross Sale Price
2 Adjusted Cost Basis at Sale
3 + Costs of Sale
4 + Excess Cost Recovery to be Recaptured
5 = Adjusted Basis Including Sale Costs & Recapture
6 Gain to be Spread over Contract Term (Line 1 minus Line 5)

Calculation of Excess of Mortgage over Basis

7 Existing Loan(s)
8 – Adjusted Basis Including Sale Costs & Recapture (Line 5)
9 = Excess of Mortgage over Basis (Must be 0 or greater - Negative # not allowed)

Principal Received at Closing and in Year of Sale

PRINCIPAL ACTUALLY RECEIVED:
10 Down Payment
11 + Option Money Applied to Purchase Price
PRINCIPAL DEEMED TO BE RECEIVED:
12 + Excess of Mortgage over Basis (Line 9)
13 + Seller's Matured Liabilities that Buyer will Pay this Year
14 + Buyer Forgiveness of Unrelated Debt of Seller to Buyer
15 = Principal Actually Received or Deemed to be Received at Closing by the Seller

16 Principal Received on Purchase Money Note during Year of Sale - but after Closing

Calculation of Contract Price and Profit Ratio

17 Gross Sale Price (Line 1)
18 + Mortgage in Excess of Basis, if any (Line 9)
19 – Existing Loan(s) (Line 7)
20 = Contract Price
21 Profit Ratio = Line 6 divided by Line 20

Figure 32

contract price = sale price + mortgage in excess of basis − existing loans

The profit ratio is used to determine the portion of principal payments received that will be taxed as gain. The profit ratio may be less than 100 percent if part of the principal received represents a return of the seller's investment and therefore, is not taxable, or if part of the principal received represents recapture of cost recovery.

REPORTING GAIN UNDER THE INSTALLMENT METHOD

Installment reporting of gain require the following steps.

1. Determine the gain in the usual manner as if the installment method were not being used.
2. Determine the contract price.
3. Divide the gain (determined in step 1) by the contract price (determined in step 2) to determine the profit ratio (the percentage of the contract price which the gain equals).
4. In each year in which principal is received from the buyer (the year of sale and subsequent years) multiply the principal amount received by the percentage determined in step 3. This procedure determines the amount of the gain to be reported in each year.

The following two examples illustrate installment reporting. The first example details a situation in which there are no existing mortgages on the property; the second deals with a case where there is an existing mortgage.

Examples

1. In March, 1988, Smith sells a parcel of land which cost her $20,000, for $50,000. The land is unencumbered. The buyer pays $10,000 in the year of sale and will pay $5,000 a year for the next eight years (plus sufficient interest on the unpaid balance to avoid imputed interest). Smith pays a broker a commission of $2,500 for bringing about the sale. The sale is reported as an installment sale, according to the following procedure:

Sale price		$50,000
Less commission	$ 2,500	
adjusted basis	20,000	
total basis		22,500
Gain on sale		$27,500

The contract price is the same as the sale price because there is no indebtedness taken over by the buyer payable to third parties. Hence, the contract price is $50,000. The gain is 55 percent of the contract price ($27,500 divided by $50,000).

In the year of sale, Smith received $10,000. Therefore, 55 percent of the $10,000, or $5,500, is reported as gain in that year. ✓

In each subsequent year, she will receive $5,000. In each of these years, Smith will report a gain of $2,750 (55 percent of $5,000). And in each of these years, she will receive interest payments. The interest will be reported separately as ordinary income.

2. In November 1988, Brown sells land and building for $100,000. His adjusted basis for the property at the time of sale is $59,600. He pays a sales commission of $5,000. Terms of the sale are

Cash paid at time of sale	$ 25,000
Existing mortgage on property assumed by buyer	40,000
Second mortgage given to seller (purchase money mortgage)	35,000
Total	$100,000

The second mortgage is to be paid in seven equal annual installments of principal plus sufficient interest to avoid imputed interest.

Brown reports the transaction as an installment sale. The gain on the sale is $35,400, determined this way.

Sale price		$100,000
Less adjusted basis	$59,600	
sales commissions	5,000	
total basis		64,600
Gain		$ 35,400

The contract price is $60,000, determined as follows.

Sale price	$100,000
Less mortgage assumed by buyer payable to third party	40,000
Contract price	$ 60,000

The gain is 59 percent of the contract price ($35,400 divided by $60,000).

In the year of sale, Brown received payments totaling $25,000. He reports 59 percent of the $25,000, or $14,750, as gain in the year of sale.

In each of the succeeding seven years, Brown will receive $5,000 as principal payment on the $35,000 second mortgage. Each year, Brown will report as gain on the sale $2,950 (59 percent of $5,000). The interest received each year will be reported separately as ordinary income.

Including the year of sale, Brown is to receive total payments of $60,000. (The remaining $40,000 of the sale price will be paid by the buyer to the mortgagee under the mortgage assumed by the buyer.) His total gain is $35,400. Under the installment method of reporting, here is how the gain is reported over the years of collection.

Year	Payment received	Taxable gain
1	$25,000	$14,750
2	5,000	2,950
3	5,000	2,950
4	5,000	2,950
5	5,000	2,950
6	5,000	2,950
7	5,000	2,950
8	5,000	2,950
Totals	$60,000	$35,400

Mortgage Over Basis and Wraparound Mortgages

If the buyer assumes or takes subject to an existing mortgage on the property and if that mortgage is greater than the seller's basis for the property, the seller is deemed to have received that excess amount in the year of sale. Two troublesome problems arise in this area. One deals with selling expenses; the other, with wraparound mortgages.

Selling expenses. Suppose the sale price of a property is $500,000 and brokers' commissions paid by the seller are $30,000. If the seller's basis for the property is $300,000, the gain on the sale is $170,000 (the $500,000 selling price minus the total of the basis plus selling expenses, $330,000). The $170,000 gain can be determined by reducing the selling price by the commissions and then subtracting the basis, or by adding the $30,000 commissions to the $300,000 basis and then subtracting the new basis of $330,000 from the selling price.

If the mortgage on the property which the buyer is assuming or taking subject to is no greater than $300,000, it would make no difference which method was used to arrive at the $170,000 gain. But suppose the mortgage on the property was $350,000.

If the selling expenses merely reduced the selling price by $30,000, the excess of the mortgage over the basis would be $50,000, and that amount would be treated as received by the seller in the year of sale. However, if the $30,000 were added to the basis to arrive at the $170,000 gain, the new basis would be $330,000 and the excess of the mortgage over the basis would be reduced to $20,000.

IRS regulations establish that the selling expenses should be added to basis. This is, of course, beneficial to sellers in that it permits them to defer a greater portion of the gain when the mortgage exceeds the seller's basis.

When a wraparound mortgage is used, the buyer gives the seller a mortgage for an amount greater than the existing mortgage on the property and purports not to assume or take subject to the existing mortgage.

Example

> Wilson has a property with a basis of $200,000. There is an existing mortgage on the property of $300,000. She sells the property for $450,000. Lynch pays $50,000 in cash and gives Wilson a mortgage of $400,000. Under the agreement, Lynch claims he is not taking subject to the $300,000 mortgage on the property. Instead, it is agreed that as he pays off the $400,000, Wilson will use the necessary portion of the payments she receives to make payments on the $300,000 mortgage. This is an example of a wraparound mortgage.

In 1987, in the case of *Professional Equities, Inc. v. Commissioner*, the court held that the IRS temporary regulations on wraparound mortgages were invalid. These regulations had been in effect since March, 1981. In essence, these regulations required sellers who used wraparound mortgages to use the same calculation in arriving at the profit ratio as sellers who allowed buyers to assume or take subject to the existing loans on the property at the time of the sale. Although it was necessary to use this profit ratio only for the year of sale, it had the effect of including a much greater portion of the gain in the year of sale than would be included if the profit ratio could be computed by the method sanctioned by court cases prior to 1981. Furthermore, a larger profit ratio caused a larger amount of principal deemed received to be taxed as gain in the year of sale. This was quite disadvantageous to sellers who sold when their mortgages exceeded the basis of the property being sold. Now that these regulations have been held invalid it will be possible to use wraparound mortgages once again to spread the gain on an installment sale more evenly over the contract term.

Related Person Sales

Suppose the seller wants an installment sale, but the buyer wants to pay all cash. One device which had been used was to have the seller sell to a related person on an installment sale basis. The related buyer would then immediately sell to the ultimate buyer for cash. The related buyer would have no gain or loss. Then, the related buyer would pay the seller according to the installment sale agreement. IRS had attacked these sales, and Congress has put some specific rules into the law to eliminate this device in certain instances.

If the seller makes an installment sale to a related person, and if that related person sells the property within two years, the original seller has to pick up the balance of the gain at the time the related person makes the sale. If the property sold is marketable securities, then it makes no difference when the related person makes the sale—even if it is more than two years after the original sale; the original seller still has to pick up the balance of the gain when the related person makes the sale. So, the sale to a related person with an immediate resale defeats the installment sale. However, if the second sale is an *involuntary conversion* (a condemnation of property), this is not a sale that triggers income to the first seller.

Who is a related person?   Related persons are defined as the seller's spouse, children, grandchildren and parents. Also included are trusts of which the seller is a beneficiary (or part of whose property the seller is deemed to own), estates in which the seller is a beneficiary, partnerships in which the seller is a partner and corporations in which the seller owns at least 50 percent of the stock. (In each of these cases, indirect ownership is also counted.) The 1986 Act expanded the definition of related persons to include any controlled entity. See §642(a)(1) of the 1986 Act amending §1239(c).

The related person rule will not apply, however, if it is established to the satisfaction of IRS that neither the original sale nor the resale "had as one of its principal purposes the avoidance of federal income tax." Of course, it will be difficult to convince IRS that there was no tax avoidance motive present when the second sale takes place almost immediately after the first, or when it is apparent that the original seller could have made an all cash sale to the ultimate buyer in the first place.

Even if the person to whom the seller makes the initial sale (with the idea that the buyer will resell) is not a related person, IRS could still attack the installment sale as a sham. Then the seller could present evidence that there was a real sale. However, if the transaction comes under the related-person rules, the installment sale is more easily knocked out.

Installment Sales which Include Like-Kind Exchanges

Gain on a like-kind exchange is not taxable. In effect, the tax on the gain is postponed. Suppose, however, that in addition to the like-kind exchange, the seller receives an amount of money which is to be paid over a period of years. It is clear that the gain attributable to the money is taxable as boot (see Chapter 11). It is also clear that if the installment sale rules apply, the gain attributable to the money received will be spread out over the period of payment. There had been some question as to how the gain should be reported. This was cleared up in the revised installment sale law for sales made after October 19, 1980.

Example

A taxpayer exchanges property with a basis of $400,000 for like-kind property worth $200,000 and an $800,000 installment obligation; $100,000 is to be paid in the year of sale and the balance in succeeding years. In effect, the total sale price is $1,000,000 and the gain is $600,000 ($1,000,000 minus the $400,000 basis). Since the seller is to receive $800,000 in cash, the entire $600,000 gain is taxable. But when?

The contract price is $800,000 (the like-kind property is not included in the contract price). Hence, the $600,000 gain is 75 percent of the contract price. *But the $200,000 value of the like-kind property is not included in the amount received in the year of sale.* So, in the year of sale, the seller reports a gain of $75,000 (75 percent of the $100,000 cash received). The balance of the gain is reported as the remainder of the $800,000 is received. Again, only $600,000 is taxable.

Cost Recovery Recapture in Installment Sales

If part of the gain on the transaction that is being reported as an installment sale is subject to cost recovery recapture, that portion of the gain is treated as ordinary income. The question arises in an installment sale as to *when* that ordinary income is to be reported. The answer depends on whether the disposition took place before June 7, 1984 (old rule), or after June 6, 1984 (new rule). The old rule also applies to dispositions taking place after June 6, 1984, if they were made pursuant to contracts that were binding on March 22, 1984.

Under the old rule, the first amounts received in the installment sale are attributable to cost recovery recapture. After the cost recovery recapture is accounted for, the balance of the payments is treated as capital gain.

Example

In Example 2, on page 252, Brown had a gain of $35,400. Assume that $15,000 of that gain was cost recovery recapture. Under the old rules, since $14,750 is reported in the year of sale which is less than the total $15,000 of depreciation recapture, the entire $14,750 would be reported as ordinary income in the year of sale. In the second year, $2,950 of the gain is reportable. Since $250 of the $15,000 depreciation recapture is still to be reported, $250 of the $2,950 gain will be reported as ordinary income in the second year, and the remaining $2,700 of gain will be reportable as long-term capital gain. In the third through the eighth years, the full $2,950 gain reported each year will be reported as long-term capital gain because the entire cost recovery recapture will have been accounted for in previous years.

The new rule takes a much more drastic approach. The amount of the cost recovery recapture is reported as ordinary income in the year of sale *regardless of when* the actual installment payments are received. The amount of the cost recovery recapture is then added to the basis of the property sold and the gain, contract price and profit ratio are calculated.

Example

Going back to Example 2, Brown has a sales price of $100,000, a basis of $64,600, and a gain of $35,400. But since $15,000 was cost recovery recapture, that amount has to be reported as ordinary income in the year of sale. The gain on the sale is recomputed by adding $15,000 to the $64,600 basis, producing a new basis of $79,600.

The gain is now $20,400, or 34 percent of the $60,000 contract price. In the year of sale, Brown receives $25,000; and reports a capital gain of 34 percent of $35,000, or $8,500. In each of the subsequent seven years, a payment of $5,000 will be received, of which 34 percent, or $1,700, will be reported as capital gain. Thus, Brown will report $15,000 of ordinary income (in the year of sale) and $20,400 of capital gain which is made up of $8,500 in the year of sale and $11,900 in the subsequent seven years ($1,700 multiplied by seven).

Overall, this is the same result as under the old rule. But under the new rule, the $15,000 cost recovery recapture has to be reported in the year of sale even if *no* payments were received in that year; and the gain attributable to the amount that *was* received in the year of sale is reported *in addition to* the cost recovery recapture reported that year.

Advantages of Installment Reporting

Under the installment method, the tax cost of the gain is matched to the collections. In other words, the taxpayer generally does not have to pay out cash in the form of taxes before actually receiving the payments in which the gain is included.

To the extent that the taxpayer can defer the payment of the tax, the taxpayer has the use of the tax money at no interest cost for the period of deferral. To the extent that the gain is spread over a number of years, it may be subject to lower marginal tax rates than if the entire gain were reported in one year.

Disadvantages of Installment Reporting

Under the installment method, the seller cannot liquidate all of the equity in the property and "cash out" at the time of sale.

The purchase money mortgage may not produce a desirable after-tax yield to the seller. The seller may have better alternative investments than this.

The real rate of return may decline in the case of inflation. Inflation may result in the receipt of installment payments with less valuable dollars.

The seller may be required to give a purchase money mortgage in order to sell the property.

All recapture of excess depreciation is taxed in the year of sale, which may result in tax payments which are greater than cash received in the year of sale.

The 1987 Act made three significant changes to the installment sale rules.

1. It repealed the use of the installment method for most dealer sales after 1987. See Figure 33 for a brief overview of these changes.

2. It accelerated the taxation of gain on nondealer sales to the extent of net loan proceeds if the seller carryback financing is pledged as collateral for a loan.

3. It imposed interest on the tax deferred to the extent attributable to the amount by which the unpaid balances to the seller on all installment sales made by the seller in any given year exceeds $5,000,000.

For an overview of the new rules see Figures 33 and 34.

Contingent Sale Price

If the sale price was not readily determinable (for example, part of the sale price depended on future events, such as the amount of income produced by the property sold), IRS took the position that the installment sale rules did not apply.

In other cases, taxpayers argued that the value of the obligations had no ascertainable value—as where the buyer's obligation was in the form of a "bare" contractual promise rather than in the form of negotiable notes. (Some courts sustained the taxpayers in this view.) Then, the seller could apply the first proceeds received to recover the basis. When the payments received had accounted for the basis, future payments were treated as gain.

Congress has finally set forth rules dealing with a contingent sales price. The law now treats as installment sales those sales which have contingent sale prices and those in which the price is not readily ascertainable. This new provision affects sales made after October 19, 1980. IRS regulations detail how the installment sale reporting should be made in these cases.

Since almost all contingent sale-price sales are to be treated as installment sales, it will be almost impossible to argue that the installment obligations do not have ascertainable values. That being the case, the seller will not have any basis for attempting to apply the first proceeds received to recover the basis and report a gain only after the basis is recovered. (As indicated above, this argument was accepted by some courts before Congress amended the law.)

Imputed Interest

Normally, an installment sale will call for interest on the unpaid installments (the seller expects the buyer to pay for the use of the money during the deferral period). In the past, transactions were structured calling for no interest or a very low rate of interest. The price was adjusted to reflect some interest (perhaps less than would normally be called for); thus

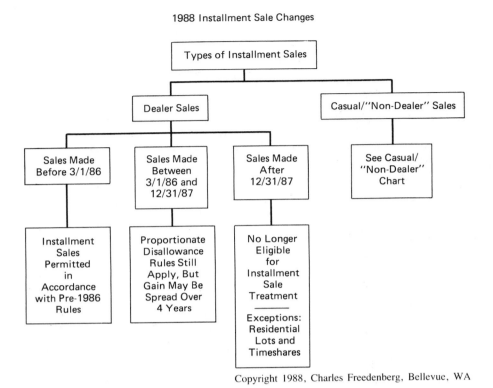

1988 Installment Sale Changes

Copyright 1988, Charles Freedenberg, Bellevue, WA

Figure 33. Overview of new rules for dealer sales

the gain on sale was increased, and the seller expected to treat this increase as a capital gain. In exchange for losing the interest deduction, the buyer was given some concession on the *interest factor* and the price was raised accordingly.

To prevent this abuse, Congress created the concept of imputed interest. If a minimum amount of interest was not called for in the sales agreement, the law would impute interest. Thus, each installment, although ostensibly all principal, is segmented into a principal payment and an *imputed interest* payment. Part of the payment becomes interest income to the seller (ordinary income) and an interest deduction to the buyer.

The rules dealing with imputed interest were substantially changed by the Tax Reform Act of 1984 for taxable years ending after July 18, 1984. Before discussing the new rules, however, it is important to see how the old rules applied to transactions governed by the old law to better understand the significance of the changes made by the new law.

Under the old law, the minimum interest rate required to avoid imputed interest was changed from time to time by IRS. If the minimum rate (in terms of simple interest) was not used, IRS imputed a rate one percentage point higher than the minimum rate and applied it on a semiannual compound interest basis. Thus, as each installment was

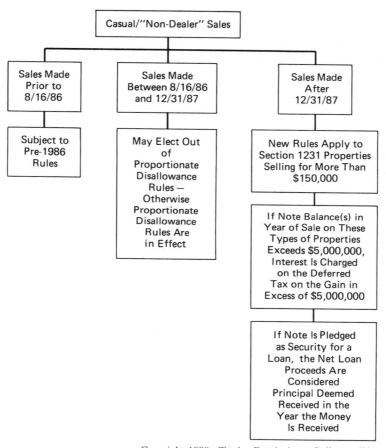

Figure 34. 1988 Changes to Non-dealer Rules

received, a portion of it, based on semiannual compound interest from the date of sale until the date of payment, was considered as interest and the balance was treated as payment of part of the purchase price. This was referred to as discounting back each installment.

Under the new law, there are two sets of rules: one deals with original issue discount, the other revises the old imputed interest rules. The revised imputed interest rules apply to a sale of a principal residence, a farm for $1,000,000 or less, other sales transactions involving total payments of $250,000 or less, and sales of land between related parties (explained below). In all other transactions, the original issue discount rules apply.

Original issue discount is the difference between the issue price of an obligation and its redemption price at maturity. If there is original issue discount, it is accrued on a daily basis and reported as income and deduction. IRS provides a formula for the accrual of the interest which uses a constant rate with periodic compounding. So the interest accruing in the earlier part of the period is relatively small, while the interest accruing in the later part of the period is relatively large.

When the original issue discount rules apply, it is first necessary to determine if the obligation has adequate stated interest. This is done by reference to an applicable rate based on interest paid on federal obligations. The present values of all payments due under the obligation are determined by discounting the payments at the applicable federal rate (AFR). (IRS regulations will explain the discounting method.) If the total of the present values are equal to or greater than the total amounts of principal to be paid under the obligation, there is adequate stated interest and no interest is imputed.

If, under this test, there is inadequate interest, the issue price of the obligation is the present value of the payments due under the obligation discounted at the applicable federal rate.

The original issue discount rules do not apply to those sales listed above to which the revised imputed interest rules apply. Under the revised imputed interest rules, the present value of all future payments is first determined and is then subtracted from the sum of the principal payments to be received. The result of this subtraction is then reduced by the interest stated in the agreement (if any). The balance is the unstated, or imputed, interest. To determine the present value of the future payments, they are discounted at the applicable federal rate.

Just as in the old law, there is a minimum amount of interest that acts as a safe harbor. If interest called for in the agreement is at least equal to that minimum, the imputed interest rules do not apply. The minimum is determined by discounting the future principal and interest payments at the applicable federal rate. If the discounted amount is not less than the principal balance, the safe harbor test is met.

A special rule applies to the sale of a principal residence for up to $250,000 or of a farm. Instead of using the applicable federal rates, the *old* imputed interest rules apply. That is, if the interest called for meets the minimum IRS rate, there is no imputed interest. If not, interest will be imputed at 9 percent compounded semiannually. (Of course, if the sale of the farm is for more than $1,000,000, the original issue discount rules apply).

Another special rule provides a safe harbor for sales of land between family members when the sales price does not exceed $500,000. (This maximum is reduced by the amounts of prior sales between the family members in the same calendar year.) Family members include brothers, sisters, spouse, ancestors (parents, grandparents, etc.) and lineal descendants (children, grandchildren, etc.). In determining the present value of future payments, a rate of 6 percent, compounded semiannually, is used. This present value is then subtracted from the total of the future payments. If the actual interest called for in the agreement is at least equal to this difference, there is no imputed interest.

While it might be thought that the original issue discount rules have lost their importance with the repeal of the capital gain exclusion, this is not necessarily true. Without a difference between the taxation of ordinary income and capital gains it would appear that sellers no longer have any reason to raise their sale prices and lower their interest rates. This ignores the recently conceded position of the IRS on the treatment of gain on an installment sale. Gain on an installment sale is now treated as passive income. Passive income can be offset by passive losses in an unlimited amount. Therefore, sellers once again have an incentive to convert ordinary income to capital gain.

Interest income from installment sales is treated as portfolio income and cannot be offset by passive losses. Therefore, the more income a seller can convert to capital gain income, the easier it will be for the seller to shelter that income. The original issue discount rules will serve to prevent flagrant abuses in this area.

SALE AND LEASEBACK

A sale and leaseback is a transaction in which the owner of the property sells the property and immediately leases it back from the new owner. Consequently, during the term of the lease, the seller-lessee's physical relationship to the property remains unchanged.

A sale-leaseback transaction is often looked upon as a financing transaction. In other words, it is often a substitute for refinancing by the owner via a new mortgage. There is one major difference between a sale-leaseback and a mortgage: at the end of the lease term the former owner (now lessee) loses possession of the property; in the case of a mortgage, the owner retains the property. Consequently, the residual value of the property (the value at the end of the lease term) is an important factor in comparing the economic results of sale-leasebacks and mortgages.

In this section we are concerned primarily with the tax consequences to the seller-lessee. The tax consequences, of course, weigh heavily in calculating the net financial results of the transaction.

Tax Consequences

Two distinct transactions are involved in a sale-leaseback.

Upon the sale, the seller realizes gain or loss in the same manner as upon any other sale. The tax consequences are the same as for any other sale: possible Section 1231 gain or loss, possible depreciation recapture.

Upon becoming a lessee, the former owner pays rent for the occupancy rights to the property. Normally, rent is a fully deductible expense for tax purposes, assuming that the property is used in the lessee's trade or business (including the business of holding the property for rent to others). If the rent agreement constitutes a Section 467 Rental Agreement, special rules apply as to when rent is deductible (and reportable as income). See the discussion in Chapter 7.

These are the general tax rules that apply to a sale-leaseback. There are, however, a number of problems that can arise which may modify these rules.

Lease term for 30 years or more.   If the lease term is for 30 years or more, IRS says the lease itself is property of a like-kind to other real estate. Hence, the sale-

leaseback is to be treated as a tax-deferred exchange. Since in a sale-leaseback the seller usually receives cash (if the result of the sale-leaseback is a gain), even if it is deemed to be a like-kind exchange, the gain would be taxable to the extent of the cash received.

The difficulty arises if the sale portion of the sale-leaseback results in a loss. In that case, if the IRS view prevails and a 30-year lease is treated as like-kind property, the loss would not be recognized for tax purposes.

The courts have sustained the IRS view in some cases, and the safer approach (when there is a loss) is to use a lease term of less than 30 years. In this respect, it should also be noted that a shorter lease term with an unrealistic renewal term (either unusual length of time or greatly reduced rent) may cause IRS to attempt to combine the lease terms for the purposes of its 30-year rule.

Repurchase option.   As has been pointed out, one of the unfavorable aspects of the sale-leaseback (from the seller's viewpoint) is that the lessee loses the property at the end of the lease term.

To overcome this objection to the sale-leaseback, the seller may be given an option to reacquire the property at the termination of the lease. The difficulty with this arrangement, from a tax viewpoint, is that it may upset the treatment of the lease as a lease. If, for example, the seller-lessee may reacquire the property at the end of the lease term for a nominal payment, IRS will likely contend that the arrangement was not a lease from the outset but rather that it was merely a financing arrangement similar to a mortgage. In that case, the rental deductions the lessee expected each year would be disallowed. Instead, the lessee would be allowed that portion of the rent payments which represent a reasonable interest rate on borrowed money as a deduction. The lessee would be entitled to cost recovery deductions (being the owner of the property).

To avoid having the lease treated as a loan, any repurchase option contained in the arrangement must call for a purchase price which can be sustained as representing the fair market value of the property at the time the lease expires. A repurchase price to be determined by professional appraisers at the time of the repurchase is probably one satisfactory approach. Other reasonable approaches resulting in the equivalent of an arm's-length purchase price at the end of the lease term may be used.

Tax Arithmetic of Leasebacks

Owners of property are entitled to cost recovery deductions and deductions for interest paid. Lessees are entitled to tax deductions for rent paid.

The owner of property recognizes that the portion of the basis allocable to the underlying land is nondepreciable for tax purposes; yet the value of the property has increased. So the owner looks to convert that appreciation into cash for use in business or for further investment. If the property is sold, the appreciation is realized, but the use of the property is lost. If the owner refinances, the amount that could be borrowed may not be as much as what could be realized on the sale. A sale-leaseback may give the best of both possible worlds (however, the loss of the property at the end of the lease term should not be overlooked).

Sale-leaseback.   Assuming that the sale is made at a gain, the seller will have a cash amount equal to the sale price minus selling costs and the tax on the gain. The cost of this after-tax cash is the net cash outlay of the rental payments over the term of the lease. Since the rent payments constitute tax deductions, the net cash outlay is the difference between the rent called for in the lease and the tax saved by the deductibility of the rent (the amount of the rent multiplied by the taxpayer's marginal rate).

The total after-tax outlay for rent over the lease term will likely exceed the net after-tax cash realized on the sale. In that sense, then, the sale-leaseback is financing. An additional cost of after-tax cash on the sale is the loss of the property at the end of the lease term.

Without the sale-leaseback, the owner's cost-recovery deductions are limited in total to the basis in the improvements (land is nondepreciable). After the sale and leaseback, the owner has realized the proceeds from the sale of both the land and improvements and is paying rent on both. To that extent, the owner has converted the nondepreciable land into an investment amortizable over the life of the lease.

Mortgage financing.   If, instead of selling and leasing back, the owner seeks to refinance, a loan must be obtained that is equal to the after-tax sale proceeds in the sale-leaseback to have the same cash availability at that point.

Assuming that the mortgage term is as long as the lease term, the after-tax cash outlay in repaying the loan may be compared with the after-tax cash outlay for the rents. In determining the after-tax cash outlay, principal payments on the loan are not considered tax deductible. However, the interest payments are deductible for income tax purposes, thereby reducing the effective cash outlay for the interest. Furthermore, when the mortgage financing route is used, the borrower continues to own the property and is therefore entitled to cash-recovery deductions. These deductions do not require a cash outlay but reduce taxable income and the cash required for tax payments. Hence, in determining the total cash outlay over the mortgage term (in order to compare it with the total net cash outlay over the lease term were a sale-leaseback employed), it is proper to subtract from the total of the principal and interest payments to be made over that period the tax savings arising from the deductibility of both the interest payments and the cost recovery on the property.

OTHER DISPOSITIONS OF PROPERTY

In addition to the more conventional dispositions of property, there are a number of less common types of disposition which have special tax consequences.

Charitable Contributions

One method of disposing of property is to contribute it to a charitable organization. Many tax factors are involved in this type of disposition; income taxes may be saved and capital gains may be avoided.

Charitable contributions can only be deducted for individuals who itemize personal deductions. The deductible amount can vary depending upon the nature of the charitable organization, the nature of the property, and, in some instances, how the organization will use the donated property.

Nature of the charity.   Certain charities are considered maximum donee organizations. These are generally charities which are religious, educational, or governmental in nature. Charities that are not maximum donee organizations are organizations such as veterans' organizations, fraternal organizations, public cemeteries, and private nonoperating foundations.

Nature of the property.   The contributed property can be

1. Appreciated ordinary income property,
2. Appreciated capital gain property,
3. Appreciated property with both ordinary income and capital gain components or
4. Property being transferred at a loss.

The nature of the contributed property will determine the amount that is allowed as a charitable deduction.

Contribution deduction amount.   Appreciated ordinary income property is property that if sold would give rise to ordinary income or short-term capital gain. This generally refers to assets held for one year or less. If an asset was held for more than one year but had excess cost recovery that was subject to recapture, the excess cost recovery would be considered an ordinary income component of the property being contributed. The deduction for ordinary income property is limited to the donor's basis in the property. The nature of the charitable organization has no bearing on this limitation.

Appreciated capital gain property is property that if sold would give rise to a long-term capital gain. This includes Section 1231 assets and capital assets that have been held for more than one year. The general rule is that the amount of the charitable deduction for appreciated capital gain property is equal to the fair market value of the property. However, there are several exceptions to these rules, also based upon the type of property being donated, the nature of the charitable organization and the use of the property by the charity that the taxpayer should consider before contributing appreciated property.

When a gift is made of property which has a capital gain component and an ordinary income component, the charitable deduction must first be reduced by the ordinary income component; then the capital gain rules are applied to the remaining value of the property.

For property that has depreciated in value, the amount of the deduction is limited to the fair market value of the property at the date of the contribution. A donor may not claim any type of loss deduction on the transaction.

Maximum Charitable Deduction Limit

The deduction ceiling for most charitable contributions is 50 percent of the contribution base. The contribution base is adjusted gross income, computed without regard to any net operating loss carryback. This 50 percent limit applies only to those charities which are considered maximum donee organizations.

There is a 30 percent of adjusted gross income limit on gifts to non-maximum donee organizations. If the contribution involves appreciated capital gain property to a non-maximum donee organization, a deduction limitation of 20 percent of the adjusted gross income applies.

If a taxpayer's contribution in any year exceeds any of these limitations, the disallowed excess contribution may be carried over for five years. If all of the contribution is not allowed within the five year period, it is lost.

11
Exchanges

MOTIVATIONS FOR EXCHANGE

Exchanging real estate, rather than selling it outright and reinvesting the proceeds, generally stems from one of two motivations. First, exchanging properties is a method of marketing real estate when a sale does not appear to be possible for one of a number of reasons, including the following:

- Buyers with cash are not available
- A sale on terms does not give the seller sufficient funds with which to acquire another property or
- The seller will not price property realistically so that it will attract a purchaser.

The second, and probably the most important, motivating force for exchanging property is the available income tax deferral. The capital gains tax that would normally be paid on the gain from the sale may be postponed or even avoided in full or in part with use of an exchange. The following example dramatically illustrates why tax deferral is such an important motivation for an exchange.

Example

Wilson, a married man filing a joint return, has property with a market value of $100,000. His adjusted basis for the property is $10,000. In 1988, were he to sell the property for

$100,000 in cash, he would have a capital gain of $90,000. Assuming the maximum tax rate applies, he would have a tax of $29,700 (33 percent of $90,000). Hence, he would have $70,300 to reinvest ($100,000 sale price minus $29,700 tax).

Were he to engage in an exchange, Wilson would receive property worth $100,000. He could, in essence, reinvest the full $100,000 value of his present property. Thus, a tax-free exchange could preserve $29,700 of his capital (the amount he would owe in taxes on a sale). Assuming a 10 percent capitalization rate on Wilson's investment, the $29,700 would produce $2,970 per year of ordinary income. Consequently, a tax deferral for ten years, for example, would build up capital for this investor of $59,400: the $29,700 of capital preserved via the tax-free exchange plus the $29,700 return on that investment at 10 percent per year. (Actually, the amount would be reduced by the taxes paid on the annual interest income and would be increased by the compounding effect of reinvesting the after-tax income.)

EXCHANGE OR SELL?

Before discussing the rules of tax deferral in detail, it is important to keep in mind that a sale at a taxable gain, coupled with reinvestment in another property, has the effect of stepping up basis. In an exchange, however (subject to adjustments discussed later), the basis of the property acquired is reduced by the amount of gain on which tax has been deferred. Consequently, a question presents itself: is the property owner better off by selling, paying tax and reinvesting to get a higher basis and larger cost recovery deductions in the future or by avoiding current taxation through a tax-deferred exchange and forego larger cost recovery deductions in the future?

The tax dollars saved currently by going through a tax-deferred exchange rather than realizing a capital gain can easily be calculated. This amount can then be compared to the total of the discounted values of the future tax savings that would arise from additional cost recovery deductions which would be available had there been a sale and reinvestment in property with a higher adjusted basis.

There cannot be one answer to the question of choosing between exchanging or selling and reinvesting. With the same properties taxpayers with different tax rates can get different tax results. Hence, individual calculations should be made.

Since the current values of future tax savings are, at best, a good guess (future tax rates can change or the taxpayer's other income streams may be altered, thus increasing or decreasing the marginal rate), many investors prefer the "bird in the hand" of a current tax saving via a tax-deferred exchange. Be that as it may, the value of future tax savings through larger cost recovery deductions (when basis is stepped up through a sale and reinvestment) is mentioned here so that it may be considered among all of the other factors in determining whether to exchange or to sell outright.

With the passage of the Tax Reform Act of 1986, tax deferred exchanges have become more attractive. Under the prior law, cost recovery deductions were taken over shorter recovery periods than are currently available (18 and 19 years as opposed to 27.5 and 31.5 years).

Also, prior tax rates on ordinary income went as high as 50 percent, while the highest tax bracket is currently 33 percent. Therefore, under the earlier law larger cost recovery deductions were allowed. The tax savings of larger deductions subject to higher tax brackets generated much higher tax savings under the prior law than under the current law. Larger tax savings made cost recovery deductions more valuable under prior law. Hence, under the earlier law, a higher basis in a piece of property had more significant tax advantages. This combination of factors made tax deferred exchanges less attractive under prior law than under current law. The trade off of a lower basis in a property acquired by exchange was more costly. Furthermore, the current passive loss rules may not permit a taxpayer to take advantage of greater cost recovery deductions even if they were available.

In connection with the future tax savings through cost recovery deductions, keep in mind that for real property put into service after January 1, 1987, the MACRS recovery rate is based on a 27.5 or 31.5 year life rather than a 15, 18, or 19-year life. This change diminishes the early-year depreciation deductions. (For a full discussion of the MACRS rules as they apply to real estate, see Chapter 9.)

Whenever a decision to exchange is made, it is important to carefully follow the tax rules set forth in this chapter.

TAX LAW REQUIREMENTS FOR TAX-DEFERRED EXCHANGES

Section 1031 of the Internal Revenue Code provides that when certain property is exchanged for other property, some or all of the gain which is *realized* economically may not have to be *recognized* for tax purposes.

Example

> Ann has property which is worth $100,000. Her adjusted basis for that property is only $40,000. If she sells that property for its value, she will *realize* a gain of $60,000. If she sells for cash, that gain will also be *recognized* for tax purposes; she would have to pay tax on a gain of $60,000. If, instead, she exchanges it for another property worth $100,000, she would still realize a gain of $60,000. However, that gain would not be recognized for tax purposes; she would pay no tax because of that transaction.

This example illustrates the difference between gain which is *realized* and that which is *recognized*. Realized is an economic concept—how much gain actually results from the transaction. Recognized is a tax concept—how much gain (if any) is taxable.

Section 1031 provides that no gain or loss is to be recognized (taxed) if certain business or investment property is exchanged solely for property of a like-kind which is also to be held for use in business or as an investment. To the extent that the exchange is not *solely* for like-kind property, some of the gain might be recognized; the balance of the gain may still be deferred.

The provisions of Section 1031 are not discretionary with the taxpayer or with the government. *If a transaction fits within the statutory requirements, no gain or loss is recognized.*

It should be made clear that when a transaction is described as tax-free in this discussion, it does not necessarily mean that the gain escapes taxation completely. What is meant is that the tax on the gain is deferred or postponed.

Example

> A owns a parcel of land with a market value of $50,000 and a basis of $10,000. She exchanges it for another piece of land which is also worth $50,000. A's basis for the new land acquired is $10,000, the same as her basis for the land she gave up. There is no tax on this exchange. But if some years later A should sell the second parcel of land for $50,000, she would have a $40,000 recognized *at that time*. Consequently, the effect of Section 1031 on that exchange was to defer the $40,000 taxable gain until the subsequent disposition; it did not eliminate the gain forever.

Of course, a tax deferral is very valuable. As was illustrated in a prior example (where the tax of $29,700 was deferred), the deferral permitted the accumulation of an additional $29,700 of income over a ten-year period. Looking at it another way, whenever a tax can be deferred, in effect, money is borrowed from the U.S. Treasury without interest. (And, should an individual die without having disposed of the property in a taxable transaction, that deferred income tax will never have to be paid. When property is inherited, the basis to the heirs is the market value of that property on the date of the owner's death.)

ELEMENTS REQUIRED FOR SECTION 1031 EXCHANGE

In order to qualify for no recognition of gain or loss on an exchange under Section 1031, certain elements must be present.

1. Both the property received and the property given up must be held either for productive use in a trade or business or for investment. Specifically excluded from the benefits of this section are stock in trade or other property primarily held for sale (inventory), stocks, bonds, notes, choses in action, certificates of trust or beneficial interest, any other securities or evidences of indebtedness or interests, and interests in a partnership transferred after March 31, 1984.
2. To qualify, both properties must be of a like-kind to each other; that is, the nature or character of both properties must be alike.
3. Finally, the properties must be exchanged for each other.

Property Used in a Trade or Business

This may include any kind of property which is used in the taxpayer's trade or business, such as machinery, office equipment, automobiles, factory buildings and land on which a building is situated. Property held for rental purposes, such as an apartment house or office building, is property used in a trade or business.

Held for Investment

This is property held for appreciation in value (and for the income therefrom) and not held for resale or in business. Since rental property (which is held for income) is defined as trade or business property, in terms of real estate, property held for investment is generally limited to vacant land. However, since property used in a trade or business also qualifies for a Section 1031 exchange, the distinction between trade or business property and investment property has no particular significance in terms of tax-free exchanges of real estate.

Like-Kind

This concept relates to the nature of the property rather than its grade or quality. Improved real estate is considered to be of the same nature as unimproved real estate. They are both of a like-kind. The fact of improvement or unimprovement relates only to the grade or quality of the property and not to its kind or class. For this purpose, real estate is considered to be the same kind of property as a leasehold for real estate if the leasehold has 30 years or more to run.

Property used in a trade or business may be exchanged for other property used in a trade or business or may be exchanged for investment property. Similarly, property held for investment may be exchanged for other investment property or may be exchanged for property used in a trade or business.

The following exchanges are illustrations of like-kind properties permitted to be exchanged: city real estate for a ranch or farm; truck for a truck; vacant lot for land and building; or a leasehold of real estate with 30 or more years to run for a parcel of real estate owned outright.

There had been considerable controversy over whether interests in partnerships qualify as like-kind property. The Tax Reform Act of 1984 provides that partnership interests exchanged after March 31, 1984 do *not* qualify as like-kind property. A partnership, however, may exchange qualifying property that it owns for other qualifying property if all members of the partnership remain in the partnership and no new members are added in the exchange.

Requirement of Exchange

To enable the gain to be deferred under Section 1031, property must actually be exchanged. Care must be taken to avoid a sale and a purchase when an exchange is intended. Under the new rules, it is permissible to close one escrow up to 180 days prior to the closing of the second escrow. If done properly, this will not be considered a cash sale. These rules will be discussed below.

A typical situation in which the exchange requirement must be carefully observed arises when the seller wants an exchange for like-kind property and the buyer does not own suitable property to exchange. In such a situation, the seller and buyer can agree that the buyer will first acquire suitable property and then exchange it for the seller's property.

In this case the seller has a tax-free exchange, but the buyer does not. The property acquired and exchanged was not held by the buyer for investment or for productive use in a trade or business. However, since the buyer has just purchased the property, chances are that the basis will be close to the fair market value and thus there will be little or no taxable gain on the transaction.

In a transaction of this sort, the seller can even direct the buyer to make specific improvements to the property the seller is to acquire, prior to the exchange. For example, the seller can direct that a plant be built on the property to specifications.

Sometimes an intermediary is used in these transactions. If, for example, the buyer does not wish to acquire the property that is then to be exchanged with the seller, the intermediary buys the property and exchanges that property for the seller's property. The buyer then buys from the intermediary the property formerly owned by the seller.

Four-Way Exchange

With three judges dissenting, the Tax Court, in *Coupe*, 52 TC 394 (1969), held a four-way exchange to be tax-free under the circumstances described in the example below.

Example

Jones owned farmland which Southern Pacific contracted to buy for $2,500 an acre, for a total of $330,000. Jones's basis in the property was only $17,000. His attorney suggested that the capital gains tax could be deferred if he were willing to take other farmlands rather than cash. Jones agreed, and the attorney obtained acceptable farmlands. Southern Pacific was not willing to take title to the other farmlands but was willing to cooperate in other ways, that is, to deposit the purchase price in escrow, payable to the titleholder of the property it had contracted to buy.

The transaction was arranged by way of simultaneous closings: (1) Jones's property was deeded to the attorney; (2) the attorney then immediately deeded that property to Southern Pacific; (3) the attorney used the escrow deposit to acquire the deeds to the other farmlands; (4) the attorney deeded the other farmlands to Jones.

Future Exchange

What can be done when the buyer has no suitable property to exchange? That problem was solved in the *Starker* case, where the court found a tax-free exchange when property was exchanged for a *promise* by the buyer to acquire suitable properties and exchange them. The court held that the promise was a fee equivalent.

However, for transfers made after March 31, 1984, the Tax Reform Act of 1984 has effectively outlawed certain future exchanges. If a taxpayer transfers property for property to be received later, the exchange will *not* qualify as like-kind unless

1. The property to be received in the future is identified no later than 45 days after the taxpayer transferred property, *and*
2. The property to be received is received no later than 180 days after the taxpayer transferred property. If the taxpayer's tax return for the taxable year in which the property was transferred is due before the end of the 180-day period, then the taxpayer must have received the property no later than the due date of that tax return which includes any extension of time allowed.

DISQUALIFICATION FROM SECTION 1031

Let us examine more closely those attributes of a transaction which will disqualify it from nonrecognition treatment of Section 1031.

The first attribute concerns the nature of the property *received*: If the property received is not the same kind as that given up, the transaction will not qualify under Section 1031. If the property received is totally cash, notes, stocks, bonds, inventory or any of the other kinds of property referred to within the section Elements Required for Section 1031 Exchange (p. 269) which are specifically excluded from the beneficial treatment accorded by the section, the transaction will not qualify.

The exclusion of inventory-type property prevents a real estate dealer from exchanging any *real estate inventory* under the umbrella of Section 1031. (For a discussion of when one is deemed to be a real estate dealer and when a dealer may be holding property for investment rather than as inventory see Chapter 10.)

Both the property received as well as that given up must have been held either for productive use in a trade or business or for investment. Thus, property which is held for personal use, such as an automobile or a yacht, does not qualify. Similarly, if the property received is immediately resold or exchanged, the inference is that the property received is not acquired for investment or for use in business but rather for the purpose of resale. This could destroy the tax-free nature of the transaction.

Also, when the property received is not the same kind as that given up, the exchange will not qualify. Thus if investment real estate is exchanged for factory machinery, the exchange would not qualify because real estate is not the same kind of property as factory machinery, which is personal property.

Computation of Indicated Gain

The presence of unlike property in the exchange may cause some gain to be taxed. Before the amount of taxable gain can be determined, however, it is necessary to compute the amount of gain *realized* on the exchange. Another term for realized is *indicated* gain. Both mean the amount of gain the property owner would have had if the property was sold rather than exchanged.

Example

Christine has a parcel with an adjusted basis to her of $6,000 and a fair market value of $10,000. On a cash sale, her realized gain would be $4,000.

Market value (cash received)	$10,000
Adjusted basis	6,000
Realized (indicated) gain	$ 4,000

If Christine had exchanged her parcel for one which also had a fair market value of $10,000, the computation and the result would be the same, so the gain is the difference between the adjusted basis of the property transferred and its fair market value. The total of what is received in exchange (net equity in real estate, cash, other property, etc.) normally will have a market value equal to the total given up.

Effect of Receipt of Unlike Property

It is a rare situation when two or more properties being exchanged will have identical equities. Before the exchange is made the equities must be balanced. The equity in a property is its market value less any encumbrances on it.

Examples

1. Property A has a market value of $50,000 and a first mortgage of $10,000. The equity in that property is $40,000. If Property B has a market value of $150,000 with a mortgage of $110,000, it too has an equity of $40,000. Thus, on the basis of equal equities, these two properties can be exchanged evenly.

2. Suppose we have this set of facts, however. Stone owns property with a market value of $100,000, subject to a mortgage of $40,000. Her equity is therefore $60,000. Brown's property has a market value of $80,000 subject to a mortgage of $40,000, giving her an equity of $40,000. Obviously, Stone and Brown cannot make an even exchange.

Brown might pay Stone $20,000 in cash *in addition* to exchanging the buildings to balance the equities. Or she might give Stone other property—a boat, a car or other property—having a total value of $20,000.

Brown might give Stone promissory notes totalling $20,000, perhaps as a mortgage on the property Brown is acquiring in the exchange.

Stone might put an additional encumbrance on her property before the exchange, borrowing another $20,000 on a second mortgage on her property, and then transferring the property to Brown subject to mortgages totaling $60,000. She thereby reduces the equity in her property to $40,000 before the exchange.

In these situations, the process of balancing the equities brings about a situation in which either something in addition to the exchange property passes from one party to the other or one party is relieved of a greater amount of loan on the property being given up than that being acquired. It is the presence of cash, other property or net loan relief that can produce a partial (or total) taxable gain in an exchange which is subject to Section 1031.

If, under the circumstances mentioned, some of the property received qualifies for the nonrecognition treatment and some does not, realized gain will be recognized and taxed only to the extent of the value of the unlike property. There are, generally speaking, three kinds of unlike property: cash, other unlike property (called *boot*) and net mortgage (loan) relief.

The mortgage debt attached to the property given up, which the former owner will no longer have to pay, is considered to be unlike property. However, a special rule applies when the former owner takes new property also subject to a mortgage. In that case, the unlike property received is deemed to be only the *net* loan relief; the two mortgages are netted and unlike property is considered to have been received only to the extent the mortgage on the property given up exceeds the mortgage on the property received. These rules apply regardless of whether the mortgage is assumed or the property received is merely taken subject to the mortgage with no personal liability assumed; it makes no difference.

Example

Arthur and Lynn wish to exchange their properties. Prior to the exchange, the pertinent facts concerning each property are as follows.

Arthur's property		Lynn's property
$50,000	Market value	$70,000
30,000	Mortgages on property	40,000
20,000	Equity	30,000

Since Lynn's equity is greater than Arthur's by $10,000, Arthur will also pay Lynn $10,000 cash. Each will acquire the other's property subject to mortgages on the properties. On the exchange, Lynn will be relieved of a $40,000 mortgage and acquire a property subject to a $30,000 mortgage. She will, therefore, have net loan relief $10,000. In addition, she will receive $10,000 cash. Hence, she will have received $20,000 of unlike property. Arthur will have an *increased* loan and will *pay* $10,000 cash. He will not have received any unlike property.

There can be situations in which one party to the exchange has net loan relief but also pays cash. In that case, the net loan relief may be reduced by the cash paid in determining the net unlike property received. On the other hand, if cash is received and one also assumes a greater loan than given up, it is not permitted to reduce the amount of cash received by the increase in loan burden. Therefore, the full amount of the cash received will be treated as unlike property in determining the amount of the recognized gain.

Effect of transaction costs.   Transaction costs (brokerage commissions paid on the transfers, excise taxes on deeds, etc.) are considered reductions of the proceeds of the sale and thereby reduce the indicated gain. They then become part of the basis of the property acquired in the exchange.

IRS has ruled that cash paid for transaction costs is to be treated as cash paid in the exchange transaction. Therefore, the IRS ruling provides that the transaction cost paid in cash reduces any cash received in the exchange in calculating the amount of unlike property received. Presumably, the same logic allows for the reduction of net loan relief by the amount of the transaction costs paid in cash in determining the amount of unlike property received in the exchange.

APPLICATION OF EXCHANGE RULES

The following example illustrates the tax effects of exchanges, including the calculation of the recognized gain and the treatment of the giving and receiving of unlike property.

Example

Dr. Brown owns an apartment house which has an adjusted basis of $100,000 and a market value of $220,000 but is subject to a mortgage of $80,000. Prof. Smith also owns an apartment house. His apartment house has an adjusted basis of $175,000 and a market value of $250,000 and is subject to a mortgage of $150,000. Dr. Brown exchanges her apartment house for Prof. Smith's apartment house and $40,000 cash. Each apartment house was exchanged subject to the mortgage on it. Dr. Brown's realized or indicated gain can be computed quickly as follows.

Market value of Brown's property		$220,000
Less adjusted basis of her property	$100,000	
Transaction costs	16,500	116,500
Indicated gain		$103,500

A similar computation would apply to Prof. Smith.

Market value of Prof. Smith's property		$250,000
Less adjusted basis of his property	$175,000	
Transaction costs	19,000	194,000
Indicated gain		$ 56,000

Dr. Brown received $40,000 in cash. She surrendered a property with an $80,000 mortgage but acquired a property subject to a mortgage of $150,000. Hence, she had no net loan relief. The only unlike property she received was the $40,000 cash. She paid $16,500 in transaction costs, which reduces the cash received by that amount. Her net unlike property received was $23,500. Since the $23,500 is less than her indicated gain of $103,500 she has a recognized (taxable) gain of $23,500.

Prof. Smith gave up property subject to a mortgage of $150,000. He acquired property subject to an $80,000 mortgage. He had a loan relief of $70,000. However, he paid out in cash $40,000 to Dr. Brown and $19,000 in transaction costs. This total of $59,000 when subtracted from the $70,000 net loan relief, gives him net unlike property received of $11,000. Thus, of his indicated gain of $56,000, $11,000 is recognized gain.

LOSSES IN A SECTION 1031 EXCHANGE

If a transaction qualifies fully under Section 1031 (if there is a like-kind exchange of qualifying property with no unlike property), neither gain nor loss is recognized. Presence of unlike property *received* may cause some gain to be recognized but will never cause the recognition of loss.

Example

Green exchanges her apartment house which as a basis of $16,000 and a market value of $12,000 for an apartment house having a $10,000 market value plus $2,000 cash. Although Green has an indicated loss of $4,000, no part of that loss is deductible.

If, however, unlike property is *transferred*, it is possible for the transferor to realize and to deduct the loss on the unlike property that is being transferred.

Example

Phillips exchanges investment real estate plus stock for another piece of real estate to be held for investment. The real estate given up has an adjusted basis of $10,000 and a market value of $11,000. The stock given up has a basis of $4,000 and a market value of $2,000. The real estate received has a fair market value of $13,000.

Phillips is deemed to have received a $2,000 portion of the new real estate in exchange for the stock he gave up because that is its fair market value at the time of the exchange. A loss of $2,000 is recognized on the transfer of the stock by Phillips. No gain or loss is recognized on the transfer of the real estate because that was an exchange completely within the provisions of Section 1031; no unlike property was *received* by Phillips.

MULTIPLE EXCHANGE

It is often difficult to find two people who are willing to exchange parcels of real estate with each other. Very often one of them will be willing to take the parcel owned by the second, but the second has no desire to receive the parcel owned by the first. In such cases, sometimes a third parcel can be found which the second individual may be willing to take. Then a three-way exchange may be executed.

For federal income tax purposes, such an exchange will still satisfy the requirements of Section 1031. Each owner will compute the realized and recognized gain in the same manner as described previously. The mechanics of the exchange may be performed as follows.

Example

A, B and C each hold parcels of real estate for investment purposes. They agree to exchange lots, with any difference in acreage to be made up the rate of $100 per acre.

In the exchange, C acquires the lot owned by B; B acquires the lot owned by A and A acquires the lot owned by C. The position of the Treasury Department, expressed in *Rev. Rul. 57-244*, is that the transaction constitutes exchanges within the scope of Section 1031 and gain, if any, is recognized only to the extent of the cash received.

The importance of this ruling is that for Section 1031 to apply, it is *not* necessary to receive the property in an exchange from the person to whom the property is being transferred. As is demonstrated in the example, although A's lot was transferred to B, A acquired the lot owned by C. In other words, only three deeds were needed to carry out the transaction: A's deed was given to B, B's deed to land was given to C and C's was given to A.

There may be a practical difficulty with the three-way exchange as described here: the difficulty of documentation. Not all exchanges are text book exchanges with all of the parties to the entire multiple exchange sitting around one table. The multiplicity of the exchange is usually developed by the broker who, after analyzing a number of different situations, is able to put together a multiple exchange for the benefit of all of the parties concerned. Consequently, a round-robin deeding of property, as described in the preceding paragraph, may not always be practical. (And where it is practical, it may be a good idea to have all the parties sign a document indicating that an exchange took place as described so that on a future tax examination, any one of the three parties can document the entire transaction.)

An alternative to the use of only three deeds, where for practical reasons not all the parties are available to do the direct deeding as would be required, is to follow a procedure such as this: (1) A deeds property to B and B deeds property to A; (2) B then deeds the property acquired from A to C and C deeds property to B.

This arrangement clearly indicates that exchanges were made. The difficulty with this type of arrangement is that B will not have a tax-free exchange on the acquisition of A's property because it has not been acquired for use in A's trade or business or for investment (it has been acquired for the purpose of exchanging it). Of course, if B wants to *cash out* or really sell the property, it makes no difference because a taxable transaction is expected. However, if B, too, wants a tax-free exchange, in order to follow the deeding procedure described above, a fourth party (probably the broker) would have to get involved. The broker would act as a conduit to whom the various parties would transfer properties and the broker would exchange with the other parties. Thus, A, B and C would deed their properties to D (the broker); D would then deed the A property to C, the B property to A and the C property to B.

ITEMS WHICH AFFECT BASIS IN AN EXCHANGE

The reason there is really only a tax deferral as the result of an exchange is that, generally, basis of the old property is reduced by the amount of gain which escapes taxation. Adjustments have to be made, however, for the unlike property that passed in the exchange, the payment of transaction costs and the recognition of some gain in many cases. Just how is the adjusted basis of the property acquired in an exchange computed?

If the gain on a transaction escapes recognition for tax purposes, the tax result is often that the new piece of property, the property received, will be penalized by having a basis that is less than its fair market value by the amount of nonrecognized or nontaxed gain. Conversely, to maintain the symmetry of the tax concepts, any loss which is not recognized will have the effect of increasing the basis of the property received.

Before the basis of the property received can be calculated, certain items of information must be known. We will now consider these items and their effects on the basis of the property acquired.

Example

Refer back to the exchange between Dr. Brown and Prof. Smith. Here is how each would calculate the basis of the property acquired in the exchange.

Dr. Brown

Gain on the property given up (realized gain)	$103,500
Less gain recognized	23,500
Equals gain not yet taxed	$ 80,000
FMV of property received	250,000
Less deferred gain	80,000
Basis of property acquired	170,000

Prof. Smith

Gain on property given up	56,000
Less gain recognized	11,000
Equals gain not yet taxed	45,000
FMV of property received	220,000
Less deferred gain	45,000
Basis of property acquired	175,000

If we now examine the situation after the new basis computations have been made, we can see the net effect of what has happened. Dr. Brown acquired an apartment house with a value of $250,000. In the process she benefited from a nonrecognized gain of $80,000. Remember that only a $23,500 gain was recognized out of her total realized (indicated) gain of $103,500. Therefore, the basis for her new property is $170,000, which is the same as the value of the property acquired ($250,000) minus the portion of the gain that was not recognized ($80,000).

Similarly, Prof. Smith acquired an apartment house with a market value of $220,000. His nonrecognized gain was $45,000 ($56,000 indicated gain minus $11,000 recognized gain). His basis for the property acquired ($175,000) is equal to the value of the property acquired ($220,000) less the nonrecognized gain ($45,000).

From this it should become apparent that the penalty for the benefit of being able to defer gain is a decrease in basis below the market value of the parcel received by the amount of the gain which is deferred.

Increases in Basis for Cost Recovery

It may be noticed from the example that it is possible for basis to be built up (actually increased) as a result of an exchange. Dr. Brown started with a parcel having an adjusted basis of $100,000. When she was finished she had a parcel of greater value, with a basis of $170,000. That increase of $70,000 was due largely to the increase in mortgage liability attributable to her new parcel.

Thus, it is possible to increase the basis of a property which is subject to cost recovery and thereby gain the advantage of additional cost recovery deductions possibly reducing taxable income without the expenditure of cash. What can be accomplished by this method is an increase in the leverage factor and the value of the investment.

Example

Green owns a property with a market value of $100,000, a mortgage of $20,000 and an adjusted basis of $45,000. She holds that parcel for the production of rental income; therefore it is property used in a trade or business. She exchanges it for another rental building which is worth $150,000 and has a mortgage of $70,000. The equity in each building is, therefore, $80,000.

Green has a tax-free exchange under Section 1031. No gain is recognized because she has received no cash, no other property and no net mortgage relief. But what about her basis for the property received? It is as follows.

FMV of property exchanged	100,000
Less adjusted basis	45,000
Equals realized gain	55,000

All of the gain can be deferred because no unlike kind property was received. Basis in the property acquired is

FMV of property acquired	150,000
Less deferred gain	55,000
Equals basis in property acquired	$95,000

As indicated, Green has increased the value of the property she holds from a $100,000 parcel to a $150,000 parcel. She has also increased her basis for cost recovery from $45,000 to $95,000. And she has not paid out any cash.

Under the Tax Reform Act of 1986, the taxpayer must use the new MACRS cost recovery rules on the new basis in the improved portion of the property acquired by exchange. This is a change from the former law where a portion of the basis might be subject to prior cost recovery rules.

Allocation of basis between land and buildings.   Another possibility for increasing the basis of property subject to the allowance for cost recovery arises from the requirement that basis be allocated between land (which is not recoverable) and building (which is recoverable).

This principle can be applied to a common situation where the adjusted basis of a building has been reduced because of cost recovery deductions to such a point that it is far below the basis for the land, and the relative market values are such that the building is worth considerably more than the land. When two such situations exist, an exchange of the properties can result in a dramatic increase in the basis for cost recovery of both buildings.

Example

Assume that Smith and Green each owns land and buildings having a value in excess of basis, as follows.

	Adjusted basis	Market value	
Smith			
Land	$40,000	$ 40,000	33⅓%
Building	10,000	80,000	66⅔
	$50,000	$120,000	100%
Green			
Land	$30,000	$ 30,000	25%
Building	30,000	90,000	75%
	$60,000	$120,000	100%

If Green and Smith should exchange properties, here are the tax results (ignoring transaction costs and assuming both properties are owned on a free and clear basis.)

Smith's basis for the total property acquired from Green would be $50,000. But he can allocate that basis between the acquired land and building according to their relative market values. Since 75 percent of the fair market value of the property acquired from Green is attributable to the building, Smith can allocate $37,500 of his $50,000 basis to the building and the remaining $12,500 to the land. Hence, as a result of the exchange, Smith has boosted his basis for cost-recovery property from $10,000 to $37,500 and stepped down his basis for land from $40,000 to $12,500.

On acquiring Smith's property, Green would use $60,000 as her basis for that property, the same basis she had for the property she exchanged. But she, too, would allocate that basis between land and building according to relative fair market values. Hence, she would allocate two-thirds of her $60,000 basis, or $40,000 to the building and the remaining one-third, or $20,000, to the land. So she, too, will have increased her basis for cost recovery property, from $30,000 to $40,000.

Hence Green and Smith *both* get stepped up bases for their buildings and increased cost recovery deductions as a result of the exchange.

Cost Recovery Recapture and the Section 1031 Exchange

As has been explained in Chapter 10, part or all of the gain on the sale or exchange of cost recovery property may be treated as the recapture of previously deducted cost recovery and taxed as ordinary income. How does this cost recovery recapture rule affect exchanges made under Section 1031 when part or all of the gain is not recognized for tax purposes?

If the property is personal property (furniture, equipment and the like) but not part of the real estate, Section 1245 provides that the amount of the cost recovery deducted after 1961 (or after June, 1963, for elevators and escalators) is compared to the portion of the gain that is taxable in the exchange. In other words, for purposes of cost recovery recapture, the *recognized* portion of the gain is treated as the total gain. That amount is the maximum amount subject to cost recovery recapture.

In the case of real property, Section 1250 applies. It provides that although cost recovery recapture can convert capital gain into ordinary income on the sale of real estate, ordinary income from cost recovery recapture can be avoided in a Section 1031 exchange. Ordinary income is recognized on the exchange due to cost recovery recapture *only if*

1. There is some recognized gain on the exchange due to the receipt of unlike property or
2. The amount of Section 1250 gain that would have been recognized had this been an outright sale rather than exchange exceeds the market value of Section 1250 property (depreciable real estate) received in the exchange.

If neither 1 nor 2 is true, there is no ordinary income due to cost recovery recapture on the exchange. If either 1 or 2 is true, the maximum amount of ordinary income due to cost recovery recapture on the exchange is the amount computed in 1 or 2. If both 1 *and* 2 are true, the larger amount is taxable.

Allocation of basis. After the exchange, if any ordinary income due to cost recovery recapture has been avoided under the above rules, basis of all the property acquired in the exchange is first computed in the usual way. Then, an allocation of the basis must be made.

First, basis is allocated between Section 1250 property and other property received in the exchange. For example, if land and building were acquired, the land is not Section 1250 property while the building is. The total basis is allocated in proportion to the properties' fair market values. But the fair market value of the Section 1250 property is reduced by the amount of ordinary income avoided on the exchange because the Section 1250 rules did not apply under the provisions explained.

Examples

1. Brown exchanges his land and building for Spencer's land and building. This is a tax-free exchange in which no gain or loss is recognized. Had this been a taxable transaction, Brown would have realized $10,000 of ordinary income under the Section 1250 cost recovery recapture rules. Since no unlike property was received in the exchange, Item 1 does not apply. Since the market value of the building received is greater than the $10,000 of ordinary income from cost recovery recapture which would have resulted in a taxable transaction, Item 2 does not apply. Hence, there is no ordinary income from cost recovery recapture recognized on this transaction.

Assume that Brown's basis for the total property he acquired, under the usual rules for computing basis in a tax-free exchange, is $42,000. Assume, too, that the market value of the building is $70,000 and the market value of the land is $30,000.

The $42,000 basis must be allocated to building and land. To do this, the market value of the building (the Section 1250 property) is reduced by the $10,000 that would have constituted ordinary income from cost recovery recapture if the transaction had been fully taxable. Thus, the market value of the building becomes $60,000 and the market value of the land remains $30,000. Since $60,000 is two-thirds of the total market value of $90,000, two-thirds of the $42,000 basis, or $28,000, is allocated to the building and one-third, or $14,000, to the land.

2. Suppose instead of getting one building in the exchange, there were two whose total value was $70,000, with the remaining $30,000 market value attributable to the land on which they stand. The $28,000 basis for buildings (calculated previously) must be allocated between the two buildings in relation to their market values. But here the market values of the buildings are not reduced by the ordinary income from cost recovery recapture which was avoided on the exchange. Thus, assume the $70,000 market value is allocable $40,000 to Building 1 and $30,000 to Building 2. In that case four-sevenths of the $28,000 basis allocable to the Section 1250 properties, or $16,000, is allocable to Building 1 and three-sevenths, or $12,000, is allocable to Building 2.

What happens to the ordinary income from cost recovery recapture that was avoided on the tax-free exchange? It carries over to the new properties as excess cost recovery. If only one building was acquired, the full $10,000 is allocated to the building. If two buildings were acquired, the allocation is made in proportion to the bases of the two buildings, i.e. four-sevenths of $10,000, or $5,715, to Building 1; and three-sevenths of $10,000, or $4,285, to Building 2.

1989 REVENUE RECONCILIATION ACT

The 1989 Revenue Reconciliation Act made a few minor changes to the laws of tax deferred exchanging. These changes are effective for transfers made after July 10, 1989, for tax years that end after that date. If a binding written contract was in effect on that date, but the transfer had not yet taken place, the new provisions of the 1989 Act will not apply.

Under the 1989 Act, real property located outside of the United States no longer qualifies as like kind property. Furthermore, if a tax deferred exchange takes place between related parties, and any property received from a related party is disposed of before two years elapses after the transfer, any gain or loss that was not recognized on the original exchange will be recognized the date the property is disposed of. This rule will not apply, however, if the subsequent disposition is due to the death of the related party, or involuntary conversion, or any other circumstance if it is determined not to involve tax avoidance. Whether or not two parties are related will be governed by IRC section 267(b).

SECTION III
Case Studies in Real Estate Brokerage

12
Cash Flow Forecasting

The real estate investment broker's role is to combine into a meaningful investment proposal all knowledge of properties, clients, investment analysis and income tax regulations available.

The previous sections of this book have been devoted to the presentation of a framework of real estate investment analysis. Much attention has been given to the methods of calculating rate of return for use in comparing all forms of investment. Income tax impact on real estate investments has been given consideration in order that the cash flow analysis can be calculated in an after-tax situation.

The purposes of this section are to discuss and demonstrate the practical aspects of cash flow analysis, to provide illustrative case studies of a limited number of important brokerage operations and to introduce and demonstrate the use of several standard forms developed by the Commercial-Investment Council of the REALTORS NATIONAL MARKETING INSTITUTE® of the NATIONAL ASSOCIATION OF REALTORS®. The purpose of using these forms is to ease and simplify the accumulation and evaluation of data necessary to understand a particular investment property.

The forms address themselves to the major problem of real estate investment analysis—defining or estimating the future income stream and measuring this stream by discounting it to a present value or measuring its rate in terms of an investment amount.

Some of the most widely used forms presented in this section are the Annual Property Operating Data form, the Cash Flow Analysis form and the Exchange Worksheet.

PRACTICAL ASPECTS OF CASH FLOW ANALYSIS

No facet of the real estate brokerage business is as controversial as that concerned with cash flow forecasting and analysis of investment real estate. Extreme views are expressed on both sides of the issue.

Rabid opponents to this kind of forecasting argue

"Future cash flows cannot be accurately predicted."

"Future resale prices are impossible to forecast."

"The process is too technical; buyers and sellers do not understand it."

"Figures can lie and liars can figure; the numbers can be made to show any desired result."

Enthusiastic advocates counter with "The only things an investor is interested in are

How much money do I put in?

When do I put it in?

How much do I get out?

When do I get it?

That's the essence of cash flow analysis."

"If real estate is acquired for its future benefit, one must estimate the annual and disposition income in order to make a decision to acquire, hold or dispose of property."

"The computer capability of cash flow analysis brings a greater professionalism to the industry."

These extremes of viewpoints create two extremes of salesperson. One is a "people person" who is never involved with numbers. This salesperson has the ability to locate properties for sale and clients who want properties. Valuation and/or analysis is left to the buyer or the buyer's advisors. The salesperson's role in the negotiation is to let the principals negotiate; sales are made (or lost) by the principals. The salesperson has little or no influence on the market or the transaction other than keeping clients happy and driving people around.

At the other end of the spectrum is the "numbers person" who is not too adept at personal relationships. This salesperson loves numbers, the computer and analyzing the properties under all possible variables. Filling out forms, passing out computer runs and stressing the percentages and ratios is how this salesperson thinks and operates. Finding clients, negotiating and compromising do not come easily. (Of these two types of salespeople, the former probably makes more money and is usually in more trouble.)

There is a great need, however, for a middle position—for the professional investment brokerage salesperson—one who recognizes that the popular rules of thumb are poor yardsticks for measuring future benefits of real estate and who understands the strengths and limitations of the internal rate of return calculations. This salesperson knows cash flow analysis thoroughly, yet understands the human aspects of brokerage. Investment clients, whether sellers or buyers, are entitled to more than a personable salesperson. They are entitled to assistance from a real estate professional as well as from the fields of law and accounting.

FORECASTING AS ART AND SCIENCE

Cash flow forecasting may be viewed as more an art than a science because of the variety of types of real estate income. The income from a long-term net lease is simplest to define because the lease itself usually states the rental stream. This estimation could become more complicated if a percentage rent is also required. At the other extreme, income from a vacant portion of land can account for a negative income stream created by real estate taxes and loan payments, until the land is sold.

Between these extremes is the apartment, the store building or other improved real estate with short-term leases where the owner pays all or most of the expenses. Other examples include vacant buildings as well as properties to be developed where all income and expense items must be estimated and projected.

The estimation of future cash flows for income-producing real estate requires a variety of judgments and assumptions concerning the future. Among these are judgments concerning the property itself, the future of the neighborhood in which it is located, the general market conditions that are expected to prevail and their impact on the specific property, future developments in the federal income tax laws that may influence the after-tax cash flows of the property and myriad other factors which may affect the cash flows of the specific property over time. The task of income estimation requires both experience in and knowledge of the operation of the real estate market. It is not simply an extrapolation of the known market behavior of preceding years, nor can the estimation problem be refined completely to objective statistical probabilities. In its final form, the estimate of future benefits from an investment in real estate must relate to the *amount, timing, duration* (or term) and *stability* of after-tax cash flows to be received by the investor.

The mathematical logic employed in discounting future cash flows is fundamentally essential in analyzing real estate investments. Of equal importance, however, is the process by which the future cash flows of a specific property (or group of properties) are estimated. Generally speaking, this process stands in marked contrast to the inexorable precision of the discounting process. Because estimates of cash flows which are generated by real estate necessarily involve estimates of the future, they are more often than not significantly less precise than the mathematical technique used to discount them to the present.

CASH FLOW ANALYSIS ASSUMPTIONS

1. The real estate investment broker uses cash flow analysis in order to determine whether or not the future benefits to be derived from the property, based on the asking price and terms, will provide a yield competitive with other real estate and non-real estate investment alternatives available in the market. If such a study indicates the property is not competitive or cannot be made competitive, the broker is foolish to waste time, money and energy trying to market the property.

2. Cash flow projections and internal rate of return calculations may or may not be used in marketing the property. How all or parts of the study are utilized with the seller, buyer and/or their advisors depends upon human factors and the education, training and experience of the parties involved.

3. Although it is impossible to predict future cash flows, it is easy to calculate yields on any series of *projected* cash flows. Therefore, it is essential that the investment broker do homework in order to make the most logical and honest projections of future cash flows. This may not necessarily be one projection. Most logically it might be three. One might be the broker's "best guesstimate" projection, the next a more optimistic one, the third a more pessimistic one. Yields can then be calculated from the three projections. Potential buyers can be shown the range of possible yields and the rationale for each projection. They can assess the future of the property based on their own viewpoints of the future and the yields available from alternative investments.

4. Cash flow analysis has no purpose other than to compare the potential yields of two or more investment opportunities. Therefore, it is essential not only that the cash flow analysis process is understood but also that clients understand under which circumstances comparisons may or may not be valid.

The case studies are grouped into three chapters:

Cash flow forecasting (Ch. 12)
Differential cash flow analysis (Ch. 13)
Special investment problems (Ch. 14)

The case studies presented are by no means an exhaustive presentation, but rather are intended to serve as a foundation for the broker who will use the fundamentals presented in solving specific brokerage or counseling problems. The potential for other applications is unlimited.

Most of the case studies presented are from actual experiences of the authors—in some instances simplified to eliminate extraneous data and calculations.

Although the case studies reflect the most recent tax changes, some studies will have interest rates and/or mortgage terms that may not be compatible with lending policies at the date of publication and/or the exact date of reading of this material. These inconsistencies, however, should not distract the reader from the principles involved in "making the transaction" nor diminish the value of the analysis process.

CASE STUDY 1: AFTER-TAX ANALYSIS OF INCOME-PRODUCING PROPERTY

The purpose of this case study is to demonstrate how the effective investment broker makes cash flow forecasts or projections and calculates yield (internal rate of return) from the projection. Two standard forms, an Annual Property Operating Data form and the Cash Flow Analysis form, are used extensively in this case study.

Situation

At a recent civic club meeting, Barbara Broker met John Seller. During the course of the meeting, Seller indicated to Broker that he had an apartment building he wanted to sell. Broker made an appointment to see the property for the following week. After the inspection, Seller indicated he wanted $1,100,000 for the property. He also gave the following information to Broker.

Rents collected in previous year	$180,000
Expenses: Taxes	$ 16,000
Insurance	5,500
Utilities	6,000
Supplies	1,000
Maintenance	5,000

Seller also said there was an existing mortgage on the property of approximately $420,000 payable at $4,600 per month, including 8 percent interest. Broker told Seller she wanted to analyze the property and would get back to him.

Owner's Statement

The first step in the process of property analysis is to obtain all possible financial and physical data about the property from the owner and his records. The Annual Property Operating Data (APOD) form acts as a checklist in the gathering of the financial data. It must be emphasized, however, that at this stage, the broker is collecting and recording data, not evaluating, interpreting, or analyzing it.

Upon returning to her office, Barbara Broker begins her analysis by preparing the Owner's Statement on an APOD. She systematically enters information supplied by the owner without verifying or evaluating it. Figure 35 shows the completed Owner's Statement. Note the indicated cash flow before income taxes of $91,300. Broker must decide whether income and expense items that are blank on the owner's statement should be investigated further.

Broker gets an overall look at the property income stream from a quantity standpoint. The owner's reported income of $180,000 and expenses of $33,500 indicate that the property produces $146,500 before debt service. Reported expenses are 18.6 percent of reported income. If this is a low expense ratio for the type of property, perhaps further investigation of the statement is needed. Is the income too high or are the expenses too

Annual Property Operating Data

Name _JOHN SELLER_
Location _5986 NE ORCHARD_
Type of Property _APARTMENT_
Size of Property _40_ ☐ Sq.Ft. ☒ Units

Date _6 15 8-_
Price $ _1,100,000_
Existing Loan _420,000_
Equity _680,000_

Purpose:
☒ Owner's Statement ☐ Broker's Reconstructed ☐ Forecast
☒ Existing Financing ☐ Potential Financing
☒ Seller's Position ☐ Buyer's Position

Existing	Balance	Payment	#Pmts/Yr.	Interest	Term
1st $	420,000	4600	12	8%	
2nd $					
3rd $					
Potential:					
1st $					
2nd $					

Assessed / Appraised Values
Land $ _____ _____ %
Improvement $ _____ _____ %
Personal Property $ _____ _____ %
Total $ _____ 100 %
Adjusted Basis as of _____ $ _____

ALL FIGURES ANNUAL	$/SQ.FT. or $/Unit	%		COMMENTS/FOOTNOTES
1 POTENTIAL RENTAL INCOME				
2 Less: Vacancy & Cr. Losses	(_____ % of $ _____)			
3 EFFECTIVE RENTAL INCOME				
4 Plus: Other Income				
5 GROSS OPERATING INCOME			180,000	
OPERATING EXPENSES:				
6 Real Estate Taxes	16 000			
7 Personal Property Taxes				
8 Property Insurance	5500			
9 Off Site Management				
10 Payroll - Onsite Personnel				
11 Expenses / Benefits				
12 Taxes / Worker's Compensation				
13 Repairs and Maintenance	5 000			
Utilities:				
14	6 000			
15				
16				
17				
18 Accounting and Legal				
19 Real Estate Leasing Commissions				
20 Advertising / Licenses / Permits				
21 Supplies	1 000			
22 Miscellaneous				
Contract Services:				
23				
24				
25				
26				
27				
28				
29 TOTAL OPERATING EXPENSES	18.6		33,500	
30 NET OPERATING INCOME			146,500	
31 Less: Annual Debt Service			55,200	
32 CASH FLOW BEFORE TAXES	13.4		91,300	

The statements and figures herein while not guaranteed are secured from sources we believe authoritative   Prepared by _BROKER_

Figure 35

low? The cash flow of 13.4 percent on equity is good, but is it too good? It is apparent that Broker should delve deeper to better understand the property. Her next step is the preparation of a broker's forecast.

Broker's Forecast (Pro Forma)

Up to this point Broker has merely organized Seller's figures in an orderly manner; however, there is no assurance that the numbers on the owner's statement are realistic or reflect the potential of the property. Last year's results may or may not be an indication of future income.

To test the validity of the information submitted by Seller and to analyze the potential income of the property in terms of quantity, quality, and durability, Broker must develop a new operating statement based upon the Owner's Statement and other market data.

This Broker's Forecast (Figures 36 through 38) is prepared by Broker on another blank APOD form. This statement reflects how the property is expected to perform financially for the next full calendar year. A projected operating statement for a shorter period is more valid than for a longer period; that is, the possibility of projecting a valid income and expense statement for the next year is greater than a projection of income and expenses fifteen years from now.

When the Broker's Forecast is completed, it is possible that not one single item of income or expense on it is the same as for any previous year; yet it should more accurately reflect than the owner's statement the income that the property will produce for the next full calendar year.

The Broker's Forecast was prepared in the following series of steps. From the local assessor's office, Broker obtained the assessed value of land and improvements and entered them on the APOD form. (The percentage of the improvement to value enables the broker to estimate the improvement value and to calculate annual depreciation from that amount.) Broker also obtained a verbal opinion from a lender concerning the amount and terms of a new loan that might be available for a qualified purchaser of the property. From the seller's accountant, it was determined that the owner's adjusted basis (depreciated value or book value) was $580,000, which is entered beside the adjusted basis.

The first item entered on the Broker's Forecast for actual operating figures is Potential Rental Income (PRI). This is the income that the property will produce during the coming year if rented at market or economic rents 100 percent of the time.

To estimate Potential Rental Income, it is necessary to know what typical rentals are in the neighborhood for a comparable apartment building. Studies must be made to estimate rents for Seller's property. This is done by analyzing competitive rents to determine unit comparability on a square-foot, cubic-foot, per-room, or per-apartment basis. The unit basis is then applied to the property being studied. In this case, Broker went to similar apartment units and inquired into rental rates and reviewed her own (or other friendly brokers') rental rates. Broker found market rents as follows.

Annual Property Operating Data

Name __JOHN SELLER__

Location __5986 NE ORCHARD__

Type of Property __APARTMENT__

Size of Property __40__ ☐ Sq.Ft. ☒ Units

Purpose:
☐ Owner's Statement ☒ Broker's Reconstructed ☐ Forecast
☒ Existing Financing ☐ Potential Financing
☒ Seller's Position ☐ Buyer's Position

Date __7/1/8—__

Price $ __1,100,000__

Existing Loan __420,000__

Equity __680,000__

Existing	Balance	Payment	#Pmts/Yr.	Interest	Term
1st	$ 420,000	4600	12	8	
2nd	$				
3rd	$				
Potential:					
1st	$ 800,000	7269.61	12	10	25
2nd	$				

Assessed / Appraised Values

		%
Land	$ 84,000	19.6 %
Improvement	$ 336,000	78.5 %
Personal Property	$ 8,000	1.9 %
Total	$ 428,000	100 %

Adjusted Basis as of __12/31__ $ __580,000__

	ALL FIGURES ANNUAL	$/SQ.FT. or $/Unit	%		COMMENTS/FOOTNOTES
1	POTENTIAL RENTAL INCOME				
2	Less: Vacancy & Cr. Losses	(____ % of $ _____)			
3	EFFECTIVE RENTAL INCOME				
4	Plus: Other Income				
5	GROSS OPERATING INCOME				
	OPERATING EXPENSES:				
6	Real Estate Taxes				
7	Personal Property Taxes				
8	Property Insurance				
9	Off Site Management				
10	Payroll - Onsite Personnel				
11	Expenses / Benefits				
12	Taxes / Worker's Compensation				
13	Repairs and Maintenance				
	Utilities:				
14					
15					
16					
17					
18	Accounting and Legal				
19	Real Estate Leasing Commissions				
20	Advertising / Licenses / Permits				
21	Supplies				
22	Miscellaneous				
	Contract Services:				
23					
24					
25					
26					
27					
28					
29	TOTAL OPERATING EXPENSES				
30	NET OPERATING INCOME				
31	Less: Annual Debt Service				
32	CASH FLOW BEFORE TAXES				

The statements and figures herein while not guaranteed
are secured from sources we believe authoritative

Prepared by _____

Figure 36

One-bedroom rents			Two-bedroom rents		
Monthly rent	Area	Rate	Monthly rent	Area	Rate
$380	600 SF	$0.63/SF/Mo	$500	900 SF	$0.55/SF/Mo
415	700 SF	.59/SF/Mo	490	870 SF	.56/SF/Mo
360	595 SF	.61/SF/Mo	510	1000 SF	.51/SF/Mo
400	700 SF	.57/SF/Mo	585	1040 SF	.56/SF/Mo
375	585 SF	.64/SF/Mo	500	1030 SF	.50/SF/Mo

Adjustments upward or downward of these figures were made by Broker, judging how the comparable units varied from those owned by John Seller and how much more or less they would rent for per month compared to the subject units. Did they have fireplaces, swimming pools, furniture, central heat, or were they in better or worse condition? Then Broker compared the adjusted rents to the square footage area to indicate unit rents. The results are as follows.

ESTIMATED RENT ROLL
(POTENTIAL RENTAL INCOME)

Area	Rate	Unit rent	Number of units	Monthly rent	Annual rent
625 SF	$0.60	$375	20	$7,500	$ 90,000
880 SF	.54	475	20	9,500	114,000
				PRI	$204,000

Vacancies and Credit Losses were determined by comparing rent rolls of several other apartment complexes to actual rents collected.

	100% rent roll	Collected rents	Indicated vacancy rate
Cavalier Apartments	$196,000	$185,612	5.3%
Thunderbird	204,000	194,820	4.5%
Celeron	152,000	144,248	5.1%
Wellman	164,000	155,308	5.3%

Broker's study estimates Vacancies and Credit Losses at five percent of Potential Rental Income or $10,200. These are deducted from the Potential Rental Income, resulting in an Effective Rental Income (ERI) of $193,800. After investigation, Broker estimates Other Income (from the use of leased washers and dryers) at $3,200 per year, thereby indicating $197,000 as the Gross Operating Income (GOI).

Operating expenses. Next, an analysis of Operating Expenses is made. Broker developed estimates of these expenses based on experience with this kind of property and by asking questions of people who had better information. Broker's investigation produced the following estimates which are shown recorded on the broker's forecast in Figure 37.

1. **Real Estate Taxes (line 6).** Although Seller reported $16,000 for the previous year, Broker determined that a new school bond levy will go into effect next year and raise the taxes to approximately $19,600.
2. **Personal Property Taxes (line 7)** are estimated at $1,300.
3. **Property Insurance (line 8)** of $6,400 is obtained from Broker's insurance agent who recommended typical coverage.
4. **Off-Site Management (line 9).** The normal professional property management fee for this type of building is five percent, with the managing office paying all advertising costs. This is $10,200.
5. **Payroll on Site (line 10)** is $10,500. Investigation indicates a resident manager could be obtained for $400 a month plus the use of a two-bedroom apartment ($475 monthly). The owner's taxes (line 12) for the manager are estimated at 10 percent, or $1,050 annually. (Although Seller now acts as resident manager and property manager, these costs must be reflected as expenses of the property. A new owner may not wish to be so actively involved.)
6. **Repairs and Maintenance (line 13).** The property is in good repair; Broker's contact with property managers indicates $240 to 265 per year per apartment should provide adequate coverage (about 5 percent of the gross operating income). This comes to $10,200.
7. **Utilities (line 14).** $6,000; Past experience and records of the utility company indicate that $500 per month, a total of $6,000 per year, will cover the cost of house electricity.
8. **Sewer-Water (line 15).** Investigation indicates $80 per month as an average, or $960 per year.
9. **Telephone (line 16).** $40 per month; $480 annually.
10. **Rubbish (line 17)** is estimated at $720.
11. **Advertising, Licenses, and Permits (line 20).** The $290 is based on experience of this property.
12. **Supplies (line 21).** $2,400 was based on an estimate of $200 per month.
13. **Miscellaneous Expense (line 22).** This is estimated at $3,000 per year.
14. **Lawn (line 23).** Broker estimates $225 a month.
15. **Security (line 24)** is estimated at $1,200.

Total Operating Expenses came to $77,000, which is 39.1 percent of Gross Operating Income. Broker's experience is that 37 to 40 percent is a typical expense ratio for properties of this type which helps confirm that the Broker's Forecast has greater validity than the Owner's Statement.

Deducting the Operating Expenses ($77,000) from the Gross Operating Income ($197,000) results in a Net Operating Income (NOI) of $120,000. From that amount the

Name ___JOHN SELLER___

Location ___5986 NE ORCHARD___

Type of Property ___APARTMENT___

Size of Property ___40___ ☐ Sq.Ft. ☒ Units

Purpose:

☐ Owner's Statement ☒ Broker's Reconstructed ☐ Forecast

☒ Existing Financing ☐ Potential Financing

☒ Seller's Position ☐ Buyer's Position

Assessed / Appraised Values

Land	$ 84 000	19.6 %
Improvement	$ 336 000	78.5 %
Personal Property	$ 8 000	1.9 %
Total	$ 428 000	100 %

Adjusted Basis as of ___12/31___ $ 580,000

Annual Property Operating Data

Date ___7/1/8—___

Price $ ___1,100,000___

Existing Loan ___420,000___

Equity ___680,000___

Existing	Balance	Payment	#Pmts/Yr.	Interest	Term
1st	$ 420,000	4600	12	8	
2nd	$				
3rd	$				
Potential:					
1st	$ 800,000	7269.61	12	10	25
2nd	$				

	ALL FIGURES ANNUAL	$/SQ.FT. or $/Unit	%		COMMENTS/FOOTNOTES
1	POTENTIAL RENTAL INCOME			204 000	20 @ 375 / mo
2	Less: Vacancy & Cr. Losses	(5 % of $ 204 000)		10 200	20 @ 475 / mo
3	EFFECTIVE RENTAL INCOME			193 800	
4	Plus: Other Income			3 200	
5	GROSS OPERATING INCOME			197 000	
	OPERATING EXPENSES:				
6	Real Estate Taxes		19 600		
7	Personal Property Taxes		1 300		
8	Property Insurance		6 400		
9	Off Site Management		10 200		5 %
10	Payroll - Onsite Personnel		10 500		475 APT + 400/mo
11	Expenses / Benefits				
12	Taxes / Worker's Compensation		1050		
13	Repairs and Maintenance		10 200		5 %
	Utilities:				
14	ELECTRIC		6 000		500 / mo
15	SEWER / WATER		960		80 / mo
16	TELEPHONE		480		40 / mo
17	RUBBISH		720		60 / mo
18	Accounting and Legal				
19	Real Estate Leasing Commissions				
20	Advertising / Licenses / Permits		290		
21	Supplies		2400		5 / mo APT
22	Miscellaneous		3000		250 / mo
	Contract Services:				
23	LAWN MAINT		2700		225 / mo
24	SECURITY		1200		100 / mo
25					
26					
27					
28					
29	TOTAL OPERATING EXPENSES	39.1		77 000	
30	NET OPERATING INCOME			120 000	
31	Less: Annual Debt Service			55200	
32	CASH FLOW BEFORE TAXES	9.5		64 800	

The statements and figures herein while not guaranteed are secured from sources we believe authoritative Prepared by ___BROKER___

Figure 37

Annual Debt Service (ADS) of $55,200 is subtracted resulting in the Cash Flow Before Taxes (CFBT) of $64,800, or 9.5 percent on the $680,000 equity. The Owner's Statement indicated a CFBT of $91,300. This discrepancy was probably caused by the owner not recognizing all costs and not differentiating between property expenses and management expenses the owner failed to compensate himself for.

The completed Broker's Forecast (shown in Figure 38) enables Barbara Broker to better understand the owner's realistic position in the property. If the property, as an investment, will produce approximately $120,000 for a new owner, it cannot be expected to produce any more than that for the present owner. Perhaps the present owner could obtain more cash flow by doing maintenance or management personally instead of hiring someone, but this is income from sources other than the investment. It is readily apparent that the owner's real Cash Flow Before Taxes for next year (assuming a valid projection) would be $64,800 under present financing if he continues to hold the property.

Using the Broker's Forecast for a Potential Client

Another important use of the Broker's Forecast is for a Potential Client Statement (Figure 38). This statement indicates the Cash Flow Before Taxes available to a potential buyer who acquires the property at the owner's asking price, while obtaining the maximum financing available. Other Potential Client Statements can be prepared using different financing assumptions (such as acquiring the property with secondary financing or *buying down* to existing financing). In any event, the Potential Client Statement forms the basis for the cash flow analysis.

Cash Flow Analysis

Before demonstrating the steps of this analysis, it is necessary to point out the purpose, the limitations and the assumptions of a cash flow analysis, as well as some suggestions for projecting future cash flows.

Purpose.   The Cash Flow Analysis is a projection of an investor's cash flows from the real estate under study after income tax. The cash flows derive from annual operations and resale proceeds. The projection is usually made for a typical real estate investment holding period of 10 to 15 years. Although some believe this period is too long, studies indicate that yield increases with the holding period up to about 12 to 14 years. Our case study's holding period will be 15 years. In real life, investors evaluate holdings periodically. They will switch investments (sell one to acquire another) only if a new one appears to have greater potential yield.

Limitations and assumptions.   No one can accurately predict exact future annual operating statements, exact holding periods or exact resale prices, but projections can be made based on certain assumptions. Therefore, the mathematics of the projections are valid if we recognize the limitations of our ability to project.

Name _POTENTIAL CLIENT_

Location _5986 NE ORCHARD_

Type of Property _APARTMENT_

Size of Property _40_ ☐ Sq.Ft. ☒ Units

Purpose:
☐ Owner's Statement ☒ Broker's Reconstructed ☐ Forecast
☐ Existing Financing ☒ Potential Financing
☐ Seller's Position ☒ Buyer's Position

Annual Property Operating Data

Date _7/5/8 —_

Price $ _1,100,000_

Existing Loan _800,000_

Equity _300,000_

Existing	Balance	Payment	#Pmts/Yr.	Interest	Term
1st $					
2nd $					
3rd $					
Potential:					
1st $	800,000	7269.61	12	10	25
2nd $					

Assessed / Appraised Values

Land	$ _____	_____ %	
Improvement	$ _____	_____ %	
Personal Property	$ _____	_____ %	
Total	$ _____	100 %	

Adjusted Basis as of _____ $ _____

	ALL FIGURES ANNUAL	$/SQ.FT. or $/Unit	%		COMMENTS/FOOTNOTES
1	POTENTIAL RENTAL INCOME			204 000	20 @ 375 / MO
2	Less: Vacancy & Cr. Losses	(5 % of $ 204 000)		10 200	20 @ 475 / MO
3	EFFECTIVE RENTAL INCOME			193 800	
4	Plus: Other Income			3 200	
5	GROSS OPERATING INCOME			197 000	
	OPERATING EXPENSES:				
6	Real Estate Taxes				
7	Personal Property Taxes				
8	Property Insurance				
9	Off Site Management				
10	Payroll - Onsite Personnel				
11	Expenses / Benefits				
12	Taxes / Worker's Compensation				
13	Repairs and Maintenance				
	Utilities:				
14					
15					
16					
17					
18	Accounting and Legal				
19	Real Estate Leasing Commissions				
20	Advertising / Licenses / Permits				
21	Supplies				
22	Miscellaneous				
	Contract Services:				
23					
24					
25					
26					
27					
28					
29	TOTAL OPERATING EXPENSES			77 000	
30	**NET OPERATING INCOME**			120 000	
31	Less: Annual Debt Service			87 235	
32	**CASH FLOW BEFORE TAXES**			32 765	

The statements and figures herein while not guaranteed
are secured from sources we believe authoritative

Prepared by _BROKER_

Figure 38

We have said that the Broker's Forecast is the best estimate for the next full calendar year's operation. Projections based on these numbers must be done cautiously, however. If it is felt that over the study period the net operating income will increase or decrease, the next year's operating statement can be adjusted accordingly. Projections can also show outlays for further capital costs (carpets, major repairs and the like) at some particular time during this study period. Reserves could be set aside each year for these purposes, thereby reducing annual cash flows. As an alternative, no funds need be set aside, but capital expenditures can be made from cash flows of the year of the improvement (and even by additional capital at that time), which can create a negative cash flow in the year that the improvement is added.

Since the projection may be made on any basis, it is imperative that each cash flow analysis be evaluated not only in terms of the final resulting numbers but also by the assumptions under which the study was made. This also pertains to the resale price. The resale price can be the same as the purchase price, or higher or lower. When the projected investment is evaluated, the broker must question how reasonable the assumptions are.

Suggestions for projections.   Projecting annual cash flows from the cash flow of the Broker's Forecast is more than a mathematical exercise. Here the investment broker's experience and knowledge of the market become important.

The major projection problems arise in determining the resale price and the pattern of the net operating income streams. If there is no long-term lease which controls the rent, there are several approaches the investment broker may take in determining these factors.

First, it can be assumed that income and expenses will increase by the same amounts, thereby projecting net operating income each year to be the same. Secondly, it can be assumed that income will increase by a greater amount than expenses. Experience may show that expenses increase annually, but rental increases may take place ever two to three years. For projection purposes it is more convenient to estimate the rent increase over five-year periods and prorate this annually. For example, if the net operating income is projected to increase 10, 15, or 20 percent over five-year periods, an annual growth rate of 2, 3, or 4 percent can be projected. It is also possible that the net operating income would be projected to decrease because of the age of the improvements or a declining or transitional neighborhood.

The resale price could be projected to be the same as the acquisition price. This would assume actual depreciation and/or declining net income were offset equally by inflation. The resale price could also be projected higher than the acquisition price which assumes an increase of net operating income and a relatively stable capitalization rate, or a stable net operating income and a decreasing capitalization rate.

A resale price less than acquisition price could be attributed to a declining income and/or increased capitalization rate. In the case of a special-purpose building, it is logical to assume the improvement at the end of a lease to be valueless and the land to have equal or greater value than it had when the building was built.

As stated previously, the assumptions of the projections are as important as the projection analysis itself. It is essential that the broker understand the ramifications of these assumptions.

Recognizing the possibilities for great differences due to the assumptions, the following are suggested guidelines to projecting cash flows.

Conservative projection.   Project net operating income as stable over the life of the projection, and the project resale prices equal to acquisition, 25 percent over acquisition, and 15 percent less than acquisition. The spread of resulting yields will give a fairly conservative projection and give the broker and client an opportunity to study a range of probabilities.

Aggressive projection.   Increase net operating income from 2 to 5 percent annually with the resale price calculated by capitalizing last year's income by the acquisition capitalization rate. Or, increase the net operating income as above, but increase the sale price by 10 to 20 percent over acquisition price.

Pessimistic projection.   Decrease net operating income from 1 to 3 percent annually and make resale price equal to the acquisition price.

It must be understood that projections may be in the range of pessimistic-conservative to overly optimistic. However, if the reader of the projection understands the assumptions made, an investment decision can be made based on what the reader feels is the probability of the projection becoming reality.

For example, if a study shows an investor can expect a 15 percent yield if the property doubles in value, an 11 percent yield if the property value remains the same, and an 8 percent return if the property declines 25 percent, the investor can make a judgment to buy or not based on some correlation of all the alternatives, not just on the optimistic one, and by comparing the property to other investments available.

Cash Flow Analysis Procedure

In our case study, Barbara Broker assumed

1. A projection period of 15 years,
2. The Net Operating Income would remain level.
3. The marginal tax bracket of the investor is 28 percent. To make an after-tax analysis, the tax bracket of the investor must be taken into account. Even if the investor's tax bracket is known, the tax position can change during the projection period. The broker can make the assumption of a constant tax bracket or a changing one. What the broker uses is less important than how the projections are interpreted.
4. Capital gain taxes will be at 28 percent of the gain. Under the 1986 Tax Act, capital gains are taxed at ordinary income rates and the minimum holding period for long-term capital gain treatment of qualifying property is more than one year.
5. Depreciation on the improvement will be straight line for a 27.5 year economic life; the first year being 11½ months to reflect the one-half month convention on

acquisition; for the personal property it will be straight line for a 7-year life, with a one-half year convention for year one.

6. Resale price will be the same as the acquisition price.
7. Purchase price is $1,100,000, with a cash down payment of $300,000 and a new mortgage of $800,000.
8. Resale costs are 6 percent.

To assist the reader, the step-by-step analysis procedures for the first five years of the projection are outlined on the respective portions of the Cash Flow Analysis Worksheet, as shown in Figures 39 through 47. A completed 15-year projection is shown in Figure 48.

Step 1. Figure 39 includes basic data from the Broker's Forecast (Figure 38) for a Potential Client using the assumptions previously discussed.

1. The mortgage data section indicates the $800,000 potential loan, its term, payments per year, interest rate, and monthly and annual debt service.
2. On lines 5 through 7 are the Gross Operating Income ($197,000), the Operating Expenses ($77,000) and the Net Operating Income ($120,000). These are also taken from the Broker's Forecast.
3. Line 8 indicates the annual mortgage interest rate of 10 percent.
4. Lines 10 and 11 indicate the cost recovery for the improvement (27.5 years) and the personal property (7 years).
5. Line 15 indicates the potential client's marginal tax bracket of 28 percent.
6. Lines 16 and 17 indicate the Net Operating Income ($120,000) minus annual debt service of $87,235 to obtain on line 20 the Cash Flow Before Taxes of $32,765.

Step 2. Figure 40 indicates the interest payable each year under the mortgage. This was calculated on a hand-held calculator and is entered on line 8 for each of the 15 years of the projection.

Step 3. Figure 41 calculates cost recovery for the 15-year projection. When the Broker's Forecast (Figure 37) was made, the following assessed values and percentages were entered:

Land	$ 84,000	19.6%
Improvements	336,000	78.5
Personal property	8,000	1.9
Total	$428,000	100 %

The investment broker can use these allocations to determine depreciation amounts for projection studies (providing the numbers are logical). This would mean that on a $1,100,000 acquisition price the allocation would be as follows:

Cash Flow Analysis Worksheet

Property Name __APARTMENT__
Prepared For __POTENTIAL CLIENT__
Prepared By __BROKER__
Date Prepared __7/1/8—__

Purchase Price __1,100,000__
Costs of Acquisition _____
Loan Points _____
Down Payment __300,000__

Mortgage Data

	1st Mortgage	2nd Mortgage
Amount	800 000	
Interest Rate	10	
Term	25	
Payments / Year	12	
Periodic Payment	7269.61	
Annual Debt Service	87 235	
Comments		

Cost Recovery Data

	Improvements	Personal Property
Value	863 500	20 900
C. R. Method	S/L	S/L
Useful Life	27.5	7
In Service Date	8/1/8—	8/1/8—
Recapture (All / None / Excess)	N	N
Investment Tax Credit ($$ or %)	0	0

Taxable Income

	Year: 1	Year: 2	Year: 3	Year: 4	Year: 5
1 Potential Rental Income	204 000				
2 − Vacancy & Credit Losses	10 200				
3 = Effective Rental Income	193 800				
4 + Other Income	3 200				
5 = Gross Operating Income	197 000				
6 − Operating Expenses	77 000				
7 = NET OPERATING INCOME	120 000				
8 − Interest - 1st Mortgage 10%	79 659				
9 − Interest - 2nd Mortgage					
10 − Cost Recovery - Improvements 27.5					
11 − Cost Recovery - Personal Property 7					
12 −					
13 −					
14 = Real Estate Taxable Income					
15 Tax Liability (Savings) @ 28 %					

Cash Flow

	Year: 1	Year: 2	Year: 3	Year: 4	Year: 5
16 NET OPERATING INCOME (Line 7)	120 000				
17 − Annual Debt Service	87 235				
18 −					
19 −					
20 = CASH FLOW BEFORE TAXES	32 765	32 765	32 765	32 765	32 765
21 − Tax Liability (Savings) (Line 15)					
22 + Investment Tax Credit					
23 = CASH FLOW AFTER TAXES					

The Statements and figures herein while not guaranteed
are secured from sources we believe authoritative

Pg _____ of _____

Figure 39

Cash Flow Analysis Worksheet

Property Name APARTMENT	Purchase Price 1,100,000
Prepared For POTENTIAL CLIENT	Costs of Acquisition
Prepared By BROKER	Loan Points
Date Prepared 7/1/8–	Down Payment 300,000

Mortgage Data / Cost Recovery Data

	1st Mortgage	2nd Mortgage			Improvements	Personal Property
Amount	800 000			Value	863 500	20 900
Interest Rate	10			C. R. Method	S/L	S/L
Term	25			Useful Life	27.5	7
Payments / Year	12			In Service Date	8/1/8–	8/1/8–
Periodic Payment	7269.61			Recapture (All / None / Excess)	N	N
Annual Debt Service	87 235			Investment Tax Credit ($$ or %)	0	0
Comments						

Taxable Income

	Year: 1	Year: 2	Year: 3	Year: 4	Year: 5
1 Potential Rental Income	204 000				
2 – Vacancy & Credit Losses	10 200				
3 = Effective Rental Income	193 800				
4 + Other Income	3 200				
5 = Gross Operating Income	197 000				
6 – Operating Expenses	77 000				
7 = NET OPERATING INCOME	120 000	120 000	120 000	120 000	120 000
8 – Interest - 1st Mortgage 10%	79 659	78 866	77 989	77 021	75 952
9 – Interest - 2nd Mortgage					
10 – Cost Recovery - Improvements 27.5					
11 – Cost Recovery - Personal Property 7					
12 –					
13 –					
14 = Real Estate Taxable Income					
15 Tax Liability (Savings) @ 28 %					

Cash Flow

16 NET OPERATING INCOME (Line 7)	120 000				
17 – Annual Debt Service	87 235				
18 –					
19 –					
20 = CASH FLOW BEFORE TAXES	32765	32765	32765	32765	32765
21 – Tax Liability (Savings) (Line 15)					
22 + Investment Tax Credit					
23 = CASH FLOW AFTER TAXES					

The Statements and figures herein while not guaranteed are secured from sources we believe authoritative

Pg _____ of _____

Figure 40

Cash Flow Analysis Worksheet

Property Name APARTMENT	Purchase Price 1,100,000
Prepared For POTENTIAL CLIENT	Costs of Acquisition
Prepared By BROKER	Loan Points
Date Prepared 7/1/8–	Down Payment 300,000

Mortgage Data			Cost Recovery Data		
	1st Mortgage	2nd Mortgage		Improvements	Personal Property
Amount	800 000		Value	863 500	20 900
Interest Rate	10		C. R. Method	S/L	S/L
Term	25		Useful Life	27.5	7
Payments / Year	12		In Service Date	1/1/8–	1/1/8–
Periodic Payment	7269.61		Recapture (All / None / Excess)	N	N
Annual Debt Service	87 235		Investment Tax Credit ($$ or %)	0	0
Comments					

Taxable Income

		Year: 1	Year: 2	Year: 3	Year: 4	Year: 5
1	Potential Rental Income	204 000				
2	– Vacancy & Credit Losses	10 200				
3	= Effective Rental Income	193 800				
4	+ Other Income	3 200				
5	= Gross Operating Income	197 000				
6	– Operating Expenses	77 000				
7	= NET OPERATING INCOME	120 000	120 000	120 000	120 000	120 000
8	– Interest - 1st Mortgage 10%	79 659	78 866	77 989	77 021	75 952
9	– Interest - 2nd Mortgage					
10	– Cost Recovery - Improvements 27.5	30 092	31 400	31 400	31 400	31 400
11	– Cost Recovery - Personal Property 7	1 493	2986	2986	2986	2986
12	–					
13	–					
14	= Real Estate Taxable Income	8756	6748	7625	8593	9662
15	Tax Liability (Savings) @ 28 %					

Cash Flow

16	NET OPERATING INCOME (Line 7)	120 000				
17	– Annual Debt Service	87 235				
18	–					
19	–					
20	= CASH FLOW BEFORE TAXES	32 765	32 765	32 765	32 765	32 765
21	– Tax Liability (Savings) (Line 15)					
22	+ Investment Tax Credit					
23	= CASH FLOW AFTER TAXES					

Pg _____ of _____

Figure 41

Cash Flow Analysis Worksheet

Property Name **APARTMENT**	Purchase Price **1,100,000**
Prepared For **POTENTIAL CLIENT**	Costs of Acquisition
Prepared By **BROKER**	Loan Points
Date Prepared **7/1/8—**	Down Payment **300,000**

Mortgage Data / Cost Recovery Data

Mortgage Data	1st Mortgage	2nd Mortgage	Cost Recovery Data	Improvements	Personal Property
Amount	800 000		Value	863 500	20 900
Interest Rate	10		C. R. Method	S/L	S/L
Term	25		Useful Life	27.5	7
Payments / Year	12		In Service Date	8/1/8—	8/1/8—
Periodic Payment	7269.61		Recapture (All / None / Excess)	N	N
Annual Debt Service	87 235		Investment Tax Credit ($$ or %)	0	0
Comments					

Taxable Income

		Year: 1	Year: 2	Year: 3	Year: 4	Year: 5
1	Potential Rental Income	204 000				
2	− Vacancy & Credit Losses	10 200				
3	= Effective Rental Income	193 800				
4	+ Other Income	3 200				
5	= Gross Operating Income	197 000				
6	− Operating Expenses	77 000				
7	= NET OPERATING INCOME	120 000	120 000	120 000	120 000	120 000
8	− Interest - 1st Mortgage 10%	79 659	78 866	77 989	77 021	75 952
9	− Interest - 2nd Mortgage					
10	− Cost Recovery - Improvements 27.5	30 092	31 400	31 400	31 400	31 400
11	− Cost Recovery - Personal Property 7	1493	2986	2986	2986	2986
12	−					
13	−					
14	= Real Estate Taxable Income	8756	6748	7625	8593	9662
15	Tax Liability (Savings) @ 28 %	2452	1889	2135	2406	2705

Cash Flow

16	NET OPERATING INCOME (Line 7)	120 000	120 000	120 000	120 000	120 000
17	− Annual Debt Service	87 235	87235	87 235	87 235	
18	−					
19	−					
20	= CASH FLOW BEFORE TAXES	32765	32 765	32765	32765	32765
21	− Tax Liability (Savings) (Line 15)	2452	1889	2135	2406	2705
22	+ Investment Tax Credit					
23	= CASH FLOW AFTER TAXES	30 313	30876	30 630	30 359	30 060

The Statements and figures herein while not guaranteed are secured from sources we believe authoritative   Pg _____ of _____

Figure 42

Land	$ 215,600	19.6%
Improvements	863,500	78.5
Personal property	20,900	1.9
Total	$1,100,000	100 %

Using a 27.5 year cost recovery schedule for the improvement with a midmonth convention for the first year and a seven-year straight line cost recovery for the personal property using a midyear convention the first year, the amounts of cost recovery are

Year	1	2–7	8	9–15
Improvements	30,092	$31,400	$31,400	$31,400
Personal property	$ 1,493	$ 2,986	$ 1,491	$ 0

These amounts are entered on lines 10 and 11, respectively. Then the cost recovery (lines 10 and 11) and the amount of interest (line 8) are subtracted from Net Operating Income (line 7) to obtain the Real Estate Taxable Income on line 14.

Step 4. Figure 43 is the calculation of Cash Flow After Taxes. Line 14 of the figure has the annual entry for Real Estate Taxable Income. Real Estate Taxable Income multiplied by the tax bracket of the potential client (28 percent) will result in the annual income tax attributable to the real estate income. This is entered on lines 15 and 21 (Tax Liability); then it is deducted from Cash Flow Before Taxes (line 20) to obtain Cash Flow After Taxes (line 23).

The next step in the analysis is to project sales proceeds after taxes, but before that is done, it is necessary to complete the Cash Flow Analysis Worksheet for the total term of the projection, in this case 15 years. Those calculations are shown in Figure 43.

Step 5. This calculates the resale proceeds (see Figure 44). Assume

1. Resale with a purchase price of $1,100,000,
2. Resale cost of 6 percent,
3. Capital gain taxes of 28 percent of the capital gain and
4. Mortgage balance at end of year 15 of $550,100.

Step 6. As an alternative, other sale prices were projected as follows. Figure 44 also shows a resale price of $950,000, which assumes a growth rate of approximately − 1% per year and a resale price of $1,280,000, which assumes a growth rate of approximately 1% per year; and Figure 45 has a price of $1,490,000, which assumes a growth rate of approximately 2% per year.

Internal Rate of Return Calculation

The broker now has completed the 1-year after-tax analysis (Broker's Forecast in Figure 37) and the 15-year After-Tax Cash Flow Analysis (Figure 43). The results of these

Cash Flow Analysis Worksheet

Property Name APARTMENT	Purchase Price 1,100,000
Prepared For POTENTIAL CLIENT	Costs of Acquisition
Prepared By BROKER	~~Loan Points~~ 15 YR PROJECTION
Date Prepared 7/1/8 –	Down Payment 300,000

Mortgage Data	1st Mortgage	2nd Mortgage
Amount	800 000	
Interest Rate	10	
Term	25	
Payments / Year	12	
Periodic Payment	7269.61	
Annual Debt Service	87 235	
Comments		

Cost Recovery Data	Improvements	Personal Property
Value	863 500	20 900
C. R. Method	S/L	S/L
Useful Life	27.5	7
In Service Date	8/1/8 –	8/1/8 –
Recapture (All / None / Excess)	N	N
Investment Tax Credit ($$ or %)	0	0

Taxable Income

		Year: 1	Year: 2	Year: 3	Year: 4	Year: 5
1	Potential Rental Income	204 000				
2	– Vacancy & Credit Losses	10 200				
3	= Effective Rental Income	193 800				
4	+ Other Income	3 200				
5	= Gross Operating Income	197 000				
6	– Operating Expenses	77 000				
7	= NET OPERATING INCOME	120 000	120 000	120 000	120 000	120 000
8	– Interest - 1st Mortgage 10%	79 659	78 866	77 989	77 021	75 952
9	– Interest - 2nd Mortgage					
10	– Cost Recovery - Improvements 27.5	30 092	31 400	31 400	31 400	31 400
11	– Cost Recovery - Personal Property 7	1 493	2986	2986	2986	2986
12	–					
13	–					
14	= Real Estate Taxable Income	8756	6748	7625	8593	9662
15	Tax Liability (Savings) @ 28 %	2452	1 889	2135	2406	2705

Cash Flow

		Year: 1	Year: 2	Year: 3	Year: 4	Year: 5
16	NET OPERATING INCOME (Line 7)	120 000	120 000	120 000	120 000	120 000
17	– Annual Debt Service	87 235	87 235	87 235	87 235	87 235
18	–					
19	–					
20	= CASH FLOW BEFORE TAXES	32765	32765	32765	32765	32765
21	– Tax Liability (Savings) (Line 15)	2452	1889	2135	2406	2705
22	+ Investment Tax Credit					
23	= CASH FLOW AFTER TAXES	30 313	30876	30 630	30 359	30060

The Statements and figures herein while not guaranteed are secured from sources we believe authoritative

Pg 1 of 3

Figure 43

Cash Flow Analysis Worksheet

Property Name _____
Prepared For _____
Prepared By _____
Date Prepared _____

Purchase Price _____
Costs of Acquisition _____
~~Loan Points~~ 15 YR PROJECTION
Down Payment _____

Mortgage Data

	1st Mortgage	2nd Mortgage
Amount		
Interest Rate		
Term		
Payments / Year		
Periodic Payment		
Annual Debt Service		
Comments		

Cost Recovery Data

	Improvements	Personal Property
Value		
C. R. Method		
Useful Life		
In Service Date		
Recapture (All / None / Excess)		
Investment Tax Credit ($$ or %)		

Taxable Income

	Year: 6	Year: 7	Year: 8	Year: 9	Year: 10
1 Potential Rental Income					
2 − Vacancy & Credit Losses					
3 = Effective Rental Income					
4 + Other Income					
5 = Gross Operating Income					
6 − Operating Expenses					
7 = NET OPERATING INCOME	120 000	120 000	120 000	120 000	120 000
8 − Interest - 1st Mortgage	74769	73464	72021	70427	68666
9 − Interest - 2nd Mortgage					
10 − Cost Recovery - Improvements	31 400	31 400	31 400	31 400	31 400
11 − Cost Recovery - Personal Property	2986	2986	1491	0	0
12 −					
13 −					
14 = Real Estate Taxable Income	10 845	12 150	15 088	18 173	19 934
15 Tax Liability (Savings) @ 28 %	3037	3402	4225	5088	5582

Cash Flow

16 NET OPERATING INCOME (Line 7)	120 000	120 000	120 000	120 000	120 000
17 − Annual Debt Service	87235	87235	87235	87235	87235
18 −					
19 −					
20 = CASH FLOW BEFORE TAXES	32765	32765	32765	32765	32765
21 − Tax Liability (Savings) (Line 15)	3037	3402	4225	5088	5582
22 + Investment Tax Credit					
23 = CASH FLOW AFTER TAXES	29728	29363	28540	27677	27183

The Statements and figures herein while not guaranteed are secured from sources we believe authoritative

Pg 2 of 3

Figure 43 (continued)

Cash Flow Analysis Worksheet

Property Name _____	Purchase Price _____
Prepared For _____	Costs of Acquisition _____
Prepared By _____	~~Loan Points~~ 15 YR PROJECTION
Date Prepared _____	Down Payment _____

Mortgage Data

	1st Mortgage	2nd Mortgage
Amount		
Interest Rate		
Term		
Payments / Year		
Periodic Payment		
Annual Debt Service		
Comments		

Cost Recovery Data

	Improvements	Personal Property
Value		
C. R. Method		
Useful Life		
In Service Date		
Recapture (All / None / Excess)		
Investment Tax Credit ($$ or %)		

Taxable Income

	Year: 11	Year: 12	Year: 13	Year: 14	Year: 15
1 Potential Rental Income					
2 − Vacancy & Credit Losses					
3 = Effective Rental Income					
4 + Other Income					
5 = Gross Operating Income					
6 − Operating Expenses					
7 = NET OPERATING INCOME	120 000	120 000	120 000	120 000	120 000
8 − Interest - 1st Mortgage	66721	64573	62200	59577	56682
9 − Interest - 2nd Mortgage					
10 − Cost Recovery - Improvements	31400	31400	31400	31400	31400
11 − Cost Recovery - Personal Property	0	0	0	0	0
12 _____					
13 _____					
14 = Real Estate Taxable Income	21879	24027	26400	29023	31918
15 Tax Liability (Savings) @ 28 %	6126	6728	7392	8126	8937

Cash Flow

16 NET OPERATING INCOME (Line 7)	120 000	120 000	120 000	120 000	120 000
17 − Annual Debt Service	87235	87235	87235	87235	87235
18 _____					
19 _____					
20 = CASH FLOW BEFORE TAXES	32765	32765	32765	32765	32765
21 − Tax Liability (Savings) (Line 15)	6126	6728	7392	8126	8937
22 + Investment Tax Credit					
23 = CASH FLOW AFTER TAXES	26639	26037	25373	24639	23828

The Statements and figures herein while not guaranteed are secured from sources we believe authoritative

Pg 3 of 3

Figure 43 (continued)

Alternative Cash Sales Worksheet

Pg _____ of _____

Mortgage Balances

	Year:	Year:	Year:	Year:	Year:
Principal Balance - 1st Mortgage					
Principal Balance - 2nd Mortgage					
TOTAL UNPAID PRINCIPAL					

Calculation of Sale Proceeds

PROJECTED SALES PRICE	1,100,000	950,000	1,280,000	

CALCULATION OF ADJUSTED BASIS:

#				
1	Basis at Acquisition	1,100,000		
2	+ Capital Additions	0		
3	− Cost Recovery (Depreciation) Taken	490,592		
4	− Basis in Partial Sales	0		
5	= Adjusted Basis at Sale	609,408	609,408	609,408

CALCULATION OF EXCESS COST RECOVERY:

#				
6	Total Cost Recovery Taken (Line 3)	490,592		
7	− Straight Line Cost Recovery	490,592		
8	= Excess Cost Recovery	0	0	0

CALCULATION OF CAPITAL GAIN ON SALE:

#				
9	Sale Price	1,100,000	950,000	1,280,000
10	− Costs of Sale	66,000	57,000	76,800
11	− Adjusted Basis at Sale (Line 5)	609,408	609,408	609,408
12	− Participation Payments	0	0	0
13	= Total Gain	424,592	283,592	593,792
14	− Excess Cost Recovery (Line 8)	0	0	0
15	− Suspended Losses	0	0	0
16	= Capital Gain or (Loss)	424,592	283,592	593,792

ITEMS TAXED AS ORDINARY INCOME:

#				
17	Excess Cost Recovery (Line 8)	0	0	0
18	− Unamortized Loan Points			
19	= Ordinary Taxable Income			
20	× Tax Rate on Ordinary Income			
21	= Tax (Savings) on Ordinary Income	0	0	0

ITEMS TAXED AS CAPITAL GAIN:

#				
22	Capital Gain (Line 16)	424,592	283,592	593,792
23	× Percentage of Capital Gain Reportable	100 %	100 %	100 %
24	= Taxable Capital Gain	424,592	283,592	593,792
25	× Tax Rate on Capital Gain	28 %	28 %	28 %
26	= Tax on Capital Gain	118,886	79,406	166,262

CALCULATION OF SALE PROCEEDS AFTER TAX:

#				
27	Sale Price (Line 9)	1,100,000	950,000	1,280,000
28	− Costs of Sale (Line 10)	66,000	57,000	76,800
29	− Participation Payments (Line 12)	0	0	0
30	− Mortgage Balance(s) (from top of form)	550,100	550,100	550,100
31	= Sale Proceeds Before Taxes	483,900	342,900	653,100
32	− Tax (Savings) on Ordinary Income (Line 21)	0	0	0
33	− Tax on Capital Gain (Line 26)	118,886	79,406	166,262
34	− Recapture of Investment Tax Credits	0	0	0
35	= SALE PROCEEDS AFTER TAX	365,014	263,494	486,838

The statements and figures herein while not guaranteed
are secured from sources we believe authoritative   Prepared by _____ BROKER

Figure 44

studies are indicated below. (Annual cash flows are based on the projection assumptions and at four resale prices.)

Period	$1,100,000 Resale Cash flows	$950,000 Resale Cash flows	$1,280,000 Resale Cash flows	$1,490,000 Resale Cash flows
0	($300,000)	($300,000)	($300,000)	($300,000)
1	30,313	30,313	30,313	30,313
2	30,876	30,876	30,876	30,876
3	30,630	30,630	30,630	30,630
4	30,359	30,359	30,359	30,359
5	30,060	30,060	30,060	30,060
6	29,728	29,728	29,728	29,728
7	29,363	29,363	29,363	29,363
8	28,540	28,540	28,540	28,540
9	27,677	27,677	27,677	27,677
10	27,183	27,183	27,183	27,183
11	26,639	26,639	26,639	26,639
12	26,037	26,037	26,037	26,037
13	25,373	25,373	25,373	25,373
14	24,639	24,639	24,639	24,639
15	23,828	23,828	23,828	23,828
Resale Proceeds After Taxes	$365,014	$263,494	$486,838	$628,966

The final calculation is now made to determine the investor's yield under the projected assumptions. Everything done thus far has been estimated, projected, or assumed. The final step will give a definitive number. The validity of the number, however, is only as good as the earlier input estimates.

By definition, the internal rate of return (IRR) is that rate which discounts an income stream so that the total equals the initial investment. The purpose of our calculation is to find and interest rate which will discount the total income stream so that the total present values will equal the initial investment (investment amount).

The calculation indicates the following internal rates of return for all the assumed resale prices, as follows:

Resale value	IRR (after income tax)
$1,100,000	10.3
950,000	9.2
1,280,000	11.4
1,490,000	12.5

In looking at the IRR above it is well to review some of the key results.

1. The Net Operating Income (NOI) remained level.
2. The acquisition price was $1,100,000 with a Net Operating Income of $120,000, resulting in a capitalization rate of 10.9 percent.
3. The mortgage interest rate was 10 percent.

Pg _____ of _____

Alternative Cash Sales Worksheet

Mortgage Balances

	Year:	Year:	Year:	Year:	Year:
Principal Balance - 1st Mortgage					
Principal Balance - 2nd Mortgage					
TOTAL UNPAID PRINCIPAL					

Calculation of Sale Proceeds

PROJECTED SALES PRICE	1,490,000	

CALCULATION OF ADJUSTED BASIS:

1	Basis at Acquisition	1,100,000	
2	+ Capital Additions	0	
3	− Cost Recovery (Depreciation) Taken	490,592	
4	− Basis In Partial Sales	0	
5	= Adjusted Basis at Sale	609,408	

CALCULATION OF EXCESS COST RECOVERY:

6	Total Cost Recovery Taken (Line 3)	490,592	
7	− Straight Line Cost Recovery	490,592	
8	= Excess Cost Recovery	0	

CALCULATION OF CAPITAL GAIN ON SALE:

9	Sale Price	1,490,000	
10	− Costs of Sale	89,400	
11	− Adjusted Basis at Sale (Line 5)	609,408	
12	− Participation Payments	0	
13	= Total Gain	791,192	
14	− Excess Cost Recovery (Line 8)	0	
15	− Suspended Losses	0	
16	= Capital Gain or (Loss)	791,192	

ITEMS TAXED AS ORDINARY INCOME:

17	Excess Cost Recovery (Line 8)	0	
18	− Unamortized Loan Points		
19	= Ordinary Taxable Income		
20	x Tax Rate on Ordinary Income		
21	= Tax (Savings) on Ordinary Income	0	

ITEMS TAXED AS CAPITAL GAIN:

22	Capital Gain (Line 16)	791,192	
23	x Percentage of Capital Gain Reportable	100 %	
24	= Taxable Capital Gain	791,192	
25	x Tax Rate on Capital Gain	28 %	
26	= Tax on Capital Gain	221,534	

CALCULATION OF SALE PROCEEDS AFTER TAX:

27	Sale Price (Line 9)	1,490,000	
28	− Costs of Sale (Line 10)	89,400	
29	− Participation Payments (Line 12)	0	
30	− Mortgage Balance(s) (from top of form)	550,100	
31	= Sale Proceeds Before Taxes	850,500	
32	− Tax (Savings) on Ordinary Income (Line 21)	0	
33	− Tax on Capital Gain (Line 26)	221,534	
34	− Recapture of Investment Tax Credits	0	
35	= SALE PROCEEDS AFTER TAX	628,966	

The statements and figures herein while not guaranteed
are secured from sources we believe authoritative   Prepared by ___BROKER___

Figure 45

Alternative T-Bars Worksheet

Alternative # _1,100,000_   Alternative # _950,000_   Alternative # _1,280,000_

n	$		n	$		n	$
0	(300 000)		0	(300 000)		0	(300 000)
1	30 313		1	30 313		1	30 313
2	30 876		2	30 876		2	30 876
3	30 630		3	30 630		3	30 630
4	30 359		4	30 359		4	30 359
5	30 060		5	30 060		5	30 060
6	29 728		6	29 728		6	29 728
7	29 363		7	29 363		7	29 363
8	28 540		8	28 540		8	28 540
9	27 677		9	27 677		9	27 677
10	27 183		10	27 183		10	27 183
11	26 639		11	26 639		11	26 639
12	26 037		12	26 037		12	26 037
13	25 373		13	25 373		13	25 373
14	24 639		14	24 639		14	24 639
15	23 828 + 365 014		15	23 828 + 263 494		15	23 828 + 486 838
IRR =	10.3		IRR =	9.2		IRR =	11.4

The statements and figures herein while not guaranteed
are secured from sources we believe authoritative

Prepared by ___BROKER___

Figure 46

Alternative T-Bars Worksheet

Alternative # 1,490,000   Alternative # _____   Alternative # _____

n	$	n	$	n	$
0	(300 000)	0	( )	0	( )
1	30 313	1		1	
2	30 876	2		2	
3	30 630	3		3	
4	30 359	4		4	
5	30 060	5		5	
6	29 728	6		6	
7	29 363	7		7	
8	28 540	8		8	
9	27 677	9		9	
10	27 183	10		10	
11	26 639	11		11	
12	26 037	12		12	
13	25 373	13		13	
14	24 639	14		14	
15	23 828 + 628 966	15		15	
IRR =	12.5	IRR =		IRR =	

The statements and figures herein while not guaranteed
are secured from sources we believe authoritative   Prepared by ____ BROKER ____

Figure 47

4. Projected resale capitalization rates at EOY 15 with the same Net Operating Income would be

Resale price	NOI	Capitalization rate
$1,100,000	$120,000	10.9
950,000	120,000	12.6
1,280,000	120,000	9.4
1,490,000	120,000	8.1

Therefore, the study is based on a constant NOI, but with a fluctuating overall capitalization rate increasing to 12.6 percent and reducing as low as 8.1 percent.

Alternative Projection

It is not at all illogical to assume that a prudent or knowledgeable investor who acquires a property with negative leverage might do so believing rents will increase (because of inflation) faster than expenses. If this happens and the overall capitalization rate remains the same, the resale price will increase, but not because of declining capitalization rates.

Another cash flow study of the property will be made, with the following changes in the assumptions.

1. Net operating income will increase 3 percent per year.
2. Two resale prices will be used. The first ($1,800,000) will be based on a 10 percent capitalization rate.
3. The second ($1,400,000) reflects an increased Net Operating Income, indicating a capitalization rate of 13 percent.

These cash flow projections are shown in Figure 48 through 50.
The resulting cash flows or yields are

N	$
0	($300,000)
1	30,313
2	33,468
3	35,892
4	38,370
5	40,904
6	43,490
7	46,129
8	48,402
9	50,725
10	53,516
11	56,353
12	59,235
13	62,158
14	65,120
15	68,116 + 838,775
Resale: $1,800,000	
IRR: 17.1%	

N	$
0	($300,000)
1	30,313
2	33,468
3	35,892
4	38,370
5	40,904
6	43,490
7	46,129
8	48,402
9	50,725
10	53,516
11	56,353
12	59,235
13	62,158
14	65,120
15	68,116 + 568,055
Resale: $1,400,000	
IRR: 15.8%	

Cash Flow Analysis Worksheet

Property Name __APARTMENT__
Prepared For __POTENTIAL CLIENT__
Prepared By __BROKER__
Date Prepared __7/1/8—__

Purchase Price __1,100,000__
Costs of Acquisition _____
~~Loan Points~~ __15 YR. PROJECTION (NOI +3%)__
Down Payment __300,000__

Mortgage Data

	1st Mortgage	2nd Mortgage
Amount	800 000	
Interest Rate	10	
Term	25	
Payments / Year	12	
Periodic Payment	7269.61	
Annual Debt Service	87 235	
Comments		

Cost Recovery Data

	Improvements	Personal Property
Value	863 500	20 900
C. R. Method	S/L	S/L
Useful Life	27.5	7
In Service Date	8/1/8—	8/1/8—
Recapture (All / None / Excess)	N	N
Investment Tax Credit ($$ or %)	0	0

Taxable Income

	Year: 1	Year: 2	Year: 3	Year: 4	Year: 5
1 Potential Rental Income	204 000				
2 − Vacancy & Credit Losses	10 200				
3 = Effective Rental Income	193 800				
4 + Other Income	3 200				
5 = Gross Operating Income	197 000				
6 − Operating Expenses	77 000				
7 = NET OPERATING INCOME	120 000	123 600	127 308	131 127	135 061
8 − Interest - 1st Mortgage 10%	79 659	78 866	77 989	77 021	75 952
9 − Interest - 2nd Mortgage					
10 − Cost Recovery - Improvements 27.5	30 092	31 400	31 400	31 400	31 400
11 − Cost Recovery - Personal Property 7	1 493	2 986	2 986	2 986	2 986
12 −					
13 −					
14 = Real Estate Taxable Income	8 756	10 348	14 933	19 720	24 723
15 Tax Liability (Savings) @ 28 %	2 452	2 897	4 181	5 522	6 922

Cash Flow

16 NET OPERATING INCOME (Line 7)	120 000	123 600	127 308	131 127	135 061
17 − Annual Debt Service	87 235	87 235	87 235	87 235	87 235
18 −					
19 −					
20 = CASH FLOW BEFORE TAXES	32 765	36 365	40 073	43 892	47 826
21 − Tax Liability (Savings) (Line 15)	2 452	2 897	4 181	5 522	6 922
22 + Investment Tax Credit					
23 = CASH FLOW AFTER TAXES	30 313	33 468	35 892	38 370	40 904

The Statements and figures herein while not guaranteed
are secured from sources we believe authoritative

Pg __1__ of __3__

Figure 48

Cash Flow Analysis Worksheet

Property Name _____	Purchase Price _____
Prepared For _____	Costs of Acquisition _____
Prepared By _____	~~Loan Points~~ 15 YR AMORTIZATION (NOI + 3%)
Date Prepared _____	Down Payment _____

Mortgage Data

	1st Mortgage	2nd Mortgage
Amount		
Interest Rate		
Term		
Payments / Year		
Periodic Payment		
Annual Debt Service		
Comments		

Cost Recovery Data

	Improvements	Personal Property
Value		
C. R. Method		
Useful Life		
In Service Date		
Recapture (All / None / Excess)		
Investment Tax Credit ($$ or %)		

Taxable Income

	Year: 6	Year: 7	Year: 8	Year: 9	Year: 10
1 Potential Rental Income					
2 − Vacancy & Credit Losses					
3 = Effective Rental Income					
4 + Other Income					
5 = Gross Operating Income					
6 − Operating Expenses					
7 = NET OPERATING INCOME	139 113	143 286	147 585	152 012	156 573
8 − Interest - 1st Mortgage	74 769	73 464	72 021	70 427	68 666
9 − Interest - 2nd Mortgage					
10 − Cost Recovery - Improvements	31 400	31 400	31 400	31 400	31 400
11 − Cost Recovery - Personal Property	2986	2986	1491	0	0
12 − _____					
13 − _____					
14 = Real Estate Taxable Income	29958	35436	42673	50185	56507
15 Tax Liability (Savings) @ 28 %	8388	9922	11 948	14052	15822

Cash Flow

16 NET OPERATING INCOME (Line 7)	139 113	143 286	147 585	152 012	156 573
17 − Annual Debt Service	87 235	87 235	87 235	87 235	87 235
18 − _____					
19 − _____					
20 = CASH FLOW BEFORE TAXES	51 878	56 051	60 350	64 777	69 338
21 − Tax Liability (Savings) (Line 15)	8388	9922	11 948	14 052	15 822
22 + Investment Tax Credit					
23 = CASH FLOW AFTER TAXES	43 490	46 129	48 402	50 725	53 516

The Statements and figures herein while not guaranteed are secured from sources we believe authoritative

Pg 2 of 3

Figure 48 (continued)

Cash Flow Analysis Worksheet

Property Name _____

Prepared For _____

Prepared By _____

Date Prepared _____

Purchase Price _____

Costs of Acquisition _____

~~Loan Points~~ 15 YR PROJECTION (NOI + 3%)

Down Payment _____

Mortgage Data

	1st Mortgage	2nd Mortgage
Amount		
Interest Rate		
Term		
Payments / Year		
Periodic Payment		
Annual Debt Service		
Comments		

Cost Recovery Data

	Improvements	Personal Property
Value		
C. R. Method		
Useful Life		
In Service Date		
Recapture (All / None / Excess)		
Investment Tax Credit ($$ or %)		

Taxable Income

	Year: 11	Year: 12	Year: 13	Year: 14	Year: 15
1 Potential Rental Income					
2 – Vacancy & Credit Losses					
3 = Effective Rental Income					
4 + Other Income					
5 = Gross Operating Income					
6 – Operating Expenses					
7 = NET OPERATING INCOME	161270	166108	171091	176224	181511
8 – Interest - 1st Mortgage	66721	64573	62200	59577	56682
9 – Interest - 2nd Mortgage					
10 – Cost Recovery - Improvements	31400	31400	31400	31400	31400
11 – Cost Recovery - Personal Property	0	0	0	0	0
12 –					
13 –					
14 = Real Estate Taxable Income	63149	70135	77491	85247	93428
15 Tax Liability (Savings) @ 28 %	17682	19638	21698	23869	26160

Cash Flow

16 NET OPERATING INCOME (Line 7)	161270	166108	171091	176224	181511
17 – Annual Debt Service	87235	87235	87235	87235	87235
18 –					
19 –					
20 = CASH FLOW BEFORE TAXES	74035	78873	83856	88989	94276
21 – Tax Liability (Savings) (Line 15)	17682	19638	21698	23869	26160
22 + Investment Tax Credit					
23 = CASH FLOW AFTER TAXES	56353	59235	62158	65120	68116

The Statements and figures herein while not guaranteed
are secured from sources we believe authoritative

Pg 3 of 3

Figure 48 (continued)

Alternative Cash Sales Worksheet

Pg _____ of _____

Mortgage Balances

	Year:	Year:	Year:	Year:	Year:
Principal Balance - 1st Mortgage					
Principal Balance - 2nd Mortgage					
TOTAL UNPAID PRINCIPAL					

Calculation of Sale Proceeds

PROJECTED SALES PRICE	1,800,000	1,400,000	

CALCULATION OF ADJUSTED BASIS:

1	Basis at Acquisition	1,100,000		
2	+ Capital Additions	0		
3	− Cost Recovery (Depreciation) Taken	490,592		
4	− Basis in Partial Sales	0		
5	= Adjusted Basis at Sale	609,408	609,408	

CALCULATION OF EXCESS COST RECOVERY:

6	Total Cost Recovery Taken (Line 3)	490,592		
7	− Straight Line Cost Recovery	490,592		
8	= Excess Cost Recovery	0	0	

CALCULATION OF CAPITAL GAIN ON SALE:

9	Sale Price	1,800,000	1,400,000	
10	− Costs of Sale	108,000	84,000	
11	− Adjusted Basis at Sale (Line 5)	609,408	609,408	
12	− Participation Payments	0	0	
13	= Total Gain	1,082,592	706,592	
14	− Excess Cost Recovery (Line 8)	0	0	
15	− Suspended Losses	0	0	
16	= Capital Gain or (Loss)	1,082,592	706,592	

ITEMS TAXED AS ORDINARY INCOME:

17	Excess Cost Recovery (Line 8)	0	0	
18	− Unamortized Loan Points			
19	= Ordinary Taxable Income			
20	x Tax Rate on Ordinary Income			
21	= Tax (Savings) on Ordinary Income	0	0	

ITEMS TAXED AS CAPITAL GAIN:

22	Capital Gain (Line 16)	1,082,592	706,592	
23	x Percentage of Capital Gain Reportable	100 %	100 %	
24	= Taxable Capital Gain	1,082,592	706,592	
25	x Tax Rate on Capital Gain	28 %	28 %	
26	= Tax on Capital Gain	303,126	197,846	

CALCULATION OF SALE PROCEEDS AFTER TAX:

27	Sale Price (Line 9)	1,800,000	1,400,000	
28	− Costs of Sale (Line 10)	108,000	84,000	
29	− Participation Payments (Line 12)	0	0	
30	− Mortgage Balance(s) (from top of form)	550,100	550,100	
31	= Sale Proceeds Before Taxes	1,141,900	765,900	
32	− Tax (Savings) on Ordinary Income (Line 21)	0	0	
33	− Tax on Capital Gain (Line 26)	303,126	197,846	
34	− Recapture of Investment Tax Credits	0	0	
35	= SALE PROCEEDS AFTER TAX	838,775	568,055	

The statements and figures herein while not guaranteed are secured from sources we believe authoritative   Prepared by _____ BROKER

Figure 49

Pg _____ of _____

Alternative T-Bars Worksheet

Alternative # _1,800,000_   Alternative # _1,400,000_   Alternative # _____

n	$	n	$	n	$
0	(300 000)	0	(300 000)	0	(_____)
1	30 313	1	30 313	1	
2	33 468	2	33 468	2	
3	35 892	3	35 892	3	
4	38 370	4	38 370	4	
5	40 904	5	40 904	5	
6	43 490	6	43 490	6	
7	46 129	7	46 129	7	
8	48 402	8	48 402	8	
9	50 725	9	50 725	9	
10	53 516	10	53 516	10	
11	56 353	11	56 353	11	
12	59 235	12	59 235	12	
13	62 158	13	62 158	13	
14	65 120	14	65 120	14	
15	68 116 + 838 775	15	68 116 + 568 055	15	
IRR =	17.1	IRR =	15.8	IRR =	

The statements and figures herein while not guaranteed
are secured from sources we believe authoritative

Prepared by _____

Figure 50

After-Tax Investment Analysis

This step-by-step analysis creates no miraculous real estate investments. In fact, some brokers dislike the method because they say it does not show real estate yields as high as do other types of investment analysis. The purpose of the procedure, however, is not to show real estate investments as high or low; it is used merely to show what happens under projected circumstances. IRR uses a yield measurement that is similar to the measurement used and understood by the public on alternative investments such as stocks and bonds.

As we have shown in our case study, the foundation of cash flow analysis is the Broker's Forecast, an estimate of the operations for the next year. If the broker finds reliability in this statement, the next step is to prepare the cash flow analysis. In making this analysis, the broker gives consideration to many factors: the type of tenant or improvement, the location and demographics of the area, increases or decreases of the quantity of income projected over succeeding years, and how these items will affect the durability of the income.

While these items are impossible to predict accurately, both the broker and the client have some ability to project future trends. They are able to understand the present condition of the property and can make some estimate about whether it can be maintained at the cost indicated in the projection for the period indicated. They have some idea as to whether the rents will increase or decrease due to the improvements, neighborhood trends and so forth. And they can form an opinion about whether the projected resale price, if it is the same as the acquisition price, is a reasonable, a conservative, or an optimistic estimate. If the property is to sell at more or less than at acquisition, one must determine if it is because of increased or decreased income or decreasing or increasing yield demands. These are all logical points of discussion between the broker and the seller or the broker and the buyer.

If a projection process is followed, such discussions can concern themselves with the assumptions; but if such a process is ignored, the negotiation process reduces itself to who is the best salesperson.

CASE STUDY 2: DISCOUNTED CASH FLOW ANALYSIS: A LISTING TOOL

One of the most common (and often the most difficult) problems that brokers face in listing income-producing property is offering it at a price that will accomplish the transaction within a reasonable period of time.

Over the years, brokers have relied on gross multipliers, overall capitalization rates and other rules of thumb to convince sellers of marketplace realities. All too often, however, a difference of only 1 percent in overall capitalization rate can stand between the seller and the agent in reaching an agreement on listing price.

This case study illustrates a situation where discounting cash flows is used as a means of bringing the sellers to list at a reasonable price.

Situation

The subject property is a small office building which the owners wish to sell for $290,000. A property analysis indicated a Net Operating Income of $24,725 and thus an overall capitalization rate of 8.5 percent at the asking price. The broker recommended a sale price of $260,000, indicating a capitalization rate of 9.5 percent. The owners disagreed and the salesperson was unable to list the property at $260,000.

A new listing approach has been conceived based on the methodology and philosophy of discounted cash flows discussed in this book. In essence, the approach is based on the idea of placing the seller in the position of a prospective buyer. What would the income stream be if the seller acquired the property? This can be projected with data and assumptions on mortgage, amortization, depreciation, interest rates, tax brackets, term of holding and resale price. These assumptions form the basis of projections which are presented to the current owner.

Mortgage Amount

Many people believe that the mortgage is always estimated as a percentage of the sale price; this is not necessarily true. Although loans may be as high as 75 percent, it is generally accepted that a $50,000 property sold at $100,000 will not necessarily command a $75,000 mortgage.

So, instead of estimating a mortgage based on a sale price for the subject property, the broker in this case used a debt coverage ratio (DCR) of 1.25 at the current interest rate (10 percent) for a loan period typical of this kind of property (25 years). Therefore

$$\frac{\text{NOI}}{\text{DCR}} = \frac{\$24,725}{1.25} = \begin{array}{l}\$19,780 \text{ available for annual debt service}\\ (\$1,648.33 \text{ per month})\end{array}$$

Payments of $1,648.33 monthly at 10 percent for 25 years will repay a loan of $181,394.15. Specifically, the broker estimated a loan of $180,000, payable at $1,635.66 per month for 25 years including 10 percent interest (which comes to $19,627.92 annual debt service).

Depreciation (Cost Recovery)

Brokers tend to think of land and building allocations in terms of ratios or percentages. Such thinking conditions them to believe that as price rises so does the amount of depreciation. It is possible, however, to change thinking habits to establish a logical amount of depreciation with a change in the price being dependent on a change in land value. Under such a premise, depreciation becomes a constant amount at various projected sale prices.

In this case study, improvements were estimated at $200,000 and the 31.5-year straight-line depreciation method was selected. Land was estimated at $60,000.

Projection Period

Experience shows that the internal rate of return (IRR) in Year One is usually negative; it generally increases until some time between 12 and 16 years when it levels off and then declines. For this case study, 15 years was selected as the projection period.

Tax Bracket of the Investor

It is unusual to find low tax-bracket investors buying million-dollar buildings; conversely, not too many duplexes are acquired by investors in high tax brackets.

In this particular case, it was assumed that a property priced in the $200,000 to $300,000 range would be sold to someone with a 28 percent marginal tax rate.

Reversion (Resale Proceeds)

Estimating the future value of a property 15 years hence is actually not as difficult as estimating current value, at least from the standpoint of present value of money. An error in judgment as to future value is minimized in terms of present value by the discounting process.

In this case the future value at the time of sale was estimated at $300,000. Marketing costs were estimated at 7 percent and capital gains taxes were calculated at 28 percent.

Projected Income Stream

A complete cash flow analysis was done on the subject property (see Figure 51), with the resulting projected income stream.

EOY	$
1	$4,896
2	4,920
3	4,865
4	4,804
5	4,737
6	4,662
7	4,580
8	4,489
9	4,389
10	4,278
11	4,155
12	4,020
13	3,871
14	3,706
15	3,523 + 123,316 (net proceeds after taxes)

This income stream becomes the total future benefits to a prospective purchaser. It therefore follows that the prospective purchaser's yield will depend upon the price paid for the income stream.

The income stream was then discounted at eight different rates to determine equity values *over* the proposed mortgage. The results were as follows.

Yield	Equity value	Mortgage	Investment value
4%	$118,104	$180,000	$298,104
6%	95,129	180,000	275,129
8%	77,630	180,000	257,630
10%	64,180	180,000	244,180
12%	53,749	180,000	233,749
14%	45,584	180,000	225,584
16%	39,134	180,000	219,184
18%	33,991	180,000	213,991

Bringing Buyer and Seller Together

It was pointed out to the sellers that a buyer of the property at $290,000 could only expect an approximate 5-percent yield. It was agreed that no one (including the sellers) buys real estate for that yield. The sellers agreed that 10 to 12 percent was a reasonable minimum expected return in light of competitive investments which a prospective purchaser could make.

The property was listed at $240,000 after these points were made, in spite of the fact that the sellers previously had refused to list at $260,000.

Within six days, Bill Lynch, who had been searching for an investment for many months was shown the analysis. He wanted to offer $225,000, but it was brought to his attention that such an offer would, if accepted, return a yield of more than 14 percent which was much higher than he could expect from competitive investments. It was also pointed out that his current equity funds were earning only 6 percent (before taxes) and that his yield could be dramatically increased by acquiring the subject property. His ultimate purchase of the property at $240,000 confirmed the broker's analysis.

It is obvious that this type of analysis by the broker lays the foundation for a more intelligent and profitable business.

Within a period of 90 days the broker did similar analyses on two apartment complexes, each having a different owner. In both instances, the yield projected, at the owner's price and terms, was less than 5 percent. Neither investment was competitive in the market; however, the broker's knowledge and experience in the market added another dimension which ultimately resulted in listing one property and rejecting the other.

The apartment building that eventually was listed consisted of two and three-bedroom units in a stable neighborhood which made the building a natural for conversion to condominiums.

The other building consisted of one-bedroom apartments in a highly transient area of the city. Condominium buyers would not be attracted to the area. The broker knew that the owner would have to revise the price and terms to dispose of the property. When the time comes for the owner to accept this fact, a transaction will probably be made.

Cash Flow Analysis Worksheet

Property Name **OFFICE**	Purchase Price **?**
Prepared For **SELLER**	Costs of Acquisition
Prepared By **BROKER**	Loan Points
Date Prepared **15yr PROJECTION**	Down Payment

Mortgage Data / Cost Recovery Data

	1st Mortgage	2nd Mortgage		Improvements	Personal Property
Amount	180000		Value	200000	
Interest Rate	10%		C. R. Method	S/L	
Term	25		Useful Life	31.5 yr	
Payments / Year	12		In Service Date	NOW	
Periodic Payment	1635.66		Recapture (All / None / Excess)	NONE	
Annual Debt Service	19628—		Investment Tax Credit ($$ or %)		
Comments					

Taxable Income

	Year: 1	Year: 2	Year: 3	Year: 4	Year: 5
1 Potential Rental Income					
2 − Vacancy & Credit Losses					
3 = Effective Rental Income					
4 + Other Income					
5 = Gross Operating Income					
6 − Operating Expenses					
7 = NET OPERATING INCOME	24725	24725	24725	24725	24725
8 − Interest - 1st Mortgage	17923	17745	17548	17330	17089
9 − Interest - 2nd Mortgage					
10 − Cost Recovery - Improvements	6084	6349	6349	6349	6349
11 − Cost Recovery - Personal Property					
12 −					
13 −					
14 = Real Estate Taxable Income	718	631	828	1046	1287
15 Tax Liability (Savings) @ **28** %	201	177	232	293	360

Cash Flow

16 NET OPERATING INCOME (Line 7)	24725				
17 − Annual Debt Service	19628				
18 −					
19 −					
20 = CASH FLOW BEFORE TAXES	5097	5097	5097	5097	5097
21 − Tax Liability (Savings) (Line 15)	201	177	232	293	360
22 + Investment Tax Credit					
23 = CASH FLOW AFTER TAXES	4896	4920	4865	4804	4737

The Statements and figures herein while not guaranteed are secured from sources we believe authoritative

Pg **1** of **4**

Figure 51

Cash Flow Analysis Worksheet

Property Name _OFFICE_
Prepared For _SELLER_
Prepared By _BROKER_
Date Prepared _15yr PROJECTION_

Purchase Price _?_
Costs of Acquisition _____
Loan Points _____
Down Payment _____

Mortgage Data	1st Mortgage	2nd Mortgage
Amount		
Interest Rate		
Term		
Payments / Year		
Periodic Payment		
Annual Debt Service		
Comments		

Cost Recovery Data	Improvements	Personal Property
Value		
C. R. Method		
Useful Life		
In Service Date		
Recapture (All / None / Excess)		
Investment Tax Credit ($$ or %)		

Taxable Income

	Year: 6	Year: 7	Year: 8	Year: 9	Year: 10
1 Potential Rental Income					
2 − Vacancy & Credit Losses					
3 = Effective Rental Income					
4 + Other Income					
5 = Gross Operating Income					
6 − Operating Expenses					
7 = NET OPERATING INCOME	24725	24725	24725	24725	24725
8 − Interest - 1st Mortgage	16823	16530	16205	15847	15451
9 − Interest - 2nd Mortgage					
10 − Cost Recovery - Improvements	6349	6349	6349	6349	6349
11 − Cost Recovery - Personal Property					
12 __					
13 __					
14 = Real Estate Taxable Income	1553	1846	2171	2529	2925
15 Tax Liability (Savings) @ 28 %	435	517	608	708	819

Cash Flow

16 NET OPERATING INCOME (Line 7)	24725				
17 − Annual Debt Service	19628				
18 __					
19 __					
20 = CASH FLOW BEFORE TAXES	5097	5097	5097	5097	5097
21 − Tax Liability (Savings) (Line 15)	435	517	608	708	819
22 + Investment Tax Credit					
23 = CASH FLOW AFTER TAXES	4662	4580	4489	4389	4278

The Statements and figures herein while not guaranteed
are secured from sources we believe authoritative

Pg _2_ of _4_

Figure 51   (continued)

Cash Flow Analysis Worksheet

Property Name **OFFICE**
Prepared For **SELLER**
Prepared By **BROKER**
Date Prepared **15YR PROJECTION**

Purchase Price **?** 0
Costs of Acquisition
Loan Points
Down Payment

Mortgage Data		
	1st Mortgage	2nd Mortgage
Amount		
Interest Rate		
Term		
Payments / Year		
Periodic Payment		
Annual Debt Service		
Comments		

Cost Recovery Data		
	Improvements	Personal Property
Value		
C. R. Method		
Useful Life		
In Service Date		
Recapture (All / None / Excess)		
Investment Tax Credit ($$ or %)		

Taxable Income

	Year: 11	Year: 12	Year: 13	Year: 14	Year: 15
1 Potential Rental Income					
2 − Vacancy & Credit Losses					
3 = Effective Rental Income					
4 + Other Income					
5 = Gross Operating Income					
6 − Operating Expenses					
7 = NET OPERATING INCOME	24725	24725	24725	24725	24725
8 − Interest - 1st Mortgage	15013	14530	13996	13407	12755
9 − Interest - 2nd Mortgage					
10 − Cost Recovery - Improvements	6349	6349	6349	6349	6349
11 − Cost Recovery - Personal Property					
12 −					
13 −					
14 = Real Estate Taxable Income	3363	3846	4380	4969	5621
15 Tax Liability (Savings) @ 28 %	942	1077	1226	1391	1574

Cash Flow

16 NET OPERATING INCOME (Line 7)	24725				
17 − Annual Debt Service	19628				
18 −					
19 −					
20 = CASH FLOW BEFORE TAXES	5097	5097	5097	5097	5097
21 − Tax Liability (Savings) (Line 15)	942	1077	1226	1391	1574
22 + Investment Tax Credit					
23 = CASH FLOW AFTER TAXES	4155	4020	3871	3706	3523

The Statements and figures herein while not guaranteed
are secured from sources we believe authoritative

Pg **3** of **4**

Figure 51   (continued)

Alternative Cash Sales Worksheet

Pg _____ of _____

Mortgage Balances

	Year: 15	Year:	Year:	Year:	Year:
Principal Balance - 1st Mortgage	123772				
Principal Balance - 2nd Mortgage	0				
TOTAL UNPAID PRINCIPAL	123772				

Calculation of Sale Proceeds

PROJECTED SALES PRICE

CALCULATION OF ADJUSTED BASIS:

1	Basis at Acquisition	260000	
2	+ Capital Additions		
3	− Cost Recovery (Depreciation) Taken	94970	
4	− Basis in Partial Sales		
5	= Adjusted Basis at Sale	165030	

CALCULATION OF EXCESS COST RECOVERY:

6	Total Cost Recovery Taken (Line 3)	94970	
7	− Straight Line Cost Recovery	94970	
8	= Excess Cost Recovery	0	

CALCULATION OF CAPITAL GAIN ON SALE:

9	Sale Price	300000	
10	− Costs of Sale	21000	
11	− Adjusted Basis at Sale (Line 5)	165030	
12	− Participation Payments		
13	= Total Gain	113970	
14	− Excess Cost Recovery (Line 8)	0	
15	− Suspended Losses		
16	= Capital Gain or (Loss)	113970	

ITEMS TAXED AS ORDINARY INCOME:

17	Excess Cost Recovery (Line 8)	0	
18	− Unamortized Loan Points		
19	= Ordinary Taxable Income		
20	x Tax Rate on Ordinary Income		
21	= Tax (Savings) on Ordinary Income	0	

ITEMS TAXED AS CAPITAL GAIN:

22	Capital Gain (Line 16)	113970	
23	x Percentage of Capital Gain Reportable	100	
24	= Taxable Capital Gain	113970	
25	x Tax Rate on Capital Gain	28	
26	= Tax on Capital Gain	31912	

CALCULATION OF SALE PROCEEDS AFTER TAX:

27	Sale Price (Line 9)	300000	
28	− Costs of Sale (Line 10)	21000	
29	− Participation Payments (Line 12)		
30	− Mortgage Balance(s) (from top of form)	123772	
31	= Sale Proceeds Before Taxes	155228	
32	− Tax (Savings) on Ordinary Income (Line 21)	0	
33	− Tax on Capital Gain (Line 26)	31912	
34	− Recapture of Investment Tax Credits		
35	= SALE PROCEEDS AFTER TAX	123316	

The statements and figures herein while not guaranteed
are secured from sources we believe authoritative

Prepared by _____ Pg. 4 of 4 _____

Figure 51 (continued)

CASE STUDY 3: THE SANDWICH LEASE

The "sandwich" lease is a further example of how value is estimated by the discounted cash flow process and, in fact, demonstrates that none of the other historically used methods of valuation are feasible when applied to this type of property.

Once a lease is executed by a tenant on a property, an income stream is defined. The stream may be above, below or equal to the rent on comparable properties at the time of execution or at later times. Therefore, care must be taken to account for the differences between contract rent and market rent when analyzing the property as a potential investment.

When the contract rent is less than market rent, an interest is established for the lessee called a leasehold interest. Such interest may be valued by the discounted cash flow techniques discussed throughout this book (applying the appropriate discount factor to the future income stream). The discount rate used will reflect the quantity, quality and durability of the income of the leasehold.

The income stream is represented by the difference between the annual contract rent and the market rent over the remaining period of the lease. If the lessee subleases the property, the income stream is defined as the difference between the rent paid and the rent received.

Situation

Twelve years have elapsed since Able leased his 50,000 square-foot warehouse to Bon Bon Corporation of America for $2,500 per month net rent for a period of 30 years. Two years ago the space became inadequate for Bon Bon; the broker subleased the building to two local tenants as follows:

Cable TV: 30,000 sq. ft.; term: 20 years, $2,400 per month net

Dental Supply: 20,000 sq. ft.; term: 20 years, $1,600 per month

Recently Dental Supply moved and the broker subleased its space for the balance of the term for $2,000 per month net to Farmer's Tractors.

Income Stream and Present Value

We will try to accomplish two aims in this case study:

1. Describe each lessor's and sublessor's projected income stream, assuming Able's resale price at the end of the lease is $400,000.
2. Estimate the present value of each leasehold interest.

The following will be our assumptions:

Able's income stream is discounted at 10 percent.

Bon Bon's stream is discounted at 15 percent because of greater risk.

Dental Supply leasehold is discounted at 25 percent to reflect the fact that Farmer's

Tractors is a new local business with untested staying power and credit.

Able has 18 years left to collect on the original 30-year lease. Thus, he will receive 216 monthly rentals of $2,500 at the beginning of the month (BOM). In addition, it is assumed that he will obtain $400,000 from resale proceeds at the end of the leases.

Able's cash flows to be discounted at 10 percent can be described as

BOM	1	$2,500
	2	2,500
	3	2,500
	4	2,500
	–	–
	–	–
	–	–
	214	2,500
	215	2,500
	216	2,500 + $400,000 (EOM)

By calculator one obtains

Present Value PV of $2,500 BOM for 216 months discounted at 10 percent on monthly basis $252,123

PV of $400,000 end of 216 months discounted at 10 percent on monthly basis   66,615

Total PV Able position $318,738

Bon Bon position (discounted at 15 percent) gives the following.

RECEIVES FROM CABLE TV		RECEIVES FROM DENTAL SUPPLY		PAYS TO ABLE		BON BON'S NET CASH FLOWS	
BOM 1	$2,400	BOM 1	$1,600	BOM 1	$2,500	BOM 1	$1,500
2	2,400	2	1,600	2	2,500	2	1,500
3	2,400	3	1,600	3	2,500	3	1,500
–	–	–	–	–	–	–	–
–	–	–	–	–	–	–	–
–	–	–	–	–	–	–	–
214	2,400	214	1,600	214	2,500	214	1,500
215	2,400	215	1,600	215	2,500	215	1,500
216	2,400	216	1,600	216	2,500	216	1,500

By calculator one obtains

$\boxed{\text{PV}}$ of \$1,500 per month BOM for 216 months discounted at 15
percent on monthly basis (leasehold interest)   \$113,197

Dental Supply Co. position (discounted at 25 percent) gives the following.

RECEIVABLE FROM FARMER'S TRACTOR		PAYABLE TO BON BON		DENTAL SUPPLY'S NET CASH FLOW	
BOM 1	\$2,000	BOM 1	\$1,600	BOM 1	\$400
2	2,000	2	1,600	2	400
3	2,000	3	1,600	3	400
–	–	–	–	–	–
–	–	–	–	–	–
–	–	–	–	–	–
214	2,000	214	1,600	214	400
215	2,000	215	1,600	215	400
216	2,000	216	1,600	216	400

By calculator one obtains

$\boxed{\text{PV}}$ of \$400 monthly BOM for 216 months discounted at 25 percent
on monthly basis (leasehold interest)   \$ 19,372

This example illustrates how a broker can create a valuable asset for a lessee who no longer needs a property by finding a sublessee who will pay a greater rent than the lessee pays the lessor. The broker should be aware of this possibility of creating a leasehold interest for the lessee when market rents exceed contract rents negotiated years before and should learn the technique of assigning value to the income stream produced.

CASE STUDY 4: AFTER-TAX YIELDS FROM WRAPAROUND LOANS

A technique of financing that has been popular, particularly in situations with owner carry-back financing, is the wraparound mortgage. As explained in Chapter 6 the wraparound mortgage is a junior loan subordinate to the underlying mortgages. The wraparound offers a potentially higher yield than the typical second or junior mortgage.

The usual problems associated with wraparound mortgages are the calculation of the true yield on the investment and the tax impact of the wraparound. This case study illustrates the calculations of the yield before and after taxes.

Situation

For purposes of illustrating the impact of wraparound financing, the present example assumes no taxable gain on sale.

Johnson is selling a property for $150,000; it has an existing loan of $81,770.50, an interest rate of 8.5 percent and monthly payments of $805.23 for the remaining 15-year term. The terms of the sale are $25,000 down with Johnson taking back a $125,000 wraparound loan at 10 percent interest with monthly payments of $1,074.59 which represents a 35-year amortization. The wraparound loan has a term of ten years. Therefore, the entire balance remaining is due and payable at the end of year 10. Johnson's marginal income tax rate is 28 percent.

Before-Tax Analysis

The before-tax analysis and calculation of rate of return for the wraparound lender is illustrated in the following table.

The before-tax yield to the wraparound lender is 11.84 percent. The borrower pays 10 percent interest on the total loan amount of $125,000. The wraparound lender (Johnson) loans $125,000 at 10 percent, but $81,770.50 of the $125,000 is borrowed at 8.5 percent. Therefore, the wraparound lender benefits from positive leverage, thus increasing Johnson's yield to 11.84 percent for the 10-year loan term.

END OF MONTH	WRAPAROUND LOAN	−	EXISTING LOAN	=	WRAPAROUND LENDER'S CASH FLOWS BEFORE TAX
0	(125,000.00)	−	(81,770.50)	=	(43,229.50)
1	1,074.59	−	805.23	=	269.36
↓	↓		↓		↓
120	1,074.59	−	805.23	=	269.36
Balloon 120	118,255.82	−	39,247.02	=	79,008.80
IRR (Monthly)	.833333		.708333		.986356
X12 =	× 12		× 12		× 12
Annualized	10.00%		8.50%		11.84%

The impact of taxes can alter both the yield and the cash flows substantially. To fully appreciate this effect, the cash flows after tax must be derived and measured. The interest collected by the wraparound lender is ordinary income and the interest paid out on the underlying (existing) loan is an ordinary deduction. Tax is calculated on the net difference. As always, cash flow after tax equals cash flow before tax less the resulting tax.

After-Tax Cash Flows

Following is an analysis of the after-tax cash flows. The analysis has been annualized to simplify the process, and thus the resulting solution will not be quite as accurate as it would be if it were calculated on a monthly basis, but it is extremely close. The calculation of net interest income and tax to the wraparound lender is summarized in the following tables.

Note that the *net* interest income increases each year in this case study. The interest portion of the wraparound loan payment is greater than the interest portion of each corresponding underlying loan payment. This relationship is explained by the greater interest rate, longer amortization term and larger principal balance of the wraparound loan compared to the underlying loan.

Cash flows before taxes were identified in the before-tax analysis of this loan. The wraparound lender's initial investment is $43,229 ($125,000 − $81,771). Total annual debt service received by the wraparound lender pays annual debt services of $9,663

SUMMARY OF NET INTEREST TO THE WRAPAROUND LENDER AND RESULTING TAX

EOY	INTEREST			Tax (28%)
	Interest Received	Interest Paid on Underlying Loan	Net Interest Income	
1	$12,481	$6,842	$5,639	$1,579
2	12,438	6,593	5,845	1,637
3	12,390	6,322	6,068	1,699
4	12,337	6,026	6,311	1,767
5	12,279	5,705	6,574	1,841
6	12,214	5,355	6,859	1,921
7	12,143	4,974	7,169	2,007
8	12,064	4,560	7,504	2,101
9	11,977	4,109	7,868	2,203
10	11,881	3,618	8,263	2,314

	SUMMARY OF CASH FLOWS BEFORE TAX AND CASH FLOWS AFTER TAX TO THE WRAPAROUND LENDER		
EOY	Cash Flows Before Tax	Tax	Cash Flows After Tax
0	($43,229)		($43,229)
1	3,232	$1,579	1,653
2	3,232	1,637	1,595
3	3,232	1,699	1,533
4	3,232	1,767	1,465
5	3,232	1,841	1,391
6	3,232	1,921	1,311
7	3,232	2,007	1,225
8	3,232	2,101	1,131
9	3,232	2,203	1,029
10	3,232 + 79,009	2,314	918 + 79,009

($805.23 × 12). The net annual cash flows before taxes to the wraparound lender from annual debt service is $3,232 ($12,895 − $9,663). The net loan balance received by the wraparound lender at the end of year 10 is $79,009 ($118,256 − $39,247). Cash flows after taxes are also summarized.

The IRR of annualized cash flows after tax is 8.71 percent, approximately 28 percent less than the before-tax IRR. Certainly, the amount of tax paid on net interest to the wraparound lender will affect the cash flows after tax and the after-tax yield. As the amount of tax increases, the cash flows after tax decreases.

Principal Amortization

Notice that the wraparound lender's initial cash investment was $43,229 and the net loan balance EOY 10 was $79,009. The wraparound lender's net balance is increased with this wraparound loan because the principal portion of each payment on the underlying loan exceeds the principal portion of each corresponding payment on the wraparound loan. The differential principal payments depend on the loan amounts, interest rates and remaining terms of both the underlying and wraparound loans. In this case, the wraparound loan payments are based on a 35-year amortization schedule at a 10-percent interest rate. The principal portion of each wraparound loan payment is less than the principal portion of each underlying loan payment at 8.5-percent interest with a 15-year remaining term. The annual principal amortization for the wraparound and underlying loans is summarized in the following table.

| | Principal Amortization | | |
EOY	Wraparound Loan*	Underlying Loan*	Difference*
1	$ 414	$2,821	($2,407)
2	457	3,070	(2,613)
3	505	3,341	(2,836)
4	558	3,636	(3,079)
5	616	3,958	(3,342)
6	681	4,308	(3,627)
7	752	4,688	(3,936)
8	831	5,103	(4,272)
9	918	5,554	(4,636)
10	1,014	6,045	(5,031)
Total			($35,779)
*Adjusted for rounding error			

With this loan, the wraparound lender receives less principal each year than the underlying lender. The difference is an additional capital investment in the loan by the wraparound lender. The sum of the increased principal during the 10-year loan term, $35,779, plus the wraparound lender's original investment of $43,229 is equal to the net loan balance EOY 10 of $79,009 (adjusted for rounding error). The annual increase of principal by the wraparound lender is taxed as ordinary income each tax period. For example, the wraparound lender's taxable income for the first year may be allocated between two elements as follows:

Net cash flow before tax EOY 1	$3,232
Net principal increase EOY 1	+2,407
Wraparound lender's taxable income EOY 1	$5,639

The wraparound lender's taxable income, as calculated above, is equal to the net interest income calculated on page 330. Taxable income exceeds cash flows before taxes for this loan. Tax is paid on the net principal increase each tax period even though the net principal increase is not received until the end of the loan term.

It is important to analyze wraparound loans on an after-tax basis. In this case study the wraparound lender is a seller. Indeed, the terms of this wraparound loan may be necessary to consummate the transaction. However, any forecast negative cash flows after tax may be unacceptable to the wraparound lender. Negative cash flows after tax could be eliminated by changing one or more of the loan terms. For example, the loan could be due at the end of year 5, the amortization term of the wraparound loan could be decreased or the wraparound loan interest rate could be increased. Each of these variables will affect the wraparound lender's cash flows and yield.

Conclusion

We have examined the seller's position when a portion of equity is "loaned" to the buyer in a wraparound loan. The same concepts apply when deriving before- and after-tax cash flows and before- and after-tax yields when negotiating a wraparound mortgage for a traditional lender who is actually putting dollars in the mortgage investment.

13
Differential Cash Flow Analysis

One of the difficulties in real estate investing is choosing among the many variables that are available with just one property or between two or more properties. Once a property has been purchased, this dilemma is not over. There are many options available almost on a daily basis during the life of the investment.

A useful process in choosing between various alternatives is differential cash flow analysis. This analysis is done by reducing each alternative to its cash flows for the entire anticipated holding period. Once the investments are reduced to cash flows, the difference between two alternatives can be derived and compared. The framework of the process will be outlined in this chapter and then various examples of application will be given.

Before the process can be outlined, an understanding of investment base, or End of Year 0 cash flow, is necessary. A detailed explanation of investment base is in Chapter 4. Simply stated, investment base is the dollar amount at risk in an investment on any given day as determined by loss of opportunity in alternative investments. For a new investment, it is the total acquisition cost or money paid for an investment by the buyer. In a currently owned investment, the investment base is equal to the proceeds of sale after tax if that investment were sold at some point in the holding period. This amount is not available for alternative investments if the present investment is held. Investment base changes during the holding period when the value of the investment, loan amounts, or owner's tax posture changes. Therefore, the investment base is probably not equal to the original cash investment amount throughout the holding period. The investment base amount is the initial investment End of Year 0 of the cash flow forecast and is usually a negative value.

The steps in the process are as follows:

Step 1. Reduce all alternatives to cash flows from EOY 0 to end of forecast period. Be consistent by using only before-tax *or* after-tax cash flows. It may be helpful to use a cash flow analysis form.

Step 2. Isolate the differential cash flows between alternatives.

Step 3. Calculate IRR of differential cash flows.

Step 4. Compare calculated IRR to other comparable investment opportunities in the marketplace.

At this point a reminder is necessary: the basic objective of any pure investment strategy is to accumulate wealth. The investor does not necessarily seek the investment which will produce the highest return, but the investment which will produce the most dollars at some time in the future. The following case studies illustrate this procedure in a variety of commercial or investment brokerage applications.

CASE STUDY 5: COMPARISON OF TWO INSTALLMENT SALE OFFERS

Very often the terms of a real estate transaction are as important as the sale price itself to the outcome of the sale. In the process of negotiating the terms of the contract, the seller may have to accept a smaller down payment in return for a higher sale price. Purchase money financing terms will also affect the sale price. Differential cash flow analysis can be used to determine which alternative purchase offer will produce the greater future wealth for the seller.

Differential cash flow analysis of two possible installment sale offers, or any financial alternative, is accomplished by comparing the cash flows created by each alternative. A forecast of cash flows after taxes produced by each sale offer is made based on the proposed terms of the offer. The differential cash flow stream is the difference between one offer and another. Usually, one offer will produce a greater initial cash flow at the time of sale and smaller future cash flows than the other offers. The IRR of the differential cash flows will indicate the minimum yield required on intermediate cash flows to produce greater future wealth by accepting the offer with a larger initial cash flow and smaller future cash flows.

Situation

In this situation, the seller is taxed at a marginal tax rate of 28 percent. The adjusted basis of the property is $500,000. There is no depreciation recapture since the straight-line method was used. Brokerage fees and other costs of sale are estimated to be 6 percent of the sale price. Each potential buyer will assume the existing mortgage balance of $400,000. Both buyers will close at the end of the seller's tax year so that only the taxable amount received at the time of closing is taxed during the year of sale. The terms of the two offers are summarized below.

	Offer A	Offer B
Sale Price	$1,100,000	$1,050,000
Cash Down Payment	$ 225,000	$ 300,000
Purchase Money Mortgage		
Amount	$ 475,000	$ 350,000
Interest Rate	11%	10%
Amortization	30 years	20 years
Monthly Payment	$ 4,168.46	$ 3,675.42

The seller requires that either of the purchase money mortgage balances is paid at the end of year 4 (balloon payment, EOY 4). Offer A has a greater sale price but a smaller cash down payment. The seller will take back a smaller purchase money mortgage at a lower interest rate and shorter amortization term if offer B is accepted.

The cash flows after taxes from each offer and the differential cash flows are summarized in the following table.

EOY	Offer A	Offer B	A–B
0	110,940	171,971	(61,031)
1	36,191	31,961	4,230
2	36,210	31,984	4,226
3	36,230	32,011	4,219
4	400,089	316,386	83,703

The IRR of A − B = 13.142660%.

Comparing the Offers

The following tables reduce both offers to a stream of cash flows after taxes for comparison.

DETAILS OF ACCUMULATION OF WEALTH

Offer A				
		FV at EOY 4		
EOY	CFAT	FV @ 10%	FV @ 15%	FV @ 13.142660%
0	110,940	162,427	194,035	181,800
1	36,191	48,170	55,042	52,418
2	36,210	43,814	47,888	46,353
3	36,230	39,853	41,664	40,992
4	400,089	400,089	400,089	400,089
Totals	619,660	694,353	738,718	721,652

Installment Sale Worksheet

Pg __1__ of __2__

Date _____
Prepared for _____
Property _____

Sale Price __1,100,000__
- Down Payment __225,000__
- Existing Loan __400,000__
= Purchase Money Note __475,000__

Amortization of Purchase Money Note

Amount __475,000__ Rate __10%__ Term __30 yrs.__ Pmt __4,168.46__ A.D.S. __50,022__

Year	Annual Debt Service	Interest	Principal	Remaining Balance
1	50,022	47,381	2,640	472,360
2	50,022	47,105	2,917	469,443
3	50,022	46,794	3,222	466,221
4	50,022	46,462	3,560	462,661
5				
6				

Calculation of Gain

1	Sale Price		1,100,000
2	Adjusted Basis at Sale	500,000	
3	+ Costs of Sale	66,000	
4	+ Excess Cost Recovery to be Recaptured	- 0 -	
5	= Adjusted Basis Including Sale Costs & Recapture		566,000
6	Gain to be Spread over Contract Term (Line 1 minus Line 5)		534,000

Calculation of Excess of Mortgage over Basis

7	Existing Loan(s)	400,000
8	- Adjusted Basis Including Sale Costs & Recapture (Line 5)	566,000
9	= Excess of Mortgage over Basis (Must be 0 or greater - Negative # not allowed)	- 0 -

Principal Received at Closing and in Year of Sale

PRINCIPAL ACTUALLY RECEIVED:

10	Down Payment	225,000
11	+ Option Money Applied to Purchase Price	- 0 -
	PRINCIPAL DEEMED TO BE RECEIVED:	
12	+ Excess of Mortgage over Basis(Line 9)	- 0 -
13	+ Seller's Matured Liabilities that Buyer will Pay this Year	- 0 -
14	+ Buyer Forgiveness of Unrelated Debt of Seller to Buyer	- 0 -
15	= Principal Actually Received or Deemed to be Received at Closing by the Seller	225,000
16	Principal Received on Purchase Money Note during Year of Sale - but after Closing	- 0 -

Calculation of Contract Price and Profit Ratio

17	Gross Sale Price (Line 1)	1,100,000
18	+ Mortgage in Excess of Basis, if any (Line 9)	- 0 -
19	- Existing Loan(s) (Line 7)	400,000
20	= Contract Price	700,000
21	Profit Ratio = Line 6 divided by Line 20	76,2857 %

The statements and figures herein while not guaranteed are secured from sources we believe authoritative

Prepared by __BROKER__

Figure 52. Offer A.

Installment Sale Cash Flow Analysis

Pg __2__ of __2__

Date _____

Prepared for _____

Property _____

Suspended Losses _____

	Closing (Mo / Yr)	(Mo / Yr)	(Mo / Yr)	(Mo / Yr)	(Mo / Yr)
	___ / ___	___ / ___	___ / ___	___ / ___	___ / ___

Taxable Income

TAXABLE INTEREST:

1 Interest Income Received		47,381	47,105	46,799	46,462
2 − Interest Expense - Paid out					
3 = Net Taxable Interest		47,381	47,105	46,799	46,462

TAXABLE GAIN:

4 Principal Payments Received	225,000	2,640	2,917	3,222	466,221
5 × Reportable Profit Ratio	76.2857%	76.2857%	76.2857%	76.2857%	76.2857%
6 = Capital Gain	171,643	2,014	2,225	2,458	355,660

USE LINES 7 - 9 ONLY IF PROPERTY HAS SUSPENDED LOSSES

7 Line 6 as % of Worksheet Line 6					
8 Suspended Losses X Line 7					
9 Net Capital Gain Reportable (6 - 8)					

CALCULATION OF TAX:

10 Net Taxable Interest (line 3)	− 0 −	47,381	47,105	46,799	46,462
11 + Cost Recovery Recapture	− 0 −				
12 = Taxable Income @ Ordinary Rate		47,381	47,105	46,799	46,462
13 × Ordinary Tax Rate	28%	28%	28%	28%	28%
14 = Tax on Ordinary Income	− 0 −	13,267	13,189	13,104	13,009
15 Capital Gain (line 6 or line 9)	171,643	2,014	2,225	2,458	355,660
16 × Capital Gain Tax Rate	28%	28%	28%	28%	28%
17 = Tax on Capital Gain	48,060	564	623	688	99,585
18 Total Tax due (line 14 + line 17)	48,060	13,831	13,812	13,792	112,594

Cash Flows

CASH RECEIVED:

19 Down Payment	225,000				
20 + Debt Service Received		50,022	50,022	50,022	512,683
21 = Total Cash Received	225,000	50,022	50,022	50,022	512,683

CASH PAID OUT:

22 Sale Costs	66,000				
23 + Debt Service Paid Out		− 0 −	− 0 −	− 0 −	− 0 −
24 = Total Cash Paid Out	66,000	− 0 −	− 0 −	− 0 −	− 0 −

CASH FLOWS AFTER TAX:

25 Total Cash Received (line 21)	225,000	50,022	50,022	50,022	512,683
26 − Total Cash Paid Out (line 24)	66,000	− 0 −	− 0 −	− 0 −	− 0 −
27 = Cash Flow Before Tax	159,000	50,022	50,022	50,022	512,683
28 − Total Tax Due (line 18)	48,060	13,831	13,812	13,792	112,594
29 = CASH FLOW AFTER TAX	110,940	36,191	36,210	36,230	400,089

The Statements and figures herein while not guaranteed
are secured from sources we believe authoritative   Prepared By _BROKER_

Figure 52. (continued).

Pg __1__ of __2__

Installment Sale Worksheet

Date _____

Prepared for _____

Property _____

Sale Price __1,075,000__

- Down Payment __300,000__

- Existing Loan __400,000__

= Purchase Money Note __375,000__

Amortization of Purchase Money Note

Amount __375,000__ Rate __11%__ Term __25 yr__ Pmt __3,675.42__ A.D.S. __44,105__

Year	Annual Debt Service	Interest	Principal	Remaining Balance
1	44,105	41,102	3,003	371,997
2	44,105	40,754	3,351	368,646
3	44,105	40,366	3,739	364,907
4	44,105	39,934	4,171	360,735
5				
6				

Calculation of Gain

1	Sale Price		1,075,000
2	Adjusted Basis at Sale	500,000	
3	+ Costs of Sale	64,500	
4	+ Excess Cost Recovery to be Recaptured	— 0 —	
5	= Adjusted Basis Including Sale Costs & Recapture		564,500
6	Gain to be Spread over Contract Term (Line 1 minus Line 5)		510,500

Calculation of Excess of Mortgage over Basis

7	Existing Loan(s)	400,000
8	− Adjusted Basis Including Sale Costs & Recapture (Line 5)	564,500
9	= Excess of Mortgage over Basis (Must be 0 or greater - Negative # not allowed)	— 0 —

Principal Received at Closing and in Year of Sale

PRINCIPAL ACTUALLY RECEIVED:

10	Down Payment	300,000
11	+ Option Money Applied to Purchase Price	— 0 —
	PRINCIPAL DEEMED TO BE RECEIVED:	
12	+ Excess of Mortgage over Basis(Line 9)	— 0 —
13	+ Seller's Matured Liabilities that Buyer will Pay this Year	— 0 —
14	+ Buyer Forgiveness of Unrelated Debt of Seller to Buyer	— 0 —
15	= Principal Actually Received or Deemed to be Received at Closing by the Seller	300,000
16	Principal Received on Purchase Money Note during Year of Sale - but after Closing	— 0 —

Calculation of Contract Price and Profit Ratio

17	Gross Sale Price (Line 1)	1,075,000
18	+ Mortgage in Excess of Basis, if any (Line 9)	— 0 —
19	− Existing Loan(s) (Line 7)	400,000
20	= Contract Price	675,000
21	Profit Ratio = Line 6 divided by Line 20	75.6294%

The statements and figures herein while not guaranteed are secured from sources we believe authoritative

Prepared by __BROKER__

Figure 53. Offer B.

Installment Sale Cash Flow Analysis

Pg __2__ of __2__

Date _____

	Closing				
Prepared for _____	(Mo / Yr)	(Mo / Yr)	(Mo / Yr)	(Mo / Yr)	(Mo / Yr)
Property _____	___ / ___	___ / ___	___ / ___	___ / ___	___ / ___
Suspended Losses _____					

Taxable Income

TAXABLE INTEREST:

1	Interest Income Received	41,102	40,754	40,366	39,934
2	− Interest Expense - Paid out	− 0 −	− 0 −	− 0 −	− 0 −
3	= Net Taxable Interest	41,102	40,754	40,366	39,934

TAXABLE GAIN:

4	Principal Payments Received	300,000	3,003	3,351	3,739.	364,907
5	× Reportable Profit Ratio	75.6296%	75.6296%	75.6296%	75.6296%	75.6296%
6	= Capital Gain	226,889	2,271	2,534	2,828	275,978

USE LINES 7 - 9 ONLY IF PROPERTY HAS SUSPENDED LOSSES

7	Line 6 as % of Worksheet Line 6	
8	Suspended Losses X Line 7	
9	Net Capital Gain Reportable (6 - 8)	

CALCULATION OF TAX:

10	Net Taxable Interest (line 3)	41,102	40,754	40,366	39,934
11	+ Cost Recovery Recapture	− 0 −			
12	= Taxable Income @ Ordinary Rate	− 0 −	41,102	40,754	40,366	39,934
13	× Ordinary Tax Rate	28%	28%	28%	28%	28%
14	= Tax on Ordinary Income	− 0 −	11,509	11,411	11,302	11,182

15	Capital Gain (line 6 or line 9)	226,889	2,271	2,534	2,828	275,978
16	× Capital Gain Tax Rate	28%	28%	28%	28%	28%
17	= Tax on Capital Gain	63,529	636	710	792	77,274
18	Total Tax due (line 14 + line 17)	63,529	12,144	12,121	12,094	88,455

Cash Flows

CASH RECEIVED:

19	Down Payment	300,000				
20	+ Debt Service Received		44,105	44,105	44,105	404,841
21	= Total Cash Received	300,000	44,105	44,105	44,105	404,841

CASH PAID OUT:

22	Sale Costs	64,500				
23	+ Debt Service Paid Out		− 0 −	− 0 −	− 0 −	− 0 −
24	= Total Cash Paid Out	64,500	− 0 −	− 0 −	− 0 −	− 0 −

CASH FLOWS AFTER TAX:

25	Total Cash Received (line 21)	300,000	44,105	44,105	44,105	404,841
26	− Total Cash Paid Out (line 24)	64,500	− 0 −	− 0 −	− 0 −	− 0 −
27	= Cash Flow Before Tax	235,500	44,105	44,105	44,105	404,841
28	− Total Tax Due (line 18)	63,529	12,144	12,121	12,094	88,455
29	= CASH FLOW AFTER TAX	171,971	31,961	31,984	32,011	316,386

The Statements and figures herein while not guaranteed
are secured from sources we believe authoritative   Prepared By ___BROKER___

Figure 53.   (continued).

		Offer B		
		FV at EOY 4		
EOY	CFAT	FV @ 10%	FV @ 15%	FV @ 13.142660%
0	171,971	251,783	300,778	281,813
1	31,961	42,540	48,609	46,291
2	31,984	38,701	42,299	40,944
3	32,011	35,212	36,813	36,218
4	316,386	316,386	316,386	316,386
Totals	584,313	684,622	744,885	721,652

SUMMARY

Offer	Accum Wealth @ 10%	Accum Wealth @ 15%	Accum. Wealth @ 13.142660%
A	694,353	738,718	721,652
B	684,622	744,885	721,652

Conclusion

Offer A has a higher sale price, a smaller cash down payment, a larger purchase money loan amount at a higher interest rate and is amortized over a longer term than offer B. As a result, offer A produces a smaller initial cash flow after tax and then greater cash flows after tax for the next four years. The IRR on the differential cash flows (summarized in the table above) is 13.1427 percent. By forgoing the difference of $61,031 if accepting offer A, the seller will receive 13.1427 percent after tax on the future differential cash flows. Therefore, if all else is equal, offer A will produce greater future wealth if cash flows after taxes can be invested at an after-tax rate of return less than 13.1427 percent. Offer B will produce greater future wealth if cash flows after taxes can be invested at an after-tax rate of return greater than 13.1427 percent. (See charts above for proofs.)

CASE STUDY 6: MEASURING THE IMPACT OF REFINANCING

A common rule of thumb used by investors in years past has been to refinance whenever possible and thus to use maximum leverage. If analyzed as an alternative investment decision, however, it might become obvious that refinancing may not always maximize the investor's future wealth.

Situation

Consider a property that has a value of $100,000 now, net operating income of $11,000 and an existing loan of $50,000 at 8 percent interest with monthly payments of $465. The owner's basis is $40,000. The straight line cost recovery amount is $2,000 per year. At the end of five years, the cost of sale will be 7 percent of the sale price. The owner's marginal tax bracket is 28 percent. Assume there is no increase in net operating income and a 5 percent annual increase in value. The anticipated holding period is five years.

A new loan is available for 75 percent of the property value with 12 percent interest, a 25-year term and monthly payments. The origination fee of this loan is three points (3 percent of the loan amount).

Reducing Alternatives to Cash Flows

The analytical process is the same as in Case Study 5. The first step is to reduce the alternatives to their cash flows after tax. The next step is to isolate the differential cash flows and then calculate the IRR on the differential cash flows.

The investment base, or end of year 0 cash flow, without refinancing is as follows.

Sale price	$100,000	
Less mortgage	50,000	
Less cost of sale	7,000	
Less tax on sale	14,840	
Proceeds of sale after tax EOY 0	$ 28,160	
Calculation of tax on Sale:		
Gross sale price		$100,000
Adjusted basis	$ 40,000	
Plus cost of sale	7,000	
Adjusted basis at sale		− 47,000
Long-term capital gain		$ 53,000
Marginal tax rate		× 28%
Tax on sale		$ 14,840

The cash flows after tax without refinancing the property are as follows.

	Without Refinance				
End of Year	1	2	3	4	5
Net Operating Income	$11,000	$11,000	$11,000	$11,000	$11,000
Interest	3,941	3,805	3,657	3,498	3,325
Cost Recovery	2,000	2,000	2,000	2,000	2,000
Taxable Income	$ 5,059	$ 5,195	$ 5,343	$ 5,502	$ 5,675
Net Operating Income	$11,000	$11,000	$11,000	$11,000	$11,000
Annual Debt Service	5,580	5,580	5,580	5,580	5,580
Cash Flow Before Tax	$ 5,420	$ 5,420	$ 5,420	$ 5,420	$ 5,420
Tax 28%	1,417	1,455	1,496	1,541	1,589
Cash Flow After Tax	$ 4,003	$ 3,965	$ 3,924	$ 3,879	$ 3,831

Proceeds of sale after tax EOY 5:

Sale price	$127,628
Less mortgage balance EOY 5	−40,326
Less cost of sale	−8,934
Less tax from sale	−24,834
Proceeds of sale after tax EOY 5	$ 53,534

Calculation of tax on sale:

Gross sale price		$127,628
Adjusted basis BOY 0	$40,000	
Less cost recovery		
(5 × $2,000)	−10,000	
Plus cost of sale	+8,934	
Adjusted basis at sale		−38,934
Capital gain		$ 88,694
Marginal tax rate		×28%
Tax on sale		$ 24,834

The new loan amount is greater than the existing loan balance. Proceeds of the new loan will first be used to repay the underlying loan. The difference between the new loan amount and the existing loan balance is a tax-free cash flow received by the owner immediately, that is, at end of year 0. Since the owner receives a portion of equity in the form of proceeds of refinancing, the investment base is reduced. The revised investment base is calculated below.

New loan amount	$75,000
Origination fee (3% × $75,000)	−2,250
Net loan proceeds	$72,750
Existing loan balance EOY 0	−50,000
Net proceeds of refinancing	$22,750
Investment base before refinancing	$28,160
Net proceeds of refinancing	−22,750
Investment base after refinancing	$ 5,410

End of Year	With Refinance 1	2	3	4	5
Net Operating Income	$11,000	$11,000	$11,000	$11,000	$11,000
Interest	8,973	8,909	8,836	8,755	8,663
Cost Recovery	2,000	2,000	2,000	2,000	2,000
Taxable Income	$ 27	$ 91	$ 164	$ 245	$ 337
Net Operating Income	$11,000	$11,000	$11,000	$11,000	$11,000
Annual Debt Service	9,479	9,479	9,479	9,479	9,479
Cash Flow Before Tax	$ 1,521	$ 1,521	$ 1,521	$ 1,521	$ 1,521
Tax 28%	8	25	46	69	94
Cash Flow After Tax	$ 1,513	$ 1,496	$ 1,475	$ 1,452	$ 1,427

Proceeds of sale after tax EOY 5

Sale price	$127,628
Less mortgage balance EOY 5	71,740
cost of sale	8,934
tax from sale	24,834
Proceeds of sale after tax	$ 22,120

The tax is the same as without refinancing because financing does not affect the amount of capital gain.

The following table is a summary of cash flows after taxes from both alternatives and the differential cash flows.

EOY	Without Refinance A	With Refinance B	Differential A–B
0	(28,160)	(5,410)	(22,750)
1	4,003	1,513	2,490
2	3,965	1,496	2,469
3	3,924	1,475	2,449
4	3,879	1,452	2,427
5	3,831 + 53,534	1,427 + 22,120	33,818
IRR	24.97%	50.66%	16.29%

Conclusion

Refinancing will reduce the investment base and increase the loan-to-value ratio. Since the investor benefits from positive leverage, additional leverage will increase the IRR. The investor is faced with the decision to do nothing and receive an after-tax yield of 24.97 percent on $28,160 or refinance the property and receive an after-tax yield of 50.66 percent on $5,410. Based on IRR alone, refinancing would appear to be the better alternative. However, the $22,750 net proceeds of refinancing should be considered.

Refinancing reduces the investment base. There is a size disparity between the two initial investment amounts. Subsequent cash flows after taxes with refinancing are less because the annual debt service is increased and the loan balance at the end of year 5 is greater with the new loan. The dollar cost to the investor of taking the $22,750 is the differential cash flows. The IRR of the differential cash flows is 16.29 percent. To maximize future wealth, the property should be refinanced at this time if the net proceeds of refinancing can be reinvested at an after-tax yield in excess of 16.29 percent. Stated another way, the opportunity cost of withdrawing capital ($22,750, in this case) is 16.29 percent. It is as if the investor borrowed $22,750 at an after-tax interest rate of 16.29 percent. To get positive leverage, these funds must be invested at a greater rate of return.

To illustrate this conclusion, assume that the most suitable investment alternative for the net proceeds of refinancing will produce an after-tax rate of return of 12 percent. In addition, all cash flows after taxes will also be reinvested at an after-tax rate of 12 percent. It should be noted that these rates may be different and changed each year according to assumptions consistent with the investor's financial planning. The future wealth from all cash flows after taxes are summarized in the following table.

		Without Refinance		With Refinance	
EOY	CFAT	$\boxed{FV}$ EOY 5 @ 12%	CFAT	$\boxed{FV}$ EOY 5 @ 12%	Net Proceeds of Refinance
0	($28,160)		($5,410)		($22,750)
1	4,003	$ 6,299	1,513	$ 2,381	
2	3,965	5,571	1,496	2,102	
3	3,924	4,922	1,475	1,850	
4	3,879	4,344	1,452	1,626	
5	3,831	57,365	1,427	23,547	40,093
	+53,534		+22,120		
Total		$78,501		$31,506 +40,093 = $71,599	

As expected, with an after-tax reinvestment rate less than the IRR on the differential cash flows, it is better not to refinance the property. In both cases, the total initial investments are the same. With refinancing, the total initial investments are the investment base in the property plus the net proceeds of refinancing. The future wealth end of year 5 is the sum of the future values of all cash flows invested at 12 percent after tax. Future wealth end of year 5 for the refinancing alternative includes the future value of net proceeds of refinancing invested at 12 percent after tax.

The future wealth position of the two alternatives can be graphed using alternative after-tax opportunity rates of return (see Figure 54). Calculation of several data points on this graph are summarized below. Note that the sum of cash flows after tax is equal to the total future value if the reinvestment rate is 0 percent.

		Without Refinance			
		$\boxed{FV}$ at End of Year 5			
EOY	CFAT	5%	10%	15%	20%
1	$ 4,003	$ 4,866	$ 5,861	$ 7,001	$ 8,301
2	3,965	4,590	5,277	6,030	6,852
3	3,924	4,326	4,748	5,189	5,651
4	3,879	4,073	4,267	4,461	4,655
5	3,831	3,831	3,831	3,831	3,831
Sale 5	53,534	53,534	53,534	53,534	53,534
Total	$73,136	$75,220	$77,518	$80,046	$82,824

With Refinance					
		FV at End of Year 5			
EOY	CFAT	5%	10%	15%	20%
1	$ 1,513	$ 1,839	$ 2,215	$ 2,646	$ 3,137
2	1,496	1,737	1,991	2,275	2,585
3	1,475	1,626	1,785	1,951	2,124
4	1,452	1,525	1,597	1,670	1,742
5	1,427	1,427	1,427	1,427	1,427
Sale 5	22,120	22,120	22,120	22,120	22,120
FV of Net Proceeds of Refinancing EOY 5	22,750	29,035	36,639	45,758	56,609
TOTAL	$52,233	$59,304	$67,774	$77,847	$89,744

The wealth positions at end of year 5 for various rates are plotted on the graph in Figure 53. The curves in Figure 53 intercept where the after-tax rate of return on reinvested cash flows equal 16.29 percent, the IRR on the differential cash flows. Figure 53 illustrates the original conclusions: to maximize future wealth, under the assumptions of this case study, the investor would refinance the property if the opportunity cost of capital exceeds 16.29 percent.

This analysis may also be useful in choosing among alternative loans available for refinancing. The interest rate, loan-to-value ratio, holding period and other variables are

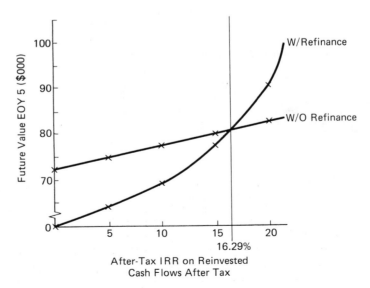

Figure 54. Future Wealth Position.

required to reduce the problem to cash flows after tax. Differential cash flow analysis is then applied to the alternative cash flows as we have done here.

CASE STUDY 7: OWN OR LEASE DECISIONS

Another useful application of differential cash flow analysis is in making the decision to own or to lease. The occupancy and/or use of any asset can be accomplished by either buying and owning the asset or by leasing it. Many individual investors or firms make the own-versus-lease decision by looking at lease payments as an operating cost. A more meaningful analysis is to view the outlays of capital for owning or leasing, either on the first or subsequent time periods, as investments. This allows the decision maker to approach the problem as one of selecting among investment alternatives. As a first step, each alternative must be reduced to after-tax cash flows. Then these flows must be compared as to their size and timing.

Leasing has several advantages. Perhaps the major advantage of leasing is that it provides *flexible financing*. Most lease arrangements tend to have fewer restrictions than loan agreements. In addition, leasing is well suited to piecemeal financing. A firm that is acquiring assets over time may find it more convenient to lease them than to negotiate term loans or sell securities each time it makes a new capital outlay.

A second advantage in the case of real estate lending is that the lessee may effectively be able to depreciate land. Generally, in leasing, the total amount of the payment is deductible in computing taxes, whereas only the interest portion of a loan payment is deductible. In real estate ownership, no cost recovery deduction is allowed on the land portion of the property. In leasing, the total cost of use and/or occupancy (rent) is deducted as an ordinary business expense.

Leasing may also allow the lessee to avoid some of the risks of obsolescence associated with ownership. The lessor will charge a lease rate intended to provide a specified return on the required net investment. The net investment is equal to the cost of the asset minus the present value of the expected salvage value at the end of the lease. If the actual salvage is less than originally expected, the lessor bears the loss. Leasing may also be the only available source of financing for the small or marginally profitable firm since the title to leased property remains with the lessor and reduces the lessor's risk in the event of failure. If the lessee does fail, the lessor can quickly recover the leased property.

Finally, leasing is said to provide 100 percent financing, whereas most borrowing requires a significant down payment. Because lease payments are normally made in advance of each period, this 100 percent financing is diminished by the amount of the first required lease payment.

The primary disadvantage of leasing is cost. For a firm with a strong earning record, good access to the credit markets, and the ability to take advantage of the tax benefits of ownership, leasing is often a more expensive alternative.

Another disadvantage of leasing is the loss of the asset's salvage value, or the value of the property at the end of the lease term. In real estate, this loss can be substantial. A lessee may also have difficulty getting approval to make property improvements on leased real estate. If the improvements substantially alter the property or reduce its potential range of uses, the lessor may be reluctant to permit them.

Finally, if a leased asset or property becomes obsolete or if the capital project financed by the lease becomes uneconomical, the lessee may not cancel the lease without paying a substantial penalty.

There are also certain tax caveats that must be considered when choosing the leasing alternative. These have to do with term, reasonable rate of return, and option of purchase. The IRS may determine that the lease is actually a financing agreement. This would limit certain tax deductions associated with the lease. It is always best to obtain competent tax advice with any transaction, but special care must be taken when arranging a lease.

Situation

This case study deals primarily with the investment decision-making process. The property under consideration is assumed to be a commercial property with cost recovery calculated on a straight-line basis over 31.5 years. If the property under consideration is a residential property, recent tax law changes require cost recovery to be calculated on a straight-line basis over 27.5 years.

Cost of asset	$100,000
Property income	None; property is occupied by user
Available financing	75% loan @ 12%, 25-year amortization, monthly payments
Lease term	10 years
Rental payments	$1,000 per month net to owner for 5 years with 15% increase in the 2nd 5 years
Value at EOY 10	$150,000
Investor's marginal tax bracket	28%
After-tax opportunity cost of money	12%
Cost recovery	31.5 years, straight-line method
Building and land allocation	80% and 20%
Holding period	10 years
Cost of sale at EOY 10	7% of sale price

Present Value Technique

There are two approaches to making the lease or own decision; the present value (or cost) approach and the differential cash flow approach. The present value approach involves three basic steps.

1. Estimate cash outflows associated with both the lease and purchase alternatives.
2. Discount these cash flows at an appropriate rate. The discount rate may be the firm's cost of capital or opportunity cost of capital. Use of the latter is more common since capital available for investment must be used for acquisition of the

Cash Flow Analysis Worksheet

Property Name OWN VS. LEASE
Prepared For OWNERSHIP ALTERNATIVE
Prepared By BROKER
Date Prepared

Purchase Price 100,000
Costs of Acquisition
Loan Points
Down Payment 25,000

Mortgage Data

	1st Mortgage	2nd Mortgage
Amount	75,000	
Interest Rate	12 %	
Term	25 yrs.	
Payments / Year	12	
Periodic Payment	789.92	
Annual Debt Service	9,479	
Comments		

Cost Recovery Data

	Improvements	Personal Property
Value	80,000	
C. R. Method	S/L	
Useful Life	31 1/2 YRS	
In Service Date		
Recapture (All / None / Excess)	N	
Investment Tax Credit ($$ or %)		

Taxable Income

	Year:	Year:	Year:	Year:	Year:
1 Potential Rental Income					
2 – Vacancy & Credit Losses					
3 = Effective Rental Income					
4 + Other Income					
5 = Gross Operating Income					
6 – Operating Expenses					
7 = NET OPERATING INCOME	– 0 –	– 0 –	– 0 –	– 0 –	– 0 –
8 – Interest - 1st Mortgage	8,973	8,909	8,836	8,755	8,663
9 – Interest - 2nd Mortgage					
10 – Cost Recovery - Improvements	2,540	2,540	2,540	2,540	2,540
11 – Cost Recovery - Personal Property					
12 –					
13 –					
14 = Real Estate Taxable Income	⟨11,513⟩	⟨11,449⟩	⟨11,376⟩	⟨11,295⟩	⟨11,203⟩
15 Tax Liability (Savings) @ 28 %	⟨3,224⟩	⟨3,206⟩	⟨3,185⟩	⟨3,163⟩	⟨3,137⟩

Cash Flow

16 NET OPERATING INCOME (Line 7)	– 0 –	– 0 –	– 0 –	– 0 –	– 0 –
17 – Annual Debt Service	9,479	9,479	9,479	9,479	9,479
18 –					
19 =					
20 = CASH FLOW BEFORE TAXES	⟨9,479⟩	⟨9,479⟩	⟨9,479⟩	⟨9,479⟩	⟨9,479⟩
21 – Tax Liability (Savings) (Line 15)	⟨3,224⟩	⟨3,206⟩	⟨3,185⟩	⟨3,163⟩	⟨3,137⟩
22 + Investment Tax Credit					
23 = CASH FLOW AFTER TAXES	⟨6,255⟩	⟨6,273⟩	⟨6,294⟩	⟨6,316⟩	⟨6,342⟩

The Statements and figures herein while not guaranteed are secured from sources we believe authoritative

Pg 1 of 2

Figure 55.

Cash Flow Analysis Worksheet

Property Name *OWN VS LEASE*
Prepared For *OWNERSHIP ALTERNATIVE*
Prepared By _____
Date Prepared _____

Purchase Price _____
Costs of Acquisition _____
Loan Points _____
Down Payment _____

Mortgage Data

	1st Mortgage	2nd Mortgage
Amount		
Interest Rate		
Term		
Payments / Year		
Periodic Payment		
Annual Debt Service		
Comments		

Cost Recovery Data

	Improvements	Personal Property
Value		
C. R. Method		
Useful Life		
In Service Date		
Recapture (All / None / Excess)		
Investment Tax Credit ($$ or %)		

Taxable Income

	Year: 6	Year: 7	Year: 8	Year: 9	Year: 10
1 Potential Rental Income					
2 – Vacancy & Credit Losses					
3 = Effective Rental Income					
4 + Other Income					
5 = Gross Operating Income					
6 – Operating Expenses					
7 = NET OPERATING INCOME	-0-	-0-	-0-	-0-	-0-
8 – Interest - 1st Mortgage	8,559	8,443	8,311	8,163	7,996
9 – Interest - 2nd Mortgage					
10 – Cost Recovery - Improvements	2,540	2,540	2,540	2,540	2,540
11 – Cost Recovery - Personal Property					
12					
13					
14 = Real Estate Taxable Income	⟨11,099⟩	⟨10,983⟩	⟨10,851⟩	⟨10,703⟩	⟨10,536⟩
15 Tax Liability (Savings) @ 28 %	⟨3,108⟩	⟨3,075⟩	⟨3,038⟩	⟨2,997⟩	⟨2,950⟩

Cash Flow

16 NET OPERATING INCOME (Line 7)	-0-	-0-	-0-	-0-	-0-
17 – Annual Debt Service	9,479	9,479	9,479	9,479	9,479
18					
19					
20 = CASH FLOW BEFORE TAXES	⟨9,479⟩	⟨9,479⟩	⟨9,479⟩	⟨9,479⟩	⟨9,479⟩
21 – Tax Liability (Savings) (Line 15)	⟨3,108⟩	⟨3,075⟩	⟨3,038⟩	⟨2,997⟩	⟨2,950⟩
22 + Investment Tax Credit					
23 = CASH FLOW AFTER TAXES	⟨6,371⟩	⟨6,404⟩	⟨6,441⟩	⟨6,482⟩	⟨6,529⟩

Pg 2 of 2

Figure 55. (continued).

Alternative Cash Sales Worksheet

Mortgage Balances

	Year: 10	Year:	Year:	Year:	Year:
Principal Balance - 1st Mortgage	65,817				
Principal Balance - 2nd Mortgage					
TOTAL UNPAID PRINCIPAL	65,817				

Calculation of Sale Proceeds

PROJECTED SALES PRICE	150,000	

CALCULATION OF ADJUSTED BASIS:

1	Basis at Acquisition	100,000
2	+ Capital Additions	
3	− Cost Recovery (Depreciation) Taken	25,400
4	− Basis in Partial Sales	
5	= Adjusted Basis at Sale	74,600

CALCULATION OF EXCESS COST RECOVERY:

6	Total Cost Recovery Taken (Line 3)	
7	− Straight Line Cost Recovery	
8	= Excess Cost Recovery	

CALCULATION OF CAPITAL GAIN ON SALE:

9	Sale Price	150,000
10	− Costs of Sale	10,500
11	− Adjusted Basis at Sale (Line 5)	74,600
12	− Participation Payments	
13	= Total Gain	64,900
14	− Excess Cost Recovery (Line 8)	
15	− Suspended Losses	
16	= Capital Gain or (Loss)	64,900

ITEMS TAXED AS ORDINARY INCOME:

17	Excess Cost Recovery (Line 8)	
18	− Unamortized Loan Points	
19	= Ordinary Taxable Income	
20	x Tax Rate on Ordinary Income	
21	= Tax (Savings) on Ordinary Income	

ITEMS TAXED AS CAPITAL GAIN:

22	Capital Gain (Line 16)	64,900
23	x Percentage of Capital Gain Reportable	100%
24	= Taxable Capital Gain	64,900
25	x Tax Rate on Capital Gain	28%
26	= Tax on Capital Gain	18,172

CALCULATION OF SALE PROCEEDS AFTER TAX:

27	Sale Price (Line 9)	150,000
28	− Costs of Sale (Line 10)	10,500
29	− Participation Payments (Line 12)	
30	− Mortgage Balance(s) (from top of form)	65,817
31	= Sale Proceeds Before Taxes	73,683
32	− Tax (Savings) on Ordinary Income (Line 21)	
33	− Tax on Capital Gain (Line 26)	18,172
34	− Recapture of Investment Tax Credits	
35	= SALE PROCEEDS AFTER TAX	55,511

The statements and figures herein while not guaranteed are secured from sources we believe authoritative

Prepared by _BECKER_

Figure 55. (continued).

asset. A hybrid weighted cost of capital, including return to equity reflecting the appropriate debt leverage, may be used.

3. The decision rule is that the alternative with the least present value is most desirable since the cash flows are the respective after-tax costs of each alternative.

The ownership cash flows after tax are derived from a cash flow analysis form (see Figure 55). Once the cash flows are derived for the end of year 0 to end of year 10, including the tenth year proceeds of sale, the present value is established by discounting these cash flows at the after-tax opportunity cost of capital. In our example, this rate is 12 percent.

The ownership after-tax cash flows, as calculated on the cash flow analysis form, are as follows.

EOY	$
0	($25,000)
1	(6,255)
2	(6,273)
3	(6,294)
4	(6,316)
5	(6,342)
6	(6,371)
7	(6,404)
8	(6,441)
9	(6,482)
10	(6,529)+ $55,511

$$\boxed{PV} = (\$42,971)$$

The present value of all cash flows after tax, discounted at 12 percent, is ($42,971). Therefore, for an investor with opportunity to invest funds at a 12 percent after-tax rate, the after-tax cost of occupancy for 10 years through the ownership alternative is $42,971 in today's dollars.

The after-tax cash flows from the leasing alternative, with the rent being paid in arrears, are calculated on another cash flow analysis form (see Figure 56).

The leasing cash flows are as follows.

EOY	$
0	–0–
1	($8,640)
2	(8,640)
3	(8,640)
4	(8,640)
5	(8,640)
6	(9,936)
7	(9,936)
8	(9,936)
9	(9,936)
10	(9,936)

$$\boxed{PV} = (\$51,469)$$

Cash Flow Analysis Worksheet

Property Name _OWN VS. LEASE_
Prepared For _LEASING ALTERNATIVE_
Prepared By _____
Date Prepared _____

Purchase Price _____
Costs of Acquisition _____
Loan Points _____
Down Payment _____

Mortgage Data	1st Mortgage	2nd Mortgage
Amount		
Interest Rate		
Term		
Payments / Year		
Periodic Payment		
Annual Debt Service		
Comments		

Cost Recovery Data	Improvements	Personal Property
Value		
C. R. Method		
Useful Life		
In Service Date		
Recapture (All / None / Excess)		
Investment Tax Credit ($$ or %)		

Taxable Income

	Year: 1	Year: 2	Year: 3	Year: 4	Year: 5
1 Potential Rental Income					
2 − Vacancy & Credit Losses					
3 = Effective Rental Income					
4 + Other Income					
5 = Gross Operating Income					
6 − Operating Expenses					
7 = NET OPERATING INCOME	⟨12,000⟩	⟨2,000⟩	⟨2,000⟩	⟨12,000⟩	⟨12,000⟩
8 − Interest - 1st Mortgage					
9 − Interest - 2nd Mortgage					
10 − Cost Recovery - Improvements					
11 − Cost Recovery - Personal Property					
12 −					
13 −					
14 = Real Estate Taxable Income	⟨12,000⟩	⟨2,000⟩	⟨2,000⟩	⟨12,000⟩	⟨2,000⟩
15 Tax Liability (Savings) @ 28 %	⟨3,360⟩	⟨3,360⟩	⟨3,360⟩	⟨3,360⟩	⟨3,360⟩

Cash Flow

	Year: 1	Year: 2	Year: 3	Year: 4	Year: 5
16 NET OPERATING INCOME (Line 7)	⟨12,000⟩	⟨12,000⟩	⟨12,000⟩	⟨2,000⟩	⟨12,000⟩
17 − Annual Debt Service					
18 −					
19 −					
20 = CASH FLOW BEFORE TAXES	⟨2,000⟩	⟨12,000⟩	⟨12,000⟩	⟨12,000⟩	⟨12,000⟩
21 − Tax Liability (Savings) (Line 15)	⟨3,360⟩	⟨3,360⟩	⟨3,360⟩	⟨3,360⟩	⟨3,360⟩
22 + Investment Tax Credit					
23 = CASH FLOW AFTER TAXES	⟨8,640⟩	⟨8,640⟩	⟨8,640⟩	⟨8,640⟩	⟨8,640⟩

Pg 1 of 2

Figure 56.

Cash Flow Analysis Worksheet

Property Name _____   Purchase Price _____
Prepared For _____   Costs of Acquisition _____
Prepared By _____   Loan Points _____
Date Prepared _____   Down Payment _____

	Mortgage Data			Cost Recovery Data	
	1st Mortgage	2nd Mortgage		Improvements	Personal Property
Amount			Value		
Interest Rate			C. R. Method		
Term			Useful Life		
Payments / Year			In Service Date		
Periodic Payment			Recapture (All / None / Excess)		
Annual Debt Service			Investment Tax Credit ($$ or %)		
Comments					

Taxable Income

		Year: 6	Year: 7	Year: 8	Year: 9	Year: 10
1	Potential Rental Income					
2	− Vacancy & Credit Losses					
3	= Effective Rental Income					
4	+ Other Income					
5	= Gross Operating Income					
6	− Operating Expenses					
7	= NET OPERATING INCOME	⟨13,800⟩	⟨13,800⟩	⟨13,800⟩	⟨13,800⟩	⟨13,800⟩
8	− Interest - 1st Mortgage					
9	− Interest - 2nd Mortgage					
10	− Cost Recovery - Improvements					
11	− Cost Recovery - Personal Property					
12						
13						
14	= Real Estate Taxable Income	⟨13,800⟩	⟨13,800⟩	⟨13,800⟩	⟨13,800⟩	⟨13,800⟩
15	Tax Liability (Savings) @ 28 %	⟨3,864⟩	⟨3,864⟩	⟨3,864⟩	⟨3,864⟩	⟨3,864⟩

Cash Flow

16	NET OPERATING INCOME (Line 7)	⟨13,800⟩	⟨13,800⟩	⟨13,800⟩	⟨13,800⟩	⟨13,800⟩
17	− Annual Debt Service					
18						
19						
20	= CASH FLOW BEFORE TAXES	⟨13,800⟩	⟨13,800⟩	⟨13,800⟩	⟨13,800⟩	⟨13,800⟩
21	− Tax Liability (Savings) (Line 15)	⟨3,864⟩	⟨3,864⟩	⟨3,864⟩	⟨3,864⟩	⟨3,864⟩
22	+ Investment Tax Credit					
23	= CASH FLOW AFTER TAXES	⟨9,936⟩	⟨9,936⟩	⟨9,936⟩	⟨9,936⟩	⟨9,936⟩

Figure 56. (continued).

The present value for all cash flows after tax discounted at 12 percent is ($51,469). Therefore, an investor who has opportunities to invest funds at a 12 percent after-tax rate has an after-tax cost of occupancy for 10 years through the leasing alternative of $51,469.

The comparison can now be made between the present values of owning and leasing. The present values of both alternatives are negative, or costs. Therefore, the least cost is the best alternative. In this case, the ownership cost of $42,971 is less than the leasing cost of $51,469. Therefore, with a 12 percent after-tax opportunity cost of capital, owning is a better alternative than leasing.

Differential Cash Flow Technique

The other approach to making the decision of own versus lease is the differential cash flow technique. The procedure is to determine the difference between the ownership cash flows and the leasing cash flows and then to calculate a rate of return on the differential cash flows. This rate of return is the after-tax opportunity cost of capital which would make the investor indifferent to either alternative. The procedure is illustrated as follows.

SUMMARY OF CASH FLOWS AFTER TAX
AND DIFFERENTIAL CASH FLOWS

EOY	Ownership	Lease	Differential
0	($25,000)	–0–	($25,000)
1	(6,255)	($8,640)	2,385
2	(6,273)	(8,640)	2,367
3	(6,294)	(8,640)	2,346
4	(6,316)	(8,640)	2,324
5	(6,342)	(8,640)	2,298
6	(6,371)	(9,936)	3,565
7	(6,404)	(9,936)	3,532
8	(6,441)	(9,936)	3,495
9	(6,482)	(9,936)	3,454
10	(6,529)+ 55,511	(9,936)	$58,918
			IRR = 16.46%

By owning the real estate in this example, the out-of-pocket net investment is the down payment of $25,000. The difference between the after-tax cash flows of ownership and the after-tax cash flows of leasing are the cash flow benefits of the net investment of $25,000 in the real estate. In other words, the investor would have an annual cash flow savings if the property were purchased instead of leased because the after-tax cost to own is less than the after-tax cost to lease. The savings is the result of an additional initial investment of $25,000 to buy the property. The cash flow savings produce an after-tax rate of return of 16.46 percent on the initial investment. Therefore, the investor should purchase the property if the after-tax opportunity cost of capital is less than 16.46 percent.

Differential cash flow analysis is useful when choosing between alternatives which produce cost savings. For example, the technique could be applied to alternative heating, ventilating and air conditioning systems where a more expensive system would produce a cost savings in energy consumption in the future. In this type of case study, future wealth is maximized by choosing the alternative which will cost less *after the time value of money has been considered*.

14
Special Investment Problems

This chapter presents case studies designed to illustrate special problems or issues in real estate investments. Case Study 8 illustrates the process used to test the feasibility of exchanging properties. The exchange worksheet form is used to organize information and to balance the equities among parties to a proposed exchange.

Case Study 9 is the analysis of a real estate exchange, comparing the financial implications of exchanging versus sale/reinvestment.

Case Study 10 is actually a collection of illustrations which sequentially analyze several key implications of investing in raw land.

Case Study 11 demonstrates the impact which holding period has on the selection of financing alternatives.

The final case study illustrates the use of financial management rate of return analysis.

CASE STUDY 8: DETERMINING EXCHANGE FEASIBILITY

The Exchange Worksheet

The investment broker involved in the exchange of real estate, whether tax deferred under Revenue Code Section 1031 or simply the barter-type exchange, must have the ability to balance equities. It is vital to understand the difference in value of respective properties and who owes whom how much.

In its simplest form, an exchange between two parties can be balanced as follows.

	Owner A (Vacant Land)	Owner B (Commercial Store)
Market Value	$100,000	$200,000
Encumbrance	55,000	100,000
Equity	45,000	100,000

A's equity is smaller than B's by $55,000. In fact, A must pay this amount to B to effect the exchange, that is, to balance equities.

However, there are other complications. What about the sale costs? How are they paid? What if A does not have $55,000? How is the loan handled? What if A wants B's property, but B does not want A's and would rather have C's? What if there are four or five parties to the exchange; will it work? Is there enough money in the transaction to pay title costs, loan costs, commissions and deficiencies in equities?

The broker's best tool for threading through this complicated maze of exchanging is the exchange worksheet. This is a simple and valuable tool for those who take the time to understand its use. In this case study, we will proceed step-by-step through the analysis of a typical two-way exchange, using the exchange worksheet as illustrated in Figures 57, 58, and 59.

Situation

Refer to A and B above, the owners respectively of the vacant land and the commercial store.

A's land is valued at $100,000. It is encumbered with a $55,000 loan. A can only put in an additional $5,000 to make the transaction. The commission to sell the property is 10 percent and other transaction costs are estimated at $800.

B's store is valued at $200,000, on which B owes $100,000. There is a potential loan available on the property for $150,000. B is willing to take the land but is not willing to add cash. She will pay a 6 percent commission "if you can get it out of the transaction," she tells the broker. Other costs are estimated at $1,500.

Is this exchange possible and, if it is made, is there sufficient money to pay the costs and the commissions? The exchange worksheet will be used to find these answers.

Step 1: Inventory the Assets of Each Party

In the first column of the worksheet (see Figure 57 and note the spacing between each party to allow for other entries) we indicate that A has land. Its market value (column 2) is $100,000. Existing loans (column 3) equal $55,000. Column 4 shows the equity of A (column 2 − column 3).

Exchange Recapitulation

Date _____

Property 1	Market Value 2	Existing Loans 3	Equity 4	Cash Gives (In) 5	Cash Gets (Out) 6	Paper Gives 7	Paper Gets 8	Comm. 9	Trans. Costs 10	Net Equity 11	New Loan 12	Old Loan 13	Net Loan Proceeds 14
1 Ashs Land	100000	55000	45000	5000				10000	800	39200			
2													
3													
4 Bhhs Stores	200000	100000	100000					12000	1500	86500	15000	100000	5000
5													
6													
7													
8													
9													
10													

The statements and figures presented
herein, while not guaranteed, are secured
from sources we believe authoritative.

Prepared by _____

Figure 57.

Exchange Recapitulation

Date _____

Property 1	Market Value 2	Existing Loans 3	Equity 4	Cash Gives (In) 5	Cash Gets (Out) 6	Paper Gives 7	Paper Gets 8	Comm. 9	Trans. Costs 10	Net Equity 11	New Loan 12	Old Loan 13	Net Loan Proceeds 14
1 A HAS LAND	100000	55000	45000	5000				10000	800	39200			
2 A GETS STORE	200000	150000	50000			10800				39200			
3													
4 B HAS STORE	200000	100000	100000					12000	1500	86500	150000	100000	50000
5 B GETS LAND	100000	55000	45000				41500			86500			
6													
7													
8													
9													
10													

The statements and figures presented herein, while not guaranteed, are secured from sources we believe authoritative.

Prepared by _____

Figure 58.

Exchange Recapitulation

Date _____

Property 1	Market Value 2	Existing Loans 3	Equity 4	Cash Gives (In) 5	Cash Gets (Out) 6	Paper Gives 7	Paper Gets 8	Comm. 9	Trans. Costs 10	Net Equity 11	New Loan 12	Old Loan 13	Net Loan Proceeds 14
1 A Has Land	100000	55000	45000	5000				10000	800	39200			
2 A Gets Stores	200000	150000	50000			10800				39200			
3													
4 B Has Stores	200000	100000	100000					12000	1500	86500	150000	100000	50000
5 B Gets Land	100000	55000	45000		30700		10800			86500			5000
6													0
7				5000	30700	10800	10800	22000	2300				
8			+	50000 +21000		−0		−22000 −2300				−1	50000
9				+2300		0		0	0				0
10				55000 55000		0							

The statements and figures presented herein, while not guaranteed, are secured from sources we believe authoritative.

Prepared by _____

Figure 59.

A is willing to put in $5,000 which is indicated in column 5. The 10 percent commission to make the transaction is indicated in column 9, and transaction costs of $800 are listed in column 10. Column 11 (Net Equity) is A's gross equity (column 4) increased $5,000 by the cash he is willing to add and diminished by the commission and transaction costs to be paid if the exchange is made. In a slightly different format, the calculation is as follows.

Market value	$100,000
Less encumbrances	− 55,000
Equity	45,000
Plus cash to be added	+ 5,000
Less commission	− 10,000
Less transaction costs	− 800
Net equity	$ 39,200 (Column 11, Figure 58)

B is similarly inventoried on line 4 of the exchange recapitulation.

Step 2: Provide for Maximum Financing of Hard Money

At this stage it is unknown how much financing is needed to make the transaction possible. It isn't even known whether or not the financing should be utilized before or after the exchange or by which party. Maximum financing may not be needed or desired, but at this stage financing is maximized, at least on paper. If, under maximum financing, the transaction is not workable, so be it. If less financing is needed, the completed worksheet will show that and the exchange can be restructured with less financing.

A owns land; in his case there are no readily available refinancing possibilities. B's property can be refinanced up to $150,000, however. This is indicated by inserting that amount under New Loan (column 12) on line 4 of Figure 57. Under Old Loan (column 13) the present loan on B's property ($100,000) is indicated, and in column 14, Net Loan Proceeds, the difference between the two previous columns ($50,000) is shown.

For simplification in this example, loan costs will be disregarded. In practice, they could be added to Transaction Costs (column 10) or reduced in Net Loan Proceeds (column 4).

Step 3: Balance Equities under Maximum Financing Available

In this step, new figures are added to the exchange recapitulation (see Figure 58). Under "A has land," "A gets store" is inserted (see line 2, column 1). Since A is to get the store, its market value of $200,000 is inserted on line 2 of column 2.

At this stage it is assumed that A will take the store with maximum financing of $150,000; that amount is inserted on line 2, column 3, making the equity (column 4) that A is to get $50,000.

Recall that the net equity A put in (column 11) is $39,200. If A put in that amount and is ready to take out $50,000 (line 2), we can see A is taking out $10,800 ($50,000 − $39,200) too much. A *must* add this amount to the exchange to keep it in balance. From the information supplied, we know A has no further money to put in. Therefore, he will put in (give) "paper" for that amount. (Paper can be a note, unsecured or secured with a mortgage, a deed of trust, a wraparound mortgage or contract or a myriad of other security instruments.) So, on line 2, column 7, $10,800 is entered. (At this stage we are not concerned with who gets the paper; we are merely indicating its need.)

As indicated in line 2, column 11, the net equity A is to receive is

Store valued at	$200,000
Less mortgage	150,000
Less paper	10,800
Net equity	$ 39,200

It is now apparent that the net equity A put in of $39,200 will be equalized by the equity A will get of $39,200; therefore, A is in balance. This is indicated by the curved line connecting the two $39,200s in column 11.

Balancing B poses another problem. On line 5, column 1, "B gets land" is inserted. In column 2 the value of the land ($100,000) is inserted and in column 3 the existing loan on the land ($55,000) is indicated, making column 4 $45,000, which is the amount of equity B is getting at this point.

Looking at column 11, line 4, it can be seen that B has a net equity of $86,500 but so far is only getting $45,000. She is $41,500 short of her net equity. We do not know if there is sufficient cash in the transaction to pay B this amount. Therefore, at this point we indicate that B is going to get paper in that amount. We are not concerned whether or not B wants paper; we just insert $41,500 on the worksheet on line 5, column 8. Line 5 is completed by inserting in column 11 (Net Equity) the total of what B gets,

$45,000	equity in the land
41,500	in paper
$86,500	Net Equity

which is equal to the net equity ($86,500) B had. We indicate that the amounts balance with a bracket (see column 11).

Step 4: Balance Paper

In Figure 58, column 7 (Gives Paper) is $10,800 while column 8 (Gets Paper) is $41,500. If the only paper coming into the transaction is $10,800, it will be impossible to take out $41,500. Therefore, $41,500 is changed to $10,800, and in order to keep column 8 in balance, we put the difference ($41,500 − $10,800 = $30,700) on line 5 of column 6, Gets Cash (see Figure 59).

Now, check to see if B is still in balance.

B put in $86,500

B will take out: Equity $45,000
                       Cash   30,700
                       Paper   10,800
                       Total $86,500

Therefore, B is in balance.

Step 5: Total the Active Columns

Again, in Figure 58 (line 7), the active columns are each totaled.

Column 5	Gives Cash	$ 5,000
Column 6	Gets Cash	30,700
Column 7	Gives Paper	10,800
Column 8	Gets Paper	10,800
Column 9	Commission	22,000
Column 10	Transaction Costs	2,300
Column 14	Net Loan Proceeds	50,000

Step 6: Close All Accounts Except Paper Account to Cash

Think of the cash columns (5 and 6) in Figure 59 as the broker's trust account. To this point the only *cash in* is the $5,000 of A. However, column 14 shows $50,000 to come from loan proceeds.

The $50,000 loan proceeds are taken out of column 14 and put in column 5 (Cash In). The commissions are to be paid from escrow; so they are subtracted from column 9 and added to column 6 (Cash Out). Transaction costs are also to be paid from escrow. They are subtracted from column 10 and added to column 6 (Cash Out).

Step 7: Check that Cash and Paper Accounts Are in Balance

Columns 5 and 6 of Figure 59 add up to $55,000, showing that cash is in balance. A glance at the Gives Paper and Gets Paper columns shows that they are also in balance. So the exchange works, on paper at least.

Step 8: Evaluation

Now is the time to review the feasibility of the exchange.

The completed worksheet in Figure 59 graphically illustrates how the exchange can be implemented.

1. A will convey his equity to B plus $5,000, and in exchange A will receive B's property with a new $150,000 mortgage and will owe an additional $10,800.

2. B will exchange her property for A's subject to the existing $55,000 loan. In addition, B will receive $30,700 in cash and a note (or other security instrument) for $10,800.

It is also evident that there will be sufficient funds for transaction costs and commissions.

What if B will not take the $10,800 in paper? That really is not too big a problem. There is $22,000 in commissions. Perhaps the broker will take the note or buy it at a discount with part of the commissions earned.

The exchange recapitulation can be used in the same manner for multiple exchanges or for a two-way exchange with a cash out. In Case Study 9, a slightly different approach is used. In that example, A's property is exchanged to B (who doesn't want it) and then B sells A's property to C, the ultimate owner. Such a procedure makes certain that A will not receive any cash, boot, or net loan relief, thereby ensuring a tax deferred exchange under Section 1031.

CASE STUDY 9: THE TAX DEFERRED EXCHANGE AND CASH FLOW ANALYSIS

The most typical tax deferred exchange under Section 1031 of the Internal Revenue Code occurs because of the following circumstances:

1. Al owns a property,
2. It has been held for some time,
3. The equity is large,
4. The adjusted basis is low because of low cost and/or the cost recovery taken,
5. The market price is substantially over basis,
6. The property no longer fits Al's investment needs,
7. Al wants to stay in real estate and is willing to step up to a larger property,
8. Al is willing to look for a property or has found one already,
9. Bea is the owner of the property Al wants, but Bea does not want Al's property and Bea wants to sell for cash or terms,
10. Cal is a person who wants to buy Al's property, and
11. Dee is an advisor to Al, probably a real estate broker, accountant or lawyer familiar with the processing of 1031 exchanges.

In order to better illustrate the actions of all parties and their resulting positions, consider the following data.

Situation

Al's property can be described as follows:

20-unit apartment building

Value	$850,000
Net operating income	85,000
Existing mortgage	350,000 (8.5%; $3,169 monthly)
Adjusted basis	380,000 (no excess depreciation)
Transaction costs	6%
Potential loan	650,000 (25 years at 10%; $5,906.55 monthly)

Al wishes to acquire an office building without further cash outlay except the loan costs, if any. Al's marginal tax bracket is 28 percent.

Bea's property can be described as follows:

Office building

Value	$1,700,000
Net operating income	175,000
Existing mortgage	530,000
Potential mortgage	1,300,000 (25 yrs at 10%; $11,813.11 monthly; $141,757 annually)
Transaction costs	6%
Land/building allocation	25/75
Depreciation schedule	31.5 years, straight line

Cal has $200,000 cash available to acquire Al's property.

In order to show the advantages of a 1031 exchange, most practitioners show Al his position in Bea's property if he acquires it by selling his own property and purchasing Bea's or if he exchanges into Bea's.

Buying and Selling Alternative

If Al sells his property, his net sales proceeds would be

Sale price		$850,000	
Less existing loan	$350,000		
transaction costs	51,000	401,000	
Gross proceeds			$449,000
Sale price		850,000	
Basis before sale	380,000		
Transaction cost	51,000		
Basis at sale		431,000	
Gain on sale		419,000	
Capital gain tax (28%)			117,320
Net proceeds (if sold)			331,680

Therefore, if Al sold to Cal, Al would have net sale proceeds of $331,680. The office building could then be acquired as follows:

Purchase price		$1,700,000
Down payment (net proceeds of apartment)	$ 331,680	
First mortgage	1,300,000	
Second mortgage	68,320	
	$1,700,000	

Exchange Alternative

On the other hand, if Al exchanges into the Bea property and Bea sells the Al property to Cal, the results would be as shown on the exchange worksheet in Figure 60. The results then can be summarized.

If Al received the $49,000 cash, he would have a taxable event; therefore it is better for Al to take a mortgage of $1,300,000 less the $49,000 ($1,251,000). For the purpose of the problem, assume the mortgage is amortized at 10.5 percent over 25 years but payable in full at the end of the fifteenth year.

Bea gets her net equity of $1,068,000 in cash. Cal acquires the Al property for $850,000 with a $650,000 mortgage. Al has exchanged his property (the apartment building) and acquired Bea's property (the office building). Bea then sells the apartment building to Cal. If Al had sold directly to Cal he would have created a taxable event that would have cost him $117,320 in capital gains taxes. Because of the exchange, Al owes a loan of $1,251,000. If he had sold instead of exchanged, paid capital gains and bought the office building, his debt would have been $1,368,320. The difference is the tax saved on the exchange.

It is apparent that the exchange avoided taxes and the equity of Al is $117,320 larger which is not bad considering the only difference was how the steps of conveyance were taken and how all the parties were educated to the transaction.

Comparing Cash Flows

It will be interesting to compare the after-tax cash flows of the property acquired by purchase and the after-tax cash flows of the property acquired by exchange and to calculate their yields to confirm the advantages of the exchange.

Figures 61 and 62 show the annual cash flows of both the sale and purchase and the exchange outlined above. The differences between these two methods are due to mortgage and cost recovery differences.

In the sale and purchase, the adjusted basis of the office building is $1,700,000 allocated $425,000 to land (25%) and $1,275,000 to improvements (75%). The improvements are depreciated on a straight-line basis for 31.5 years.

In the exchange (see Figure 60), the adjusted basis is $1,700,000 minus the unrecognized gain of $419,000, or $1,281,000. Of this, 75 percent is allocated to improvements ($960,750) and depreciated over 31.5 years on a straight-line basis.

Exchange Recapitulation

Date _____

Property 1	Market Value 2	Existing Loans 3	Equity 4	Cash Gives (In) 5	Cash Gets (Out) 6	Paper Gives 7	Paper Gets 8	Comm. 9	Trans. Costs 10	Net Equity 11	New Loan 12	Old Loan 13	Net Loan Proceeds 14
A has apt.	850,000	350,000	500,000						51,000	449,000			
A gets	1,700,000	1,300,000	400,000		49,000					449,000			
B has office	1,700,000	530,000	1,170,000						102,000	1,068,000	1,300,000	530,000	770,000
B gets apt.	850,000	350,000	500,000		568,000					1,068,000			
B has apt.	850,000	350,000	500,000							500,000	650,000	350,000	300,000
B gets					500,000					500,000			
C has				200,000						200,000			
C gets apt.	850,000	650,000	200,000						153,000	200,000			1,070,000
				200,000	1,117,000				153,000				1,070,000
				1,070,000	153,000				153,000				1,070,000
				1,270,000	1,270,000				-0-				-0-
					-0-								

The statements and figures presented
herein, while not guaranteed, are secured
from sources we believe authoritative.

Prepared by _____

Figure 60.

Cash Flow Analysis Worksheet

Property Name _OFFICE_
Prepared For _CLIENT_
Prepared By _BROKER_
Date Prepared _SALE/PURCHASE ALTERNATIVE_

Purchase Price _1,700,000_
Costs of Acquisition _____
Loan Points _____
Down Payment _331 680_

Mortgage Data	1st Mortgage	2nd Mortgage	Cost Recovery Data	Improvements	Personal Property
Amount	1,300,000	68320	Value	1,275,000	
Interest Rate	10.5	11	C. R. Method	SL	
Term	25 yr	25 yr	Useful Life	31.5	
Payments / Year	12	12	In Service Date		
Periodic Payment	12274 —	669 —	Recapture (All / None / Excess)	NONE	
Annual Debt Service	147292 —	8033 —	Investment Tax Credit ($$ or %)		
Comments	15 yr BALLOON	15 yr BALLOON			

Taxable Income

	Year: 1	Year: 2	Year: 3	Year: 4	Year: 5
1 Potential Rental Income					
2 − Vacancy & Credit Losses					
3 = Effective Rental Income					
4 + Other Income					
5 = Gross Operating Income					
6 − Operating Expenses					
7 = NET OPERATING INCOME	175000	178500	182070	185711	189426
8 − Interest - 1st Mortgage	135965	134717	133331	131793	130085
9 − Interest - 2nd Mortgage	7488	7425	7354	7275	7187
10 − Cost Recovery - Improvements	38790	40476	40476	40476	40476
11 − Cost Recovery - Personal Property					
12 −					
13 −					
14 = Real Estate Taxable Income	⟨7243⟩	⟨4118⟩	909	6167	11 678
15 Tax Liability (Savings) @ 28 %	⟨2028⟩	⟨1153⟩	255	1727	3270

Cash Flow

16 NET OPERATING INCOME (Line 7)	175000	178500	182070	185711	189426
17 − Annual Debt Service	155325	155325	155325	155325	155325
18 −					
19 −					
20 = CASH FLOW BEFORE TAXES	19675	23175	26745	30386	34101
21 − Tax Liability (Savings) (Line 15)	⟨2028⟩	⟨1153⟩	255	1727	3270
22 + Investment Tax Credit					
23 = CASH FLOW AFTER TAXES	21703	24328	26490	28659	30831

The Statements and figures herein while not guaranteed are secured from sources we believe authoritative

Pg _____ of _____

Figure 61.

Cash Flow Analysis Worksheet

Property Name _____   Purchase Price _____
Prepared For _____   Costs of Acquisition _____
Prepared By _____   Loan Points _____
Date Prepared _____   Down Payment _____

Mortgage Data			Cost Recovery Data		
	1st Mortgage	2nd Mortgage		Improvements	Personal Property
Amount			Value		
Interest Rate			C. R. Method		
Term			Useful Life		
Payments / Year			In Service Date		
Periodic Payment			Recapture (All / None / Excess)		
Annual Debt Service			Investment Tax Credit ($$ or %)		
Comments					

Taxable Income

		Year: 6	Year: 7	Year: 8	Year: 9	Year: 10
1	Potential Rental Income					
2	− Vacancy & Credit Losses					
3	= Effective Rental Income					
4	+ Other Income					
5	= Gross Operating Income					
6	− Operating Expenses					
7	= NET OPERATING INCOME	193214	197078	201020	205040	209141
8	− Interest - 1st Mortgage	128188	126082	123745	121150	118269
9	− Interest - 2nd Mortgage	7089	6980	6858	6722	6570
10	− Cost Recovery - Improvements	40476	40476	40476	40476	40476
11	− Cost Recovery - Personal Property					
12	−					
13	−					
14	= Real Estate Taxable Income	17461	23540	29941	36693	43826
15	Tax Liability (Savings) @ 28 %	4889	6591	8383	10274	12271

Cash Flow

16	NET OPERATING INCOME (Line 7)	193214	197078	201020	205040	209141
17	− Annual Debt Service	155325	155325	155325	155325	155325
18	−					
19	−					
20	= CASH FLOW BEFORE TAXES	37889	41753	45695	49715	53816
21	− Tax Liability (Savings) (Line 15)	4889	6591	8383	10274	12271
22	+ Investment Tax Credit					
23	= CASH FLOW AFTER TAXES	33000	35162	37312	39441	41545

The Statements and figures herein while not guaranteed
are secured from sources we believe authoritative

Pg _____ of _____

Figure 61.   continued

Cash Flow Analysis Worksheet

Property Name _____

Prepared For _____

Prepared By _____

Date Prepared _____

Purchase Price _____

Costs of Acquisition _____

Loan Points _____

Down Payment _____

Mortgage Data			Cost Recovery Data		
	1st Mortgage	2nd Mortgage		Improvements	Personal Property
Amount			Value		
Interest Rate			C. R. Method		
Term			Useful Life		
Payments / Year			In Service Date		
Periodic Payment			Recapture		
Annual Debt Service			(All / None / Excess)		
Comments			Investment Tax Credit ($$ or %)		

Taxable Income

		Year: 11	Year: 12	Year: 13	Year: 14	Year: 15
1	Potential Rental Income					
2	− Vacancy & Credit Losses					
3	= Effective Rental Income					
4	+ Other Income					
5	= Gross Operating Income					
6	− Operating Expenses					
7	= NET OPERATING INCOME	213324	217591	221942	226381	230909
8	− Interest - 1st Mortgage	115071	111520	107578	103201	98342
9	− Interest - 2nd Mortgage	6399	6210	5999	5763	5501
10	− Cost Recovery - Improvements	40476	40476	40476	40476	40476
11	− Cost Recovery - Personal Property					
12	−					
13	−					
14	= Real Estate Taxable Income	51378	59385	67889	76941	86590
15	Tax Liability (Savings) @ 28 %	14386	16628	19009	21543	24245

Cash Flow

16	NET OPERATING INCOME (Line 7)	213324	217591	221942	226381	230909
17	− Annual Debt Service	155325	155325	155325	155325	155325
18	−					
19	−					
20	= CASH FLOW BEFORE TAXES	57999	62266	66617	71056	75575
21	− Tax Liability (Savings) (Line 15)	14386	16628	19009	21543	24245
22	+ Investment Tax Credit					
23	= CASH FLOW AFTER TAXES	43613	45638	47608	49513	51330

The Statements and figures herein while not guaranteed are secured from sources we believe authoritative

Pg _____ of _____

Figure 61.   continued

Alternative Cash Sales Worksheet

Pg _____ of _____

Mortgage Balances

	Year: 15	Year:	Year:	Year:	Year:
Principal Balance - 1st Mortgage	909650				
Principal Balance - 2nd Mortgage	48611				
TOTAL UNPAID PRINCIPAL	958261				

Calculation of Sale Proceeds

PROJECTED SALES PRICE _____ _____ _____

CALCULATION OF ADJUSTED BASIS:

1	Basis at Acquisition	1700000	
2	+ Capital Additions		
3	− Cost Recovery (Depreciation) Taken	605456	
4	− Basis in Partial Sales		
5	= Adjusted Basis at Sale	1094544	

CALCULATION OF EXCESS COST RECOVERY:

6	Total Cost Recovery Taken (Line 3)	605456	
7	− Straight Line Cost Recovery	605456	
8	= Excess Cost Recovery	0	

CALCULATION OF CAPITAL GAIN ON SALE:

9	Sale Price	2,000,000	
10	− Costs of Sale	120000	
11	− Adjusted Basis at Sale (Line 5)	1094544	
12	− Participation Payments		
13	= Total Gain	785456	
14	− Excess Cost Recovery (Line 8)		
15	− Suspended Losses		
16	= Capital Gain or (Loss)	785456	

ITEMS TAXED AS ORDINARY INCOME:

17	Excess Cost Recovery (Line 8)	0	
18	− Unamortized Loan Points		
19	= Ordinary Taxable Income		
20	x Tax Rate on Ordinary Income		
21	= Tax (Savings) on Ordinary Income	0	

ITEMS TAXED AS CAPITAL GAIN:

22	Capital Gain (Line 16)	785456	
23	x Percentage of Capital Gain Reportable	100	
24	= Taxable Capital Gain	785456	
25	x Tax Rate on Capital Gain	28	
26	= Tax on Capital Gain	219928	

CALCULATION OF SALE PROCEEDS AFTER TAX:

27	Sale Price (Line 9)	2,000,000	
28	− Costs of Sale (Line 10)	120000	
29	− Participation Payments (Line 12)	0	
30	− Mortgage Balance(s) (from top of form)	958261	
31	= Sale Proceeds Before Taxes	921739	
32	− Tax (Savings) on Ordinary Income (Line 21)	0	
33	− Tax on Capital Gain (Line 26)	219928	
34	− Recapture of Investment Tax Credits	0	
35	= SALE PROCEEDS AFTER TAX	701811	

The statements and figures herein while not guaranteed
are secured from sources we believe authoritative   Prepared by _____

Figure 61.   continued

Pg _____ of _____

Alternative T-Bars Worksheet

Alternative # _SALE /_ _PURCHASE_

Alternative # _____

Alternative # _____

n	$	n	$	n	$
0	(331680)	0	( )	0	( )
1	21703	1		1	
2	24328	2		2	
3	26490	3		3	
4	28659	4		4	
5	30831	5		5	
6	33000	6		6	
7	35162	7		7	
8	37312	8		8	
9	39441	9		9	
10	41545	10		10	
11	43613	11		11	
12	45638	12		12	
13	47608	13		13	
14	49513	14		14	
15	51330+ 701811	15		15	
IRR =	12.66	IRR =		IRR =	

The statements and figures herein while not guaranteed
are secured from sources we believe authoritative

Prepared by _____

Figure 61.   continued

Cash Flow Analysis Worksheet

Property Name __OFFICE__   Purchase Price __1700000__
Prepared For __CLIENT__   Costs of Acquisition _____
Prepared By __BROKER__   Loan Points _____
Date Prepared __EXCHANGE ALTERNATIVE__   Down Payment __449000__

Mortgage Data			Cost Recovery Data		
	1st Mortgage	2nd Mortgage		Improvements	Personal Property
Amount	1,251,000		Value	960750	
Interest Rate	10.5		C. R. Method	SL	
Term	25YR		Useful Life	31.5	
Payments / Year	12		In Service Date		
Periodic Payment	11811.71		Recapture (All / None / Excess)	NONE	
Annual Debt Service	141741		Investment Tax Credit ($$ or %)		
Comments	15YR BALLOON				

Taxable Income

	Year: 1	Year: 2	Year: 3	Year: 4	Year: 5
1 Potential Rental Income					
2 − Vacancy & Credit Losses					
3 = Effective Rental Income					
4 + Other Income					
5 = Gross Operating Income					
6 − Operating Expenses					
7 = NET OPERATING INCOME	175000	178500	182070	185711	189426
8 − Interest - 1st Mortgage	130841	129639	128305	126825	125181
9 − Interest - 2nd Mortgage					
10 − Cost Recovery - Improvements	29229	30500	30500	30500	30500
11 − Cost Recovery - Personal Property					
12 −					
13 −					
14 = Real Estate Taxable Income	14930	18361	23265	28386	33745
15 Tax Liability (Savings) @ 28 %	4180	5141	6514	7948	9449

Cash Flow

16 NET OPERATING INCOME (Line 7)	175000	178500	182070	185711	189426
17 − Annual Debt Service	141741	141741	141741	141741	141741
18 −					
19 −					
20 = CASH FLOW BEFORE TAXES	33259	36759	40329	43970	47685
21 − Tax Liability (Savings) (Line 15)	4180	5141	6514	7948	9449
22 + Investment Tax Credit					
23 = CASH FLOW AFTER TAXES	29079	31618	33815	36022	38236

The Statements and figures herein while not guaranteed are secured from sources we believe authoritative

Pg _____ of _____

Figure 62.

Cash Flow Analysis Worksheet

Property Name _____   Purchase Price _____
Prepared For _____   Costs of Acquisition _____
Prepared By _____   Loan Points _____
Date Prepared _____   Down Payment _____

Mortgage Data			Cost Recovery Data		
	1st Mortgage	2nd Mortgage		Improvements	Personal Property
Amount			Value		
Interest Rate			C. R. Method		
Term			Useful Life		
Payments / Year			In Service Date		
Periodic Payment			Recapture		
Annual Debt Service			(All / None / Excess)		
Comments			Investment Tax Credit ($$ or %)		

Taxable Income

	Year: 6	Year: 7	Year: 8	Year: 9	Year: 10
1 Potential Rental Income					
2 − Vacancy & Credit Losses					
3 = Effective Rental Income					
4 + Other Income					
5 = Gross Operating Income					
6 − Operating Expenses					
7 = NET OPERATING INCOME	193214	197078	201020	205040	209141
8 − Interest - 1st Mortgage	123356	121330	119081	116583	113811
9 − Interest - 2nd Mortgage					
10 − Cost Recovery - Improvements	30500	30500	30500	30500	30500
11 − Cost Recovery - Personal Property					
12 −					
13 −					
14 = Real Estate Taxable Income	39358	45248	51439	57957	64830
15 Tax Liability (Savings) @ 28 %	11020	12669	14403	16228	18152

Cash Flow

16 NET OPERATING INCOME (Line 7)	193214	197078	201020	205040	209141
17 − Annual Debt Service	141741	141741	141741	141744	141741
18 −					
19 −					
20 = CASH FLOW BEFORE TAXES	51473	55337	59279	63299	67400
21 − Tax Liability (Savings) (Line 15)	11020	12669	14403	16228	18152
22 + Investment Tax Credit					
23 = CASH FLOW AFTER TAXES	40453	42668	44877	47071	49248

The Statements and figures herein while not guaranteed
are secured from sources we believe authoritative

Pg _____ of _____

Figure 62.   continued

Cash Flow Analysis Worksheet

Property Name _____

Prepared For _____

Prepared By _____

Date Prepared _____

Purchase Price _____

Costs of Acquisition _____

Loan Points _____

Down Payment _____

Mortgage Data

	1st Mortgage	2nd Mortgage
Amount		
Interest Rate		
Term		
Payments / Year		
Periodic Payment		
Annual Debt Service		
Comments		

Cost Recovery Data

	Improvements	Personal Property
Value		
C. R. Method		
Useful Life		
In Service Date		
Recapture (All / None / Excess)		
Investment Tax Credit ($$ or %)		

Taxable Income

	Year: 11	Year: 12	Year: 13	Year: 14	Year: 15
1 Potential Rental Income					
2 – Vacancy & Credit Losses					
3 = Effective Rental Income					
4 + Other Income					
5 = Gross Operating Income					
6 – Operating Expenses					
7 = NET OPERATING INCOME	213324	217591	221942	226381	230909
8 – Interest - 1st Mortgage	110733	107316	103522	99311	94635
9 – Interest - 2nd Mortgage					
10 – Cost Recovery - Improvements	30500	30500	30500	30500	30500
11 – Cost Recovery - Personal Property					
12 –					
13 –					
14 = Real Estate Taxable Income	72091	79774	87920	96570	105774
15 Tax Liability (Savings) @ 28 %	20185	22337	24618	27040	29617

Cash Flow

16 NET OPERATING INCOME (Line 7)	213324	217591	221942	226381	230909
17 – Annual Debt Service	141741	141741	141741	141741	141741
18 –					
19 –					
20 = CASH FLOW BEFORE TAXES	71583	75850	80201	84640	89168
21 – Tax Liability (Savings) (Line 15)	20185	22337	24618	27040	29617
22 + Investment Tax Credit					
23 = CASH FLOW AFTER TAXES	51398	53513	55583	57600	59551

Pg _____ of _____

Figure 62. continued

Alternative Cash Sales Worksheet

Pg _____ of _____

Mortgage Balances

	Year: 15	Year:	Year:	Year:	Year:
Principal Balance - 1st Mortgage	875363				
Principal Balance - 2nd Mortgage					
TOTAL UNPAID PRINCIPAL					

Calculation of Sale Proceeds

PROJECTED SALES PRICE

CALCULATION OF ADJUSTED BASIS:

1	Basis at Acquisition	1,281,000	
2	+ Capital Additions	0	
3	− Cost Recovery (Depreciation) Taken	456229	
4	− Basis in Partial Sales	0	
5	= Adjusted Basis at Sale	824771	

CALCULATION OF EXCESS COST RECOVERY:

6	Total Cost Recovery Taken (Line 3)	456229	
7	− Straight Line Cost Recovery	456 229	
8	= Excess Cost Recovery	0	

CALCULATION OF CAPITAL GAIN ON SALE:

9	Sale Price	2000000	
10	− Costs of Sale	120000	
11	− Adjusted Basis at Sale (Line 5)	824771	
12	− Participation Payments	0	
13	= Total Gain	1055229	
14	− Excess Cost Recovery (Line 8)	0	
15	− Suspended Losses	0	
16	= Capital Gain or (Loss)	1055229	

ITEMS TAXED AS ORDINARY INCOME:

17	Excess Cost Recovery (Line 8)	0	
18	− Unamortized Loan Points		
19	= Ordinary Taxable Income		
20	x Tax Rate on Ordinary Income		
21	= Tax (Savings) on Ordinary Income	0	

ITEMS TAXED AS CAPITAL GAIN:

22	Capital Gain (Line 16)	1055229	
23	x Percentage of Capital Gain Reportable	100	
24	= Taxable Capital Gain	1055229	
25	x Tax Rate on Capital Gain	28	
26	= Tax on Capital Gain	295464	

CALCULATION OF SALE PROCEEDS AFTER TAX:

27	Sale Price (Line 9)	2000000	
28	− Costs of Sale (Line 10)	120000	
29	− Participation Payments (Line 12)	0	
30	− Mortgage Balance(s) (from top of form)	875363	
31	= Sale Proceeds Before Taxes	1004637	
32	− Tax (Savings) on Ordinary Income (Line 21)		
33	− Tax on Capital Gain (Line 26)	295464	
34	− Recapture of Investment Tax Credits	0	
35	= SALE PROCEEDS AFTER TAX	709153	

The statements and figures herein while not guaranteed
are secured from sources we believe authoritative

Prepared by _____

Figure 62. continued

Alternative T-Bars Worksheet

Pg _____ of _____

n	$		n	$		n	$
	Alternative # *EXCHANGE*			Alternative # _____			Alternative # _____
0	(331680)		0	( )		0	( )
1	29079		1			1	
2	31618		2			2	
3	33815		3			3	
4	36022		4			4	
5	38236		5			5	
6	40453		6			6	
7	42668		7			7	
8	44877		8			8	
9	47071		9			9	
10	49248		10			10	
11	51398		11			11	
12	53513		12			12	
13	55583		13			13	
14	57600		14			14	
15	59551 + 709173		15			15	
IRR =	14.43		IRR =			IRR =	

The statements and figures herein while not guaranteed are secured from sources we believe authoritative   Prepared by _____

Figure 62. continued

COST RECOVERY CALCULATIONS

Sale and Purchase	$1,700,000
Improvement	1,275,000
Term	31.5 years
Per year	40,476
First year	38,790*
15-year cost recovery	605,456
Basis at disposition	$1,094,544

Exchange Price	$1,700,000
Unrecognized gain	419,000
Basis at acquisition	1,281,000
Improvements (75%)	960,750
Term	31.5 years
Per year	30,500
First year	29,229*
15-year cost recovery	456,229
Basis at disposition	824,771

*(1/2 month convention)

Other assumptions of the cash flow studies are as follows.

1. The Net Operating Income is projected to increase at 2 percent per year.

2. The resale price at end of year 15 will be $2,000,000 and sale costs will be 6 percent.

3. Resale capital gains tax will be 28 percent.

4. The second mortgage loan on the sale and purchase will be amortized on a 25-year, 11 percent monthly schedule, payable in full at the end of the fifteenth year.

5. Al's annual qualifying adjusted gross income is less than $100,000; therefore, tax losses are completely deductible.

The t-charts on p. 380 have been extracted from the cash sale worksheets in Figures 61 and 62.

The equal initial investment for each projection is based on the premise from Chapter 6 that the investment base for an alternative investment analysis is the net sale proceeds after taxes plus any cash added or minus any cash received. In both the exchange and the sale and purchase the transaction was made from the net after-tax equity of $331,680.

The comparative cash flows show that under the assumptions made, the sale and purchase would result in a 12.66 percent internal rate of return and the exchange would result in a 14.43 percent return, approximately a 14 percent greater projected yield for the latter. It is interesting to note here that a similar problem in the previous edition of this

Sale and Purchase		Exchange	
n	$	n	$
0	(331,680)	0	(331,680)
1	21,703	1	29,079
2	24,328	2	31,618
3	26,490	3	33,815
4	28,659	4	36,022
5	30,831	5	38,236
6	33,000	6	40,453
7	35,162	7	42,668
8	37,312	8	44,877
9	39,441	9	47,072
10	41,545	10	49,248
11	43,613	11	51,398
12	45,638	12	53,513
13	47,608	13	55,584
14	49,513	14	57,601
15	51,330 + 701,811	15	59,552 + 709,173

IRR = 12.66   IRR = 14.43

book did not show the same advantage for the exchange. The difference has been the 1986 Tax Act which lengthened cost recovery periods and reduced the availability of tax savings by reducing tax rates.

Conclusion

Much of the literature of 1031 exchanging only takes the tax consequences of the sale into consideration and completely omits the after-tax cash flows of the property's operation over the holding period. Investment brokers would be wise, however, to test the future after-tax benefits of the exchange with those of the sale/purchase so that they completely understand the differences.

While the 1031 exchange has prevailed and probably will do so in the future, other tax rules and regulations regarding disposition of real estate should be taken into consideration before making the decision to sell and purchase or to exchange.

Some major points to be learned from this case are

1. Changes in cost recovery terms and tax rates can affect the decision to sell and purchase or exchange.
2. The investment broker should be able to make the cash flow analyses of both the potential sale and purchase and the potential exchange, as well as calculate the tax savings on disposition by the exchange.
3. Investors should demand (and pay for) such studies before they attempt the complicated negotiations and paperwork of a technically complex exchange.

CASE STUDY 10: LAND AND LAND ANALYSIS

Land is the most misunderstood and the most mysterious of investments. There is very little literature on the subject, but what is available often quotes platitudes of wealthy historical figures.

John Jacob Astor	"Buy land near a growing city."
Andrew Carnegie	"The wise young man or wage earner of today invests his money in real estate, suburban real estate."
Grover Cleveland	"No investment on earth is so safe, so sure, so certain to enrich its owner as undeveloped realty. I always advise my friends to place their savings in realty near some growing city. There is no such savings bank anywhere."

Most investors' opinions about land as an investment result in additional statements.

"Land is a good investment because it always increases in value. In fact, if I'm not satisfied with an offer on my land because it's too low, all I have to do is wait and prices will catch up to mine."

"Land is a bad investment—it's not liquid, it's an alligator, it keeps eating and I, as owner, have to support it."

"Land is a good investment. As an owner I can write off the interest and taxes I pay. As a result Uncle Sam is paying my costs. It's a good tax shelter."

"Land is a bad investment—it lacks cash flow—and any investment without cash flow is foolhardy."

"Land is a good investment. God stopped making land, but He didn't stop making people; therefore land prices must go up. In fact, I have a friend who doubled his money in land in only ten years. Not only that, but land can be bought on leverage."

Such thinking results in some people buying, some people not buying, and some people buying, accomplishing their goals, but losing money. In fact, ask a room full of people if investment in land is a good long-term investment or a good short-term investment. You will find the answers mixed. We shall try to resolve the conflicting opinions.

First, let us define investment land (or speculative land). Investment lands are vacant properties acquired with no specific plan in mind except to hold them for appreciation. This is quite different from acquiring land to subdivide or to build a specific building on within a relatively short period of time.

Investment in land is unique. When land is acquired, all cash flows are negative: the down payment, the debt service, and the carrying charges. The only positive cash flow (excluding the possibility of rental income) comes from the eventual disposition of the property.

The following is a t-chart of a land acquisition.

n	$
0	(Initial Investment)
1	(Annual Debt Service + Carrying Costs)
2	(AD + CC)
3	(AD + CC)
—	
—	
—	
Year of Sale	(AD + CC) + Resale Proceeds

Most investors are aware that investment land has greater risk than most other investments, as well as less liquidity and negative cash flows; because of these factors, land should yield greater returns than savings (5 to 7 percent) or mortgages (10 to 15 percent). Investors are often unable to translate this awareness into the price necessary to obtain the yield they desire for the period they expect to hold the property. Furthermore, they are unable to evaluate this type of investment on a before- or after-tax basis and to make comparisons with alternative investments available. Therefore, most tend to rely on platitudes to justify their Go or No Go decisions on a land investment opportunity.

An interesting comparison for a land investment can be found in zero coupon bonds. Although each has different risks, basically both are for investors who are willing to invest money now for a future lump sum, for appreciation.

Zero coupon bonds are bonds which have no annual return in cash but rather the annual return is held for the investor and accrues interest each compounding period until the bond matures.

The bonds could be municipal (tax free) or corporate (interest subject to tax). The bonds are usually compounded semiannually.

Situation

The purpose of this section then is to provide some guidelines and processes for understanding land investment. This will be done by comparing similar size investments in land and in a tax-free zero coupon bond and relating the appreciation necessary in a land investment to equal the yield on the bond.

The assumptions used to make the comparisons are as follows.

	Land	Tax Free 0 Bond
Future value	To be determined	$100,000
Term	10 years	10 years
Tax rate		
Ordinary	28%	28%
Capital gain	28%	28%
Yield	Same as bond	7%
Carrying costs	$3,000 annual	0
Disposition cost	10%	0
Compounded	Semiannually	Semiannually
Original cost	Same as bond	$50,257

When investment in land is compared to the tax-free zero coupon bond we find that to yield 7% compounded semiannually in 10 years, a $100,000 tax free bond would cost $50,257. To determine the resale price of land necessary to obtain a similar yield, the following calculations were made.

Step 1   Determine the annual cash flow. The down payment and carrying costs are all outflows (or negative cash flows).

Step 2   Tax savings were calculated at 28 percent of the annual carrying costs.

Step 3   Net annual negative cash flows were calculated by reducing the carrying cost cash flows by the tax savings.

Step 4   The net annual negative cash flows were discounted at a safe rate of 5 percent to determine a single sum deposit necessary to fund the outflows when due.

Step 5   The deposit was added to the original costs to determine the initial investment needed for the transaction.

Step 6   The initial investment was compounded semiannually at 7 percent to determine the after-tax proceeds necessary to have the same yield as the tax-free bond.

Step 7   A net price before sale costs was calculated as follows:

$$\text{net sale price} = \text{after-tax proceeds} + 0.28 \,(\text{sales price} - \text{basis})$$

Step 8   The gross sales price was calculated by increasing the net sales price by the sales costs:

$$\text{gross sale price} = \text{sale price} \div 0.90$$

The year by year after tax cash flows for land are

EOY	Annual Cash Flow Before Taxes	Tax Savings	Cash Flow After Taxes	Deposit Needs @ 5%	Adjusted Initial Investment
0	(50,257)			(16,678)	(66,935)
1	(3,000)	840	(2,160)	(2,057)	
2	(3,000)	840	(2,160)	(1,959)	
3	(3,000)	840	(2,160)	(1,866)	
4	(3,000)	840	(2,160)	(1,777)	
5	(3,000)	840	(2,160)	(1,692)	
6	(3,000)	840	(2,160)	(1,612)	
7	(3,000)	840	(2,160)	(1,535)	
8	(3,000)	840	(2,160)	(1,462)	
9	(3,000)	840	(2,160)	(1,392)	
10	(3,000)	840	(2,160)	(1,326)	

For step 6, $66,935 is compounded semiannually at 7% which indicates that $133,187 return is needed after taxes. Below are the calculations of sales price before taxes (step 7).

$$SP = \$133,187 + 0.28 \, (SP - Basis)$$

$$SP = \$133,187 + 0.28 \, (SP - \$50,257)$$

$$SP = \$133,187 + 0.28SP - \$14,072$$

$$0.72 \, SP = \$119,115$$

$$SP = \$165,437$$

And step 8 reveals

$$\text{gross sales price} = \frac{\$165,437}{0.90} = \$183,819$$

Because the land investment takes additional cash to fund the annual carrying costs, to make a fairer comparison, the zero coupon bond should be funded with the same investment as the land. The $16,678 additional needed for the land investment, if invested in additional bonds, would compound at 7 percent semiannually to $33,187.

More simply, for both investments to yield 7 percent, the bond would return $133,187 and the land would have to sell for $183,819, which requires an annual growth rate of 10.6 percent.

As a further comparison, it is not logical that one would invest in a speculative land transaction with the same yield as a zero coupon bond having a guaranteed maturity as to amount and time. Rather, it is more realistic to assume that a minimum expected yield would exceed the savings bank rate or mortgage interest rate, say 15 percent. For such a rate of return, the gross resale price would be $417,065, making the growth rate 20.1 percent annually. The calculations are, for step 6, $66,935 is compounded semiannually at 15 percent to yield = $284,330. The calculations for step 7 are

$$SP = \$284,330 + 0.28 \, (SP - Basis)$$

$$SP = \$284,330 + 0.28 \, (SP - \$50,252)$$

$$SP = \$284,330 + 0.28SP - \$14,072$$

$$0.72 \, SP = \$270,258$$

$$SP = \$375,358$$

And step 8 yields

$$\text{gross sales price} = \frac{\$375,358}{0.90} = \$417,065$$

Using the same technique, comparisons of land investments to zero coupon bonds were made under the same assumptions for holding periods of 5, 10, and 20 years.

Item	5 Year	10 Year	15 Year	20 Year
Bond cost (7% yield)	$ 70,892	$ 50,257	$ 35,628	$ 25,257
Land: Initial investment (adjusted)	80,244	66,935	58,048	52,175
Resale price at 7%	144,047	183,819	236,039	307,873
Growth rate at 7%	12.4	10.6	9.8	9.3
Resale price at 15%	224,591	417,065	768,876	1,441,954
Growth rate at 15%	22.9	20.1	18.8	18.1

According to the results above, to obtain a return commensurate with the risk of holding speculative land, it must have a growth rate of 18 to 23 percent annually. It becomes evident that land values must more than double every five years to obtain an after tax yield commensurate with risk.

Many land investors have conflicting investment strategies which usually result in working against their best interests. Most wish a high yield, say 20 to 40 percent, because of the speculative nature and lack of liquidity of investment land, and they couple these dreams with the concept that the investment is the small price they originally paid for the property instead of its worth today. In addition, they are reluctant to sell the property because of the capital gains that would be created; so they keep it for long periods of time (15 to 30 years). This ensures the impossibility of attaining the yields they originally hoped for.

This study did not take into consideration the IRS limitation on investment interest. The interest limitation, in effect, delays the tax savings caused by the deduction, which must be deferred, thereby increasing early negative cash flows and requiring higher resale prices.

The study also disregards syndicators' portions of profits and perhaps even management fees. Real estate taxes in the example are considered level, but they could increase as the property value increases. These additional costs would require an even further boost in sale price to obtain the desired yield.

One who wishes to acquire speculative land must understand that profit comes from appreciation. If a 15 percent yield is satisfactory, the investor in the examples above must undertake an $80,000 investment, must resell for $225,000 in five years or nearly double that in 10 years, and must project what trends, zoning, utilities capability and development potential will have to occur to make the needed sales price a probability.

The potential purchaser might want to relate these findings with the land investment platitudes discussed earlier.

"Land is a good investment because it always goes up in value."

"Land is a bad investment—it's not liquid. . . ."

There is nothing wrong with a nonliquid investment, if it has a good yield; in land, that means a good and rapid growth.

"Land is a good investment. I can write off carrying costs; it's a good shelter."

The costs written off are not a shelter. They are actual out-of-pocket expenses. They can be deducted from ordinary income and this results in tax savings which can be described as the government paying a portion of the costs. But the deduction is not like depreciation, which is a noncash expense against ordinary income. Land is sold at an amount over the original basis, and if qualified, the gain is taxed at long-term capital gain rates. This, however, is not tax shelter.

"Land is a good investment—its amount is finite and it must go up in value."

As before, the *timing* of the growth is the overriding factor. There are some who believe that getting an appraisal is the answer, but that only indicates what others have been doing in the past. It does not indicate what will happen.

If there are any conclusions about land investments they must be the following.

1. Because investment land has all negative cash flows until it is sold; because it is difficult to project when it can be sold and to whom and because such land is difficult to borrow against, it has greater risk than many other traditional investments and, therefore, should have a potential for greater yield than these other investments.

2. The longer land is held the longer is the period for compounding all the negative cash flows that increase in total each year. This means that the sale price needed increases more rapidly with each additional year of holding, especially after the first four or five years. Therefore, investment land tends to be a better short-term investment than a long-term one.

3. Although an investor in land may not be able to project when or at what price it will resell; prior to acquisition, the investor should have some idea what it must sell for at some future time in order to earn a yield commensurate with the risks.

4. Nothing here should be construed to imply that land is not or cannot be an attractive investment. However, in order for land to be an intelligent investment decision, it should be acquired with a basic understanding of what it must sell for.

5. The greatest error committed by many investors who hold speculative land is their tendency to regard what they paid for it many years ago as their investment in the property. In reality, their investment today is the amount they would *net* from a sale after expenses, including taxes.

6. The decision to keep or sell should not be based on potential income taxes, but rather on whether the proceeds *after* taxes would earn more by investing in the land for a further period (holding on to it) or by investing in some other holding that will yield a larger return.

CASE STUDY 11: IMPACT OF HOLDING PERIOD ON EQUITY YIELD

Before-tax equity yield will virtually always change throughout the holding period of an investment. Yield is affected by changes in income and expenses during the holding period, the sale price at the end of the holding period, and the financing. Interest rates, amortization terms and loan-to-value ratio will each affect the equity return on investment. For any investment financed with an amortizing loan, the loan-to-value ratio changes after each payment which includes principal; thus, leverage will change each period. The related equity yield, if calculated for each individual period, will be different for each period if only because of the constantly changing financial structure. Therefore, holding period can be an important variable when choosing among alternative financing with different amortization terms.

Situation

To illustrate the impact of holding period on equity yield, consider a property with constant NOI of $12,000 and a constant value of $100,000. Constant value and income are assumed in order to isolate the impact of financing. Notice that this property would produce a 12 percent equity yield for any holding period if it were acquired without any debt financing. The investors' cash flows before taxes are summarized below.

EOY	$
0	($100,000)
1	12,000
↓	↓
$\boxed{n}$	12,000 + 100,000

The income will be the same for any number of periods, and the sale price will be $100,000 no matter when it is sold. Equity yield, in this case, is calculated as if the cash flows were a perpetuity or interest-only loan.

$$y = \frac{\text{NOI}}{\text{value}} = \frac{\$12,000}{\$100,000} = 12\%$$

The IRR of these cash flows will be 12 percent for any number of years exceeding zero.

Financing Alternatives

Consider three alternative loans to finance this property.

Loan A   An $85,000 loan at 10.75 percent interest per year with a balloon payment of $80,000 due EOY 15 and monthly payments of $772.71. The annual debt constant is

0.1091 [($772.71 × 12) ÷ $85,000]

Loan B   An $85,000 loan at 10 percent interest per year with monthly payments of $913.41 which will fully amortize the loan in 15 years. The annual debt constant is

0.1290 [($913.41 × 12) ÷ $85,000].

Loan C   An $85,000 loan at 9.5 percent interest per year plus 2.5 points at origination and 20-year amortization with monthly payments of

$792.31. Loan proceeds are $82,875 (85,000 less 2.5 percent). The annual debt constant is

0.1147 [($792.31 × 12) ÷ $82,875].

If equity yield before tax is used as the decision criterion, the highest yielding choice will depend on the *investment holding period*. Monthly cash flows before taxes (CFBT) for each financing alternative are constant for each month the property is owned. (CFBT is the monthly NOI of $1,000 less the monthly loan payment.) Proceeds before taxes (PBT) are equal to the constant sale price of $100,000 less the outstanding loan balance at the end of the month. The initial investment end of month (EOM) 0 is equal to the $100,000 purchase price less the loan proceeds. In the case of loan C, the 2.5 points have been added to the initial investment. The cash flows before taxes and proceeds before taxes for all three financing alternatives have been summarized below for 3-, 8- and 15-year holding periods.

EOM	Loan A	
	CFBT	PBT
0	($15,000.00)	
1	$227.29	
3 × 12 = 36	$227.29	$15,475.69
8 × 12 = 96	$227.29	$16,701.40
15 × 12 = 180	$227.29	$20,000.00

EOM	Loan B	
	CFBT	PBT
0	($15,000.00)	
1	$86.59	
3 × 12 = 36	$86.59	$23,568.66
8 × 12 = 96	$86.59	$44,978.96
15 × 12 = 180	$86.59	$100,000.00

EOM	Loan C	
	CFBT	PBT
0	($17,125.00)	
1	$207.69	
3 × 12 = 36	$207.69	$19,950.80
8 × 12 = 96	$207.69	$32,070.50
15 × 12 = 180	$207.69	$62,274.22

Equity yields before taxes are summarized in the following table, using the monthly cash flows above. The resulting monthly IRRs have been annualized.

SUMMARY OF EQUITY YIELD BEFORE TAXES

Holding Period (Years)	Financing Alternative		
	A	B	C
3	19.0%	20.8%*	18.7%
8	18.8%	18.2%	19.2%*
15	18.6%*	16.0%	18.0%

The asterisk indicates the financing alternative that will produce the highest equity yield before taxes for each holding period. The best of these financing alternatives actually depends on holding period. The original loan-to-value ratio is the same for each alternative, but the interest rate and terms vary for each.

Effects of Holding Period

The effects, over time, of the different financing alternatives can be seen in Figure 63. The equity yields before taxes for each financing alternative for holding periods up to 15 years have been summarized in this graph. Each point on each curve indicates the equity yield for that corresponding holding period. This graph also illustrates the highest-yielding financing alternative for every holding period during the 15-year projection.

Figure 63 shows that loan B would be higher for holding periods less than five years. If the property is held for approximately 5 to 11 years, loan C has the highest yield; for holding periods beyond 11 years, loan A would provide the highest yield.

Note that each loan shown on Figure 63 would maximize equity yield before tax for some holding periods, but not for all holding periods. Some generalizations can be made for each of these loans which may clarify the equity yield trends.

Loan A has the highest interest rate but the lowest monthly payment. Among the three financing alternatives monthly CFBT is greater for this loan. Proceeds before taxes, for any holding period, is less for loan A, compared to B and C. The $80,000 balloon payment EOY 15 reduces the amount of amortization required as part of the debt service. Alternatively stated, it would take more than 39 years to amortize $85,000 at 10.75 percent interest with monthly payments of $772.71. Thus, the loan-to-value ratio does not decline a great deal during the 15-year projection due to the small amount of principal amortization. Since the loan-to-value ratio is fairly constant, the resulting equity yield is likewise relatively stable during the 15-year projection. (Recall from Chapter 6 that the equity yield would be constant over time with an interest-only loan.)

Loan B illustrates the impact of a short amortization term. The 10 percent interest rate is less than for loan A. Equity yields for holding periods less than about five years are greatest with loan B because of the low effective interest rate. Monthly cash flows before taxes are less for loan B than the other loans because B requires the greater debt service.

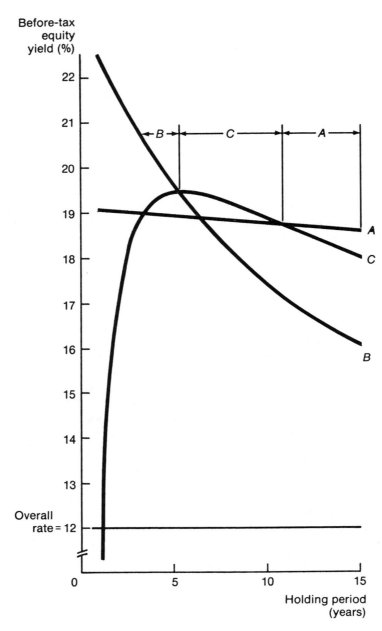

Figure 63. Financing Alternatives.

The high debt service is required to fully amortize the loan balance in 15 years, the shortest term among the three loans.

For any holding period, the equity proceeds before taxes are greater for loan B. The benefit of positive leverage decreases as equity increases. The rate of equity increase per period, from loan amortization, is greatest for loan B. Therefore, the equity yield will decrease more rapidly for longer holding periods. The equity yields for holding periods up to 15 years decline over 470 basis points (a basis point is 1/100th of a percentage point) for loan B compared to about 38 basis points for loan A.

The steady decline in equity yields for longer holding periods for loans A and B can be explained by changes in the loan-to-value ratios over time. The effective interest rates for these alternatives are constant over any holding period. This is not the case, however, for loan C.

Loan C produces a humped equity yield curve (see Figure 63) which indicates that it is the highest-yielding financing alternative for holding periods over five years and less than eleven years. Loan C's cash flows before taxes and sales proceeds before taxes, for any holding period, are always between those resulting from the other two financing alternatives. The shape of the equity yield curve for loan C is caused by two variables which change for different holding periods, the loan-to-value ratio and the effective interest rate.

Loan C has the lowest nominal interest rate among the three choices, but it is the only loan with discount points payable at origination. Recall that the effective interest rate of a loan with discount points decreases as the term of the loan is increased. If loan C is paid in full after a short holding period, the effective interest rate will be very high; therefore, the equity yield will be low. The effective interest rate of loan C is more than 10 percent, the interest rate of loan B, for holding periods of less than eight years.

The equity yields produced with this financing alternative increase for holding periods of less than approximately five years because the effective interest rate decreases significantly for each additional period up to that time. The decreasing loan-to-value ratio becomes the dominant influence on equity yield for longer holding periods. The benefit of positive leverage declines for long holding periods as it does for the other alternative loans; therefore, the equity yield will be less for longer holding periods.

Conclusion

It is obvious that the anticipated holding period of an investment can be an important consideration in the selection among financing alternatives. The effective interest rate and amortization terms affect the volatility of equity yield over time. An understanding of the influence of interest rates and repayment terms over time will assist in negotiating financing terms which are most consistent with investment objectives.

CASE STUDY 12: FMRR ANALYSIS

The financial management rate of return (FMRR) model was designed to provide a flexible analytical framework which can reflect present and anticipated market realities in the form of cash flow projections.

Recall from Chapter 4 that all cash flows processed within the context of the FMRR model are after tax and after all available financing. Cash flows may be modified with after-tax discount and compounding rates commensurate with the investment amount, level of risk and duration of the investment. The "safe rates" used to discount projected after-tax cash outflows are chosen to reflect anticipated after-tax market yields for investments which provide *both* liquidity and preservation of capital.

After-tax yields on reinvested after-tax cash inflows are based on the investor's risk and liquidity preferences. Yields on safe or speculative investments change with market conditions. An analyst may choose a reinvestment rate based on treasury bill or municipal bond yields as of the date of the analysis or he may use the average yield on AA utility bonds in the past ten years. FMRR analysis can incorporate an investor's total investment portfolio management strategy, including risk preference, with the current and anticipated economic environment in choosing among investment alternatives based upon estimated future wealth.

Situation

Consider a client with a total of $100,000 available to invest who is trying to choose between two investment alternatives. The cash flows after taxes for each are summarized in the following table.

FMRR Analysis

Investment A has a greater IRR with half the initial investment of investment B. If A is acquired, some provisions must be made to meet the $30,000 cash outflow EOY 2. Investment B has a duration of only four years, compared to six years for investment A. The after-tax cash flows must be modified for the time and size disparities in order to compare the investment alternatives on a par basis, assuming that each has similar risk characteristics.

EOY	Investment A	Investment B
0	($50,000)	($100,000)
1	5,000	–0–
2	(30,000)	–0–
3	10,000	–0–
4	30,000	200,000
5	35,000	–0–
6	115,000	–0–
IRR	22.3%	18.9%

Three after-tax investment rates will be used to adjust the cash flows. Cash required to meet future obligations will be invested in treasury bonds at an after-tax yield of 7 percent. After-tax income from investments will be reinvested at an after-tax rate of 12 percent. At any time in the future the investor can buy limited partnership shares in block amounts of $60,000 which will produce an after-tax yield of 18 percent.

The after-tax cash flows for investment A are modified in a three-step procedure.

Step 1 Modify cash outflows. The $5,000.00 received EOY 1 will be invested at the safe rate of 7 percent and will grow to $5,350 by EOY 2. The $30,000 cash outflow at EOY 2 will be reduced by that amount, leaving a balance of ($24,650). This amount must be available EOY 2 from a safe investment of $21,530.26 (the present value of $24,650 discounted at 7 percent for two years) made EOY 0 to anticipate the payment. The actual initial investment is $71,530.26: $50,000 plus the reserve account balance EOY 0 of $21,530.26.

EOY	Cash Flows	Adjustments			Modified Cash Flows
0	($50,000)		+($21,530.26)		($71,530.26)
1	5,000	7%	↑ 7%		–0–
2	(30,000)	↓	= ($24,650)		–0–
3	10,000	+$5,350			10,000
4	30,000				30,000
5	35,000				35,000
6	115,000				115,000

Step 2 Adjust for investment size disparity. Investment B required an initial investment of $100,000 compared to $71,530.26 for investment A. If investment A is acquired, the investor will have $28,469.74 ($100,000 − $71,530.26) to invest at 12 percent.

Step 3 Adjust for reinvestment income. The remaining $28,469.74 of the $100,000 investment base grows at 12 percent to $39,997.93 by EOY 3. The $10,000 after-tax investment income plus $39,997.93 grows at 12 percent to $55,997.68 by EOY 4. The $55,997.68 plus investment income of $30,000 totals $85,997.68 by EOY 4. At EOY 4 the investor will purchase one limited partnership share for $60,000 which grows at 18 percent to $83,544 by EOY 6. The remaining $25,997.68 grows at 12 percent to $29,117.40 by EOY 5. The $35,000 investment income EOY 5 plus $29,117.40 is $64,117.40, enough money to buy another limited partnership share for $60,000. The balance of $4,117.40 ($64,117.40 − $60,000) is invested at 12 percent and grows to $4,611.49 by EOY 6. Total wealth by EOY 6 from investment alternative A is estimated to be $273,955.49. This is the sum of the $115,000 investment income, plus $4,611.49, plus $70,800 (from the second limited partnership share), plus $83,544 (from the first limited partnership share).

Investment A				
EOY	Cash Flows	Adjustments		Modified Cash Flows
0	($71,530.26) + ($28,469.74)		=	($100,000)
1	–0–			–0–
2	–0–	↓ 12%		–0–
3	10,000 +	39,997.93 = 49,997.93		–0–
		12% ↙ ↓		
4	30,000 +	55,997.68 = 85,997.68		–0–
		= 25,997.68 +	60,000	
		↓ 12%		
5	35,000 +	29,117.40 = 64,117.40	↓	–0–
		= 4,117.40 + 60,000	18%	
		↓ 12% 18%	↓	
6	115,000 +	4,611.49 + 70,800 +	83,544 =	$273,955.49

Step 4 Adjust cash flows of Investment B for the time disparity.   The $200,000 received at EOY 4 will be used to buy three limited partnership shares at $60,000 each. Thus, $180,000 (three shares times $60,000) is compounded forward at 18 percent for two years at $250,632. The remaining $20,000 ($200,000 − $180,000) is compounded at 12 percent to $25,088. Total wealth at EOY 6 from investment alternative B is estimated to be $275,720: the $250,632 from limited partnership shares plus $25,088.

Investment B				
EOY	Cash Flows	Adjustments		Modified Cash Flows
0	($100,000)			($100,000)
1	–0–			–0–
3	–0–			–0–
4	$200,000	= $180,000 + $20,000		–0–
5	–0–	↓ 18% ↓ 12%		–0–
6	–0–	$250,632 + $25,088 =		$275,720

Comparing the Investment Alternatives

Investment alternatives A and B can now be compared. The total available initial investment base of $100,000 was assumed to have been fully invested in both investment analyses. Only after-tax cash flows and after-tax rates of return were used. Some cash was invested in a safe and liquid investment to meet the $30,000 future obligation for alternative A. After-tax income was reinvested to earn yields consistent with the economic environment and the investor's financial objectives and risk preferences. Cash flows from investment B were adjusted for the time disparity between the alternatives. Results of the comparison are summarized below.

	Investment A		Investment B	
EOY	Cash Flows	Modified Cash Flows	Cash Flows	Modified Cash Flows
0	($50,000)	(100,000)	($100,000)	($100,000)
1	$5,000	–0–	–0–	–0–
2	($30,000)	–0–	–0–	–0–
3	$10,000	–0–	–0–	–0–
4	$30,000	–0–	$200,000	–0–
5	$35,000	–0–	–0–	–0–
6	$115,000	$273,955.49	–0–	$275,720
IRR	22.3%		18.9%	
FMRR	18.3%		18.4%	

Future wealth will be maximized with investment B based upon the assumptions employed in this analysis. The IRR of investment A is greater than the IRR of investment B. However, the IRR is the *internal* rate earned on capital which remains at risk in the investment. The geometric mean compound rate of growth of wealth, measured by FMRR, will be lower if investment income is reinvested at a rate lower than the IRR. Different financial management assumptions with regard to the after-tax yields on safe or more speculative investments may indicate a different conclusion.

To summarize, the factors which may be imputed in the estimate of future wealth using the FMRR model are

- Alternative reinvestment and safe rates may be used to reflect the economic environment.

- Several criteria should be considered when selecting after-tax reinvestment rates for cash flows.

- Before-tax market yields should be adjusted for the investor's particular tax posture.

- Investment duration may affect the yield as well as the amount of capital available for investment.

- Risk and liquidity have a fundamental impact on the reinvestment rates used in the analysis.

APPENDIX A
Compound Interest Tables

The tables are reprinted from *Ellwood Tables for Real Appraising and Financing,* 4th edition, by L. W. Ellwood, with the permission of the American Institute of Real Estate Appraisers.

EFFECTIVE RATE = 5/12%   **BASE = 1.00416666 +**

MONTHS	1 Amount of 1 at Compound Interest $S^n = (1 + i)^n$	2 Accumulation of 1 Per Period $S_n = \dfrac{S^n - 1}{i}$	3 Sinking Fund Factor $1\,S_n = \dfrac{i}{S^n\,1}$	4 Pres. Value Reversion of 1 $V^n = \dfrac{1}{S^n}$	5 Present Value Ord. Annuity 1 Per Period $e_n = \dfrac{1 - V^n}{i}$	6 Instalment to Amortize 1 $1\,e_n = \dfrac{i}{1 - V^n}$	n MONTHS
1	1.004167	1.000000	1.000000	.995851	.995851	1.004167	1
2	1.008351	2.004167	.498960	.991718	1.987569	.503127	2
3	1.012552	3.012517	.331948	.987603	2.975173	.336115	3
4	1.016771	4.025070	.248443	.983506	3.958678	.252610	4
5	1.021008	5.041841	.198340	.979425	4.938103	.202507	5
6	1.025262	6.062848	.164939	.975361	5.913463	.169106	6
7	1.029534	7.088110	.141081	.971313	6.884777	.145248	7
8	1.033824	8.117644	.123188	.967283	7.852060	.127355	8
9	1.038131	9.151467	.109272	.963269	8.815329	.113439	9
10	1.042457	10.189599	.098139	.959272	9.774602	.102306	10
11	1.046800	11.232055	.089031	.955292	10.729894	.093198	11
YEARS							
1	1.051162	12.278855	.081441	.951328	11.681222	.085608	12
2	1.104941	25.185921	.039705	.905025	22.793898	.043872	24
3	1.161472	38.753336	.025804	.860976	33.365701	.029971	36
4	1.220895	53.014885	.018863	.819071	43.422956	.023030	48
5	1.283359	68.006083	.014705	.779205	52.990706	.018872	60
6	1.349018	83.764259	.011938	.741280	62.092777	.016105	72
7	1.418036	100.328653	.009967	.705201	70.751835	.014134	84
8	1.490585	117.740513	.008493	.670877	78.989441	.012660	96
9	1.566847	136.043196	.007351	.638225	86.826108	.011518	108
10	1.647010	155.282280	.006440	.607161	94.281350	.010607	120
11	1.731274	175.505671	.005698	.577609	101.373733	.009865	132
12	1.819849	196.763730	.005082	.549496	108.120917	.009249	144
13	1.912956	219.109392	.004564	.522751	114.539704	.008731	156
14	2.010826	242.598300	.004122	.497308	120.646077	.008289	168
15	2.113704	267.288945	.003741	.473103	126.455243	.007908	180
16	2.221845	293.242810	.003410	.450076	131.981666	.007577	192
17	2.335519	320.524524	.003120	.428170	137.239108	.007287	204
18	2.455008	349.202023	.002864	.407331	142.240661	.007031	216
19	2.580611	379.346717	.002636	.387505	146.998780	.006803	228
20	2.712640	411.033670	.002433	.368645	151.525313	.006600	240
21	2.851424	444.341789	.002251	.350702	155.831531	.006418	252
22	2.997308	479.354014	.002086	.333633	159.928159	.006253	264
23	3.150656	516.157530	.001937	.317394	163.825396	.006104	276
24	3.311850	554.843985	.001802	.301946	167.532948	.005969	288
25	3.481290	595.509712	.001679	.287250	171.060047	.005846	300
26	3.659400	638.255975	.001567	.273269	174.415476	.005734	312
27	3.846622	683.189218	.001464	.259968	177.607590	.005631	324
28	4.043422	730.421330	.00'369	.247315	180.644338	.005536	336
29	4.250291	780.069928	.001282	.235278	183.533282	.005449	348
30	4.467744	832.258641	.001202	.223827	186.281617	.005369	360
31	4.696323	887.117429	.001127	.212933	188.896185	.005294	372
32	4.936595	944.782896	.001058	.202569	191.383497	.005225	384
33	5.189161	1005.398638	.000995	.192709	193.749748	.005162	396
34	5.454648	1069.115596	.000935	.183330	196.000829	.005102	408
35	5.733719	1136.092435	.000880	.174407	198.142346	.005047	420
36	6.027066	1206.495936	.000829	.165918	200.179632	.004996	432
37	6.335423	1280.501414	.000781	.157843	202.117759	.004948	444
38	6.659555	1358.293153	.000736	.150160	203.961554	.004903	456
39	7.000270	1440.064865	.000694	.142852	205.715609	.004861	468
40	7.358417	1526.020172	.000655	.135899	207.384290	.004822	480
41	7.734888	1616.373117	.000619	.129284	208.971754	.004786	492
42	8.130620	1711.348689	.000584	.122992	210.481953	.004751	504
43	8.546598	1811.183392	.000552	.117006	211.918649	.004719	516
44	8.983858	1916.125828	.000522	.111311	213.285417	.004689	528
45	9.443489	2026.437318	.000493	.105893	214.585663	.004660	540
46	9.926636	2142.392554	.000467	.100739	215.822623	.004634	552
47	10.434501	2264.280279	.000442	.095836	216.999379	.004609	564
48	10.968350	2392.404012	.000418	.091171	218.118860	.004585	576
49	11.529512	2527.082798	.000396	.086734	219.183853	.004563	588
50	12.119383	2668.652007	.000375	.082512	220.197012	.004542	600

EFFECTIVE RATE = 1¼% BASE = 1.0125

	1 Amount of 1 at Compound Interest $S^n = (1 + i)^n$	2 Accumulation of 1 Per Period $S_n = \dfrac{S^n - 1}{i}$	3 Sinking Fund Factor $1\,S_n = \dfrac{i}{S^n\,1}$	4 Pres. Value Reversion of 1 $V^n = \dfrac{1}{S^n}$	5 Present Value Ord. Annuity 1 Per Period $e_n = \dfrac{1 - V^n}{i}$	6 Instalment to Amortize 1 $1\,e_n = \dfrac{i}{1 - V^n}$	n QUARTERS
QUARTERS							
1	1.012500	1.000000	1.000000	.987654	.987654	1.012500	1
2	1.025156	2.012500	.496894	.975461	1.963115	.509394	2
3	1.037971	3.037656	.329201	.963418	2.926534	.341701	3
YEARS							
1	1.050945	4.075627	.245361	.951524	3.878058	.257861	4
2	1.104486	8.358888	.119633	.905398	7.568124	.132133	8
3	1.160755	12.860361	.077758	.861509	11.079312	.090258	12
4	1.219890	17.591164	.056847	.819746	14.420292	.069347	16
5	1.282037	22.562979	.044320	.780009	17.599316	.056820	20
6	1.347351	27.788084	.035987	.742197	20.624235	.048487	24
7	1.415992	33.279384	.030049	.706219	23.502518	.042549	28
8	1.488131	39.050441	.025608	.671984	26.241274	.038108	32
9	1.563944	45.115506	.022165	.639409	28.847267	.034665	36
10	1.643619	51.489557	.019421	.608413	31.326933	.031921	40
11	1.727354	58.188337	.017186	.578920	33.686395	.029686	44
12	1.815355	65.228388	.015331	.550856	35.931481	.027831	48
13	1.907839	72.627097	.013769	.524153	38.067734	.026269	52
14	2.005034	80.402736	.012437	.498745	40.100431	.024937	56
15	2.107181	88.574508	.011290	.474568	42.034592	.023790	60
16	2.214532	97.162593	.010292	.451563	43.874992	.022792	64
17	2.327353	106.188201	.009417	.429673	45.626178	.021917	68
18	2.445920	115.673621	.008645	.408844	47.292474	.021145	72
19	2.570529	125.642280	.007959	.389025	48.877995	.020459	76
20	2.701485	136.118795	.007347	.370167	50.386657	.019847	80
21	2.839113	147.129040	.006797	.352223	51.822185	.019297	84
22	2.983753	158.700206	.006301	.335148	53.188125	.018801	88
23	3.135761	170.860868	.005853	.318902	54.487850	.018353	92
24	3.295513	183.641059	.005445	.303443	55.724570	.017945	96
25	3.463404	197.072342	.005074	.288733	56.901339	.017574	100
26	3.639849	211.187886	.004735	.274737	58.021064	.017235	104
27	3.825282	226.022551	.004424	.261419	59.086509	.016924	108
28	4.020162	241.612973	.004139	.248746	60.100305	.016639	112
29	4.224971	257.997654	.003876	.236688	61.064957	.016376	116
30	4.440213	275.217058	.003633	.225214	61.982847	.016133	120
31	4.666421	293.313711	.003409	.214297	62.856242	.015909	124
32	4.904154	312.332304	.003202	.203909	63.687298	.015702	128
33	5.153998	332.319805	.003009	.194024	64.478068	.015509	132
34	5.416570	353.325577	.002830	.184619	65.230505	.015330	136
35	5.692519	375.401494	.002664	.175669	65.946467	.015164	140
36	5.982526	398.602077	.002509	.167153	66.627722	.015009	144
37	6.287308	422.984621	.002364	.159051	67.275953	.014864	148
38	6.607617	448.609342	.002229	.151340	67.892760	.014729	152
39	6.944244	475.539523	.002103	.144004	68.479668	.014603	156
40	7.298021	503.841671	.001985	.137023	69.038124	.014485	160
41	7.669821	533.585681	.001874	.130381	69.569509	.014374	164
42	8.060563	564.845011	.001770	.124061	70.075135	.014270	168
43	8.471211	597.696857	.001673	.118047	70.556250	.014173	172
44	8.902779	632.222352	.001582	.112324	71.014042	.014082	176
45	9.356334	668.506759	.001496	.106879	71.449643	.013996	180
46	9.832996	706.639689	.001415	.101698	71.864128	.013915	184
47	10.333941	746.715313	.001339	.096768	72.258520	.013839	188
48	10.860408	788.832603	.001268	.092078	72.633794	.013768	192
49	11.413695	833.095572	.001200	.087614	72.990876	.013700	196
50	11.995169	879.613534	.001137	.083367	73.330649	.013637	200
51	12.606267	928.501369	.001077	.079326	73.653950	.013577	204
52	13.248498	979.879811	.001021	.075480	73.961580	.013521	208
53	13.923447	1033.875745	.000967	.071821	74.254296	.013467	212
54	14.632781	1090.622520	.000917	.068340	74.532824	.013417	216
55	15.378253	1150.260278	.000869	.065027	74.797849	.013369	220
56	16.161704	1212.936303	.000824	.061875	75.050027	.013324	224
57	16.985067	1278.805378	.000782	.058875	75.289980	.013282	228
58	17.850377	1348.030176	.000742	.056021	75.518302	.013242	232
59	18.759771	1420.781655	.000704	.053306	75.735556	.013204	236
60	19.715494	1497.239482	.000668	.050722	75.942278	.013168	240

EFFECTIVE RATE = 2½%   BASE = 1.025

HALF YEARS	1 Amount of 1 at Compound Interest $S^n = (1 + i)^n$	2 Accumulation of 1 Per Period $S_{\overline{n}} = \dfrac{S^n - 1}{i}$	3 Sinking Fund Factor $1\,S_{\overline{n}} = \dfrac{i}{S^n\,1}$	4 Pres. Value Reversion of 1 $V^n = \dfrac{1}{S^n}$	5 Present Value Ord. Annuity 1 Per Period $e_{\overline{n}} = \dfrac{1 - V^n}{i}$	6 Instalment to Amortize 1 $1\,e_{\overline{n}} = \dfrac{i}{1 - V^n}$	n HALF YEARS
1	1.025000	1.000000	1.000000	.975610	.975610	1.025000	1

YEARS							
1	1.050625	2.025000	.493827	.951814	1.927424	.518827	2
2	1.103813	4.152516	.240818	.905951	3.761974	.265818	4
3	1.159693	6.387737	.156550	.862297	5.508125	.181550	6
4	1.218403	8.736116	.114467	.820747	7.170137	.139467	8
5	1.280085	11.203382	.089259	.781198	8.752064	.114259	10
6	1.344889	13.795553	.072487	.743556	10.257765	.097487	12
7	1.412974	16.518953	.060537	.707727	11.690912	.085537	14
8	1.484506	19.380225	.051599	.673625	13.055003	.076599	16
9	1.559659	22.386349	.044670	.641166	14.353364	.069670	18
10	1.638616	25.544658	.039147	.610271	15.589162	.064147	20
11	1.721571	28.862856	.034647	.580865	16.765413	.059647	22
12	1.808726	32.349038	.030913	.552875	17.884986	.055913	24
13	1.900293	36.011708	.027769	.526235	18.950611	.052769	26
14	1.996495	39.859801	.025088	.500878	19.964889	.050088	28
15	2.097568	43.902703	.022778	.476743	20.930293	.047778	30
16	2.203757	48.150278	.020768	.453771	21.849178	.045768	32
17	2.315322	52.612885	.019007	.431905	22.723786	.044007	34
18	2.432535	57.301413	.017452	.411094	23.556251	.042452	36
19	2.555682	62.227297	.016070	.391285	24.348603	.041070	38
20	2.685064	67.402554	.014836	.372431	25.102775	.039836	40
21	2.820995	72.839808	.013729	.354485	25.820607	.038729	42
22	2.963808	78.552323	.012730	.337404	26.503849	.037730	44
23	3.113851	84.554034	.011827	.321146	27.154170	.036827	46
24	3.271490	90.859582	.011006	.305671	27.773154	.036006	48
25	3.437109	97.484349	.010258	.290942	28.362312	.035258	50
26	3.611112	104.444494	.009574	.276923	28.923081	.034574	52
27	3.793925	111.756996	.008948	.263579	29.456829	.033948	54
28	3.985992	119.439694	.008372	.250879	29.964858	.033372	56
29	4.187783	127.511329	.007842	.238790	30.448407	.032842	58
30	4.399790	135.991590	.007353	.227284	30.908656	.032353	60
31	4.622529	144.901164	.006901	.216332	31.346728	.031901	62
32	4.856545	154.261786	.006482	.205908	31.763691	.031482	64
33	5.102407	164.096289	.006094	.195986	32.160563	.031094	66
34	5.360717	174.428663	.005733	.186542	32.538311	.030733	68
35	5.632103	185.284114	.005397	.177554	32.897857	.030397	70
36	5.917228	196.689122	.005084	.168998	33.240078	.030084	72
37	6.216788	208.671509	.004792	.160855	33.565809	.029792	74
38	6.531513	221.260504	.004520	.153104	33.875844	.029520	76
39	6.862170	234.486817	.004265	.145726	34.170940	.029265	78
40	7.209568	248.382713	.004026	.138705	34.451817	.029026	80
41	7.574552	262.982087	.003803	.132021	34.719160	.028803	82
42	7.958014	278.320556	.003593	.125659	34.973620	.028593	84
43	8.360888	294.435534	.003396	.119605	35.215819	.028396	86
44	8.784158	311.366333	.003212	.113941	35.446348	.028212	88
45	9.228856	329.154253	.003038	.108356	35.665768	.028038	90
46	9.696067	347.842687	.002875	.103135	35.874616	.027875	92
47	10.186931	367.477223	.002721	.098165	36.073400	.027721	94
48	10.702644	388.105758	.002577	.093435	36.262606	.027577	96
49	11.244465	409.778612	.002440	.088933	36.442694	.027440	98
50	11.813716	432.548654	.002312	.084647	36.614105	.027312	100
51	12.411786	456.471430	.002191	.080569	36.777257	.027191	102
52	13.040132	481.605296	.002076	.076686	36.932546	.027076	104
53	13.700289	508.011564	.001968	.072991	37.080354	.026968	106
54	14.393866	535.754649	.001867	.069474	37.221039	.026867	108
55	15.122556	564.902228	.001770	.066126	37.354944	.026770	110
56	15.888135	595.525404	.001679	.062940	37.482398	.026679	112
57	16.692472	627.698877	.001593	.059907	37.603710	.026593	114
58	17.537528	661.501133	.001512	.057021	37.719177	.026512	116
59	18.425366	697.014628	.001435	.054273	37.829080	.026435	118
60	19.358150	734.325993	.001362	.051658	37.933687	.026362	120

EFFECTIVE RATE = 5%   BASE = 1.05

YEARS	1 Amount of 1 at Compound Interest $S^n = (1 + i)^n$	2 Accumulation of 1 Per Period $S_{\overline{n}} = \dfrac{S^n - 1}{i}$	3 Sinking Fund Factor $1\,S_{\overline{n}} = \dfrac{i}{S^n - 1}$	4 Pres. Value Reversion of 1 $V^n = \dfrac{1}{S^n}$	5 Present Value Ord. Annuity 1 Per Period $e_{\overline{n}} = \dfrac{1 - V^n}{i}$	6 Instalment to Amortize 1 $1/e_{\overline{n}} = \dfrac{i}{1 - V^n}$	n YEARS
1	1.050000	1.000000	1.000000	.952381	.952381	1.050000	1
2	1.102500	2.050000	.487805	.907029	1.859410	.537805	2
3	1.157625	3.152500	.317209	.863838	2.723248	.367209	3
4	1.215506	4.310125	.232012	.822702	3.545951	.282012	4
5	1.276282	5.525631	.180975	.783526	4.329477	.230975	5
6	1.340096	6.801913	.147017	.746215	5.075692	.197017	6
7	1.407100	8.142008	.122820	.710681	5.786373	.172820	7
8	1.477455	9.549109	.104722	.676839	6.463213	.154722	8
9	1.551328	11.026564	.090690	.644609	7.107822	.140690	9
10	1.628895	12.577893	.079505	.613913	7.721735	.129505	10
11	1.710339	14.206787	.070389	.584679	8.306414	.120389	11
12	1.795856	15.917127	.062825	.556837	8.863252	.112825	12
13	1.885649	17.712983	.056456	.530321	9.393573	.106456	13
14	1.979932	19.598632	.051024	.505068	9.898641	.101024	14
15	2.078928	21.578564	.046342	.481017	10.379658	.096342	15
16	2.182875	23.657492	.042270	.458112	10.837770	.092270	16
17	2.292018	25.840366	.038699	.436297	11.274066	.088699	17
18	2.406619	28.132385	.035546	.415521	11.689587	.085546	18
19	2.526950	30.539004	.032745	.395734	12.085321	.082745	19
20	2.653298	33.065954	.030243	.376889	12.462210	.080243	20
21	2.785963	35.719252	.027996	.358942	12.821153	.077996	21
22	2.925261	38.505214	.025971	.341850	13.163003	.075971	22
23	3.071524	41.430475	.024137	.325571	13.488574	.074137	23
24	3.225100	44.501999	.022471	.310068	13.798642	.072471	24
25	3.386355	47.727099	.020952	.295303	14.093945	.070952	25
26	3.555673	51.113454	.019564	.281241	14.375185	.069564	26
27	3.733456	54.669126	.018292	.267848	14.643034	.068292	27
28	3.920129	58.402583	.017123	.255094	14.898127	.067123	28
29	4.116136	62.322712	.016046	.242946	15.141074	.066046	29
30	4.321942	66.438848	.015051	.231377	15.372451	.065051	30
31	4.538039	70.760790	.014132	.220359	15.592811	.064132	31
32	4.764941	75.298829	.013280	.209866	15.802677	.063280	32
33	5.003189	80.063771	.012490	.199873	16.002549	.062490	33
34	5.253348	85.066959	.011755	.190355	16.192904	.061755	34
35	5.516015	90.320307	.011072	.181290	16.374194	.061072	35
36	5.791816	95.836323	.010434	.172657	16.546852	.060434	36
37	6.081407	101.628139	.009840	.164436	16.711287	.059840	37
38	6.385477	107.709546	.009284	.156605	16.867893	.059284	38
39	6.704751	114.095023	.008765	.149148	17.017041	.058765	39
40	7.039989	120.799774	.008278	.142046	17.159086	.058278	40
41	7.391988	127.839763	.007822	.135282	17.294368	.057822	41
42	7.761588	135.231751	.007395	.128840	17.423208	.057395	42
43	8.149667	142.993339	.006993	.122704	17.545912	.056993	43
44	8.557150	151.143006	.006616	.116861	17.662773	.056616	44
45	8.985008	159.700156	.006262	.111297	17.774070	.056262	45
46	9.434258	168.685164	.005928	.105997	17.880067	.055928	46
47	9.905971	178.119422	.005614	.100949	17.981016	.055614	47
48	10.401270	188.025393	.005318	.096142	18.077158	.055318	48
49	10.921333	198.426663	.005040	.091564	18.168722	.055040	49
50	11.467400	209.347996	.004777	.087204	18.255925	.054777	50
51	12.040770	220.815395	.004529	.083051	18.388977	.054529	51
52	12.642808	232.856165	.004294	.079096	18.418073	.054294	52
53	13.274949	245.498974	.004073	.075330	18.493403	.054073	53
54	13.938696	258.773922	.003864	.071743	18.565146	.053864	54
55	14.635631	272.712618	.003667	.068326	18.633472	.053667	55
56	15.367412	287.348249	.003480	.065073	18.698545	.053480	56
57	16.135783	302.715662	.003303	.061974	18.760519	.053303	57
58	16.942572	318.851445	.003136	.059023	18.819542	.053136	58
59	17.789701	335.794017	.002978	.056212	18.875754	.052978	59
60	18.679186	353.583718	.002828	.053536	18.929290	.052828	60

EFFECTIVE RATE = 5/6%   **BASE = 1.00833333**

MONTHS	1 Amount of 1 at Compound Interest $S^n = (1 + i)^n$	2 Accumulation of 1 Per Period $S_{\overline{n}} = \dfrac{S^n - 1}{i}$	3 Sinking Fund Factor $1/S_{\overline{n}} = \dfrac{i}{S^n - 1}$	4 Pres. Value Reversion of 1 $V^n = \dfrac{1}{S^n}$	5 Present Value Ord. Annuity 1 Per Period $e_{\overline{n}} = \dfrac{1 - V^n}{i}$	6 Instalment to Amortize 1 $1/e_{\overline{n}} = \dfrac{i}{1 - V^n}$	n MONTHS
1	1.008333	1.000000	1.000000	.991735	.991735	1.008333	1
2	1.016736	2.008333	.497925	.983539	1.975274	.506258	2
3	1.025208	3.025069	.330570	.975410	2.950685	.338904	3
4	1.033752	4.050278	.246896	.967349	3.918035	.255229	4
5	1.042366	5.084030	.196694	.959355	4.877390	.205027	5
6	1.051053	6.126397	.163228	.951426	5.828817	.171561	6
7	1.059812	7.177450	.139325	.943563	6.772380	.147658	7
8	1.068643	8.237262	.121399	.935765	7.708146	.129732	8
9	1.077549	9.305906	.107458	.928031	8.636177	.115791	9
10	1.086528	10.383456	.096307	.920362	9.556540	.104640	10
11	1.095583	11.469984	.087184	.912755	10.469295	.095517	11
YEARS							
1	1.104713	12.565568	.079582	.905212	11.374508	.087915	12
2	1.220390	26.446915	.037811	.819409	21.670854	.046144	24
3	1.348181	41.781821	.023933	.741739	30.991235	.032267	36
4	1.489354	58.722491	.017029	.671432	39.428160	.025362	48
5	1.645308	77.437072	.012913	.607788	47.065369	.021247	60
6	1.817594	98.111313	.010192	.550177	53.978665	.018525	72
7	2.007920	120.950418	.008267	.498027	60.236667	.016601	84
8	2.218175	146.181075	.006840	.450820	65.901488	.015174	96
9	2.450447	174.053712	.005745	.408088	71.029355	.014078	108
10	2.707041	204.844978	.004881	.369406	75.671163	.013215	120
11	2.990504	238.860492	.004186	.334391	79.872985	.012519	132
12	3.303648	276.437875	.003617	.302695	83.676528	.011950	144
13	3.649584	317.950100	.003145	.274003	87.119542	.011478	156
14	4.031743	363.809198	.002748	.248031	90.236200	.011082	168
15	4.453919	414.470344	.002412	.224521	93.057438	.010746	180
16	4.920303	470.436373	.002125	.203239	95.611258	.010459	192
17	5.435523	532.262776	.001878	.183974	97.923008	.010212	204
18	6.004693	600.563212	.001665	.166536	100.015632	.009998	216
19	6.633463	676.015596	.001479	.150750	101.909902	.009812	228
20	7.328073	759.368830	.001316	.136461	103.624619	.009650	240
21	8.095418	851.450237	.001174	.123526	105.176801	.009507	252
22	8.943114	953.173772	.001049	.111817	106.581857	.009382	264
23	9.879575	1065.549089	.000938	.101218	107.853729	.009271	276
24	10.914096	1189.691570	.000840	.091624	109.005045	.009173	288
25	12.056944	1326.833392	.000753	.082939	110.047230	.009087	300
26	13.319464	1478.335753	.000676	.075078	110.990629	.009009	312
27	14.714186	1645.702391	.000607	.067961	111.844605	.008940	324
28	16.254954	1830.594505	.000546	.061519	112.617636	.008879	336
29	17.957060	2034.847238	.000491	.055688	113.317391	.008824	348
30	19.837399	2260.487900	.000442	.050409	113.950820	.008775	360
31	21.914633	2509.756088	.000398	.045631	114.524207	.008731	372
32	24.209382	2785.125915	.000359	.041306	115.043244	.008692	384
33	26.744421	3089.330559	.000323	.037390	115.513303	.008657	396
34	29.544911	3425.389403	.000291	.033846	115.938387	.008625	408
35	32.638649	3796.638004	.000263	.030638	116.323378	.008596	420
36	36.056343	4206.761180	.000237	.027734	116.671875	.008571	432
37	39.831913	4659.829611	.000214	.025105	116.987341	.008547	444
38	44.002835	5160.340233	.000193	.022725	117.272903	.008527	456
39	48.610506	5713.260852	.000175	.020571	117.531398	.008508	468
40	53.700662	6324.079483	.000158	.018621	117.765390	.008491	480
41	59.323823	6998.858807	.000142	.016856	117.977204	.008476	492
42	65.535802	7744.296352	.000129	.015258	118.168940	.008462	504
43	72.398257	8567.790939	.000116	.013812	118.342502	.008450	516
44	79.979301	9477.516170	.000105	.012503	118.499611	.008438	528
45	88.354179	10482.501530	.000095	.011318	118.641830	.008428	540
46	97.606016	11592.721980	.000086	.010245	118.770568	.008419	552
47	107.826641	12819.197020	.000078	.009274	118.887103	.008411	564
48	119.117499	14174.100030	.000070	.008395	118.992592	.008403	576
49	131.590658	15670.879080	.000063	.007599	119.088082	.008397	588
50	145.369919	17324.390450	.000057	.006879	119.174520	.008391	600

EFFECTIVE RATE = 2½%   BASE = 1.025

	1 Amount of 1 at Compound Interest $S^n = (1 + i)^n$	2 Accumulation of 1 Per Period $S_n = \dfrac{S^n - 1}{i}$	3 Sinking Fund Factor $1/S_n = \dfrac{i}{S^n - 1}$	4 Pres. Value Reversion of 1 $V^n = \dfrac{1}{S^n}$	5 Present Value Ord. Annuity 1 Per Period $e_n = \dfrac{1 - V^n}{i}$	6 Instalment to Amortize 1 $1/e_n = \dfrac{i}{1 - V^n}$	n
QUARTERS							QUARTERS
1	1.025000	1.000000	1.000000	.975610	.975610	1.025000	1
2	1.050625	2.025000	.493827	.951814	1.927424	.518827	2
3	1.076891	3.075625	.325137	.928599	2.856024	.350137	3
YEARS							
1	1.103813	4.152516	.240818	.905951	3.761974	.265818	4
2	1.218403	8.736116	.114467	.820747	7.170137	.139467	8
3	1.344889	13.795553	.072487	.743556	10.257765	.097487	12
4	1.484506	19.380225	.051599	.673625	13.055003	.076599	16
5	1.638616	25.544658	.039147	.610271	15.589162	.064147	20
6	1.808726	32.349038	.030913	.552875	17.884986	.055913	24
7	1.996495	39.859801	.025088	.500878	19.964889	.050088	28
8	2.203757	48.150278	.020768	.453771	21.849178	.045768	32
9	2.432535	57.301413	.017452	.411094	23.556251	.042452	36
10	2.685064	67.402554	.014836	.372431	25.102775	.039836	40
11	2.963808	78.552323	.012730	.337404	26.503849	.037730	44
12	3.271490	90.859583	.011006	.305671	27.773154	.036006	48
13	3.611112	104.444494	.009574	.276923	28.923081	.034574	52
14	3.985992	119.439695	.008372	.250879	29.964858	.033372	56
15	4.399790	135.991590	.007353	.227284	30.908657	.032353	60
16	4.856545	154.261786	.006482	.205908	31.763692	.031482	64
17	5.360717	174.428664	.005733	.186542	32.538311	.030733	68
18	5.917228	196.689123	.005084	.168998	33.240078	.030084	72
19	6.531513	221.260505	.004520	.153104	33.875844	.029520	76
20	7.209568	248.382713	.004026	.138705	34.451817	.029026	80
21	7.958014	278.320556	.003593	.125659	34.973620	.028593	84
22	8.784158	311.366333	.003212	.113841	35.446348	.028212	88
23	9.696067	347.842688	.002875	.103135	35.874616	.027875	92
24	10.702644	388.105759	.002577	.093435	36.262606	.027577	96
25	11.813716	432.548655	.002312	.084647	36.614105	.027312	100
26	13.040132	481.605297	.002076	.076686	36.932546	.027076	104
27	14.393866	535.754651	.001867	.069474	37.221039	.026867	108
28	15.888135	595.525406	.001679	.062940	37.482398	.026679	112
29	17.537528	661.501135	.001512	.057021	37.719177	.026512	116
30	19.358150	734.325996	.001362	.051658	37.933687	.026362	120
31	21.367775	814.711016	.001227	.046799	38.128022	.026227	124
32	23.586026	903.441037	.001107	.042398	38.304081	.026107	128
33	26.034559	1001.382378	.000999	.038410	38.463581	.025999	132
34	28.737282	1109.491294	.000901	.034798	38.608080	.025901	136
35	31.720583	1228.823308	.000814	.031525	38.738989	.025814	140
36	35.013588	1360.543523	.000735	.028560	38.857586	.025735	144
37	38.648450	1505.937994	.000664	.025874	38.965030	.025664	148
38	42.660657	1666.426286	.000600	.023441	39.062368	.025600	152
39	47.089383	1843.575332	.000542	.021236	39.150552	.025542	156
40	51.977868	2039.114732	.000490	.019239	39.230442	.025490	160
41	57.373841	2254.953642	.000443	.017430	39.302818	.025443	164
42	63.329985	2493.199414	.000401	.015790	39.368388	.025401	168
43	69.904454	2756.178168	.000363	.014305	39.427790	.025363	172
44	77.161438	3046.457506	.000328	.012960	39.481606	.025328	176
45	85.171790	3366.871582	.000297	.011741	39.530361	.025297	180
46	94.013719	3720.548769	.000269	.010637	39.574530	.025269	184
47	103.773555	4110.942208	.000243	.009636	39.614545	.025243	188
48	114.546588	4541.863516	.000220	.008730	39.650797	.025220	192
49	126.438000	5017.520012	.000199	.007909	39.683639	.025199	196
50	139.563895	5542.555784	.000180	.007165	39.713393	.025180	200
51	154.052426	6122.097036	.000163	.006491	39.740348	.025163	204
52	170.045054	6761.802144	.000148	.005881	39.764768	.025148	208
53	187.697922	7467.916888	.000134	.005328	39.786892	.025134	212
54	207.183386	8247.335444	.000121	.004827	39.806934	.025121	216
55	228.691692	9107.667692	.000110	.004373	39.825092	.025110	220
56	252.432838	10057.313520	.000099	.003961	39.841542	.025099	224
57	278.638621	11105.544820	.000090	.003589	39.856445	.025090	228
58	307.564901	12262.596050	.000082	.003251	39.869946	.025082	232
59	339.494103	13539.764110	.000074	.002946	39.882178	.025074	236
60	374.737967	14949.518680	.000067	.002669	39.893259	.025067	240

EFFECTIVE RATE = 5%   BASE = 1.05

	1 Amount of 1 at Compound Interest $S^n = (1+i)^n$	2 Accumulation of 1 Per Period $S_{\overline{n}|} = \dfrac{S^n - 1}{i}$	3 Sinking Fund Factor $1/S_{\overline{n}|} = \dfrac{i}{S^n - 1}$	4 Pres. Value Reversion of 1 $V^n = \dfrac{1}{S^n}$	5 Present Value Ord. Annuity 1 Per Period $e_{\overline{n}|} = \dfrac{1 - V^n}{i}$	6 Instalment to Amortize 1 $1/e_{\overline{n}|} = \dfrac{i}{1 - V^n}$	n
HALF YEARS							HALF YEARS
1	1.050000	1.000000	1.000000	.952381	.952381	1.050000	
YEARS							
1	1.102500	2.050000	.487805	.907029	1.859410	.537805	2
2	1.215506	4.310125	.232012	.822702	3.545951	.282012	4
3	1.340096	6.801913	.147017	.746215	5.075692	.197017	6
4	1.477455	9.549109	.104722	.676839	6.463213	.154722	8
5	1.628895	12.577893	.079505	.613913	7.721735	.129505	10
6	1.795856	15.917127	.062825	.556837	8.863252	.112825	12
7	1.979932	19.598632	.051024	.505068	9.898641	.101024	14
8	2.182875	23.657492	.042270	.458112	10.837770	.092270	16
9	2.406619	28.132385	.035546	.415521	11.689587	.085546	18
10	2.653298	33.065954	.030243	.376889	12.462210	.080243	20
11	2.925261	38.505214	.025971	.341850	13.163003	.075971	22
12	3.225100	44.501999	.022471	.310068	13.798642	.072471	24
13	3.555673	51.113454	.019564	.281241	14.375185	.069564	26
14	3.920129	58.402583	.017123	.255094	14.898127	.067123	28
15	4.321942	66.438847	.015051	.231377	15.372451	.065051	30
16	4.764941	75.298829	.013280	.209866	15.802677	.063280	32
17	5.253348	85.066959	.011755	.190355	16.192904	.061755	34
18	5.791816	95.836323	.010434	.172657	16.546852	.060434	36
19	6.385477	107.709546	.009284	.156605	16.867893	.059284	38
20	7.039989	120.799774	.008278	.142046	17.159086	.058278	40
21	7.761588	135.231751	.007395	.128840	17.423208	.057395	42
22	8.557150	151.143005	.006616	.116861	17.662773	.056616	44
23	9.434258	168.685164	.005928	.105997	17.880066	.055928	46
24	10.401270	188.025393	.005318	.096142	18.077158	.055318	48
25	11.467400	209.347996	.004777	.087204	18.255925	.054777	50
26	12.642808	232.856165	.004294	.079096	18.418073	.054294	52
27	13.938696	258.773922	.003864	.071743	18.565146	.053864	54
28	15.367412	287.348249	.003480	.065073	18.698545	.053480	56
29	16.942572	318.851445	.003136	.059023	18.819542	.053136	58
30	18.679186	353.583718	.002828	.053536	18.929290	.052828	60
31	20.593802	391.876049	.002552	.048558	19.028834	.052552	62
32	22.704667	434.093344	.002304	.044044	19.119124	.052304	64
33	25.031896	480.637912	.002081	.039949	19.201019	.052081	66
34	27.597665	531.953298	.001880	.036235	19.275301	.051880	68
35	30.426426	588.528511	.001699	.032866	19.342677	.051699	70
36	33.545134	650.902683	.001536	.029811	19.403788	.051536	72
37	36.983510	719.670208	.001390	.027039	19.459218	.051390	74
38	40.774320	795.486404	.001257	.024525	19.509495	.051257	76
39	44.953688	879.073761	.001138	.022245	19.555098	.051138	78
40	49.561441	971.228821	.001030	.020177	19.596460	.051030	80
41	54.641489	1072.829775	.000932	.018301	19.633978	.050932	82
42	60.242241	1184.844827	.000844	.016600	19.668007	.050844	84
43	66.417071	1308.341422	.000764	.015056	19.698873	.050764	86
44	73.224821	1444.496418	.000692	.013657	19.726869	.050692	88
45	80.730365	1594.607301	.000627	.012387	19.752262	.050627	90
46	89.005227	1760.104549	.000568	.011235	19.775294	.050568	92
47	98.128263	1942.565265	.000515	.010191	19.796185	.050515	94
48	108.186410	2143.728204	.000466	.009243	19.815134	.050466	96
49	119.275517	2365.510344	.000423	.008384	19.832321	.050423	98
50	131.501258	2610.025154	.000383	.007604	19.847910	.050383	100
51	144.980137	2879.602732	.000347	.006897	19.862050	.050347	102
52	159.840601	3176.812012	.000315	.006256	19.874875	.050315	104
53	176.224262	3504.485244	.000285	.005675	19.886508	.050285	106
54	194.287249	3865.744982	.000259	.005147	19.897060	.050259	108
55	214.201692	4264.033842	.000235	.004668	19.906630	.050235	110
56	236.157366	4703.147310	.000213	.004234	19.915311	.050213	112
57	260.363496	5187.269910	.000193	.003841	19.923184	.050193	114
58	287.050754	5721.015076	.000175	.003484	19.930326	.050175	116
59	316.473456	6309.469122	.000158	.003160	19.936804	.050158	118
60	348.911985	6958.239706	.000144	.002866	19.942679	.050144	120

EFFECTIVE RATE = 10%   BASE = 1.10

	1 Amount of 1 at Compound Interest $S^n = (1 + i)^n$	2 Accumulation of 1 Per Period $S_{\overline{n}} = \dfrac{S^n - 1}{i}$	3 Sinking Fund Factor $1/S_{\overline{n}} = \dfrac{i}{S^n - 1}$	4 Pres. Value Reversion of 1 $V^n = \dfrac{1}{S^n}$	5 Present Value Ord. Annuity 1 Per Period $e_{\overline{n}} = \dfrac{1 - V^n}{i}$	6 Instalment to Amortize 1 $1/e_{\overline{n}} = \dfrac{i}{1 - V^n}$	
YEARS							n YEARS
1	1.100000	1.000000	1.000000	.909091	.909091	1.100000	1
2	1.210000	2.100000	.476190	.826446	1.735537	.576190	2
3	1.331000	3.310000	.302115	.751315	2.486852	.402115	3
4	1.464100	4.641000	.215471	.683013	3.169865	.315471	4
5	1.610510	6.105100	.163797	.620921	3.790787	.263797	5
6	1.771561	7.715610	.129607	.564474	4.355261	.229607	6
7	1.948717	9.487171	.105405	.513158	4.868419	.205405	7
8	2.143589	11.435888	.087444	.466507	5.334926	.187444	8
9	2.357948	13.579477	.073641	.424098	5.759024	.173641	9
10	2.593742	15.937425	.062745	.385543	6.144567	.162745	10
11	2.853117	18.531167	.053963	.350494	6.495061	.153963	11
12	3.138428	21.384284	.046763	.318631	6.813692	.146763	12
13	3.452271	24.522712	.040779	.289664	7.103356	.140779	13
14	3.797498	27.974983	.035746	.263331	7.366687	.135746	14
15	4.177248	31.772482	.031474	.239392	7.606080	.131474	15
16	4.594973	35.949730	.027817	.217629	7.823709	.127817	16
17	5.054470	40.544703	.024664	.197845	8.021553	.124664	17
18	5.559917	45.599173	.021930	.179859	8.201412	.121930	18
19	6.115909	51.159090	.019547	.163508	8.364920	.119547	19
20	6.727500	57.274999	.017460	.148644	8.513564	.117460	20
21	7.400250	64.002499	.015624	.135131	8.648694	.115624	21
22	8.140275	71.402749	.014005	.122846	8.771540	.114005	22
23	8.954302	79.543024	.012572	.111678	8.883218	.112572	23
24	9.849733	88.497327	.011300	.101526	8.984744	.111300	24
25	10.834706	98.347059	.010168	.092296	9.077040	.110168	25
26	11.918177	109.181765	.009159	.083905	9.160945	.109159	26
27	13.109994	121.099942	.008258	.076278	9.237223	.108258	27
28	14.420994	134.209936	.007451	.069343	9.306567	.107451	28
29	15.863093	148.630930	.006728	.063039	9.369606	.106728	29
30	17.449402	164.494023	.006079	.057309	9.426914	.106079	30
31	19.194342	181.943425	.005496	.052099	9.479013	.105496	31
32	21.113777	201.137767	.004972	.047362	9.526376	.104972	32
33	23.225154	222.251544	.004499	.043057	9.569432	.104499	33
34	25.547670	245.476699	.004074	.039143	9.608575	.104074	34
35	28.102437	271.024368	.003690	.035584	9.644159	.103690	35
36	30.912681	299.126805	.003343	.032349	9.676508	.103343	36
37	34.003949	330.039486	.003030	.029408	9.705917	.103030	37
38	37.404343	364.043434	.002747	.026735	9.732651	.102747	38
39	41.144778	401.447778	.002491	.024304	9.756956	.102491	39
40	45.259256	442.592556	.002259	.022095	9.779051	.102259	40
41	49.785181	487.851811	.002050	.020086	9.799137	.102050	41
42	54.763699	537.636992	.001860	.018260	9.817397	.101860	42
43	60.240069	592.400692	.001688	.016600	9.833998	.101688	43
44	66.264076	652.640761	.001532	.015091	9.849089	.101532	44
45	72.890484	718.904837	.001391	.013719	9.862808	.101391	45
46	80.179532	791.795321	.001263	.012472	9.875280	.101263	46
47	88.197485	871.974853	.001147	.011338	9.886618	.101147	47
48	97.017234	960.172338	.001041	.010307	9.896926	.101041	48
49	106.718957	1057.189572	.000946	.009370	9.906296	.100946	49
50	117.390853	1163.908529	.000859	.008519	9.914814	.100859	50
51	129.129938	1281.299382	.000780	.007744	9.922559	.100780	51
52	142.042932	1410.429320	.000709	.007040	9.929599	.100709	52
53	156.247225	1552.472252	.000644	.006400	9.935999	.100644	53
54	171.871948	1708.719477	.000585	.005818	9.941817	.100585	54
55	189.059142	1880.591425	.000532	.005289	9.947106	.100532	55
56	207.965057	2069.650567	.000483	.004809	9.951915	.100483	56
57	228.761562	2277.615624	.000439	.004371	9.956286	.100439	57
58	251.637719	2506.377186	.000399	.003974	9.960260	.100399	58
59	276.801490	2758.014905	.000363	.003613	9.963873	.100363	59
60	304.481640	3034.816395	.000330	.003284	9.967157	.100330	60

15%   **ANNUAL COMPOUND INTEREST TABLE**   **15%**

EFFECTIVE RATE = 15%   BASE = 1.15

	1 Amount of 1 at Compound Interest $S^n = (1 + i)^n$	2 Accumulation of 1 Per Period $S_{\overline{n}|} = \dfrac{S^n - 1}{i}$	3 Sinking Fund Factor $1/S_{\overline{n}|} = \dfrac{i}{S^n - 1}$	4 Pres. Value Reversion of 1 $V^n = \dfrac{1}{S^n}$	5 Present Value Ord. Annuity 1 Per Period $e_{\overline{n}|} = \dfrac{1 - V^n}{i}$	6 Instalment to Amortize 1 $1/e_{\overline{n}|} = \dfrac{i}{1 - V^n}$	
YEARS							n YEARS
1	1.150000	1.0000	1.000000	.869565	.869565	1.150000	1
2	1.322500	2.1500	.465116	.756144	1.625709	.615116	2
3	1.520875	3.4725	.287976	.657516	2.283225	.437976	3
4	1.749006	4.9934	.200265	.571753	2.854978	.350265	4
5	2.011357	6.7424	.148315	.497177	3.352155	.298315	5
6	2.313061	8.7537	.114236	.432328	3.784483	.264236	6
7	2.660020	11.0668	.090360	.375937	4.160420	.240360	7
8	3.059023	13.7268	.072850	.326902	4.487322	.222850	8
9	3.517876	16.7858	.059574	.284262	4.771584	.209574	9
10	4.045558	20.3037	.049252	.247185	5.018769	.199252	10
11	4.652391	24.3493	.041068	.214943	5.233712	.191068	11
12	5.350250	29.0017	.034480	.186907	5.420619	.184480	12
13	6.152788	34.3519	.029110	.162528	5.583147	.179110	13
14	7.075706	40.5047	.024688	.141329	5.724476	.174688	14
15	8.137062	47.5804	.021017	.122894	5.847370	.171017	15
16	9.357621	55.7175	.017947	.106865	5.954235	.167947	16
17	10.761264	65.0751	.015366	.092926	6.047161	.165366	17
18	12.375454	75.8364	.013186	.080805	6.127966	.163186	18
19	14.231772	88.2118	.011336	.070265	6.198231	.161336	19
20	16.366537	102.4436	.009761	.061100	6.259331	.159761	20
21	18.821518	118.8101	.008416	.053131	6.312462	.158416	21
22	21.644746	137.6316	.007265	.046201	6.358663	.157265	22
23	24.891458	159.2764	.006278	.040174	6.398837	.156278	23
24	28.625176	184.1678	.005429	.034934	6.433771	.155429	24
25	32.918953	212.7930	.004699	.030378	6.464149	.154699	25
26	37.856796	245.7120	.004069	.026415	6.490564	.154069	26
27	43.535315	283.5688	.003526	.022970	6.513534	.153526	27
28	50.065612	327.1041	.003010	.019974	6.535508	.153010	28
29	57.575454	377.1697	.002651	.017369	6.550877	.152651	29
30	66.211772	434.7451	.002300	.015103	6.565980	.152300	30

20%   ANNUAL COMPOUND INTEREST TABLE   **20%**

EFFECTIVE RATE = 20%   BASE = 1.20

	1 Amount of 1 at Compound Interest $S^n = (1 + i)^n$	2 Accumulation of 1 Per Period $S_{\overline{n}} = \dfrac{S^n - 1}{i}$	3 Sinking Fund Factor $1/S_{\overline{n}} = \dfrac{i}{S^n - 1}$	4 Pres. Value Reversion of 1 $V^n = \dfrac{1}{S^n}$	5 Present Value Ord. Annuity 1 Per Period $e_{\overline{n}} = \dfrac{1 - V^n}{i}$	6 Instalment to Amortize 1 $1/e_{\overline{n}} = \dfrac{i}{1 - V^n}$	
YEARS							n YEARS
1	1.200000	1.000000	1.000000	.833333	.833333	1.200000	1
2	1.440000	2.200000	.454545	.694444	1.527777	.654545	2
3	1.728000	3.640000	.274725	.578704	2.106481	.474725	3
4	2.073600	5.368000	.186289	.482253	2.588734	.386289	4
5	2.488320	7.441600	.134380	.401878	2.990612	.334380	5
6	2.985984	9.929920	.100706	.334898	3.325510	.300706	6
7	3.583181	12.915904	.077424	.279082	3.604592	.277424	7
8	4.299817	16.499085	.060609	.232568	3.837160	.260609	8
9	5.159780	20.798902	.048079	.193807	4.030967	.248079	9
10	6.191736	25.958682	.038523	.161506	4.192473	.238523	10
11	7.430083	32.150418	.031104	.134588	4.327061	.231104	11
12	8.916100	39.580501	.025265	.112157	4.439218	.225265	12
13	10.699320	48.496601	.020620	.093464	4.532682	.220620	13
14	12.839184	59.195921	.016893	.077887	4.610569	.216893	14
15	15.407021	72.035105	.013882	.064905	4.675474	.213882	15
16	18.488514	87.442126	.011436	.054088	4.729562	.211436	16
17	22.186217	105.930640	.009440	.045073	4.774635	.209440	17
18	26.623460	128.116857	.007805	.037561	4.812196	.207805	18
19	31.948153	154.740317	.006462	.031301	4.843497	.206462	19
20	38.337783	186.688470	.005357	.026085	4.869582	.205357	20
21	46.005340	225.026253	.004444	.021737	4.891319	.204444	21
22	55.206408	271.031593	.003690	.018114	4.909433	.203690	22
23	66.247690	326.238001	.003065	.015095	4.924528	.203065	23
24	79.497228	392.485691	.002548	.012579	4.937107	.202548	24
25	95.396675	471.982919	.002119	.010483	4.947590	.202119	25
26	114.476010	567.379594	.001762	.008735	4.956325	.201762	26
27	137.371212	681.855604	.001467	.007280	4.963605	.201467	27
28	164.845454	819.226816	.001221	.006066	4.969671	.201221	28
29	197.814545	984.072270	.001016	.005055	4.974726	.201016	29
30	237.377454	1181.886815	.000846	.004213	4.978939	.200846	30

25%   ANNUAL COMPOUND INTEREST TABLE   **25%**

EFFECTIVE RATE = 25%   BASE = 1.25

YEARS	1 Amount of 1 at Compound Interest $S^n = (1 + i)^n$	2 Accumulation of 1 Per Period $S_{\overline{n}} = \dfrac{S^n - 1}{i}$	3 Sinking Fund Factor $1/S_{\overline{n}} = \dfrac{i}{S^n - 1}$	4 Pres. Value Reversion of 1 $V^n = \dfrac{1}{S^n}$	5 Present Value Ord. Annuity 1 Per Period $e_{\overline{n}} = \dfrac{1 - V^n}{i}$	6 Instalment to Amortize 1 $1/e_{\overline{n}} = \dfrac{i}{1 - V^n}$	n YEARS
1	1.250000	1.000000	1.000000	.800000	.800000	1.250000	1
2	1.562500	2.250000	.444444	.640000	1.440000	.694444	2
3	1.953125	3.812500	.262295	.512000	1.952000	.512295	3
4	2.441406	5.765625	.173442	.409600	2.361600	.423442	4
5	3.051758	8.207031	.121847	.327680	2.689280	.371847	5
6	3.814697	11.258789	.088819	.262144	2.951424	.338819	6
7	4.768372	15.073486	.066342	.209715	3.161139	.316342	7
8	5.960465	19.841858	.050399	.167772	3.328911	.300399	8
9	7.450581	25.802323	.038756	.134218	3.463129	.288756	9
10	9.313226	33.252904	.030073	.107374	3.570503	.280073	10
11	11.641532	42.566130	.023493	.085899	3.656402	.273493	11
12	14.551915	54.207662	.018448	.068719	3.725121	.268448	12
13	18.189893	68.759577	.014544	.054976	3.780097	.264544	13
14	22.737366	86.949470	.011501	.043980	3.824077	.261501	14
15	28.421708	109.686836	.009117	.035184	3.859261	.259117	15
16	35.527134	138.108544	.007241	.028147	3.887408	.257241	16
17	44.408918	173.635678	.005759	.022518	3.909926	.255759	17
18	55.511147	218.044596	.004586	.018014	3.927940	.254586	18
19	69.388934	273.555743	.003656	.014412	3.942352	.253656	19
20	86.736167	342.944677	.002916	.011529	3.953881	.252916	20
21	108.420208	429.680844	.002327	.009223	3.963104	.252327	21
22	135.525260	538.101052	.001858	.007379	3.970483	.251858	22
23	169.406575	673.626312	.001485	.005903	3.976386	.251485	23
24	211.758219	843.032887	.001186	.004722	3.981108	.251186	24
25	264.697727	1054.791106	.000948	.003778	3.984886	.250948	25

Appendix B
Conversion and Expansion
of Tables and Use
of Financial Calculators

The compound interest tables, as published in *Ellwood Tables* (see Appendix A), may be modified or expanded quite simply for use in solving an even greater variety of compound interest and discount problems.

CONVERTING TABLE FACTORS FROM EOP TO BOP

In many instances, compound interest problems involve the receipt or investment of funds at the "beginning of the period" (BOP) rather than at the end of the period (EOP). Of course, column 1 factors of the tables are already based upon the assumption that the investment takes place at the beginning of the period or at the present. Thus, there is generally no need to convert such factors to BOP, although it is possible to do so.

Of much greater relevance is the conversion of those columns which are based upon either receipt or payment (investment) at EOP, columns 2 through 6. Conversion of all columns may be accomplished using the base of the factor as follows.

Columns					
1	2	3	4	5	6
$F_1 \div$ Base	$F_2 \times$ Base	$F_3 \div$ Base	$F_4 \times$ Base	$F_5 \times$ Base	$F_6 \div$ Base

Example

Suppose an investor wishes to invest $10,000 today and each year thereafter for three years at 10-percent compounded annually. How much is accumulated by the end of the third year? It is not appropriate to use the column 2 factor at 10 percent interest compounded annually for three years because this factor of 3.310000 is based on the assumption that the first investment takes place at the end of the first period, not the beginning.

EOP	Amount Invested	Interest Earned From Prior Period	EOP Balance
1	$10,000	–0–	$10,000
2	$10,000	$1,000	$21,000
3	$10,000	$2,100	$33,000

The case described, however, indicates that the first $10,000 investment is made at the beginning of the first period, or at the period zero (0), as follows:

BOP	Amount Invested	Interest Earned During Period	EOP Balance
1	$10,000	$1,000	$11,000
2	$10,000	$2,100	$23,100
3	$10,000	$3,310	$36,410

It may be seen that when the series of three investments of $10,000 each is made at the beginning of each period rather than at the end, the amount accumulated by the end of three years with 10 percent annual compoundng is $36,410. This same result is achieved using the following procedure:

$$\underset{3.310000}{\underset{10\%,\; n\;=\;3}{\text{EOP Factor}}} \times \underset{(1.10)}{\underset{\text{(Annual, 10\%)}}{\text{Base}}} = \underset{3.641000}{\underset{10\%,\; n\;=\;3}{\text{BOP Factor}}}$$

and

$$3.641000 \times \$10,000 = \$36,410$$

The conversion of all factors at 10 percent, annual compounding, $n = 3$, is shown this way:

Column	EOP Factors	Function	Base	BOP Factors
1	1.331000	÷	1.1	1.210000
2	3.310000	×	1.1	3.641000
3	.302115	÷	1.1	.274650
4	.751315	×	1.1	.826447
5	2.486852	×	1.1	2.735537
6	.402115	÷	1.1	.365559

Converting EOP to BOP factors for compounding periods of less than a year is accomplished in exactly the same manner as for annual compounding. It is also possible to convert the present value of a variable income stream from EOP to BOP receipts by multiplying the proper base value times the present value (originally calculated using EOP factors).

EXPANSION OF COMPOUND INTEREST FACTORS

It is often necessary to obtain factors which extend into periods beyond the published tables. This situation can occur if a factor is needed for a greater number of periods than provided for in the table. A similar situation occurs when a factor is needed for a fractional compounding period beyond one year (such as nine years, seven months) since only annual factors are provided beyond the first year. In either situation, the expansion procedure is exactly the same.

Columns 1 and 4

These columns may be expanded *directly* by multiplication of those factors where the sum of the number of periods is equal to the desired number of periods. For example, suppose that a column 1 factor at 10 percent annual compounding is needed for a period of 65 years. This may be calculated as follows:

Column 1 factor		Column 1 factor		Column 1 factor
$(10\%, n = 60)$		$(10\%, n = 5)$		$(10\%, n = 65)$
304.481640	$\times$	1.610510		490.37072

or

Column 1 factor		Column 1 factor		Column 1 factor
$(10\%, n = 35)$		$(10\%, n = 30)$		$(10\%, n = 65)$
28.102437	$\times$	17.449402		$= 490.37072$

or

Any combination of two or more factors whose periods' sum is equal to $n = 65$ multiplied times each other:

$$F_1^n \times F_1^m = F_1^{n+m}$$

and

$$F_4^n \times F_4^m = F_4^{n+m}$$

If a column 1 factor for three years, seven months, (43 months) at 5 percent compounded monthly, is needed, it would be calculated in the following manner:

Column 1 factor		Column 1 factor		Column 1 factor
$(5\%, n = 36)$		$(5\%, n = 7)$		$(5\%, n = 43)$
1.161472	$\times$	1.029534	$=$	1.195775

Columns 2 and 3

The procedure for expanding columns 2 and 3 may be generalized as follows.

$$F_2^n + (F_1^n \times F_2^m) = F_2^{n+m}$$

and

$$\frac{1}{F_2^{n+m}} = F_3^{n+m}$$

Thus, the column 2 factor for three years, seven months, (43 months) at 5 percent, compounded monthly, is calculated this way:

Column 2 factor (5%, $n = 36$)		Column 1 factor (5%, $n = 36$)		Column 2 factor (5%, $n = 7$)		Column 2 factor (5%, $n = 43$)
38.753336	$+$	(1.161472	$\times$	7.088110)	$=$	46.985977

To calculate the comparable column 3 factor, simply find the reciprocal:

$$\frac{1}{46.985977} = .021283 = F_3^{43}$$

Columns 5 and 6

Expanding columns 5 and 6 may be generalized:

$$F_5^n + (F_4^n \times F_5^{n+m})$$

and

$$\frac{1}{F_5^{n+m}} = F_6^{n+m}$$

Thus, the column 5 factor for three years, seven months, (43 months) at 5 percent compounded monthly, would be calculated this way:

Column 5 factor (5%, $n = 36$)		Column 4 factor (5%, $n = 36$)		Column 5 factor (5%, $n = 7$)		Column 5 factor (5%, $n = 43$)
33.365701	$+$	(.860976	$\times$	6.884777)	$=$	39.293328

To calculate the comparable column 6 factor, simply find the reciprocal:

$$\frac{1}{39.293328} = .0254496 = F_6^{43}$$

INTERPOLATION

It is often necessary to "interpolate" between compound interest rates as a means of estimating an intermediate value not found in the tables or as a short-cut means of finding an approximate rate of return. The concept of interpolation is simple; it involves applying proportionate distances between known quantities so that the corresponding values found between such quantities can be estimated.

Example

Suppose that the following relationships are given:

	Production Time	Output of Product
	10.0 hours	90 units
	4.0 hours	30 units
Distance (value dffi.)	6.0 hours	60 units

How much time would be required to produce 45 units?

The distance between the lower production level and 45 units is 15 units or a distance of 25 percent (15 ÷ 60) of the total distance. The same percentage of distance on the time scale would be 25 percent of the total distance—1.5 (6 × .25). When this amount is added to the minimum time of four hours, the suggested solution is that it would take 5.5 hours to produce 45 units.

The same technique may be used to *estimate* compound interest factors, but again it must be recognized that the method of estimation assumes a proportionate (linear) relationship between factors and values which does not actually exist. Thus, while the technique is reasonably useful, it loses accuracy as the distance between rates increases.

Example

The following rates and factors are given:

n	Rate	Factor (Column 1)
10	15	4.045558
	10	
10	5	1.628895
Diff.	10	2.416663

Suppose now that the interpolation method is used to calculate the factor for 10 percent. The estimated factor would be as follows:

$$5 \div 10 \times 2.416663 = 1.208332$$
$$+ 1.628895$$
$$\overline{2.837227}$$

However, the actual factor is 2.593742. If the same estimate of the ten-year, 10-percent factor is made with an interpolation between 20 and 5 percent, the resulting solution is 3.149842, producing an even greater error than the earlier estimate.

Perhaps the most useful and frequent application of the interpolation technique is the calculation of Internal Rate of Return (IRR).

Example

Assume an investment of $10,000 in return for the following after-tax cash flows:

n	After-Tax Cash Flows
1	$2,000
2	1,500
3	1,200
4	1,000
5	800
6	600
7	300 + $10,700 sales proceeds

		Present Values of After-Tax Cash Flows			
		Discounted at 10%		Discounted at 15%	
End of Year	After-Tax Cash Flow	PV of 1	Amount	PV of 1	Amount
1	$ 2,000	.909091	$ 1,818	.869565	$1,739
2	1,500	.826446	1,240	.756144	1,134
3	1,200	.751315	902	.657516	789
4	1,000	.683013	683	.571753	572
5	800	.620921	497	.497177	398
6	600	.564474	339	.432328	259
7	11,000	.513158	5,645	.375937	4,135
Total			$11,124		$9,026

	Interpolation		
% Rate	Present Value Amount		
Smaller .10	$11,124	⟶	$11,124
Larger .15	$ 9,026	Initial investment	$10,000

Absolute difference [.05 ÷ $2,098] × $1,124 + smaller rate .10 = .126787

or

12.68% IRR (correct answer is 12.48%)

Short-cut Method for Calculating the Present Value of a Variable Cash Flow

The typical method of calculating the present value of a variable stream of cash flows is to find the sum of the present values of each cash flow using the appropriate column 4 factors.

Example

The following procedure would be used to calculate the present value of the indicated cash flows with a discount rate of 8.5 percent.

EOP (Year)	Cash Flows	×	Discount Factor Column 4, 8.5%	=	Present Value
1	$ 2,000		.921659		$1,843.32
2	–0–		—		–0–
3	(3,000)		.782908		(2,348.72)
4	11,000		.721574		7,937.31
					$7,431.91

The "short-cut" procedure is designed for speed of calculation but also eliminates the need for any compound interest tables, thus reducing the risk of errors from copying factors. The procedure is based upon the table below.

Thus, by utilizing the following procedure, each cash flow is divided by $(1 + i)$ n times according to when it is received. The steps are as follows:

Step 1. Enter the *last* period cash flow and divide by the appropriate base. (Enter the base in the calculator as a constant if possible.)

$$\$11,000 \div 1.085 = \$10,138.25$$

EOP (Years)	Cash Flows	×	Discount Factors	=	Present Value
1	$ 2,000	×	$1/(1 + i)$	=	PV
2	–0–	×	$1/(1 + i) \times 1/(1 + i)$	=	PV
3	(3,000)	×	$1/(1 + i) \times 1/(1 + i)$ $\times 1/(1 + i)$	=	PV
4	11,000	×	$1/(1 + i) \times 1/(1 + i)$ $\times 1/(1 + i) \times 1/(1 + i)$	=	PV

Step 2. Add *next* cash flow to the previously calculated product and divide the sum by the constant base.

$$(\$3,000) + \$10,138.25 = \$7,138.25$$

$$\$7,138.25 \div 1.085 = \$6,579.03$$

Step 3. Repeat Step 2 for each remaining cash flow.

$$0 + \$6,579.03 = \$6,579.03$$

$$\$6,579.03 \div 1.085 = \$6,063.62$$

and

$$\$2,000 + \$6,063.62 = \$8,063.62$$

$$\$8,063.62 \div 1.085 = \$7,431.91$$

This procedure illustrates the treatment of positive, zero and negative cash flows and can save a considerable amount of time in most present value calculations.

Example

The cash flows in the previous problem under "Interpolation" were the following:

n	$
1	$ 2,000
2	1,500
3	1,200
4	1,000
5	800
6	600
7	11,000

The present value of this cash flow stream discounted at 10 percent may be calculated, with modest practice, in less than 40 seconds using the short-cut procedure. Compare this time with the conventional method using column 4 factors.

FINANCIAL CALCULATORS

Financial calculators can solve a multitude of quantitative financial problems. To maximize the utility of any calculator, it is certainly very helpful to read the instruction manual of the particular calculator model. Many manuals have detailed explanations of procedures to solve common financial problems.

The following discussion will present an analytical format for financial problem-solving with financial calculators. The first step in any analytical process is to determine what data are known. For simple financial problems, there are three categories of data: the number of time *periods* during the holding period, the effective compound interest or discount *rate per period* and the cash flows. The appropriate data can usually be matched easily to the financial input of the financial calculator.

Number of Time Periods

The number of time periods $\boxed{n}$ for an investment is the only measure of time. Each period is assumed to be of equal duration and consistent with the periodic interest rate. When the number of periods is not given directly, it is usually easy to determine. The number of time periods is equal to the number of compounding periods per year times the number of years. For example, $\boxed{n}$ is 360 months for an amortizing loan for 30 years with 12 monthly payments per year. If the number of periods is the unknown value, an interest rate and a minimum of two cash flow values (explained below) are required.

Periodic Interest Rate

The periodic interest rate $\boxed{i}$ is usually stated as an annualized value. It must be consistent with the duration of the compounding period used (e.g., monthly, semiannual). Some financial calculators require input of $\boxed{i}$ as a decimal value (0.0075 for ¾ percent). Check the operating manual for the input format for a specific calculator. If the interest rate is stated as an annualized value, compute $\boxed{i}$ by dividing the annualized rate by the number of compounding periods per year. For example, the periodic interest rate for a problem with 12-percent interest per year and quarterly compounding would be

$$12\% \div 4 = 3\% \text{ per period}$$

If $\boxed{i}$ is the unknown value, the number of compounding periods and at least two cash flows are required. The result of the calculation will be the effective *periodic* interest rate. The annualized effective interesr rate is the periodic rate times the number of compounding periods per year. For example, the annualized effective interest rate (or yield) for a problem with a monthly rate of 1.25 percent is

$$12 \times 1.25\% = 15\%$$

Check the manual to determine if the calculated rate is displayed as a percentage or a decimal value. Some calculators will display the calculated rate as a percentage when it is calculated, but display the rate as a decimal if it is recalled from memory.

Cash Flows

Financial calculators will require and calculate the three types of cash flows described below:

> Present Value $\boxed{PV}$ is always one lump sum cash flow that occurs at the *beginning* of the *first* compounding period (sometimes labeled EOP O).
>
> Future Value $\boxed{FV}$ is always one lump sum cash flow that occurs at the *end* of the *last* compounding period.
>
> Periodic Payment $\boxed{PMT}$ is always assumed to be the amount of equal periodic cash flows made at the end of each and every compounding period during the investment time horizon. Some calculators have a built-in function to accommodate payments made at the beginning of each period. If not, see the discussion on cash flows received at the beginning of each period on page 408.

Required Data Input

The following combinations of data input are required to solve for the listed unknown financial quantity. Most financial calculators can solve for one unknown financial value from any three known values.

> To solve for $\boxed{n}$: known values for $\boxed{i}$ and two cash flows are required.
> To solve for $\boxed{i}$: known values for $\boxed{n}$ and two cash flows are required.
> To solve for $\boxed{PV}$: known values for $\boxed{n}$, $\boxed{i}$ and either $\boxed{PMT}$ *or* $\boxed{FV}$ are required.
> To solve for $\boxed{PMT}$: known values for $\boxed{n}$, $\boxed{i}$ and either $\boxed{PV}$ *or* $\boxed{FV}$ are required.
> To solve for $\boxed{FV}$: known values for $\boxed{n}$, $\boxed{i}$ and either $\boxed{PV}$ *or* $\boxed{PMT}$ are required.

Notice that n and i are *always* required to solve for an unknown cash flow value.

The data input combinations above are true for all financial calculators. However, some financial calculators, such as the Hewlett-Packard HP-38E, can solve for one unknown financial value from three *or* four known financial values. The above generalizations are also true for such calculators.

One other type of known cash flow *may* be input for any of the five types of calculations generalized above. Consult the owner's manual of your calculator regarding algebraic sign convention. In some cases, the calculator will distinguish cash flow receipts as positive values and cash flow payments as negative values.

Rounding

Financial calculators vary in the number of digits in the display, the number of internal significant digits and the method of automatic rounding of the last significant digit in the display. Consequently, results may vary slightly between calculators. The result of a particular problem may also be slightly different if rounded results are input into the same calculator to verify a calculation. The rounding error will be a small part of 1 percent of the answer. It should not negate the validity of the analysis. Of course, a large error may *not* be a rounding error.

Example

A loan will be paid in full at the end of six years and 11 months. The balance today is $6,210.37 and monthly payments are $100. What is the annual interest rate?

The unknown value is i, the periodic interest rate. The known values are

n = 83 months ((6 × 12) + 11 months)

PV = $6,210.37, loan balance today

PMT = $100 per month

Input the known values above and solve for i. The result is 0.729165 percent, the *monthly* periodic interest rate. The annual interest rate is:

$$\begin{array}{ll} 0.729165\% & \\ \times \quad 12 & \text{months per year} \\ \hline 8.749980\% & \text{rounded to 8.75\% per year} \end{array}$$

Summary

Using a financial calculator to solve simple financial problems is a matter of determining the known values and the unknown value. The known values must be input in the correct format. The periodic interest rate, i, must be consistent with the number of compounding periods per year. The total number of compounding periods, n, must likewise be consistent with the periodic interest rate. It is always advisable to consult the owner's manual of a particular calculator to identify specific operating characteristics.

FINANCIAL CALCULATIONS WITH HANDHELD ELECTRONIC CALCULATORS

Many of the financial calculations discussed in this book may be performed easily with any one of the many handheld electronic financial calculators currently avaiable. Financial calculators have at least five "financial keys":

$\boxed{n}$ or $\boxed{N}$ = number of compounding periods

$\boxed{i}$ or $\boxed{\%i}$ = interest rate *per period* (this will be stated as a percent, not a decimal)

$\boxed{PMT}$ = equal payment made at the end of each period

$\boxed{PV}$ = present value of an amount invested at the beginning of the first investment period

$\boxed{FV}$ = future value of a cash flow invested or received at the end of the last compounding period

Financial calculators vary in operating logic and data input format. Some calculators use an algebraic sign convention to indicate cash inflows (positive cash flows) and cash outlays or payments (negative cash flows). We will use this sign convention. Computation of the unknown value may be automatic (as with Hewlett-Packard calculators) or may require some kind of "compute" instruction (as do certain Texas Instrument calculators) to initiate the computation. The "compute" instruction will be used here.

Most financial calculators will take only three known financial values to solve for the fourth unknown value; they are called "four value" calculators. For example, with the givens, (1) number of payments $\boxed{n}$; (2) periodic interest rate $\boxed{i}$; and (3) present value of a loan $\boxed{PV}$, these calculators can compute the payment to amortize the loan $\boxed{PMT}$, the unknown fourth value. In contrast, some calculators will accept any four known values, although only three are required, and solve for the fifth value; these are called "five value" calculators.

Some of the following procedures may not function with some calculators. Again, the reader is advised to consult the operating manual of a particular calculator to identify subtle data input requirements and other operating characteristics. In many cases, financial calculators will have additional preprogrammed financial functions that will save steps in some financial calculations. For example, many financial calculators have preprogrammed internal rate of return, net present value, loan balance and amortization functions. Most financial problems may be solved with any one of many keystroke procedures; however, only one procedure will be given here.

In most cases, the format of this section will list the type of financial problem and the known values, with the instruction to solve for the unknown values. All of these problems usually may be solved by merely identifying the known values and the unknown value.

Unless otherwise indicated, it is assumed that the calculator is reset and/or all financial registers are cleared at the beginning of each problem.

Compound Interest and Discount Factors

All compound interest and discount factors are calculated with three known values; therefore, only one set of keystrokes will be summarized here. In each case [n] and [i] are known. Recall that the interest per period, [i], must be consistent with the period (e.g., monthly interest for monthly compounding of payments). Here are the factors:

Elwood Column Number	Factor	Input these Known Values	Input 1 Into this Register	Solve for this Value
1	Amount of 1 at compound interest	[n], [i]	[PV]	[FV]
2	Accumulation of 1 per period	[n], [i]	[PMT] *	[FV]
3	Sinking fund factor	[n], [i]	[FV]	[PMT] *
4	Present value reversion of 1	[n], [i]	[FV]	[PV]
5	Present value of an ordinary annuity of 1 per period	[n], [i]	[PMT] *	[PV]
6	Installment to amortize 1	[n], [i]	[PV]	[PMT] *

*All calculations involving [PMT] assume that payments are received or paid at the *end* of each period.

Converting Factors for Payments to Be Received or Paid at the Beginning of Each Period

In many instances, compound interest problems involve the receipt or investment of funds at the beginning of the period (BOP) rather than at the end of the period (EOP). Many financial calculators have a preprogrammed instruction or function to make these adjustments. For example, Hewlett-Packard financial calculators have a ''Begin/End'' switch, and Texas Instruments financial calculators have an annuity ''DUE'' instruction to use prior to the calculation. Of course, the amount of 1 at compound interest and the present value reversion of 1 factors are based on the assumptions that the investment takes place at the beginning of the first period and reversion, [FV], is received at the end of the last period. Thus, there is generally no need to convert these factors to BOP, although it is possible to do so.

Loan Analysis

To calculate the payment for a fully amortized loan input the known values:

[n] = number of payments during loan term

[i] = interest rate per period

[PV] = loan amount

Solve for [PMT] = periodic loan payment

To calculate the payment for a partially amortized loan with known balloon payments, do the following: For a five-value calculator, input the known values:

$$\boxed{n} = \text{number of payments during loan term (including last payment)}$$

$$\boxed{i} = \text{interest rate per period}$$

$$\boxed{PV} = \text{loan amount}$$

$$\boxed{FV} = \text{dollar amount of balloon payment}$$

Solve for $\boxed{PMT}$ = periodic loan payment

Examples

1. Calculate the quarterly payment for a $100,000 loan at 12 percent per annum with a balloon payment of $95,000 due EOY 15.

$$\boxed{n} = 60 \text{ (15 years} \times 4 \text{ quarterly payments per year)}$$

$$\boxed{i} = 3 \text{ percent (12 percent} \div 4)$$

$$\boxed{PV} = \$100,000$$

$$\boxed{FV} = (\$95,000) \text{ (negative because it will be } \textit{paid} \text{ EOY 15)}$$

Solve for $\boxed{PMT}$ = ($3,030.66)

For a four-value calculator, first compute the payment on total amount, then compute the sinking fund payment of the balloon payment. The payment is the difference of the payment on the total amount less the sinking fund payment on the balloon. The process is as follows:

Step 1.   Compute the payment on total amount from known values:

$$\boxed{n} = \text{number of payments}$$

$$\boxed{i} = \text{periodic interest rate}$$

$$\boxed{PV} = \text{loan amount}$$

Solve for $\boxed{PMT}$ = payment for fully amortized loan

Step 2.   Compute sinking fund factor of the balloon payment:

$$\boxed{n} = \text{number of payments (same as Step 1)}$$

$$\boxed{i} = \text{periodic interest rate (same as Step 1)}$$

$$\boxed{FV} = \text{amount of balloon payment}$$

Solve for $\boxed{PMT}$ = sinking fund factor for balloon

Step 3.   Compute the payment by simple subtraction:

Payment for fully amortized loan
Less sinking fund payment for balloon
Equals loan payment

2. Use the facts in the preceding example.

Step 1. Compute the payment on total amount from known values:

$$\boxed{n} = 60$$
$$\boxed{i} = 3\%$$
$$\boxed{PV} = \$100,000$$
$$\text{Solve for } \boxed{PMT} = \$3,613.30$$

Step 2. Compute the sinking fund payment on the balloon payment from known values:

$$\boxed{n} = 60$$
$$\boxed{i} = 3\%$$
$$\boxed{FV} = \$95,000$$
$$\text{Solve for } \boxed{PMT} = \$582.63$$

Step 3. Compute the loan payment:

Payment to fully amortize the loan	$3,613.30
Less sinking fund payment for balloon	582.63
Loan payment	$3,030.67

Remaining Term of a Fully Amortized Loan

The remaining term of a straight amortizing loan is calculated using the same procedure for both four-value and five-value calculators from the following known data:

$$\boxed{i} = \text{periodic interest rate}$$
$$\boxed{PMT} = \text{periodic payment}$$
$$\boxed{PV} = \text{current loan balance}$$

The remaining term is the unknown value $\boxed{n}$.

Example

Calculate the remaining term of a loan at 12-percent interest, with monthly payments of $100 and a remaining balance of $7,000.

The known values are

$$\boxed{i} = 1\% \ (12\% \div 12)$$
$$\boxed{PMT} = \$100$$
$$\boxed{PV} = \$7,000$$

Solving for the unknown value, $\boxed{n} = 121$ months.
The remaining term is 121 months or 10 years, 1 month.

Loan Balance

The procedure for figuring loan balances is the same for both four-value and five-value calculators. The loan balance is equal to the present value of the *remaining* payments, discounted at the nominal rate of the loan. Therefore, the known values are

$$\boxed{n} = \text{remaining number of payments}$$

$$\boxed{i} = \text{periodic nominal interest rate}$$

$$\boxed{PMT} = \text{periodic loan payment}$$

$$\text{Solve for } \boxed{PV} = \text{loan balance}$$

Example

Calculate the loan balance of a loan with a remaining term of nine years, 11 months; monthly payments are $1,780.91 at 11⅞ percent (11.875 percent). The known values are

$$\boxed{n} = 119 \text{ months } [(9 \times 12) + 11]$$

$$\boxed{i} = 0.99\% \ (11.875 \div 12)$$

$$\boxed{PMT} = \$1,780.91$$

Solving for the unknown value, $\boxed{PV} = \$124,211.58$.

Number of Payments to Reduce the Loan Balance to a Specified Balance

For a four-value calculator, first calculate the number of payments from the *end* of the loan term to a specified balance. The number of payments to reduce a loan balance to a specific sum is the total remaining payments less the number of payments from the end of the loan term to the specified balance.

Calculate the number of payments from the end of the loan term to the specified balance from the known values:

$$\boxed{i} = \text{periodic interest rate}$$

$$\boxed{PMT} = \text{periodic loan payment}$$

$$\boxed{PV} = \text{specified loan balance}$$

Solve for number of payments $\boxed{n}$ until the *end* of the loan term from the specified loan balance. The number of payments to reduce the loan balance to a specified balance is the total remaining term less the number of payments until the end of the loan term from the specified loan balance.

Example

How many monthly payments of $1,028.61 are required to reduce a $100,000 loan at 12 percent to a balance of $50,000? This loan would be fully amortized in 30 years (360 months).

Calculate the number of payments from the end of the loan term from the known values:

$$\boxed{i} = 1\% \ (12\% \div 12)$$
$$\boxed{PMT} = 1,028.61$$
$$\boxed{PV} = 50,000$$
$$\text{Solve for } \boxed{n} = 66.90.$$

The loan balance will be \$50,000 when there are 66.90 remaining payments. The number of payments required to reduce the loan balance to \$50,000 is

Total remaining payments	360.00
Payments to the end of the loan term from the specified balance	66.90
Number of payments to reduce loan balance to \$50,000	293.10

The fractional portion of the result indicates that the balance is slightly more than \$50,000 after the 293rd payment.

For a five-value calculator, solve for $\boxed{n}$ from the known values:

$$\boxed{i} = 1\% \ (12\% \div 12)$$
$$\boxed{PMT} = (\$1,028.61)$$
$$\boxed{PV} = \$100,000$$
$$\boxed{FV} = (\$50,000)$$
$$\text{Solve for } \boxed{n} = 293.11 \ (\text{difference due to rounding})$$

Amortization Schedules*

Amortization may be computed for any number of periods. The basic principal reduction formula is

Loan balance at the beginning of amortization period
Less loan balance at the end of amortization period
Equals principal reduction during amortization period

Accumulated interest is

Total of loan payments during amortization period
Less principal reduction during amortization period
Equals accumulated interest during amortization period

Calculation of the loan balances is the only financial calculation required.

*Some handheld financial calculators, such as the HP-12c, have a built-in amortization function which can calculate the interest and principal accumulated over any period directly and much more quickly than this section illustrates.

Example

An investor assumes a loan balance of $75,000 at 12.6 percent interest with monthly payments of $824.97 for the remaining term of 24 years, eight months (296 months). Calculate the principal reduction and accumulated interest for the last four months of the current tax year and for the next tax year.

Amortization for the remaining four months of the current tax year is calculated first. Loan balance at the beginning of the amortization period is $75,000. The loan balance after four payments is calculated from the following known data:

$$\boxed{n} = 292 \ (296 - 4 \text{ remaining payments})$$

$$\boxed{i} = 1.05\% \ (12.60\% \div 12)$$

$$\boxed{PMT} = \$824.97$$

To find the balance after the first four payments, solve for $\boxed{PV} = \$74,847.71$. Principal reduction for the first four months is

Beginning balance	$75,000.00
Ending balance	− 74,847.71
Principal reduction	$152.29

Accumulated interest is

Total loan payments (4 × $824.97)	$ 3,299.88
Principal reduction	− 152.29
Accumulated interest	$ 3,147.59

Amortization in the following tax year (12 months) is calculated as follows. Beginning balance is $74,847.71 from above. Ending balance, after 12 payments, is calculated from the following known data:

$$\boxed{n} = 280 \ (292 - 12 \text{ remaining payments at the end of the next tax year})$$

$$\boxed{i} = 1.05\% \ (12.60\% \div 12)$$

$$\boxed{PMT} = \$824.97$$

Calculate the ending balance by solving for $\boxed{PV} = \$74,350.83$. Principal reduction during the next tax year is

Beginning balance	$ 74,847.71
Ending balance	− 74,350.83
Principal reduction	$ 496.88

Accumulated interest is

Total loan payments (12 × $824.97)	$ 9,899.64
Principal reduction	− 496.88
Accumulated interest	$ 9,402.76

Calculation of IRR

Many financial calculators can solve for the periodic interest rate, $\boxed{i}$. The IRR for three types of cash flows can be calculated directly on such four-value financial calculators: (1) a present lump sum and a future sum, (2) a present lump sum and an ordinary annuity and (3) a future lump sum and an ordinary annuity. In each case, the number of periods, $\boxed{n}$, must be known. Simply input the three known values and solve for $\boxed{i}$.

Examples

      1. An investor bought a vacant site five years ago for $100,000 and recently sold it for $250,000. Holding costs were paid by a nominal rent for a billboard on the property. What is the investor's before-tax yield? The known values are

$$\boxed{n} = 5 \ (\text{number of periods})$$
$$\boxed{PV} = \$100,000 \ (\text{initial investment})$$
$$\boxed{FV} = \$250,000 \ (\text{future value of reversion})$$

Solving for the yield, $\boxed{i} = 20.11$ percent

      2. An investor pays $10,000 for quarterly payments of $875 for four years. Calculate the yield. The known values are

$$\boxed{n} = 16 \ (4 \times 4 \ \text{payments})$$
$$\boxed{PV} = \$10,000$$
$$\boxed{PMT} = \$875$$

The quarterly yield is calculated by solving for $\boxed{i} = 4.264$ percent. The annual yield is 17.06 percent (4×4.264 percent).

      3. A condominium association will make monthly deposits of $100 for ten years for the roof replacement reserve account. The new roof is expected to cost $20,000. What minimum rate of return will produce the required funds EOY 10? The known values are

$$\boxed{n} = 120 \ (10 \times 12 \ \text{periods})$$
$$\boxed{PMT} = \$100 \ \text{per month}$$
$$\boxed{FV} = \$20,000$$

Solving for the unknown yield, $\boxed{i} = 0.7984$ percent per month. The annual minimum required yield is 9.58 percent (12×0.7984 percent).

Compound Rate of Growth

The compound rate of growth of populations, company earnings, securities values, land or other values over time may be figured with a financial calculator. The known values are

$$\boxed{n} = \text{number of periods during growth}$$
$$\boxed{PV} = \text{value at beginning of projection}$$
$$\boxed{FV} = \text{value at end of projection}$$

Solve for $\boxed{i}$ to get the geometric mean compound rate of growth during the projection period.

Example

During the past five years, the population of a certain market area has grown from 121,000 to 162,000 people. Calculate the geometric mean compound rate of growth of the population for the five-year period. The known values are

$$\boxed{n} = 5 \text{ years}$$

$$\boxed{PV} = 121,000 \text{ (population at beginning of projection)}$$

$$\boxed{FV} = 162,000 \text{ (population at the end of projection)}$$

The compound rate of growth is $\boxed{i} = 6.01$ percent per year.

IRR of Cash Flows with Level Annuities, Present Value Sum and a Sum in the Future for Four-Value Calculators

We will present two procedures for estimating IRR. The first will work for a cash flow with an annuity, present sum and future sum, which can be described as follows:

EOY	$
0	$\boxed{PV}$
1	$\boxed{PMT}$
↓	↓
$\boxed{n}$	$\boxed{PMT}$ + $\boxed{FV}$

Note that the last payment is *not* included in the future reversion.

Step 1. Calculate the "cash-on-cash" (c/c) per period (not annualized) as a percent:

$$\frac{\boxed{PMT}}{\boxed{PV}} \times 100 = \text{c/c (save this value in the calculator's memory)}$$

Step 2. Calculate the change in value (Δ V—positive or negative) from the $\boxed{PV}$ to $\boxed{FV}$ as a percent:

$$\frac{\boxed{FV} - \boxed{PV}}{\boxed{PV}} \times 100 = \Delta V$$

This value is $\boxed{FV}$ for this calculation.

Step 3. Input the following values:

$$\boxed{n} = \text{number of periods}$$

$$\boxed{i} = \text{c/c from Step 1 and save this value}$$

$$\boxed{FV} = \Delta V \text{ from Step 2}$$

Step 4. Solve for $\boxed{\text{PMT}}$, then add result to c/c. This will produce an approximation of the yield.

Step 5. Replace the value of $\boxed{\text{i}}$ with the result of Step 4.

Step 6. Repeat Steps 4 and 5 until the same value is repeated after Step 4.

Example

A bank loans $100,000 at 12 percent per annum with monthly payments of $1,028.61. The lender charges four points to make the loan. The borrower repays the loan balance of $97,663.43 at EOY 5. Calculate the lender's IRR on this loan. The lender's cash flows are summarized in the following T-chart:

EOM	$
0	(96,000) = ($100,000 less 4 pts)
1	$1,028.61
↓	↓
12 × 5 = 60	$1,028.61 + $97,663.43

Step 1. Calculate the "cash-on-cash" as a percent:

$$c/c = \frac{\$1,028.61}{\$96,000} \times 100 = 1.0715\% \text{ (use internal answer from calculator, not rounded value)}$$

Save in memory if possible.

Step 2. Calculate the change in value as a percent:

$$\Delta V = \left[\frac{\$97,663.43 - \$96,000}{\$96,000} \right] \times 100 = 1.7327\%$$

Step 3. Input the following data (to improve estimate of IRR, do not use rounded values):

$$\boxed{\text{n}} = 60 \ (12 \times 5 \text{ periods})$$
$$\boxed{\text{i}} = 1.0715\% \ (c/c)$$
$$\boxed{\text{FV}} = 1.7327\% \ (\Delta V)$$

Step 4.

Solve for PMT =	0.0207
Add c/c	+ 1.7327
First approximation of IRR	1.0922

Step 5. Replace $\boxed{\text{i}}$ with approximation of IRR from above.

Step 6. Repeat Steps 4 and 5 until the same result from Step 4 is repeated (to more decimal places for more accuracy). The steps may be repeated several times, depending on the particular calculation.

First approximation   1.0922
Second approximation   1.0921
Third approximation   1.0921

The monthly IRR is approximately 1.0921 percent. The lender's annual yield is 13.10 percent.

Estimation of IRR of Variable Cash Flows by Interpolation

The following procedure is based on the definition of IRR—that rate at which all future cash flows are discounted to equal the initial investment.

Step 1.   Discount cash flows at a trial rate. Save results. Use a periodic discount rate consistent with the cash flows.

Step 2.   Discount cash flows at a second trial rate, preferably closer to the IRR based on the first estimate. If the $\boxed{\text{PV}}$ of the cash flows discounted at the first trial rate is greater than the initial investment, try a greater discount rate, and vice-versa. The estimate of IRR will be better for smaller intervals between the trial rates.

Step 3.   Compute:

> First trial discount rate
> Less second trial rate
> Difference in discount rates

Step 4.   Compute:

> $\boxed{\text{PV}}$ of cash flows at first trial discount rate
> Less $\boxed{\text{PV}}$ of cash flows at second trial discount rate
>
> Difference in trial $\boxed{\text{PV}}$s

Step 5*.   Compute:

> Initial investment
> Less $\boxed{\text{PV}}$ of cash flows at first trial discount rate
>
> Difference of first trial $\boxed{\text{PV}}$ to initial investment

Step 6*.   The estimated IRR is:

$$\text{First trial rate} + \left[\frac{\text{Difference in discount rates} \times \text{difference of trial } \boxed{\text{PV}} \text{ to initial investment}}{\text{Difference in trial } \boxed{\text{PV}}} \right]$$

*These values must correlate to first and second trial discount rates although they may be reversed if done consistently.

Examples

1. Estimate the IRR of the following cash flows:

EOY	$	
0	$10,000	(treat initial investment as
1	1,000	a positive number)
2	(2,000)	
3	3,000	
4	4,000	
5	11,000	

Step 1. Discount cash flows at first trial rate, say 10 percent:

EOY	$	PV @ 10%
1	$1,000	$ 909.09
2	(2,000)	(1,652.89)
3	3,000	2,253.94
4	4,000	2,732.05
5	11,000	6,830.13
Total PV @ 10%		$11,072.32

Notice that the negative cash flow EOY 2 maintains the negative algebraic sign.

Step 2. Discount the cash flows at a second trial rate. The first trial rate, 10 percent, is too low because the PV of $11,072.32 is greater than the initial investment of $10,000. Therefore, a greater trial rate will be used, say 15 percent.

EOY	$	PV @ 15%
1	$1,000	$ 869.57
2	(2,000)	(1,512.29)
3	3,000	1,972.55
4	4,000	2,287.01
5	11,000	5,468.94
Total PV @ 15%		$ 9,085.78

The IRR is between 10 percent and 15 percent since the total PV of the cash flows is greater and less than, respectively, the initial investment.

Step 3. Difference in discount rates:

First trial discount rate	10%	
Second trial discount rate	15%	
Difference in discount rates	−5%	(keep appropriate algebraic signs)

Step 4.   Difference in trial $\boxed{\text{PV}}$s:

First trial $\boxed{\text{PV}}$ @ 10%	$11,072.32
Second trial $\boxed{\text{PV}}$ @ 15%	9,085.78
Difference in trial $\boxed{\text{PV}}$s	$1,986.54

Step 5.   Difference of first trial $\boxed{\text{PV}}$ to initial investment:

Initial investment	$10,000.00
First trial $\boxed{\text{PV}}$ @ 10%	11,072.32
	($-$1,072.32)

Step 6.   The estimated IRR is

$$10 + \left[\frac{(-.05) \times (-1,072.32)}{1,986.54}\right] = .10 + .0272 = .1270 = 12.7\%$$

The actual IRR is 12.54 percent.

2. This procedure could be used to estimate the IRR of the lender from the previous example on page 427. Recall that the *monthly* cash flows were

EOM	$	
0	$96,000.00	(treat initial investment
1	1,028.61	as a positive number)
60	1,028.61 + 97,663.43	

Step 1. $\boxed{\text{PV}}$ at first trial rate of say 12 percent per annum, or 1 percent per month:

$\boxed{\text{PV}}$ @ 1% of annuity of $1,028.61 for 60 months is	$46,241.20
$\boxed{\text{PV}}$ @ 1% of loan balance EOM 60 of $97,663.43 is	53,758.80
Total	$100,000.00

This result could have been predicted because the payments and balance were based on a $100,000 loan at 12 percent per year with monthly payments.

Step 2.   The IRR is greater than 12 percent per year since the $\boxed{\text{PV}}$ at 12 percent, $100,000, is greater than the initial investment of $96,000. Try 1.1 percent per month.

$\boxed{\text{PV}}$ @ 1.1% per month of annuity of $1,028.61 per month is	$45,004.75
$\boxed{\text{PV}}$ @ 1.1% of loan balance EOM 60 of $97,663.43 is	50,659.70
Total	$95,664.45

Step 3.   Difference in discount rates:

First trial discount rate	1.0%
Second trial discount rate	1.1%
Difference in discount rates	$-$0.1%

Step 4.   Difference in trial $\boxed{PV}$s:

First trial $\boxed{PV}$ @ 1.0%	$100,000.00
Second trial $\boxed{PV}$ @ 1.1%	95,664.45
Difference in trial $\boxed{PV}$s	$4,335.55

Step 5.   Difference in first trial $\boxed{PV}$ to initial investment:

Initial investment	$96,000
First trial $\boxed{PV}$ @ 1.0%	100,000
	$4,000

Step 6.   The estimated monthly IRR is

$$.010000 \ + \ \left[\ \frac{(-.001000 \ \times \ (-4,000)}{4,335.55} \ \right] \ = \ .010000 \ + \ .000923 \ + \ .010923$$
$$= \ 1.0923\%$$

The estimated *annual* IRR is

$$\begin{array}{r} 1.0923\% \\ \times \quad 12 \\ \hline 13.1076\% \end{array}$$

This is close to the estimate of 13.1 percent found on page 428. The calculations were carried to several decimal places because of the small difference in the trial discount rates. This procedure is valid for discount rates for any consistent time period (quarter, semi-annual, etc.).

The estimate of IRR is improved by using trial discount rates which produce a small difference in discount rates (Step 3). The estimated IRR for cash flows using trial discount rates with a one-percentage-point difference is better than using discount rates with a five-percentage-point difference.

Bibliography

Allen, Roger H. *Real Estate Investment and Taxation*. Cincinnati: South-Western Publishing Co., 1984.

——— *Real Estate Investment Strategy*, 3rd ed. Cincinnati: South-Western Publishing Co., 1989.

American Institute of Real Estate Appraisers. *American Institute of Real Estate Appraisers Financial Tables*, ed. and comp. by James J. Mason. Chicago, 1981.

American Institute of Real Estate Appraisers. *Readings in Real Estate Investment Analysis*. Chicago, 1977.

Andersen (Arthur) & Co. *Federal Taxes Affecting Real Estate*, 5th ed. New York: Matthew Bender, 1981.

Aronsohn, Alan J. B. "Real Estate Investment and the Economic Recovery Tax Act of 1981." *Journal of Real Estate Taxation*, Spring 1981, pp. 291–300.

Bagby, Joseph R. *Real Estate Financing Desk Book*, 3d ed. Englewood Cliffs, N.J.: Institute for Business Planning, 1981.

Blitz, E., and R.J. Spiegel. "Rich Man, Poor Man: The Impact of the 1986 Tax Reform Act on Low-income Housing Values." *Real Estate Appraiser Analyst* 53, Spring 1987, pp. 153–190.

Boykin, James H. *Financing Real Estate*. Lexington, Mass.: D.C. Heath & Co., 1979.

Britten, James A. and Kerwood, Lewis O., ed. *Financing Income-Producing Real Estate: A Theory and Casebook*. New York: McGraw-Hill, 1977.

432

Brown, Gary Alan. "Real Estate Investment Trusts." *The Real Estate Handbook*, edited by Maury Selden. Homewood, IL: Dow Jones-Irwin, 1980, pp 686–87.

Brueggeman, William B., and Stone, Leo D. *Real Estate Finance*, 7th ed. Homewood, Ill.: Irwin, 1981.

Bruss, Robert J. *Effective Real Estate Investing*. Orem, Utah: Investment and Taxation Publications, Inc., 1984.

Casino, J.J. Del, "An Overview of the Real Estate Investment Marketplace." *Appraisal Journal* 55, October 1987, pp. 558–566.

Commerce Clearing House. *U.S. Master Tax Guide*. Chicago, Ill. Annual.

Cooney, B.D. "REMIC: An Idea Whose Time Has Come." *Mortgage Banking* 47, November, 1986, pp. 39–41.

Cooper, James R. *Real Estate Investment Analysis*. Lexington, MA: Lexington Books, 1974.

Corgel, John B., and Goebel, Paul R. "Useful Life, Component Depreciation, and the Economic Characteristics of Real Estate." *Journal of Real Estate Taxation*, Winter 1981, pp. 125–141.

Crean, Michael J. "Are Capitalization Rates Obsolete?" *Appraisal Journal*, Apr. 1981, pp. 248–257.

Dasso, Jerome J., William N. Kinnard, and Stephen D. Messner. *Valuation and Analysis of Interests in Participation Financed Properties*. Chicago: Society of Real Estate Appraisers, 1972.

Dasso, Jerome, and Kuhn, Gerald. *Real Estate Finance*. Englewood Cliffs, N.J.: Prentice Hall, 1983.

"DCF Analysis: The Other Side of the Coin." *Mortgage and Real Estate Executives Report*, Jan. 15, 1981, pp. 6–7.

Dennis, Marshall. *Fundamentals of Mortgage Lending*. Reston, VA: Reston Publishing Co., 1978.

Dilmore, Gene. *The New Approach to Real Estate Appraising*. Englewood Cliffs, NJ: Prentice Hall, 1970.

———— *Quantitative Techniques in Real Estate Counseling*. Lexington, Mass: Heath, 1981.

Edwards, Charles E., and Gaines, James P. "Alternative Accelerated Depreciation Methods and Rates of Return on Real Estate Investments." *Real Estate Appraiser and Analyst*, Fall 1981, pp. 13–22.

Ellwood, L.W. *Ellwood Tables for Real Estate Appraising and Financing*, 4th ed. Chicago: American Institute of Real Estate Appraisers, 1977.

Emory, Meade, and Hjorth, Roland L. "An Analysis of the Changes Made by the Installment Sales Revision Act of 1980." *Journal of Taxation*, Feb. 1981, pp. 66–71; Mar. 1981, pp. 130–137.

Epley, Donald R., and James A. Miller. *Basic Real Estate Finance and Investments*. New York: John Wiley & Sons, 1980.

Epley, Donald R., and Joseph Rabianski. *Principles of Real Estate Decisions*. Englewood Cliffs, NJ: Prentice Hall, 1986.

Feder, Jack M. "Starker: The Deferred Tax-free Exchange Resurrected." *Journal of Real Estate Taxation*, Spring 1980, pp. 218–240.

Ferguson, Jerry T. *Fundamentals of Real Estate Investing*. Glenview, Ill.: Scott, Foresman and Company, 1984.

Fisher, Jeffrey D., and Lusht, Kenneth M. "Mortgage Equity Analysis with a Debt Coverage Constraint." *Real Estate Appraiser and Analyst*, Fall 1981, pp. 5–12.

Fisher, Jeffrey D., and Sanders, Anthony B. "Capitalization Rates and Market Information." *Appraisal Journal*, Apr. 1981, pp. 186–198.

Floyd, Charles F. *Real Estate Principles, 2nd ed.* Chicago: Longman Financial Services Publishing Inc., 1987.

Follain, J.R. "The Impact of the 1986 Tax Reform Act on Real Estate." *Real Estate Review* 17, September 1987, pp. 76–83.

Gabriel, S.A. "Housing Mortgage Markets: The Post-1982 Expansion." *Federal Reserve Bulletin* 73, December 1987, pp. 893–903.

Gibbons, J.E. "Current Financial Markets." *Appraisal Journal* 55, April 1987, pp. 297–306.

Gibbons, James E. "Equity Yield." *Appraisal Journal*, Jan. 1980, pp. 31–55.

Goodman, Richard A. "The New Starker Case: How It Will Revolutionize Tax Deferred Exchanges." *Real Estate Securities Journal*, Spring 1980, pp. 33–43.

Greer, Gaylon E. and Michael D. Farrell. "Individual Investors' Attitudes Towards Real Estate" (survey). *Real Estate Review* 17, Fall 1987, pp. 101–108.

———— *Investment Analysis for Real Estate Decisions*, 2nd ed. Chicago: Longman Financial Services Publishing, Inc., 1988.

Gross, E.L. "Understanding Wraparound Loans: A Closer Examination." *Mortgage Banking* 47, October 1986, pp. 123ff.

Harris, Bridget McInerney. "The Effect of the Installment Sales Revision Act of 1980 on Like-kind Exchanges: Nonsimultaneous Exchanges." *Taxes*, July 1981, pp. 448–456.

Harris, Jack, and Jack P. Friedman. *Tax-free Exchanges under Section 1031*. College Station, TX: Texas A & M University, College of Agriculture, Texas Real Estate Center, 1981.

Howell, A. Harold, and Smith, David A. "Independent Component Analysis; a New Way to Analyze Real Estate Shelter Opportunities." *Real Estate Review*, Spring 1981, pp. 53–64.

"Investment Analysis: What's the Return?" *Real Estate Investment Ideas*, May 1981, 1st issue, pp. 1–3.

Jaffe, Austin J. "A Note on the Use of Capitalization, Discount, and Forward Rates." *Appraisal Journal*, Jan. 1980, pp. 24–30.

Johnson, Ross H., and Henderson, Thomas P. *Real Estate Finance*. Columbus, OH: Charles E. Merrill Publishing Co., 1985.

Kane, Carl. "Still Infant, Securitization Is Long-Term Development; Commercial Market Benefits by Following Residential." *National Real Estate Investor* 29, August 1987, pp. 63ff.

Koelsch, James P. "Discounting Projected Cash Flows." *Appraisal Journal*, Oct. 1981, pp. 522–533.

Kurn, Neal, and Nutter, Jack O., II. ''The Installment Sales Revision Act of 1980: In the Name of Simplification Has a Measure of Complexity Been Added?'' *Journal of Real Estate Taxation*, Spring 1981, pp. 195–212.

Levine, Howard J. ''Tax-free Real Estate Transactions.'' *Journal of Real Estate Taxation*, Spring 1981, pp. 354–358.

Levine, Mark Lee. ''Multiple Party Exchanges: Recent Decisions Support Flexibility Under Section 1031.'' *Taxes*, Mar. 1981, pp. 194–200.

———— *Real Estate Exchanges*. Chicago, Ill.: REALTORS NATIONAL MARKETING INSTITUTE®, 1981.

Levitin, C.M. ''REMICS: Removing Tax Obstacles.'' *Real Estate Review* 17, Fall 1987, pp. 26–34.

Lipscomb, Joseph B. ''Discount Rates for Cash Equivalent Analysis.'' *Appraisal Journal*, Jan. 1981, pp. 23–33.

''A Look at the Accelerated Cost Recovery System.'' *Real Estate Investment Ideas*, Oct. 1981, 2d issue, pp. 1–3.

Luscombe, George A., II, and Chevis, Cheryl A. ''Faster, Simpler Depreciation Rules Available for All Property under the New Tax Legislation.'' *Journal of Taxation*, Oct. 1981, pp. 194–201.

Lusht, Kenneth M. ''Measuring Rate of Return: Two Rules of Thumb v. the Internal Rate.'' *Appraisal Journal*, April 1978, pp. 245–256.

Martin, William B., Jr. ''A Risk Analysis Rate-of-Return Model for Evaluating Income-Producing Real Estate Investments.'' *Appraisal Journal*, July 1978, pp. 424–442.

McBirney, James J. ''Real Estate Financing in an Inflationary Economy.'' *Appraisal Journal*, Oct. 1981, pp. 494–521.

McGuire, John A. ''Tax Aspects of Income Reservations in Real Estate Transactions.'' *Journal of Real Estate Taxation*, Spring 1981, pp. 213–232.

McMullen, Charles W. *Tax Deferred Exchanges of Real Estate Investments*. New York: Wiley, 1981.

Montgomery, J. Thomas, and Raper, Charles F. ''Equity Yields and the Reinvestment Issue.'' *Appraisal Journal*, Oct. 1981, pp. 509–521.

Nutter, Jack O., II. ''Regulations under the Installment Sales Revision Act.'' *Journal of Real Estate Taxation*, Fall 1981, pp. 46–56.

Peterson, Charles H. ''Are Capitalization Rates Obsolete?'' *Appraisal Journal*, Apr. 1981, pp. 179–185.

Pyhrr, Stephen A., and Cooper, James R. Real Estate Investment: *Strategy, Analysis, Decisions*. Boston, Mass.: Warren, Gorham and Lamont, Inc., 1982.

Ring, Alfred A. *The Valuation of Real Estate*. Englewood Cliffs, NJ: Prentice Hall, 1970.

Rohan, Patrick J. *Real Estate Financing: Text; Forms; Tax analysis*. New York: Matthew Bender.

Sear, Michael. ''Choosing a Recovery Method for Non-residential Property: An Internal Rate of Return Approach.'' *Real Estate Securities Journal*, Fall 1981, pp. 38–49.

Seldin, Maury. *Real Estate Investment for Profit Through Appreciation.* Reston, Va.: Reston, 1980.

Shenkman, Martin M. *Real Estate after Tax Reform.* New York: John Wiley & Sons, 1987.

Shlaes, Jared, and Young, Michael S. "Evaluating Major Investment Properties." *Appraisal Journal,* Jan. 1978, pp. 101–111.

Sirota, David. *Essentials of Real Estate Investment.* Chicago Ill.: Longman Group U.S.A., Inc., 1984.

Smith, Halbert C. and others. *Real Estate and Urban Development,* 3d ed. Homewood, Ill.: Irwin, 1981.

Smith, Keith V., and David K. Eiteman. *Essentials of Investing.* Homewood, IL: Richard D. Irwin, Inc., 1974.

"Special Issue: New Tax Law Benefits Real Estate." *Real Estate Tax Ideas,* Oct. 1981 (entire issue).

"Special Report: Depreciation and Recapture Under New Tax Law." *Mortgage and Real Estate Executives Report,* Oct. 1, 1981, pp. 3–8.

"Special Report: New Tax Law Is Good News for Investors." *Mortgage and Real Estate Executives Report,* Sept. 1, 1981, pp. 1–7.

Tornga, David L. "Tax Consequences on the Disposition of Real Property or Interests Therein by Limited Partnerships and Partners." *Journal of Real Estate Taxation,* Winter 1981, pp. 166–182.

Valachi, Donald J. "On Interpreting the Internal Rate of Return on a Real Estate Investment." *Real Estate Appraiser and Analyst,* First Quarter 1981, pp. 35–42.

Viscione, Jerry A., and Porter, Ronald. "IRR Analyses May Not Yield the Best Results." *Real Estate Review.* Summer 1980, pp. 97–101.

Walters, David W. *Real Estate Exchanges.* New York: Wiley, 1982.

Webb, James R. "Negative Cash Flows: A Current Appraisal Problem." *Appraisal Journal,* Jan. 1981, pp. 95–101.

Weimer, Arthur M., Homer Hoyt, and George F. Bloom. *Real Estate,* 7th ed. New York: John Wiley & Sons, 1978.

Weinstein, Marvin W. "Real Estate—The "Unquestionable" Tax Shelter." *Real Estate Law Journal,* Summer 1981, pp. 67–71.

"Which Depreciation Method Should You Use?" *Real Estate Investment Ideas,* Dec. 1981, 1st issue, pp. 5–6.

Whitmire, Robert L., and Reynolds, Kerry M. "Selecting the Optimum Depreciation Method for Real Estate under the New ACR System." *Journal of Taxation,* Dec. 1981, pp. 360–363.

Young, Michael S. "FMRR: A Clever Hoax?" *Appraisal Journal,* July 1979, pp. 359–369.

Zerbst, Robert H. "Evaluating Risks by Partitioning the Internal Rate of Return." *Real Estate Review,* Winter 1980, pp. 80–84.

Index